WESLEY
AND THE PEOPLE
CALLED METHODISTS

Richard P. Heitzenrater

Abingdon Press
Nashville

WESLEY AND THE PEOPLE CALLED METHODISTS

Library of Congress Cataloging-in-Publication Data

Heitzenrater, Richard P., 1939—
    Wesley and the people called Methodists / Richard P. Heitzenrater
       p.   cm.
    Includes bibliographical references and index.
    ISBN 0-687-01682-7 (alk. paper)
    ISBN 0-687-44311-3 (pbk: alk. paper)
    1. Methodist Church—History—18th century. 2. Wesley, John, 1703–1791. 3. Great Britain—Church history—18th century. I. Title.
    BX8276.H45   1995   95-4049
    287'.09'033—dc20   CIP

ISBN - 13: 978-0-687-44311-6

Unless otherwise noted, all Scripture quotations reflect John Wesley's own patterns of use, and are from the Authorized (King James) Version of the Bible or from the Psalter in The Book of Common Prayer.

Appreciation is extended to the following institutions for permission to reproduce illustrations on the listed pages:

The British Museum, Prints and Drawings Department—pp. 93, 98.

Drew University Libraries—p. 116.

Duke University, Special Collections, Perkins Library—pp. xiv, 272, 316.

Methodist Archives, The John Rylands University Library of Manchester—pp. 37, 53, 105, 162, 183, 185, 190, 210, 279, 304, 306.

The National Gallery of Canada, Ottawa—p. 114.

Southern Methodist University, Bridwell Library, Perkins School of Theology—pp. 157, 189, 200, 231, 288.

The University of Georgia, Hargrett Rare Book and Manuscript Library—pp. 63, 65.

This book is printed on acid-free recycled paper.

09 10 11 12 13 14 15 — 25 24 23 22 21 20

Manufactured in the United States of America

Wesley
and the People
Called Methodists

To my mother and father

who personify in their life and faith

the Wesleyan heritage

of the people called Methodists

Contents

Preface

Every account of origins is laden with myths and legends. Christianity is said to have been brought to England by Joseph of Arimathea, who placed his staff in the ground at Glastonbury and said, "This is the place." The rod supposedly sprouted into a tree. It is a tribute to human credulity that the guidebooks to Glastonbury today locate the living descendant of that tree with the same confidence that they point out the location of King Arthur's grave, both within the confines of the medieval abbey ruins.

John Wesley is much closer to us in time, of course, than Joseph or Arthur, but the story of his influence on English religion is not untouched by twice-told tales that have at times taken on the easy ring of truth. Wesley himself was anxious to be the historian of his own movement—"who is more suited to the task?" he asked his readers. But his usual intent was as much to defend as to describe the people called Methodists and his rôle in their rise and development. His detractors quite naturally were more interested in painting a dark picture of the movement, and cannot be accused of attempting an accurate portrayal of its rise and design. Wesley's friends unabashedly put the best side forward in describing Methodism and its leader. We discover, in sifting through the vast amount of material left us by Wesley and his contemporaries, that it is fairly easy to distinguish attack from defense, or diatribe from devotion. It is not always so easy, however, to disentangle propaganda from polemic, or fact from fantasy, on either side of the fence.

Wesley was self-conscious of his own spiritual and theological development; he was equally concerned about the religious and intellectual pilgrimage of his followers. We must remember that the story of the Wesleyan movement in the eighteenth century is more than a description of a spreading organization, a developing theology, and a widening mission. It is the story of the people called Methodists for whom and with whom Wesley spent his time and energy. Therefore, many individuals are mentioned by name in this survey who traditionally have not been considered significant enough to mention. Unfortunately, in many cases we know nothing more about them than their names. Nevertheless, I have tried to rescue them from the fate of being anonymous participants in the story of Methodism's development.

This book, then, is not a biography of Wesley; many of the classic stories of his life (especially the early years) are not told here: his childhood rescue from the burning rectory, his ill-fated romance with Sophy Hopkey, and the like. These may be found in the standard biographies. Our focus here is Wesley's relationship to the movement that would become characterized as a religious revival among the people called Methodists.

Part of our task in reviewing the early history of the Wesleyan revival is to recognize the roots both from which the movement sprouted and upon which it relied for continuing nourishment. Wesley, in his later reflections upon the rise and growth of Methodism, emphasized the spontaneity of its origins and the open-endedness of its development (see his *Short History of Methodism*). In his view, God raised up the people called Methodists for a purpose that was specific and appropriate but in a manner that was not necessarily predictable or predetermined. And Wesley's best intentions to reform the Church and spread scriptural holiness often led to actions that had consequences he neither desired nor anticipated.

Wesley's anecdotal recollections about the rise and development of his movement tended at times to oversimplify or to embellish the facts (for apologetic or didactic reasons), but the form and content of the stories have become fixed in Methodist lore by subsequent repetition by biographers and historians. Having taken on the aura of truth, the twice-told tales are both difficult to distinguish from historical facts and, when identified, are even more difficult to correct and dislodge from the popular narratives.

The present-day historian, however, benefits from the insights gained from hindsight and can analyze historical developments in ways that would have been nearly impossible for the participants of those events (and in ways that were not of concern to the many subsequent denominational historians). The cultural climate, the intellectual ambience, the subtle influences, the unforeseen consequences—these are often more clearly perceived by latter-day spectators of past events.

A careful review of the Wesleyan revival reveals that while there may have been no preconceived *shape* for Methodism, the movement does seem to have gone in a specific and determined *direction*. And it seems that Wesley is much more interested in maintaining the momentum in the proper direction than in creating or preserving any preconceived format.

To understand the rise of Methodism, then, we must not try to see an unfolding of Wesley's "design" so much as to understand the dynamics of the movement's development and its effects upon the lives of the people. We must look at the historical context—the *situation*, its people, its problems, its resources. We must look at particular persons who confront this situation—their experience and understanding of the problems, their choice of resources, the manner of applying their solutions in concrete situations.

In many cases, John Wesley had an intellectual conviction about what was right or true before he had an experiential verification (assurance) that such was the case—empirical verification became important, even for religious or spiritual truths. Propositional faith and experiential faith were in some ways congruent, in others conjunctive, that is, met at a given point. His Aldersgate experience, for instance, was in some ways the experiential confirmation of the truth he was both proclaiming and searching for: one could have an assurance of divine forgiveness that would be transforming. The primary importance of this event is in its verification of this central concept in his spiritual/theological self-understanding—the event itself (time, place, actions) is not of lasting memorable importance in Wesley's own mind, not really an event the anniversary of which he would celebrate (he remarks much more regularly about his birthday). It was, however, a crucial step toward a fuller understanding of how one can *know and experience* the truth of the gospel.

It is this truth that he will continue to celebrate, elaborate, propagate, qualify, along with a series of other truths that he had experienced in one way or another—the whole of which amounted to a view of God, salvation, and the Christian life that he was compelled to preach to the people of his day—to open to them the vision of the Christian life which his experience of the gospel had made real in his life and would be confirmed in the lives of thousands of others.

We will tell the story of the rise of Methodism as a narrative of unfolding developments, without describing subsequent consequences until they occur. The history of early Methodism is best understood in terms of the emergence and interrelatedness of theological, organizational, and missional developments—each aspect is shaped over a period of many years, and none of these elements is fully understood without seeing its dependence upon the other two.

Wesley's own personal pilgrimage of faith is, of course, centrally and inextricably intertwined with the development of the theology, the organization, and the mission of Methodism in the eighteenth century. But his is neither the only nor the whole story. Many of the ideas that he incorporated into Methodism came from other people; many of the activities that characterized the movement were started by other persons. And although Wesley kept a close personal control of the movement, not everyone responded positively to his direction. The story of the Wesleyan movement in the eighteenth century is the story of Wesley and the people called Methodists.

I have intended this book to be scholarly without being pedantic, in the sense that the latest research has been used without belaboring the revisions that new discoveries have brought to old stereotypes. This work has benefited especially from the decades of work by many scholars that has gone into the *Bicentennial Edition of the Works of John Wesley*, which is cited as the source for Wesley's writings whenever possible. Quotations from other primary sources are cited in modern collections that are readily available to the modern reader, such as volume 4 of *The History of The Methodist Church in Great Britain*. British spelling is maintained within quotations. Significant terms (names, places, publications, concepts) are printed in bold type at their initial use or in an important context. Abbreviated references to sources cited within the text are expanded at the end of the first chapter in which they appear, as well as in the Bibliography at the end. References to common sources that are obvious from the text (such as *Minutes* for a particular year or *Journal* for a specific date) are not cited. Illustrations in this work are, whenever possible, woodcuts of contemporary art-work or reproductions of contemporary documents; acknow-ledgments, when required, are collected on the copyright page.

I would like to give appreciation to many persons who have critiqued all or parts of this work, especially Karen Heitzenrater, Wanda Smith, Frank Baker, John Vickers, Kenneth Rowe, Jean Miller Schmidt, Russell Richey, Rex Matthews, Frederick Maser, John Wells, and several classes of seminary students at Southern Methodist University, Drew University, Iliff School of Theology, and Duke University. I also appreciate the support of a faculty development grant from the Lilly Foundation through Perkins School of Theology.

This book is dedicated to my parents, who have constantly encour-aged my pursuit of scholarly excellence for half a century. I hope that this work will prove to be a useful resource for persons in both the church and the academy who are attempting to discern the signifi-cance of the Wesleyan heritage for both present and future genera-tions.

R. P. H.
Durham, NC
March 2, 1994

BELIEVE LOVE OBEY

St. Michael's Church, Stanton Harcourt, with Pope's Tower of Harcourt House.

CHAPTER 1

Methodism and the Christian Heritage in England

John Wesley, the Oxford don, frequently walked the eight miles from the University to the hamlet of Stanton Harcourt to preach for the local vicar, his friend John Gambold. He could not have foreseen the way in which his preaching in that quiet pastoral setting might later be seen as a manifest confluence of forces that converge upon and express themselves in Wesley himself and in the Methodist movement he began during the second quarter of the eighteenth century. One of those occasions does, however, provide for us a striking historical vignette that captures much of the nature and dynamic of the origins of the Wesleyan revival.

On a late spring day in 1738, when Wesley preached "Salvation by Faith" in this little rural church, the past, present, and future of English religion met in an intriguing conjunction of forces. The long course of English ecclesiastical history met the force of a new concern for renewal, both individual and institutional. A long tradition of propositional certainty of faith met the power of a personal experience of faith. An institution built by and for the establishment met a concern for the souls and bodies of the disenfranchised. Although the preacher and his host were both already known as Methodists at the time, none of the small congregation on that Sunday morning in Stanton Harcourt could have known that Gambold, the host vicar, would eventually become a Moravian bishop and that Wesley, the guest preacher, would shortly become the leader of an evangelical revival that would, during his lifetime, spread across the lands and become a trans-Atlantic movement.

Relatively unspoiled in the rural preserve of Oxfordshire, the eleventh-century church of St. Michael in Stanton Harcourt contains in its very stone and mortar the traditions of its Roman Catholic founders. Seclusion was, however, not able to protect or preserve the faith of the members or the fabric of the building from the iconoclastic zeal of the Anglican and Puritan reformers—the carvings in wood, stone, and brass did manage to survive more intact than either the

1

stained glass or the Roman faith of the medieval patrons. The wooden rood-screen, still in place today, as it was in Wesley's day, is the oldest extant in England, a relic of medieval Catholicism dating from the thirteenth century. But the stone carvings preserve in their chips and missing appendages the marks of destructive zeal typical of the Henrician reformers. Most of the monumental brasses remain intact, but occasional indentions in the stone with orphaned brass rivets, are vivid reminders of the Cromwellian zealots who thought the brass more appropriate for bullets than burials. The medieval stained glass is gone, the unrecapturable victim of several generations of sixteenth and seventeenth-century reformers who exemplified the typical Protestant shift in spiritual and aesthetic sensitivity away from things representative or mystical.

When Wesley climbed the steps of the pulpit of St. Michael's on June 11, 1738, those visual reminders of his Church's history were spread before his eyes, signs of the power and glory, the storm and stress, the triumphs and failures that the Church in England had experienced in the previous centuries and in which Wesley himself had participated in his own pilgrimage of faith. A firm rootage in the early Christian tradition, a meditative spirituality typical of the medieval pietists, an unembarrassed adherence to the Church of England, a moral conviction drawn from the Puritan ethos—these had left their mark on the mind and heart of Wesley, as they had also on the fabric of St. Michael's.

The ideas and forces that gave shape and direction to early Methodism are by and large manifest in the various upheavals of Reformation England in the sixteenth and seventeenth centuries. To understand the Wesleyan movement, we must first sift the soil which gave it life, look for the seeds from which it sprang, and notice the resources which sustained and nourished it.

The English Reformation:
The Church in England to the Church of England

England was introduced to Christianity in the sixth century by St. Augustine of Canterbury, whose strategy was to convert the Saxon king Ethelbert, whose queen, Bertha, was a Christian. The English monarchs have since then played an important role in the religious affairs of the British Isles. The interface between religion and politics was certainly not without friction. Thomas à Becket's confrontations with Henry II, Anselm's compromise in the investiture controversy, John Ball's sermon against Richard II, and a host of other incidents testify to the continuing tension between church and crown. But the essential relationship of the two seemed to both somehow necessary and natural, if not divinely ordained, throughout most of England's history.

The influence of the Church of Rome, Augustine's legacy to medieval England, faced many tests in the lands north of the Channel. In the feudal period, the monarchy challenged the pope's prerogative to invest English bishops (who were in fact the monarch's vassals); in the early days of parliament, protectionist (if not xenophobic) tendencies resulted in several acts restraining the powers of, or appeals to, foreign powers such as the pope; a rising national self-consciousness, congenitally anti-French, led John Wycliffe to claim the Bible as an alternate authority to the pope, who was (during much of the fourteenth century) under French influence. An insular mindset pervaded the consciousness of the developing English nation. It is not surprising that Sir Thomas More would portray the ideal community, in *Utopia*, as an island kingdom. It is also no surprise that the English, the natural boundaries of their consciousness defined in part by the ever-present shoreline (never more than seventy-five miles away) and their developing national identity centered in large part in their monarchy, would eventually develop a religious establishment that was unabashedly nationalistic, legally centered in the monarchy, and strongly anti-papal.

The monarchy is the central feature of English history through at least the eighteenth century. This is perhaps most evident during the period of the English Reformation, the time of Henry VIII, Edward VI, Mary I, and Elizabeth I. Although religious reformers gained some renown for their ideas and programs, especially on the continent, the implementation of their reforms depended in large part upon the wishes and whims of the political power structure—in many areas, such as Germany, France, and England, the fate of reform movements hinged upon the positive or negative inclinations of individual monarchs or princes. The Reformation in England goes through a series of stages, determined in large part by the attitudes of the monarchs, shaped to some degree by the advice of courtiers, and put in place in every case by acts of Parliament.

Henry VIII took the first major step—separating the English Church from the Church of Rome and establishing it under the monarch. A series of personal and political problems moved Henry from a position of "Defender of the Faith," supporting the papacy against the writings of Luther (in the *Assertion of the Seven Sacraments*, 1521), to a stance a decade later of declaring himself the head of the

The vernacular translation of the Bible became an important feature of the English Reformation. Henry VIII supported the publication of the "Great Bible" in 1539 and is portrayed on its title-page distributing the Word of God through Thomas Cranmer and Thomas Cromwell.

Church of England. The Reformation Parliament (1532–35) established an **Erastian** form of government; that is, they declared Henry VIII to be head of both church and state in England (by the **Act of Supremacy**) and made the Church of England the official religion of the state and an integral part of the political structure. These actions set the boundaries of power for the future—all matters of church doctrine, structure, policy would have to pass through Parliament. In addition to these steps which asserted English ecclesiastical independence, Parliament (with the encouragement and guidance of Henry's counselor, Thomas Cromwell) also vented its anti-papalism by reiterating the prohibitions of earlier parliaments against interference in English affairs by foreign powers, including most obviously the See of Rome.

Theologically, the Henrician Church was not typically "Protestant" in the Lutheran or Calvinist sense. The first official statement of the English faith, the **Ten Articles** of Religion (1536), was a fairly brief statement of traditional beliefs, omitting the (by this time) typical Protestant bias against transubstantiation, celibacy of the clergy, etc. The two most notable changes in the transition from Church *in* England to Church *of* England were in polity and liturgy—the monarch rather than the pope was now the head of the Church, and the service was to be in English rather than Latin. A revision of the doctrinal statement in 1539, the **Six Articles**, reflects an even more conservative trend in the Henrician Church, reaffirming the doctrine of transubstantiation and reasserting the need for a celibate clergy. The soteriological doctrines, such as justification, good works, grace, etc., as published in *The King's Book* (1543), are typical of the more irenic compromises arrived at by the Protestant and Roman Catholic negotiators at the colloquies of 1539–41 on the continent (e.g., the *Regensburg Book*).

The early attempts at doctrinal formulation were revised and extended by Henry's closest religious advisor, Archbishop Thomas Cranmer, at the close of the monarch's reign. His first important step was to publish a collection of sermons or homilies that would present models of correct theological exposition for the clergy. The first **Book of Homilies** (1546) contained twenty-one sermons that could be read from the pulpits to assure that the people would on occasion hear solid interpretation of orthodox doctrines, regardless of the homiletical or doctrinal inadequacy of the local parish priest or curate.

During the reign of Edward VI, the influence of the continental reformers became more noticeable, both at the royal court and in the countryside. Cranmer himself was not untouched by this development. In 1532, he had secretly married Margaret Osiander, the niece of Andreas Osiander the Lutheran reformer, and brought to England some of the continental theologians, mostly Calvinist and noticeably irenic, such as Martin Bucer and Peter Martyr. The Archbishop's next major production was the official prayerbook for the Church—the **Book of Common Prayer** (1549, rev. 1552). By an act of Parliament, the BCP became the official liturgy of the Established Church. Cranmer also helped develop a revised doctrinal statement, the **Forty-Two Articles**, which was much more Protestant than any previous English standard of orthodoxy. The Calvinistic bent of these Articles can be seen in their assertion of supralapsarian predestination (decreed by God before the Fall) and their clear opposition to good works apart from a proper faith in Christ. These Articles received royal acceptance in June 1553, less than a month before Edward VI died and his sister Mary acceded to the throne.

As a result of its history and nature, the Church of England would continue to assume a position somewhere between the more radical views of continental Protestantism and the more traditional views of Roman Catholicism. The reign of Mary was really too short to effect a permanent return to Roman Catholicism in England. The incipient Protestantism of Edward's reign, culminating twenty years of slow shifts in the religious winds of England, seems to have pervaded the country sufficiently to present a broad challenge to Mary's program of religious re-formation, effected as usual by acts of Parliament. Even her firm-handed disposal of the opposition through the traditional methods used earlier by her father and later by her sister, in the end worked against her. The persons she forced into exile because of their Protestant inclinations came back to England at her death with a reforming zeal that saw even the Henrician Church as having need of further reform. And the execution of those who stayed in England served not only to solidify the opposition to Mary in her own day, but also to provide her most unfortunate legacy—the nickname "bloody" Mary. In particular, the burning of the three bishops, Cranmer, Latimer, and Ridley, ignited a lasting spark for the continuing spirit of anti-Roman reform in England, a spark fanned by the writings of John Foxe, Thomas Cartwright, and others.

Mary's untimely death, without heirs, left the throne to her sister, Elizabeth, whose political savvy and religious inclinations (or lack thereof) led to the **Elizabethan Settlement**—a series of parliamentary acts (1559) that defined once again the nature of and relationship between the English crown and church. Elizabeth's desire was to turn the clock back to the time of her father, Henry VIII. The march of time and events would not permit that. The intervening years had seen the rise of Calvin in Geneva and the redefinition of Roman Catholicism at Trent. She found it necessary to confront both realities in her own country—the reinstituted Roman faith of her sister's reign and the revitalized Calvinism of the returning **Marian exiles**. The latter brought with them two books that would influence the English-speaking world for generations—Foxe's *Book of Martyrs* and the Geneva Bible.

The first of these was a detailed description, in the tradition of the "lives of the saints," of the martyrdom of those persecuted under Mary's reign. The blatant anti-Catholic tone of the book is exemplified in the conclusion of the account of a pregnant woman who was burned at the stake and whose unborn child burst unexpectedly into the fire, first to be retrieved but then to be cast back into the flames, as Foxe says, "to make up the number of those countless innocents who by their tragic death display to the whole world the Herodian cruelty of this graceless generation of Catholic tormentors." The widespread popularity of Foxe's work is largely responsible for implanting in the English consciousness a vibrant anti-Catholic sentiment.

The Marian exiles also came carrying their Calvinist Bibles as the

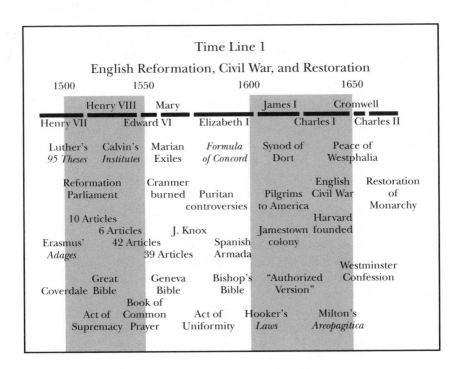

Time Line 1

English Reformation, Civil War, and Restoration

1500	1550	1600	1650
Henry VIII	Mary	James I	Cromwell
Henry VII	Edward VI	Elizabeth I	Charles I	Charles II
Luther's 95 *Theses*	Calvin's *Institutes*	Marian Exiles	*Formula of Concord*	Synod of Dort	Peace of Westphalia
	Reformation Parliament	Cranmer burned	Puritan controversies	Pilgrims to America	English Civil War	Restoration of Monarchy
	10 Articles				Harvard	
	6 Articles	J. Knox		Jamestown founded	
Erasmus' *Adages*	42 Articles	Spanish	colony	
		39 Articles	Armada		Westminster Confession
	Great Coverdale Bible	Geneva Bible	Bishop's Bible	"Authorized Version"	
	Book of				
	Act of Supremacy	Common Prayer	Act of Uniformity	Hooker's *Laws*	Milton's *Areopagitica*

handbook for church reform. The Geneva (or "Breeches") Bible—small in size compared with the editions of the official Bishop's Bible; printed in clear Roman type rather than the heavy black-lettering of previous English bibles; verses numbered for convenience—was considered not only a source of devotional study and Protestant (anti-Catholic) theological interpretation, but also in good Calvinist terms a practical guidebook for church reform. The returning Marian exiles had already determined from their place of exile that the Church of England, even in its Henrician or Edwardian form, needed further reform of its Roman tendencies. Hence some English Calvinists became known popularly as **"Puritans"** and worked to effect reforms that would purify the church of its non-scriptural corruptions. They saw no scriptural support for such things as vestments in worship services, or archbishops (much less monarchs) in ecclesiastical leadership.

The task of the religious settlement under Elizabeth was to establish a balanced approach that would protect the national church, formed (if not fully "reformed") under Henry, from the traditional "catholic" claims of Rome on the one side and from the more radical "reform" tendencies of the Puritans on the other, a stance traditionally expressed as the *via media* ("middle way") between Rome and Geneva. Elizabeth's role in this process was not determined so much by strong personal religious sentiments, if indeed she had any, as by her political astuteness; she was, in this as in most matters, thoroughly *politique.* Her concern was to establish stability in her reign, following the turmoil of her siblings' reigns. A unified country would need a settled order in the Church.

The parliamentary measures that settled the religious question under Elizabeth used the Henrician Church as a model and set the basic framework for English religion for generations to come. A new **Act of Supremacy** (1559) established Elizabeth as head of state and "Supreme Governor" of the Church, carefully chosen words that indicated an appreciation for the problems Henry had encountered in proclaiming himself "head" of the Church (in the light of Eph. 5:23 and Col. 1:18). The **Act of Uniformity** (1559) defined the standards for liturgy and doctrine—requiring that churches use the **Book of Common Prayer,** requiring clergy and other officials to subscribe to the doctrines in the **Thirty-Nine Articles of Religion,** and providing a standard exposition of accepted teachings in an enlarged **Book of Homilies** (to be read regularly from pulpits across the realm). These three basic sources of theological identity came primarily from the pen of Thomas Cranmer a decade earlier; the BCP and the Articles were only slightly revised from the Edwardian prayerbook and articles, and

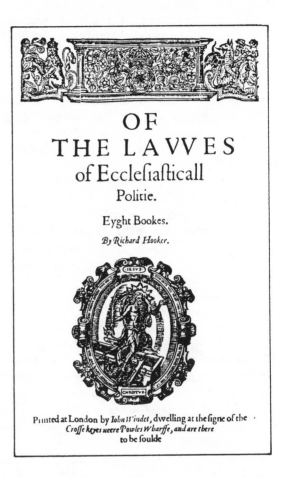

OF
THE LAVVES
of Ecclefiafticall
Politie.

Eyght Bookes.

By Richard Hooker.

Printed at London by *Iohn Windet*, dwelling at the figne of the
Croffe keyes neere Powles Wharffe, and are there
to be foulde

Title page of the first edition of Hooker's exposition of the polity and theology of the Elizabethan Settlement.

the homilies were doubled in number from the edition first produced in 1546.

Neither the Puritans nor the Roman Catholics took kindly to these developments. As the Puritans' numbers increased (returning from the continent and gaining converts), they protested the political and theological structures put in place by Elizabeth and her advisors, their tempers boiling over in the controversies of the 1570s and 1580s concerning liturgy, episcopacy, and doctrine (Thomas Cartwright, Walter Strickland, the Marprelate Tracts, etc.). Pope Pius V excommunicated Elizabeth in 1570, calling upon her subjects to depose her. This forced the English Roman Catholics to choose between loyalty to the queen (thus denying papal authority) and obedience to the pope (thus inviting treason to England).

In the face of these tensions, Richard Hooker undertook to provide an exposition of church polity and doctrine in a work that became a definitive explication of the Elizabethan Settlement, *Of The Laws of Ecclesiastical Polity* (1595). In his work, Hooker first raises the crucial question as to what the authorities should be for answering basic questions of ecclesiastical structure and thought. His answer, self-consciously walking a line between the poles of thought in his day (to become a model of the mediating, *via media* tradition of the Church of England), was three-fold: (1) **Scripture** (but not as used by the Puritans) provides the main source of truth and the basic test of Christian veracity, but was not to be used in the manner of the Puritans' understanding of *sola scriptura*—scripture was *not* a handbook that provided specific answers to all questions, to be followed to the letter: doing all the things spelled out there, omitting all the things not found there. Hooker suggested that the scriptures, the primary source of truth, should be seen whole and could provide guidelines for thought and action in many areas. (2) **Tradition** (but not as used by the Roman Catholics) provides a view of life and thought from the earliest centuries of Christianity, closest to the purity of the apostolic witness and most liable to be (in its consensus) an authentic reflection and explication of the biblical testimony—certainly *not* to be venerated equally with scripture (as the Council of Trent had decreed), and by all means limited to the first few centuries of the church, excluding the "innovations" of the medieval church. Hooker saw the value of tradition as an early authoritative explanation of scriptural truths. (3) **Reason** (but not as used by the Platonists) furnishes the means by which scripture and tradition can be scrutinized and understood by thoughtful persons—revealed truth may at times be above reason, but can never be contrary to reason. Hooker was willing to discern connections between revelation and reason as sources and measures of truth in order to develop doctrines that were cogent and credible.

Hooker's delineation of theology and polity supplied the definitive outline and defense of the *via media* of the **Elizabethan Settlement** for generations to come. By the eighteenth century, Hooker was a standard authority. Samuel Wesley's *Advice to a Young Clergyman* (1735) assumes that any aspiring cleric will be well-grounded in Hooker, and John Wesley's own framework for authority owes an obvious debt to the Hookerian perspective that had become pervasive by his day. The tensions between Calvinism and Catholicism that Hooker had addressed were soon superseded by a growing antagonism between

Puritans and Arminians—a dispute that first erupted in the Low Countries at the turn of the seventeenth century as an intra-Calvinistic squabble.

In the late sixteenth century, Jacob Arminius (1560–1609) challenged the Calvinist theology that had developed under the influence of Theodore Beza and others who had stressed divine determinism (predestination). While Calvin's thought had indeed been grounded in the concept of God's sovereignty, which implied omniscience, omnipotence, omnipresence, and other attributes of total power and control, Arminius was concerned that an overemphasis upon divine sovereignty destroyed what he considered to be the reality of human choice—in a pre-determined world, how could one talk about human responsibility? In order to reassert human free will without negating divine sovereignty, Arminius suggested that persons do make real, free choices and that God, while not causing such decisions, does know ahead of time what is going to happen. Thus, divine foreknowledge supplants divine determination as the basis of God's sovereign relationship to creation and humanity. The argument, at its root, might seem to hinge on conflicting views of the Divine Being (the question of whether causation is a necessary corollary to sovereignty), but the issue for the traditional Calvinists was focused on the implications of such a view upon the nature and role of humanity in the process of salvation. The assertion of free will, when associated with the question of salvation, seemed to imply that human beings, of their own free will, could *do* something that would effect their salvation. The battle-cry of the reformers had been *sola gratia* and *sola fide*—by God's *grace alone* are we saved, and that salvation is effected by *faith alone*. Both Luther and Calvin had asserted predestination as a basic belief: that God chooses those to whom salvation will be given, and that persons can do nothing to earn this gift—the only human action that is possible is for those who have been chosen (the "elect") to respond in faith. Arminius challenged this view which implied that Christ died only for the elect; his view of "universal atonement" (Christ died for all) centered the question in the human will—those who *chose* to respond in faith and accepted God's gift of grace would be saved.

Hardline Calvinists reacted by decrying the Arminian allowance for human free will and human action as yet another form of semi-Pelagian works-righteousness. Arminius, of course, would never claim that persons are saved *by* their decisions, works, or any other human action. But the threat to traditional Calvinist views of God, humanity, and salvation, seen in the spreading views of Arminius, was enough to bring about the Synod of Dort (1619) in the Netherlands to deal with these matters. Arminius himself had died; his followers (the Remonstrants) lost the day on every point. The decisions of the Synod, defining and affirming "orthodox" Calvinism in the Canons of Dort, are often summarized under the acronym TULIP—*T*otal depravity, *U*nconditional election, *L*imited atonement, *I*rresistible grace, *P*erseverance of the saints. The first point, based on the doctrine of original sin, Arminians would have little trouble accepting, but the other four, props to predestination, would be attacked in future years by many who could not accept the "horrible decrees" of predestination. Those who chose to oppose predestination, or who asserted free will, or held to the view of universal atonement, or stressed human responsibility, were tagged by their Calvinist opponents as "Arminians," whether or not they held a theological position entirely congruent with that of Jacob Arminius. The terms "semi-Pelagian" and "works-righteousness" were not self-descriptions by any party, but always charges made by an opponent (no one claims the title "heretic"), and such was frequently the case with the term "Arminian." On the other side, the Calvinists and Lutherans were often tagged by their opponents as "**solifidians**" and "**antinomians**"—persons who carried *sola fide* to an extreme and who, by their radical opposition to legalism (viewing law and grace strictly as a dialectic), promoted moral laxity. It is easy to see, then, how anyone who stressed the disciplines of the Christian life, the necessity of holy living, and the importance of conversion, stood a chance of being called an **Arminian**, especially by the Calvinists.

In the Church of England, then, it was to be expected that this conflict would arise between the Calvinists (particularly the Puritans) and the high-Church party that seemed, in the Anglo-Catholicism of the seventeenth century, to perpetuate the semi-Pelagianism of medieval Roman Catholicism, now given a home and a name within Protestantism as "Arminianism." Early in the century, both James I and Charles I (and especially the latter's archbishop, William Laud) were the focus of Puritan attacks. James had hoped, upon moving from Scotland, to escape the snarls of the Calvinists (in Scotland, Presbyterians—a vocal and pestering opposition to his mother, Mary Stuart, and himself), but he discovered in the English Puritans a new brand of the same challenge. James would have liked to suppress them, but instead tried theological dialogue (e.g., the Hampton Court Conference). The most tangible result of these encounters was the production of a new version of the Bible, long-since desired by the Puritans who clung to their Geneva versions. The new "Authorized" ("King James") version of 1611 helped placate the Calvinists for a time. But the gradual slip of James and his son, Charles I, into a more

Roman Catholic religious sensitivity led to an increasingly vehement opposition among more radical Protestants, such as the Puritans.

Charles I was, in the end, the primary victim of the increasing political and religious tensions that fractured for a time the fragile *via media* that Elizabeth had established. The successful military ventures of the antiroyalist army mounted by Parliament (where Puritans held a majority) brought down the monarchy and the Church of England with it. Ironically, Charles met his end at the Banqueting House in Whitehall, walking to his execution under the great ceiling paintings by Rubens portraying the "Apotheosis of James I," his father, whose policies he had continued. In the face of a crowd hungry for vengeance, Charles met his death with such grace and dignity that ten years later, after a decade with no monarchy and no established church, even the revolutionary forces that made up the Parliament recognized that England would fare better under its former system of government than under the conditions of political and religious precariousness that Oliver Cromwell had tried to manage (and that his successor and son, Richard, could not control). Religious freedom had resulted, in the view of an increasing number of people, in the rise of religious fanaticism—the country was becoming infested by every type of group imaginable: Presbyterians, Baptists, Congregationalists, Quakers . . . all, in their tendencies toward singularity of religious expression, quite foreign to the mediating tendencies of the by then traditional English mindset.

The restoration of the monarchy under Charles II (invited back to the throne by Parliament itself!) meant the reestablishment of the Church as well. The Stuart monarchy, self-consciously authorized by "divine right," followed the traditional ritual of self-authorization through a series of Parliamentary acts, including the usual Act of Supremacy and Act of Uniformity. Thereby the liturgy and doctrine of the Church of England were once again put in place: the Book of Common Prayer authorized (with only minor revisions), the Thirty-Nine Articles accepted, the Book of Homilies reaffirmed. The monarch was again Supreme Governor of the Church, and bishops were reappointed.

The main difference between the religious ethos of the Restoration period and of the earlier Stuart reign was that by the latter part of the seventeenth century the English exhibited a conscious fear of explicit religiosity. Any expression of spiritual zeal they associated with religious fanaticism, which in hindsight was easily tied to political and social upheaval and was fresh in their experience. The general tenor of spiritual lethargy and moral laxity that resulted in many parts of

The execution in 1649 of Charles I, in later prayerbooks called "the Martyrdom of the Blessed King Charles the First," whose dignity and royal demeanor on that occasion later helped reinforce the divine-right perspective of Stuart supporters.

the country is typified by the licentious style of life at the royal court and signaled by Charles II's own long list of mistresses. Not everyone, of course, followed the royal model in this regard. In fact, before Charles' reign was over, the reaction against the disintegration of England's moral and religious fiber would inspire the formation of small societies intended to promote piety and Christian discipline.

Not everyone in the Church agreed with the reinstatement of the traditional guidelines for polity and doctrine. The influx of more radical Protestant thinking during the Cromwellian interregnum, for all its tendencies toward "fanaticism," had infused a new zeal for reforming further the life and thought of the Church. Clergy who held a theology that was more radical than the Thirty-Nine Articles allowed, and who had flourished during the disestablishment at mid-century, now were forced to make the decision to conform or, as **nonconformists** (dissenters), to lose their positions ("livings" or bene-fices). With the presence of continuing large numbers of persons in nonconforming traditions (many of them filling the pews and pulpits of Established churches), the ideal of "uniformity" was tested as it never had been before. One minister brought before the Bishop of Bristol, Gilbert Ironside, to answer for his nonconforming views was John Westley (*sic*), paternal grandfather of the founder of Methodism. The confrontation is recorded in Edmund Calamy's *The Noncon-formists Memorial*, a work that would become the eighteenth-century nonconformists' sequel to Foxe's martyrology. In his mid-twenties, Westley was accused of irregular worship and preaching, as well as lack of proper ordination. He defended himself on scriptural grounds that he was sent to preach the gospel (Romans 10). For his views, John Westley was ejected from his living and, as was typical of many nonconformists, spent the remaining years of his life in a variety of pulpits and prisons.

The increasing tendencies of the monarch to exhibit publicly his Roman Catholic sympathies not only exacerbated the tensions be-tween the religious establishment (headed by the monarch) and the reforming parties, but even made the Parliament uncomfortable. With the accession of James II, matters became worse. James made little attempt to hide his Roman Catholic inclinations—he married an Italian princess, his personal chaplain was a Catholic priest, and he made no pretence of his religious preference. Any inclinations of the Parliament to challenge the Stuart concept of divine right and replace the king with a more acceptable monarch were held in abeyance by, among other things, the royal inability to produce a male heir. Parliament's willingness to sit out the reign was brought up short by the "miracle" of a royal birth, thought by some (but how could they prove it?) to be a "warming pan baby," brought in from outside. The predicament was therefore clearly presented to them: face the possibility of a continuing Stuart line of "absolute monarchs" taking them increasingly closer to Rome, or do something drastic before matters proceeded any further.

The decision of Parliament to invite James's Protestant daughter, Mary, to the throne and to accept her husband, William of Orange, as king, presented a problem of political logistics to the Parliament: how does one dismiss a king who understands himself to be on the throne by God's design and who feels that he is the law (namely, that he is above the laws or whims of a Parliament)? James decided not to challenge the armies of William and Mary when they crossed the English Channel, and thereby spared a great deal of English blood. Instead, he fled to France, where he and his progeny (his son James, known in Wesley's day as "The Old Pretender," and his grandson, "Bonnie Prince Charlie") awaited their chance to return to their "rightful" place on the English throne.

While this bloodless revolution (seen later by the Whigs as a "Glorious Revolution") of 1688 solved some problems, it created others. The traditional parliamentary acts consequent to a royal succession forced the supporters of the Stuart line to a hard decision. Bishops and other leaders of the Church who supported James (and were therefore called "**Jacobites**") but who were required to sign an oath of allegiance to the new monarchs under the Act of Supremacy, had to choose between their conscience and their living. Those unable to sign were called "**nonjurors**" and lost their positions in church and government. By and large, the nonjurors represented a major segment of the opposition to the monarchy of William and Mary.

At the same time, the continuing presence of nonconformist sentiments in the land raised the dilemma of how the Church would handle diversity in its midst. Some leaders, characterized as **Latitudinarians**, while conforming to the Church, did not think that orthodoxy of doctrine or uniformity of liturgy should be a major concern. One group of influential clergy, known as the Cambridge Platonists, felt that reason could be used to arbitrate between different positions and that toleration was desirable within the Church.

Two major options were debated. A national church that was *comprehensive* in nature might include a variety of theological opinions under one large umbrella. This umbrella approach would be one way of officially recognizing the diversity that existed, though at the expense of uniformity. The other option was to maintain a national church that was *uniform* in its doctrine and liturgy, and at the same time somehow allow other groups to exist legally. Many Puritans and high-Church Anglicans favored this approach even though they could not always agree on the specific content of that uniformity.

Nevertheless, the latter approach prevailed and was implemented not only by the usual Act of Uniformity, but also by an **Act of Toleration** (1689). Under this latter act, those who could not subscribe to the Thirty-Nine Articles, those (nonconformists) who thus opted to dissent from the official religion were "tolerated" in the sense that they were allowed to exist legally under certain prescribed conditions: (1) meeting houses must be registered with the government; (2) dissenting preachers must be licensed; (3) meetings for worship must be held in the registered meeting houses, not in private homes; (4) Roman Catholic or Unitarian groups were not to be included under these provisions (i.e., not allowed to exist legally). Many privileges of English citizenship thereby became dependent upon conformity to the official doctrines of the Church—subscription to the Articles was required of all who matriculated at the universities, of all who held public office, of all who held commissions in the armed forces, and of all who wished to vote in elections.

Thus, while the Act of Toleration did allow legal protection for a variety of dissenting groups, freedom of doctrine and polity was gained at a price. In a variety of ways, nonconformity now meant disenfranchisement. The alternatives that faced many were clear—subscription to the Articles or registration under the Act. It is no wonder on these grounds alone that Wesley would vehemently oppose those in his movement who favored separation from the Church of England—ironically, the "toleration" allowed to dissenters by their registering under the Act of Toleration also seriously circumscribed their political and religious freedom.

Pietism and the Religious Societies

Puritans often added a typical Calvinist concern for promoting individual piety, which then became typical of many of the nonconformists. The theological grounding for the Puritan interest in morality was, of course, quite different from the common "moralism" that simply emphasized the necessity of being a "good person," or the "Arminianism" of the high-Church party that emphasized the necessity of holy living. Both would be charged with relying upon "works-righteousness" for salvation (see Allison). The Calvinists were not promoting "good works" as such, but rather wanted persons to recognize their "elect" status and evidence it in their lives, as the human response to God's grace. The order (divine action, human response) was important, though not always kept straight in the popular mind—the Puritans at times seemed to be "proving" (if not earning) their salvation by their good works. The Arminians were not claiming any meritorious value for "good works" either, but were emphasizing the human opportunity to accept the empowerment of God's grace. The primacy of grace was central to their position, though the implication of divine/human cooperation (synergism) led many to criticize the Arminians for stressing human activity in salvation.

The controversies that developed over this issue toward the end of the seventeenth century led to some interesting "name-calling" that is of importance to an understanding of the name "Methodist." As early as the 1670s, both in the Low Countries and in England, a few orthodox Calvinists began to write vigorously against the Arminians and their "new method" of doing theology, especially relative to their views of justification and sanctification. Those designated as "**New Methodists**," persons using this new (i.e., wrong) method, included Moses Amyraldus, Peter Baro, Richard Baxter, and Daniel Williams. The Calvinist critics (such as Johannes Vlak, Theophilus Gale, and Tobias Crisp) saw the Arminian view of free will as laying too much emphasis upon the necessity of obedience to God's law even under the New Covenant, leading to "neonomianism" (new-legalism) and reliance upon works-righteousness for salvation. The Arminians, however, saw the Calvinist view of predestination and election as dispensing with the demands of obedience, leading to "antinomianism" (anti-legalism) and consequent moral laxity. These terms and names were generally used by the opposition to designate what they considered to be dangers in the other parties' positions; one would hardly *claim* to rely on works-righteousness or claim to be an antinomian. So also the term "New Methodist" (one who uses this new, wrong method) was a derogatory name applied to some of the Arminians by their theological opponents in writings such as Theophilus Gale's *Court of the Gentiles* (1678) and an anonymous pamphlet by "A Country Presbyter" entitled *A War Among the Angels of the Churches; wherein is shewed the Principles of the New Methodists in the great Point of Justification* (1693). The controversy died out at the turn of the eighteenth century but may have provided the terminology for a derogatory designation of Wesley's preaching at Oxford, which fitted the Arminian "New Methodist" mold rather precisely.

Although the disputants in these controversies felt that important issues of faith were at stake, their arguments often focused upon

theological *minutiae* and their methodology rivalled medieval scholas-
ticism in its rigor. This tendency was fully in keeping with the growing
rationalism of the age, which was flowering into various patterns of
scientific, philosophical, and religious thinking. Debates between em-
piricists and intuitionists could be found in many overlapping circles
of thought: the boundaries of disciplines were not sharply drawn. The
emergence of **Deism,** which portrayed a view of God and creation
based on reason, was accompanied by the rise of modern scientific
fields. Deists such as John Ray and William Derham became pioneers
in the fields of botany and astronomy. Sir Isaac Newton and John
Locke saw no conflict between their scientific or philosophical observations and their religious assumptions or conclusions. These early
stages of "enlightened" thinking were pervasive and influential
enough at the end of the seventeenth century to bring many philosophical issues (such as epistemology) to the forefront of religious
discussions for several generations. Every serious theologian would
have to deal with these issues.

This trend was accompanied by a growing fear among some that
the increasing prevalence of rational speculation in place of faithful
repetition in matters of faith was causally related to the decreasing
evidence of traditional moral values in society. In spite of certain
theological differences, therefore, the possibility existed of an alliance
among many of the Puritans, Nonconformists, and Arminians on the
matter of improving the spiritual temper and moral fiber of society.
The reaction to the spiritual lethargy and moral laxity of the Restoration period was to be a revival of emphasis on piety and holy living
among small groups of Christians dotting the English countryside. In
many ways, this development reflected a parallel development in
Germany that gave the name to the whole movement—**Pietism.**

German Pietism was an attempt to renew the Lutheran Church
in Germany by reinstating several of the traditional Reformation
themes. Philipp Jacob Spener was among the first to spell out a
program for the movement. His book, *Pia desideria* (1675), outlined
six "desires of piety" for the church. First, in order to ground its life
in the proper authority, the church needed to reemphasize the study
of scripture—this was a reiteration of the Reformation theme of *sola
scriptura* (scripture as the sole authority for Christian life and thought).
Second, Spener suggested that renewal of the church required the
active involvement and concern of laity—a way of restating Luther's
theme of the priesthood of all believers. Third, more emphasis should
be placed on evangelical zeal than on debating skill. Fourth, there
should be a practical focus on Christian living rather than intellectual

acumen. Fifth, preaching should be aimed at the salvation of the listener, not simply for instruction or correction. And sixth, ministerial training should emphasize the development of moral and spiritual qualities in the life of the pastor. This program generally attempted to refocus the center of religious sensitivity upon the heart rather than the mind. German Pietist theology, as seen in such writers as Spener, August Hermann Francke, and particularly Nicholas Ludwig von Zinzendorf (patron of the Moravians), would become characterized as "heart theology."

Spener's plan for renewal was effected through small groups known as ***collegia pietatis***—"colleges of piety." (Francke started similar groups known as *collegia philobiblia*—"groups of bible-lovers.") These were of course, not really colleges as we think of institutions of higher learning; they were small groups of lay persons, gathered together in homes for Bible study and prayer. The fellowship of Christian nurture that developed therein provided the base from which these groups then carried on a mission of Christian concern—to the poor, the ignorant, the sick, the elderly (similar to the groups under Gaston de Renty in France).

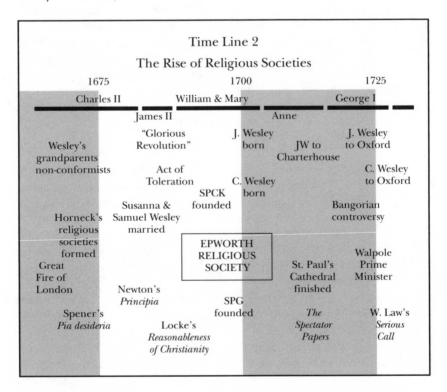

Time Line 2

The Rise of Religious Societies

1675	1700	1725
Charles II	William & Mary	George I
	James II	Anne
	"Glorious Revolution"	J. Wesley born / JW to Charterhouse	J. Wesley to Oxford
Wesley's grandparents non-conformists	Act of Toleration	C. Wesley born	C. Wesley to Oxford
Horneck's religious societies formed	SPCK founded / Susanna & Samuel Wesley married		Bangorian controversy
Great Fire of London	Newton's *Principia*	EPWORTH RELIGIOUS SOCIETY / St. Paul's Cathedral finished	Walpole Prime Minister
Spener's *Pia desideria*	Locke's *Reasonableness of Christianity*	SPG founded	*The Spectator Papers*	W. Law's *Serious Call*

The English counterparts to the *collegia* were the **religious societies**. The religious societies began during the period following the Restoration when English society was in the throes of a reaction to its recent encounter with politicized Puritanism. The effects of the nation-wide sigh of relief that accompanied the return of the Stuart monarchy seem to have permeated the life of the nation quite beyond the political level. The return to the principles of the Elizabethan Settlement brought with it a measured abhorrence for the fanaticism, moral as well as political, of the Puritan Commonwealth. Within two decades, the debilitating effect of this sentiment upon the moral fiber of the nation was viewed with alarm by Anthony Horneck and other English pietists who saw the growth of immorality and irreligion as a crisis that must be met by a rejuvenation of religious life within the Church. The organization of concerned persons into religious societies in England followed some of the basic patterns evident in certain pietistic and mystical tendencies on the continent at that time. Such European models as may have been transferred to British soil, however, were also transformed by their adaptation to the life and thought of the Church of England.

Started by Anthony Horneck in the 1670s, the religious societies were also small groups of laity who represent an almost spontaneous fusion of moralism and devotionalism, with a zeal for the promotion of "real holiness of heart and life." This outcropping of pietism contrasted sharply with the sentiment of the age. These societies and their reforming zeal were generally secured to the Established Church by means of rules that stipulated that each local group be under the guidance of "a pious and learned divine of the Church" (Legg, 292). Within twenty years, this form of religious organization had established itself within the structure of the Church of England as a viable expression of Christian piety and social concern. Around the turn of the eighteenth century, the movement gave rise to centralized organizations such as the **Society for Promoting Christian Knowledge** (SPCK), which in turn became the model (and source of encouragement) for local societies throughout the realm. Samuel Wesley, rector of the Epworth parish, became involved in this movement. And the fact that his son John became a corresponding member of the SPCK is also of some consequence to the origins of the people called Methodists.

The religious societies attacked the problem of immorality on a personal, individualistic basis. Theirs was no social program to reform England in one grand stroke. The approach instead was to work toward the transformation of society by changing one person at a time.

They worked first with those for whom there seemed to be some hope of moral improvement. The method for such an endeavor was grounded in the development of a life of personal piety. The movement was not marked by an evangelistic zeal to bring vast numbers of persons into the societies. Rather, their approach was aimed more toward quality than quantity and was grounded more in the process of nurture than conversion. In many ways the program of the religious societies resembles the development of the lay "third orders" within the Roman Catholic Church.

The stated purpose of the societies was to promote "real holiness of heart and life." To this end, the meetings were designed primarily to offer mutual encouragement in the development of devotional piety based on a study of the Bible and other works of divinity, and to assist the promotion of a life of personal holiness and morality. The Orders of one society furnished a list of particular duties (and the biblical citation) which the members were expected to make "their serious endeavor" as a guide to holy living, including the following:

> 2. To pray many times every day, remembering our continual dependence upon God, both for spiritual and temporal things. 1 Thess. 5:17.
> 3. To partake of the Lord's Supper at least once a month, if not prevented by a reasonable impediment. 1 Cor. 11:26. Luke 22:19.
> 4. To practise the profoundest meekness and humility. Matt. 11:29.
> 6. To accustom themselves to holy thoughts in all places. Ps. 2, 3.
> 10. To shun all foreseen occasions of evil; as evil company, known temptations, etc. 1 Thess. 5:22.
> 12. To examine themselves every night, what good or evil they have done in the day past. 2 Cor. 13:5.
> 13. To keep a private fast once a month (especially near their approach to the Lord's Table), if at their own disposal; or to fast from some meal when they may conveniently. Matt. 6:16; Luke 5:35.
> 14. To mortify the flesh with its affections, and lust. Gal. 5:19,24.
> 16. To shun spiritual pride, and the effects of it; as railing, anger, peevishness, and impatience of contradiction, etc.
> 18. To read pious books often for their edification.
> 19. To be continually mindful of the great obligation of this special profession of religion, and to walk so circumspectly, that none may be offended or discouraged from it by what they see in them, nor occasion be given to any, to speak reproachfully of it (*M&M*, 38).

The fellowship of the society not only supported Christian nurture, but also exercised discipline—those found to be walking "disorderly" were to be privately admonished by one or more members or, if necessary, reproved by the whole society. This inclination to repri-

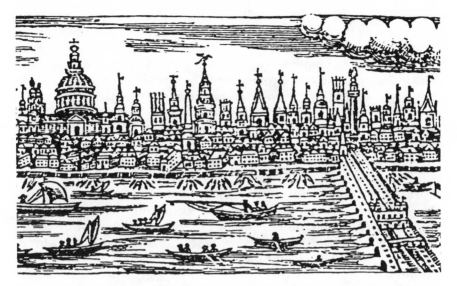

London, the center of the religious societies, was a city full of churches, shown here in a mid-eighteenth century woodcut from the masthead of *The London Magazine*, with the recently completed St. Paul's cathedral dominating the skyline around London Bridge.

mand immorality occasionally extended beyond the limits of the society's own small gathering into the public realm. Every member of the Cripplegate Society was to be ready to do what might be advisable "towards the punishment of publick prophaneness."

Upon this rather exclusivistic base, the societies attempted in some small measure to spread their influence within English society. The motivation for their endeavors was self-consciously circumspect—never for "popular applause or malice to any man," but rather their activities should arise out of "pure Love to God and Charity to men's souls" (Legg, 312).

The religious societies also encouraged certain charitable causes, for which the members subscribed regularly as their circumstances would allow. This was not the promotion of general philanthropy in the simple humanitarian sense of the word, but rather the dispensing of funds to promote more narrowly the goals and purposes of the societies. Their charitable exercises were a natural outgrowth of the concern members exhibited for each other, such as visiting sick members. At a very early stage in their development, the societies began to demonstrate a special interest in the needs of the poor and disadvantaged, giving food and money to the needy, visiting the sick and imprisoned, and teaching the children of the unfortunate.

In working with the poor, the religious societies intended not so much to raise their standard of living in an economic sense, but rather to improve their life in a spiritual and moral sense. Illiteracy and poverty in the burgeoning lower classes of England at the time were seen by many as the major contributing factors to growing immorality and vice. The religious societies, in trying to help improve this situation, found it necessary to take an apologetic stance in supporting such programs as the development of charity schools, pointing out very carefully that such schools were not seedbeds of discontent or revolution, but rather were designed "to instruct [the poor] very carefully in the duties of servants, and submission to superiors." Workhouses, established in many cities as another means of helping the poor, had a dual emphasis upon work and education, so designed that "the next generation of persons in lower life [would] be made better." In this setting, the children of the poor, "instead of being bred up in irreligion and vice, to an idle, beggarly, and vagabond life, [would have] the fear of God before their eyes, get habits of virtue, be inured to labour, and thus become useful to their country."

In addition to these programs of nurture, welfare, and education, the religious societies did encourage vigilance in promoting private and public morality. The latter was institutionalized in the formation of the **Society for the Reformation of Manners** (SRM) in 1691. Concerned with neighborhood morality, this society was designed to encourage and assist the Justices of the Peace to perform their duties in the enforcement of laws respecting moral offenses, especially "profaneness and debauchery." These ends were achieved by means of members who acted as secret informers and witnessed against the offenders. The generally negative approach of the Society (especially the use of informers) tended to bring reproach upon the organization from several quarters, which subsequently contributed to the decreasing influence of all the religious societies after the first three decades of the eighteenth century.

The program of the SPCK (1698) and its sister group, the **Society for the Propagation of the Gospel** (1701), was more specific than the general purpose of the religious societies to encourage holy living among the membership. The SPCK attempted to attack what it considered to be the root of the problem (ignorance) by developing channels of educating the public in Christian principles. While the impetus of the program lay also in the qualities of charity, virtue, and piety which characterized the religious societies in general, the program of the SPCK consisted mainly of encouraging the establishment of charity schools for teaching the poor, promoting the spread of lending libraries, and visiting the prisons to instruct the inmates and to give them religious services and books. To this end, the Society entered upon an extensive publishing program. The dispersing of "pious books and catechisms" among the public, particularly the poor, was fervently advocated as a means of bringing "the generality of the common people to a true knowledge of God, a sense of the great importance of religion, and a serious concern for their everlasting welfare." Within the first two or three years of the Society's existence, its leaders estimated that they had given away nearly a million books of all sorts—Bibles, Common-Prayer Books, Catechisms, Treatises on the Sacrament, and a multitude of practical and devotional pieces (including those in their book catalog under one of the main subheadings, "Anti-popery"). The expense of such a program was underwritten by the regular subscriptions of the "residing members" (later called "subscribing members") of the Society, bolstered by the casual benefactions of friends, and promoted by a host of "corresponding members" in the countryside.

In addition to their publishing enterprise, the SPCK supported the growing missionary movement of the day. Not only were the first members of the Society instrumental in the incorporation of the SPG, but they independently encouraged particular mission projects with money, books, and other forms of assistance. From the beginning, the SPCK supported the mission work in the "Plantations" of America. In 1732, the Society undertook to assist the persecuted Salzburgers in Germany and provided for their relief by helping to transport them to the colony of Georgia in America.

The program of the SPCK continued to flourish in spite of the general demise of the religious societies in the second quarter of the eighteenth century. For although the SPCK had grown out of the religious society movement, the outward thrust of its program carried it beyond the introspective and elitist tendencies of the private societies. Its publishing interests and its educational endeavors in the charity schools and the mission field laid a foundation of service and usefulness to the general public that encouraged further support and development of the Society as an important and lasting institution in British life.

The Wesley Family at Epworth

Although the story of Methodism is much more than the biography of John Wesley, the influence upon him of the Wesley household was certainly a formative factor in the rise of the movement that later bore his name. Susanna Wesley is traditionally given much of the credit for raising and nurturing her sons Charles and John in such a fashion that the Methodist movement might seem a natural outgrowth of the devotional life and thought of the Epworth rectory. That view tends to overlook the fact that, for all their differences, Samuel and Susanna held very similar theological and political views and were of a mind in the methods of raising their children. Susanna was in charge of the early education of the children, and did institute a weekly evening hour with each of the five or six children at home at any given time. But the influence of the weekly sermon, which the children were no doubt expected to attend faithfully, would certainly leave its mark on the developing theology of the children. The surviving letters of Susanna to her children contain a preponderance of theological issues perhaps surprising to behold in an age when women were not expected to be educated.

But the Wesleys were not what one would normally expect to find in a remote rural parish. Samuel was of a scholarly and literary bent. His university degree at Oxford was earned through Exeter College. Then, when he lived near London shortly thereafter, he was the resident cleric in an urbane literary society, the Athenian Society, and seems to have written theological treatises for the *Athenian Gazette* on their behalf. He also wrote poetry, publishing, among other things, a metrical version of the life of Christ (the Gospels) that went through several editions well into the nineteenth century and producing as his last work a tedious scholarly linguistic study of the book of Job.

Susanna was also interested in learning and education, though of course not university-educated herself—women could not enroll at the universities. But she extended her own training to all her children. Susanna is often best remembered in this regard for her hard-nosed approach: "In order to form the minds of children, the first thing to be done is to conquer their will and bring them to an obedient temper." What is often overlooked is that she was ahead of her day in one particular area; Susanna was very concerned that girls be taught to read as well as boys. One of her household "by-laws" stipulated "that no girl be taught to work till she can read very well, [since] the putting children to learn sewing before they can read perfectly is the very reason why so few women can read fit to be heard, and never to be well understood." We should remember that when John Wesley was a young boy in the Epworth rectory, he was the only boy at home with four or five sisters until he was four and his little brother Charles was born. Given this context for his rearing, John's later eagerness to accept the leadership abilities of women is as understandable as his inability to develop a lasting intimate relationship with a woman is perplexing.

Samuel and Susanna both came from nonconformist backgrounds. As we have already seen, Samuel's father (John Westley) had been excluded from his living by the Bishop of Bristol in the seventeenth century. Susanna was the daughter of Samuel Annesley, a noted nonconformist minister in London in the late seventeenth century. Both Samuel and Susanna, however, as young adults became "converts" to the Established Church. As is often the case, their change of loyalty was accompanied by a zeal for their new position—they became ardent supporters of the establishment and arch-Tories as well (nonconformists tended to have Whig sympathies). Samuel and Susanna even supported the general position of the nonjuring bishops and their Jacobite support for the Old Pretender, James.

One illustration of domestic differences in the Epworth rectory arose over Samuel's somewhat tempered position—willing to be loyal to the monarchy in spite of questioning the validity of the person on the throne. He was not able to accept Susanna's refusal to say "Amen" to the prayer for the monarch during family prayers. The resulting argument ("if we have different monarchs, we shall sleep in different beds") led Samuel to leave Epworth for an extended visit to London, purportedly to attend the Convocation of Clergy. His return home to prepare for a proposed naval chaplaincy was simultaneous with the accession of a new monarch, Anne, whose mutual acceptability to the couple led him to forget the navy and stay at Epworth. Within a year, John Wesley was born, the "fruits of reconciliation."

The Wesleys were among the many persons who were influenced by the SPCK. John's relationship with the Society will be noted later. In many ways, however, his own direct connection with the SPCK was anticipated by his father's interest both in the work of that Society in particular and in the development of the religious societies in general. In 1700 Samuel Wesley attempted to set up a small religious society in Epworth built upon the model of the societies in London. Books and tracts were ordered from the SPCK, of which Samuel had become a corresponding member (*SPCK*, 87–88). Within two years, he had established a small society, begun with a few of "the most sensible and well dispos'd persons" from the choir in his parish. He founded the group upon a set of rules and orders substantially the same as those of the London society, including the expected guidance by "a pious and learned divine of the Church" (Legg, 292). He reported in a letter to the London-based Society that the intent of his circle of friends was "First to pray to God; secondly, to read the Holy Scriptures and discourse upon religious matters for their mutual edification; and thirdly, to deliberate about the edification of our neighbour and the promoting of it."

Following the generally accepted pattern, the members of the society at Epworth were not hasty to admit new members, especially those "of whose solid piety they [were] not yet sufficiently apprised." To this end, and to prevent their religious design from falling of its own weight, the group was limited to twelve members. However, a procedure was adopted in case the providence of God should stir up more persons with a powerful desire for the same edification. A new society could be formed around two members who would separate themselves from the first society. This second group also would be

The parish church of St. Andrew's at Epworth.

limited to twelve members, with the provision from that group another could grow, following the pattern established in the first case. This provision prefigures the general pattern of organization that John Wesley would follow with his company of friends at Oxford three decades later.

Within this organizational scheme set up at Epworth, the "first Society" had priority in matters of policy. Thus any debate which should happen to arise about any question of "amending or reforming" the Church in point of "manners" or public morality, was referred to the first society. While Samuel was careful to point out that the first group should in no wise assume any prerogative to itself, members of the other societies were obliged to bring any matter tending toward public edification to the attention of the first society. It appears also from the rector's comments that, with the above precedence in mind, the membership of this first society was to be quite select, admitting only such "as are able to help the Church by their wisdom and good advices."

All of these stipulations represent an attempt to keep the society within the boundaries of Church doctrine and polity. Samuel's concern in this regard can be seen in his later reaction to Susanna's inviting neighbors to her kitchen for Sunday evening prayers in 1711/12. Such a gathering might appear to some as a worship service in a private home, i.e. a "conventicle," strictly forbidden by the Act of Toleration and subsequent legislation as a threat to established religion and perceived as an underground means of circumventing the registration laws for dissenters. Samuel's strong words to his wife (in a letter from London) were met by a typically strong retort by the strong-willed Susanna, who felt that if Samuel had not left the parish in the hands of such an inept curate, she would not have had the neighbors begging to come into her home for spiritual nourishment. She ended her letter to Samuel by saying, "If you do, after all, think fit to dissolve this assembly, . . . send me your positive command, in such full and express terms as may absolve me from all guilt and punishment for neglecting this opportunity of doing good, when you and I shall appear before the great and awful tribunal of our Lord Jesus Christ." Samuel's response is lost, as it probably was also on Susanna.

The design for the Epworth society is especially interesting with respect to the close manner in which Samuel attempted to emulate the outward thrust of the SPCK within his remote country parish. Five of the fourteen rules of order he wrote for the society dealt with the charitable activities he hoped their subscriptions would support, as did their following statement of purpose:

> Their first care is to set schools for the poor, wherein children (or if need be, adult persons) may be instructed in the fundamentals of Christianity by men of known and approved piety.
> Their second design is to procure little practical treatises from Holland, England, and Germany, etc., to translate them into the vulgar tongue, print them, and so to give or lend them to those who are less solicitous of their own and others edification.
> The third is to establish a correspondence with such societies in England, Germany, etc., that so they may mutually edify one another.
> The fourth is to take care of the sick and other poor, and to afford them spiritual as well as corporal helps (*M&M*, 44).

To what extent these rather ambitious goals were realized in the Epworth society is difficult to assess on the basis of records now available. It is important to note, however, that the vision of such possibilities, even within the rather remote setting of the Isle of Axholme, was a part of the Wesley family heritage. Samuel was by no means a stranger to the publishing world himself, and his own personal correspondence included many of the ecclesiastical and political leaders in England. Whether or not this personal participation in the scholarly and literary pursuits of his day, exemplified in part by his association with the Athenian Society in London, was effectually transferred to the group at Epworth, his attempt to encourage these pursuits within his society no doubt had some bearing on the direction his sons would take three decades later at Oxford.

The design of the religious societies of the early eighteenth century "to promote real holiness of heart and life" was characterized by a high-Church piety that depended upon an intense study of Scripture and other works of practical divinity, that demanded personal moral discipline, and that expressed itself in charitable acts toward the disadvantaged elements of society. The practice of the societies to meet regularly to encourage each other in "practical holiness" was part of a larger design to retreat from the snares of "the world." In this respect there was more than a passing similarity with the purposes of the medieval monastic orders. As Samuel Wesley noted in his "Letter Concerning the Religious Societies,"

> I know few good men but lament that after the destruction of monasteries, there were not some societies founded in their stead, but reformed from their errors and reduced to the primitive standard. None who had but looked into our own church history, can be ignorant how highly instrumental such bodies of men as these were to the first planting and propagating Christianity amongst our forefathers. . . . A great part of the good effects of that way of life may be attained without many of the inconveniencies of it, by such societies as we are now discoursing of (*M&M*, 44).

Such sentiments, combined with certain tendencies of the high-Church party, were construed by some to indicate a dangerous element of Jacobitism among the supporters of the societies. The stipulation that new members be well-affected toward both church and state did little to allay the suspicions of some. On the other hand, such inclinations within the societies did not bother Samuel Wesley or his family, most of whom had a tendency to lean in that direction anyway.

Although there is no evidence of John or Charles Wesley having had any contact with the Epworth religious society as such when they were children, their parents' concern for the family was certainly of a piece with their nurture of the congregation. All the children were given careful training in piety and learning. They learned a traditional theology that combined faith and good works in a fashion that reflected the orthodox doctrinal perspective and Puritan ethical inclinations of Samuel and Susanna. After sitting at their mother's knee and in their father's church, at about ten years of age the boys were sent off to London for more formal schooling at excellent schools: young Samuel and Charles to Westminster, John to Charterhouse. All three then followed their father's footsteps to Oxford.

Oxford University in the early eighteenth century reflected many of the problems that characterized English society as a whole. While one contemporary observer felt that Oxford was a "seat of good manners, as well as of learning" (the people being "more civilized than the inhabitants of any other town in Great Britain"), it must be said that "a comfortable slackness" prevailed in the spiritual and academic endeavors of the University, representing a low point in the history of the school. The problems that beset England in general thus confronted John Wesley at Oxford, both in his relationships within the University and in the conditions of the city and surrounding area. When in 1725 the direction of his life began to change toward a more vital expression of practical piety, he began a spiritual and intellectual pilgrimage that led him through the pages of hundreds of books, into dozens of country parishes and city prisons, across the paths of a multitude of new acquaintances, and even to the shores of the New World within the ensuing decade. Wesley found himself not only pursuing the goals expressed by the religious societies in their search for "real holiness," but also adopting some of their methods. In this pursuit he was perhaps led, if not encouraged, by the earlier experience of his father.

Wesley's search during this period for a meaningful understanding of the demands of Christian living eventually led him to tie together the perfectionism of the pietists, the moralism of the Puritans, and the devotionalism of the mystics in a pragmatic approach that he felt could operate within the structure and doctrine of the Church of England. Many of the historic movements that had left their mark on the fabric of so many churches in England like St. Michael's, Stanton Harcourt, were still a part of the living traditions in European Christianity that would influence Wesley's development and from which would emerge his own conception of the nature and design of Christian life and thought. The manner in which Wesley and his company of friends at Oxford proceeded in this search and the methods they developed during these early years were important in helping to determine the later shape of the Wesleyan movement. This story of the Oxford Methodists is aptly referred to, by Wesley himself, as "the first rise of Methodism."

CHAPTER 1—Suggested Additional Reading

Abbey, Charles John, and John H. Overton, *The English Church in the Eighteenth Century* (London: Longmans, Green, 1878).

Allison, Christopher F., *The Rise of Moralism; the Proclamation of the Gospel from Hooker to Baxter* (New York: Seabury Press, 1966).

Bangs, Carl, *Arminius* (Nashville: Abingdon Press, 1971).

Butterfield, Herbert, "The Eighteenth Century Background," in *A History of the Methodist Church in Great Britain*, Vol. 1, ed. Rupert Davies and Gordon Rupp (London: Epworth Press, 1965).

Clarke, W. K. Lowther, *Eighteenth-Century Piety* (London: SPCK, 1944).

Cragg, Gerald R., *The Church and the Age of Reason* (Baltimore: Penguin Books, 1966).

Dickens, Arthur G., *The English Reformation* (New York: Schocken, 1964).

Legg, J. Wickham, *English Church Life from the Restoration to the Tractarian Movement* (London: Longmans, Green, 1914).

M&M—Heitzenrater, Richard P., *Mirror and Memory: Reflections on Early Methodism* (Nashville: Kingswood Books, 1989).

McAdoo, Henry R., *The Spirit of Anglicanism* (New York: Charles Scribner's Sons, 1965).

More, Paul E., and F. L. Cross, *Anglicanism* (London: SPCK, 1962).

Plumb, J. H., *England in the Eighteenth Century, 1714–1815* (Baltimore: Penguin Books, 1964).

Portus, Garnet Vere, *Caritas Anglicana* (London: Mowbray & Co., 1912).

Rupp, Gordon, *Religion in England, 1688–1791* (Oxford: Clarendon Press, 1986).

SPCK — Allen, W. O. B., and Edmund McClure, *Two Hundred Years: The History of the Society for Promoting Christian Knowledge, 1698–1898* (London: SPCK, 1898).

Walsh, John, "Origins of the Evangelical Revival," *Essays in Modern English Church History* (New York: Oxford University Press, 1966).

Willey, Basil, *The Eighteenth Century Background* (Boston: Beacon Press, 1964).

CHAPTER 2

The Rise of Methodism (1725–1739)

In his various reflections upon the rise and growth of Methodism, Wesley often emphasized the spontaneity of its origins and the open-endedness of its development. In his view, God raised up the people called Methodists for a purpose that was specific and appropriate but in a manner that was not necessarily predictable or predetermined.

The task of determining the actual beginning of a movement that arose spontaneously and without design or preconception is difficult at best. As early as 1765 John Wesley noticed, "It is not easy to reckon up the various accounts which have been given of the people called Methodists" (*Short History of Methodism*). And yet, when he decided to write a history of the Methodists in his *Ecclesiastical History* (1781), Wesley was very specific in pointing out three stages in the rise of Methodism prior to 1739: Oxford, Georgia, and London. This suggestion of an explicit progression of early developments provides a useful framework within which to examine the origins of Methodism.

The First Rise of Methodism—Oxford

The story of the beginnings of "the people called Methodists" is quite naturally bound up with the personal story of John and Charles Wesley. John was, as his contemporaries acknowledged, the "chief manager" of the Oxford Methodists (*EMW*, 2:38). In more recent years, Charles has been claimed by some to be the founder of the group. At least one account has pointed out that William Morgan has a valid claim on the title, the "first Methodist" (*M&M*, 233). The search for the first Methodist is not simple; the beginnings of a movement are not often easy to pinpoint. A specified "date of origin" might be the pedagogue's delight, a list of "charter members" the archivist's dream, and a designated "founder" the hagiographer's necessity. But the historian is generally satisfied to describe the developments as they happened and allow the complexities of the situation to define what questions are appropriate to answer.

John Wesley had gone up to Oxford (one never goes over or down

The southwest prospect of the city of Oxford in the eighteenth century, dominated by the towers of All Saints' Church (11), St. Mary's Church (12), Christ Church (16), Merton College (17), Christ Church Cathedral (another 16), and Magdalen College (18).

to Oxford) in June 1720 from Charterhouse School in London, where he had spent seven years in a program of classical education designed to train him for the university. His college was Christ Church (one never says Christ Church College), the largest and, some say, the most prestigious of the schools that constitute the University. The majority of scholars at Oxford were preparing for a position in government, medicine, law, or the Church. The tutors and fellows of the various colleges, responsible for implementing the curriculum were, by statute, almost exclusively men of the cloth. It is no surprise, then, that when in 1724 John Wesley received his baccalaureate degree and had aspirations of continuing at Oxford as a Fellow of a college, he faced the prospect of proceeding toward ordination. With his father's hesitant support and his mother's concurrence (she thought it would induce him toward the study of "practical divinity," whereas Samuel was encouraging him in critical learning), he began reading for the ordination examination (*Letters*, 25:158–60).

Ministerial training in the Church of England entailed, after the attainment of a Bachelor of Arts degree, examination under the bishop prior to ordination as a deacon; then, after two years probation in that status (including continuation of academic studies toward an M.A. while reading for the next exam), another examination under the bishop and ordination as a presbyter or priest. While the academic and ecclesiastical processes were parallel, they were distinctly separate. The Bachelor of Divinity degree was not a normal expectation (much less a prerequisite) for parish ministers, but was a statutory requirement for most Fellows of colleges within seven years of receiving their master's degree. The Doctor of Divinity degree was pursued only by those interested in further preferment within the academy.

During Lent of 1725, Wesley began his studies toward ordination as a deacon. At this point, he entered what he later described as the third stage of his theological development. First, at Epworth and at Charterhouse, he had been raised in the theological tradition of the Church of England. The mediating emphasis of the *via media* can be seen in his comment that he was "early warned against laying, as the Papists do, too much stress . . . on outward works, or [as the radical Protestants do] on a faith without works, which, as it does not include, so it will never lead to, true hope or charity" (*J&D*, 18:212). The balance between faith and good works, the following of virtuous tempers, and the use of all the means of grace which God provided, would help one "have the mind that was in Christ and walk as he walked."

Then, sometime prior to 1725, Wesley "fell among some Lutheran and Calvinist authors whose confused and undigested accounts magnified faith to such an amazing size that it quite hid all the rest of the commandments." In retrospect, his confusion was understandable: "this was the natural effect of their overgrown fear of Popery; being so tempted with the cry of 'merit and good works' that they plunged at once into the other extreme." He describes his plight: "in this labyrinth I was utterly lost, not being able to find out what the error was, nor yet to reconcile this uncouth hypothesis either with Scripture or common sense" (*J&D*, 18:212).

Wesley now entered a third stage of influence in his theological development. His reading in 1725 began to focus on the pietists of the holy living tradition. **Thomas à Kempis** provided the foundation for this perspective; Wesley began reading *De Imitatione Christi* regularly. From the typical pietist bibliography, he picked up Jeremy Taylor's *Rule and Exercises of Holy Living and Holy Dying* (1650), Robert Nelson's *The Practice of True Devotion* (1708), and William Beveridge's *Private Thoughts Upon Religion* (1709?). These, and similar writings, relieved him, as he said, from those "well-meaning, wrong-headed Germans."

Jeremy Taylor provided one of the most crucial suggestions that Wesley adopted: the first rule of holy living is care of your time. The most visible consequence of Taylor's advice was Wesley's beginning to keep a **diary** as a record and measure of his progress in holy living. The most significant theological consequence of the pietist influence was Wesley's discovery that holiness was an inner reality—"that true religion was seated in the heart and that God's law extended to all our thoughts as well as words and actions." Wesley's recollection of his self-evaluation at that point nevertheless was that "I doubted not but I was a good Christian" (*J&D*, 18:244).

Some historians and biographers have suggested that this change of temper on Wesley's part, coincident with his preparation for holy orders in 1725, marks his "conversion." The entries in Wesley's diary certainly indicate the seriousness of his attempts at **holy living** and the pervasiveness of his concern for inward purity of intention, all grounded in an understanding of Christian virtue that was essentially scriptural. But the question of "conversion" hinges on the definition of "Christian," and not only will Wesley's own definition undergo subsequent modifications, but the application of the definition as a personal measure will change with his own fluctuations of spiritual sensitivity from time to time.

At the very least, what can be seen in 1725 is the first outward manifestations of a conviction that holy living is essential to the nature of true Christianity. Even the beginning implementation of this perspective in Wesley's life and thought displays many of the characteristic features of what will come to be called "Methodist."

This spiritual quest for **holiness** provided the focus for Wesley's theology. Wesley already had some convictions that would shape his theological framework and provide a lifelong spiritual impetus. He was convinced as early as 1725 that one should certainly be able to sense God's forgiveness; this became the basis for his concern for a perceptible assurance of salvation (*Letters*, 25:174–75). He was just as convinced that such certainty of pardon was not a guarantee that sin would not rise up again; this is the basis for his constant concern for backsliding (and for part of his antipathy toward predestination). He also felt that the means of grace should be used constantly; this provided a basis for his lifelong battle against antinomianism. At this point, Wesley was beginning to work through these issues with the help of several books and the advice of his parents. The concerns were only personal and had no broader implications beyond his own life at the University.

By exercising a certain amount of political leverage and social grace, Wesley succeeded in winning election to a fellowship at Lincoln College on March 17, 1726. Parental pride shines through his father's response to the news: "Wherever I am, my Jacky is Fellow of Lincoln." John could now also be assured of basic support: a roof over his head, food on his plate, students under his charge—all gratis to a Fellow (along with a yearly stipend for life) so long as he remained unmarried.

Wesley found little camaraderie in his spiritual pilgrimage either among his colleagues or his students, however. Even his brother Charles, who came up to the University as a Scholar at Christ Church in June 1726, was of a frivolous bent of mind and spirit, and not inclined toward serious religious pursuits. The same was true of the brothers' closest friend, Robert Kirkham, brother of Wesley's closest female friend during this period, Sarah Kirkham of Stanton (also known as "Varanese"). The one person at Oxford who appears to have shared Wesley's vision of Christian commitment and holy living, Robin Griffiths, died that winter; John preached his funeral sermon on January 15, 1727 (*Sermons*, 4:236–43).

Having received his M.A. on February 14, 1727, John decided the following summer to accept his father's invitation to serve as curate in Epworth and Wroot. Besides assisting in the ministerial duties of the parish, John could help Samuel with his scholarly *magnum opus*, *Dissertationes in Librum Jobi*. John's only trip back to Oxford during the next two years would be for his ordination as **presbyter** (priest) on September 22, 1728. John was not hesitant to admit to Charles that

John Wesley's personal diary contained many entries written in cipher and shorthand, such as these lists of rules inspired by Jeremy Taylor's book, *Holy Living*. Charles also began keeping a diary, which acted as a record of activities and a basis for self-examination.

this new situation in the parish setting was to his liking, and that he was perhaps "settled for life—at least for years" (*Letters*, 25:230).

Charles Wesley, continuing at Christ Church and feeling his brother's absence keenly, soon reported to John that he had "awoke out of [his] lethargy." Later that year, the officials of the University decided to combat openly the influence of Deism and irreligion at Oxford, proclaiming that the tutors would be diligent in explaining to their students the Articles of Religion and recommending to them the "frequent and careful reading the Scriptures." Charles, now conscientiously trying to take this course of action, had to report to John what his older brother had already learned three years earlier, that at Christ Church "a man stands a very fair chance of being laughed out of his religion at his first setting out." Charles asked John for help, pointing out that " 'tis through your means, I firmly believe, God will establish what He has begun in me, and there is no one person I would so willingly have to be the instrument of good to me as you." Now quickened in spirit, Charles asked for specific advice from his brother, especially regarding the keeping of a spiritual logbook, a diary: what should he record? should he mark both the good and bad? keep track of learning as well as religion? use a cipher? what books should he read? If John was already a Methodist in spirit (though not yet in name), Charles was now his willing companion: "If you would direct me to the same, or a like method with your own, I would gladly follow it."

The word from Charles in May 1729 that he had convinced a colleague to join him in serious study and weekly attendance at church encouraged John to visit Oxford, where he arrived on his birthday, June 17. For the next two months, John, Charles, Charles's friend, **William Morgan** (and occasionally their old friend Bob Kirkham), encouraged each other in their scholarly and religious pursuits, getting together occasionally for study and going to church every week. John's diary reveals no regular meetings among the friends during his ten-week stay at Oxford during the summer of 1729; but the seeds of an organizational pattern began to germinate during this period. The little band of friends, encouraged by the presence of John, occasionally met together for study, prayer, and religious conversation, attended the Sacrament regularly, and kept track of their lives by daily notations in a diary. These fairly innocuous activities represent the first manifestations of what would become **Oxford Methodism**. The gatherings were not regular, not everyone attended each meeting, the daily routine was not set, the light recreation was still evident now and then; but some of the marks of the Wesleyan movement were present in the group. At the end of the summer, as the students scattered to their homes for the holiday between terms, the Wesleys headed north for Epworth and the annual fair.

John's return to Oxford ten weeks later was precipitated by a call from the head of his college, who voiced the other Fellows' concern that John take up his share of tutorial duties at the college. The October letter containing this message had to pursue John into Yorkshire, where it found him traveling with his father, the pair of them trying to raise subscriptions for Samuel's book on Job. The prospect of being at Oxford and having paying students must have looked attractive to John in that setting for a variety of reasons. A spare page in his diary at this point reveals that he calculated the deficit in his curate's stipend from his father—over a year in arrears, even when subtracting the value of a pair of gift boots. Within days, John and Charles begin the walk south, adding another fifty or sixty miles to the journey in order to visit their brother Samuel in London.

The Wesleys took up their activities at Oxford just where they left off in the summer. There is no noticeable change in the configuration of their associations, no visible alteration in their schedule of occasional gatherings for study and worship. The date of their arrival back in Oxford (November 22) has little intrinsic significance, save that John later mentions it in his recollection of the beginnings of Methodism as the time when he resumed residence in Oxford. For several weeks, John, Charles, and William Morgan continue as in the summer.

Organizational Beginnings of the Oxford Society

The actual beginnings of regular activities that John himself mentions as definitive of their purpose and design can be seen in the late winter of 1729/30 when, much to John's surprise, **Bob Kirkham** "left off his society" and began to meet with the Wesleys and Morgan regularly. John's diary clearly reveals the pattern that developed in early March 1730: evening meetings on Tuesdays at Charles's room, Thursdays at Kirkham's, Saturdays at John's, and Sundays at Morgan's. Aside from this notable regularity, the diary entries which refer to these meetings (e.g., "at Charles's, with Morgan and Kirkham, read Tully"), contain no indication of anything other than an occasion for study. At the weekday sessions, the four friends studied the classics, such as Horace, Juvenal, and Terence. On Sunday evening, they read works of divinity, such as Milton, de Renty, and Prior. And on frequent occasions, the group attended the University sermon and Sacrament on Sunday, although John himself was more often preaching in the country parish churches of Oxfordshire on the weekends.

Aside from occasionally jibing at what was seen as a **"sacramentarian"** tendency, the university community hardly noticed this small band of students who were trying faithfully to fulfill the expectations of the University Statutes. Although they did not represent the typical student at Oxford in the early eighteenth century, they were hardly the first or only group to attend diligently to the serious pursuits of the academic community; similar groups meeting in a tutor's room for prayer and study are evident in the previous decade and were also meeting concurrently with the Wesleyan group in the early 1730s in other colleges (*Ingham,* 12). While such scholarly and devotional activities characterize the Wesleyan group, the movement is obviously not entirely defined by such activities. The manifestations of the unique blend of life and thought that come to typify the Wesleyan approach at Oxford become more apparent in the late summer of 1730.

In August, William Morgan suggested repeatedly to John that the group visit the debtors and condemned felons in the **Castle prison**. Morgan had been carrying on a wide range of charitable activities for some time: teaching orphan children, caring for the poor and aged, visiting the prisons. The Wesley brothers accompanied Morgan to the old fortifications of the Castle on the afternoon of August 24 and were so satisfied by the experience with the prisoners that they agreed to go thereafter at least weekly. The group, growing slowly to five or six members, began to set a schedule for such visits; John's time was Saturday afternoons.

Following Morgan's lead, the Wesleyan group soon incorporated other charitable activities into their growing schedule of social concern. A week after visiting the Castle, John visited Mrs. Vesey, one of the many elderly and poor folk in Oxford who relied on the sometime charity of their parish church for what support and spiritual sustenance they could receive. This activity was not a new experience for the Fellow of Lincoln, who had spent two years as a curate in a country parish. But the credit for seeing the possibility of this sort of regular service within the activities of an academic community (and in particular for the Methodists at Oxford) seems to go also to his friend, William Morgan. Before long, the Methodists were spending several hours a week with the poor and needy in the town.

In December 1730, the group expanded their concerns to include those persons incarcerated in the city jail at the North Gate **(Bocardo),** the way once again having been opened for them by Morgan. The

Bocardo, the Oxford city jail, extended over the North Gate of the city wall at St. Michael's Church (which also served as part of the wall). The prisoners at times lowered a basket from their window (as shown in this woodcut) for passers-by to give them food or money.

young Irishman, who was the designer of a great portion of the Methodists' scheme of social action, also began bringing together children of poor families in Oxford as least as early as the spring of 1731. When he left town for a time to recover from an illness, Wesley and his friends attempted to fill the void which their Irish friend had left. John realized quite soon that the situation called for more permanent arrangements and toward the end of June 1731 hired Mrs. Plat to take care of the children. The Methodists continued, however, to take an active interest and role in the progress of the children.

These actions within the community gained a certain notoriety for the group among their university peers. Kirkham was the first to feel the brunt of his colleagues' vicious mirth at Merton College for being a member of what they derisively called "**The Holy Club**." This epithet was soon displaced by a series of other scornful names that chided their attempted virtues: Godly Club, Bible-Moths, Supererogation-Men. As was often to be the case, the rumors about their activities as a group had exceeded their actual scheme of endeavors, with the result that they had gained the reputation for being (as John reported to his father) "friends to none but what are as queer as ourselves." Wesley disliked their being called a "club," and despite his own occasional use of the term, was hesitant to adopt any formal designation as a "society." It was to be two years before the term "Methodist" would be applied to them, but the small group of students was beginning to display many of the characteristics that would identify the movement throughout the rest of the century.

It is of crucial importance in trying to understand the dynamics of Oxford Methodism to note that the various activities which characterize their public image were in most cases not originated by Wesley himself, as we shall continue to notice. It must be remembered that Wesley was deeply engaged in the search for "a right state of soul." Consequently his method was not a static, settled scheme, but rather an approach to life that grew and developed and changed as he confronted different crises, had further insights, and met new friends. John's acknowledged leadership within the movement came from an ability to fit these various pursuits together with a sense of purpose, which gave direction and spiritual impulse to the Methodists' search for salvation. To catch the essence of Methodism at Oxford is to recognize this impulse as well as the developing lifestyle which it elicited.

For the next year, John's attention was increasingly focused on the Oxford scene. The frequent preaching trips to country parishes, typical of the previous years, abruptly ceased; he even sold the horse he had acquired for this purpose a year before. Part of John's continuing involvement at the Castle prison included preaching there at least once a month for the next four and a half years. He noted his own weekly schedule of visiting in the front of his diary for 1731: Monday, Bocardo; Tuesday, Castle; Wednesday, children; Thursday, Castle; Friday, Bocardo; Saturday, Castle; Sunday, poor and elderly. Wesley was aware of the ease with which such busyness could become an end in itself, and perhaps for his own recollection as much as his father's, told the aging counselor that the main point they needed to establish to make all their activity manageable was "to have an habitual lively sense of our being only instruments in His hand, who can do all things either with or without any instrument" (*Letters*, 25:257–58).

Wesley's sermon before the university in November 1729 gives us a clue as to the impetus and rationale behind his increasingly evident concern for others, which was beginning to draw him beyond his own desire for personal salvation. This sermon on Genesis 1:27 ends with the comment, "They who have saved others from sin and its attendant death 'shall shine as the brightness of the firmament'; they who have reprinted the image of God on many souls, 'as the stars for ever and ever'" (*Sermons*, 4:303). John's methods and activities, perhaps best characterized as **meditative piety**, were all designed to promote "holiness of heart and life" (in the typical terminology of the religious societies) in himself as well as in others. His seemingly frantic attempt to "omit no duty either to God or man" evidenced his inner search for a sense of assurance, a desired conviction that he was a child of God.

By 1730, John had begun reading **William Law**'s *Serious Call to a Devout and Holy Life* (1729), which reinforced and extended his previous understanding of "the exceeding height and breadth and depth of the law of God." Again, Wesley himself expressed the significance of this influence in terms that imply a drastic change in his life—"The light flowed in so mightily upon my soul, that everything appeared in a new view" (*J&D*, 18:244). Some twentieth-century authors have pointed to this comment as an indication that Wesley at that point certainly had a drastic re-orientation in his spiritual life—a real conversion, by most definitions of the term.

At that time, Wesley's hope for salvation was grounded in a reliance upon the **sincerity** of his own desire to lead the Christian life and a trust in God's promises as he understood them. His **assurance** of salvation rested upon what he defined as "the hope of our calling: to know that our hope is sincerity, not perfection; not to do well, but to do our best" (*Letters*, 25:318). This guideline, to do the best one can, undergirded Wesley's activities at this time and gave him some measure of strength to persevere in spite of both adverse criticism from many quarters and the nagging awareness of his own shortcomings. It was hardly the sort of hope or assurance, however, that could calm an honest and introspective soul convinced (as Wesley was) that there were no indifferent acts—that every action had moral value, good or evil. Even though he was disclaiming **perfection** (here understood as perfect obedience) as either a measure or goal of life, the intensive reliance upon his own sincerity in the face of constant moral choices placed an equal burden of responsibility upon him. This combination of views would for a time produce more anxiety than assurance in Wesley and lead to an increasingly compulsive pattern of activity that had an apparent design but no clear goal. His primary concern was inner purity of heart promoted by meditation on the virtues, but he and his friends were often characterized by their concern for the outward manifestation of these virtues conforming to certain rules and methods. Meditative piety among the Methodists became seen as legalistic works-righteousness by their colleagues.

In 1732, the design of the Wesleyan society at Oxford changed rather notably in conjunction with a dramatic change in personnel. Morgan, weakened from continuing sickness, went home to Ireland in early June. Kirkham and John Boyce left Oxford, and William Haward, their only other compatriot, gradually disassociated from the group, leaving John and Charles Wesley as the only original participants still active in these pursuits at the University. But, as was frequently to happen in the following years, this discouraging trend was offset by a positive development.

As William Morgan was preparing to leave Oxford, Wesley made the acquaintance of **John Clayton**, whose subsequent association with the Methodists made a lasting mark on the movement. Clayton, who had many of the same social concerns as Morgan, also had a little society of his own at Brasenose College, and opened up several new friendships and associations for Wesley. He introduced Wesley to the program of the Manchester nonjurors (Thomas Deacon, John Byrom, *et al.*), who focused their interests on the life and thought of early Christianity. The son of a Manchester bookseller, Clayton helped John develop closer relationships with publishers and booksellers in London and Oxford. He also seems to have introduced John into a new circle of friends in the London area which included influential supporters of the religious society movement. Sir John Phillips, a prime mover in the SPCK, became a substantial contributor to the Oxford Methodists' causes. Wesley in turn purchased from the Society's book-list many tracts, Bibles, and other works for distribution among his friends. Wesley's life and thought was influenced by his connection with the Society, of which he became a "corresponding member" in 1732: the Society not only functioned to some degree as a model for his own group, but also initiated and encouraged his interest in the Georgia colony.

Although Clayton was associated with Wesley at Oxford for less than six months, his influence brought some important changes. Signs of increased discipline appear in the Wesleyan schedule of works of piety and mercy. Their weekly routine was altered to observe the **"Stationary fasts"** every Wednesday and Friday, following the pattern of the Early Church: nothing to eat before breaking the fast at 3:00 p.m. on those days. With the ardor of a new convert to this idea, Wesley held unerringly to this practice for months to come, the habit becoming so ingrained by the end of the summer that when visiting his parents at Epworth he noted in his diaries on Wednesday and Friday mornings (perhaps with a little bit of pride, if not disdain), *"they breakfast."*

Clayton also renewed an interest in "collecting" prayers among the Wesleyans, which eventuated in Wesley's first entrance into the publishing world at the end of 1733 with his *Collection of Forms of Prayers for Every Day in the Week*. And just as William Morgan had done before him, Clayton opened up some new areas of social activity for the group. In August 1732, Clayton obtained leave to go to St. Thomas' Workhouse twice a week, providing yet another venture in which Wesley and his friends could help the poor. With Clayton at Oxford, Wesley had an associate to whom he could with confidence entrust the leadership of his group while he was out of town—no small consideration in the light of the rather noticeable negative impact that Wesley's absence occasionally had upon the movement.

A very significant organizational impact of Clayton's association with Wesley was the introduction of *subsidiary groups* to the scheme, a provision stipulated in the rules of many religious societies (see above, the Epworth society rules) and a format that would characterize the subsequent development of the Wesleyan movement at Oxford and beyond. The increased necessity for structure and organization as the movement grew in size and complexity is reflected in Wesley's diary summary of a meeting in late June 1732: "divided men and business."

Increasingly, the life and thought of the Oxford Wesleyans manifested a theology and praxis that amounted to an Arminian methodology spelled out in a complex pattern of rules and expectations. The Wesleyan lifestyle was grounded upon a brand of Arminian theology that required continuing obedience to God's will even within the context of the New Covenant. An astute observer of the Wesleyans would have noted the applicability of the term "New Methodist" both to John Wesley's sermons and his society's scheme of activities (*M&M*, 27–31).

It was, in fact, just about this time that John Bingham, M.A., of Christ Church, noticed "a new set of Methodists sprung up amongst us," as John Wesley later recalled the phrasing (did he in fact say "a set of New Methodists"?). Wesley never associated the title "**Methodist**" with the nomenclature of the previous generation's theological disputes, apparently being unfamiliar with the obscure usage, but instead strained his imagination to draw a parallel with an ancient sect of doctors so denominated, a school of first century Greek medics who promoted good health through a regimen of diet and exercise. In any case, the first contemporary reference to the term comes in a letter from John Clayton, at Oxford, to John Wesley, visiting London in

St. Mary's Church was the site of most official religious services of the university, including the weekly sermons before the university, the sacrament at the opening of term, and the special feasts and festivals, as well as several other official ceremonies of the university.

August 1732, and implies that the term is directly associated with Wesley himself: "Now you are gone, we have in good part lost the honorable appellation of Methodists" (*JWJ*, 8:281). The name was not gone from everyone's mind, however. It seemed to many to be an appropriate designation for the group of Wesleyans, for a variety of reasons, derogatory and otherwise. Within a few weeks, carried by fast-spreading rumors, the term was to be on the lips of many Oxford folks. After being used in a critical letter published in a London newspaper (*Fog's Weekly Journal*) in December, the term "Methodist" soon became widely recognized as the tag for the Wesleyan movement at Oxford.

When Clayton left the University in the fall of 1732 to take a living at Salford, near Manchester, Wesley and the Methodists were in the midst of a period of trial. Word had reached Oxford that William Morgan had died, and the rumor spread that the ascetic rigors of the Methodist lifestyle had killed him. The occasional note of ridicule or passing smirk of the detractors throughout the University became more frequent and more intense as the life and work of the group now called Methodists had taken on an increasingly visible dimension. Many began noticing with some alarm the seemingly fanatical practices of fasting on Wednesdays and Fridays, the annoying habit of getting up at four and five o'clock in the morning, and the radical extent to which Wesley and his friends carried their frugality and their various methods of self-denial.

In this situation, Wesley assumed the responsibility for defending the Methodists against slanderous attacks. His defense would take many forms, but the most important were (1) a letter to Morgan's father explaining the rise and design of the movement, and (2) a sermon preached at St. Mary's outlining their theological rationale. The first document was transcribed and used continually by Wesley as he visited a variety of persons throughout the University in his attempt to explain his position and to gain broader support. This **"Morgan letter"** became a particularly useful document throughout the fall and winter in his continuing defense among friend and foe alike.

The sermon, preached in St. Mary's on January 1, 1733, the Festival of the Circumcision of Our Lord, was a pivotal document in the development of the Wesleyan movement. Hammered out in the midst of controversy and based upon the text for the day ("Circumcision is that of the heart, in the spirit, and not in the letter," Romans 2:29), this sermon is a clearly positive outline of the theology upon which Wesley was attempting to develop a distinctly Christian life style (*Sermons*, 1:401–14). Contrary to the impression carried by many of his contemporaries and perpetuated by subsequent analysts, Wesley's life style (and that of the Oxford Methodists) was neither circumscribed by negative injunctions nor impelled primarily by a set of prescriptive rules. Their actions were guided by lists of questions for self-examination that were arranged according to the virtues for each day of the week: love of God, love of neighbor, humility, mortification and self-denial, resignation and meekness, and thanksgiving. The "one thing needful" was a soul renewed in the image of God. The main focus of the Oxford Methodist spirituality, then, was on an inward state of the soul that would be reflected in (and measured by) their Christian life style.

This sermon is not, as one might suspect (given the circumstances), a point by point rebuttal of various attacks currently aimed at him and his friends, but rather a vibrant and positive proclamation of his understanding of "the distinguishing mark of a true follower of Christ . . . that habitual disposition of the soul which in the sacred writings is termed holiness." The inward emphasis of this sermon is disarming—focused on the virtues, cultivated through meditation, manifest in the centrality of faith, confirmed by the witness of the Spirit, and exercised through self-denial. The climax is a clarion call for love as "the sum of the perfect law [and] the true circumcision of the heart." It is training all of one's affections upon the will of God, having "the mind in us which was also in Christ Jesus." This definition of Wesley's doctrine of holiness, **Christian perfection**, would not only become the distinctive hallmark of Methodist theology in the eighteenth century, but also act as a compass for his own lifelong spiritual pilgrimage.

The reaction to this sermon was mixed: Thomas Wilson thought it was "enthusiastic," the rector of Lincoln looked upon it with favor. In the following weeks, however, the sermon took a secondary role to the Morgan letter in the public's attention. The surreptitious printing of the letter as the heart of an anonymously produced pamphlet, *The Oxford Methodists* (1733), caused Wesley some concern because of some less than flattering comments accompanying the description of his movement therein. Wesley never discovered the source who "leaked" his letter; nor was he thereafter ever able to escape the terminology fixed by this pamphlet in the minds of the public. He and his friends would henceforth be called Methodists, a term applied first in derision, but a term which Wesley himself turned to their advantage.

The events of the fall and winter of 1732/33 emphasize a basic characteristic that would become evident throughout Wesley's life— his ability generally to thrive in periods of turmoil and crisis, made possible in part by his knack of turning aside the personal bite of criticism and claiming such occasions as opportunities for sharpening his proclamation of the Gospel in the face of challenge.

Oxford Methodism, 1733–1735

Wesley used the Morgan letter as the basic explanation of the rise of Methodism at Oxford and, since it was prefixed to most editions of Wesley's *Journal*, it has continued to serve as a seemingly definitive description of Methodist beginnings. Nevertheless, several important developments within the movement at Oxford took place after Wesley's writing of this letter. The changes become evident through a study of the diaries of John Wesley and two others, Benjamin Ingham and George Whitefield, who became Methodists in the period after Clayton left.

The most obvious change is in organization. Clayton had not only altered the character of the group by introducing a subsidiary level of group participation, he had also intentionally promoted a scheme of spreading the movement, encouraging his acquaintances (as he told Wesley) to "fall upon all their friends, by which means I hope in God we shall get at least an advocate for us, if not a brother and fellow laborer, in every College in town" (*JWJ*, 8:281). After some initial falling off (it seemed to Wesley as if the "walls were falling in about them," "the torrent . . . rolling down from all sides upon me"), Wesley's group had grown back to its more usual size of five or six regular members by the end of 1733. Other groups under the general aegis of the Wesleyan banner began cropping up around Oxford as well.

Following Clayton's lead and the pattern of the religious societies, individual members of John's group formed other cells of persons interested in pursuing serious study and holy living. Charles set up at least one group at Christ Church, made up of his colleague Henry Evans and a friend from Queen's College, **Benjamin Ingham**. Before the next year was out, there would be other groups around the University, so that in all, over forty persons were associated with Oxford Methodism in the five years of the Wesleys' involvement at the University. Some of these were age twenty or so, but many were in their teens, some as young as fourteen. These university men represented eight colleges: Christ Church, Lincoln, Queen's, Brasenose, Pembroke, Merton, Magdalen, and Exeter. In addition, the Methodists also related to a group in town headed by Miss Potter, who had some differences with Wesley and attracted away some of his disaffected followers.

Some of the groups subdivided further. Ingham started his own group at Queen's, which involved over a dozen persons primarily from his own college. Ingham's diary indicates that they met regularly in several different combinations, with as many as six or seven in some groups and as few as two or three in other little bands. Some individuals met in two or three of the different groups every week; Ingham seems to have met regularly with most of these groups himself, in addition to meeting with Charles Wesley's group at Christ Church. Ingham never met with John Wesley's core group, even though he was an active Methodist for a year at Oxford.

Another characteristic of Oxford Methodism becomes evident in

OVERLEAF: The city of Oxford as seen from the north in David Loggan's map (1698). Familiar landmarks are Christ Church at the top (13), the Castle on the right, St. Mary's Church (31), the Theatre (28), and St. Michael's at the North Gate (37). Methodists were enrolled in several colleges, including Lincoln (8), Brasenose (11), Queen's (6), Merton (3), Pembroke (18), and Exeter (4), in addition to Magdalen (off left) and Christ Church.

Ingham's diary. The various rules and methods that guided the Methodists' activities generally originated in John Wesley's group (though not necessarily, as we have seen, with John Wesley personally) and were passed on to the other groups after being tried. Ingham learned from Charles the method of keeping a diary, the general resolutions, the resolutions for Lent, the lists of questions for self-examination, and a variety of other practices, which he then passed on to members of his own group at Queen's.

However, the impression of uniform harmonious groups of Methodists around the University is not a fully accurate picture. On the one hand, some of Ingham's friends were not interested in following all the suggested rules. Fasting, early rising, frequent Communion were difficult for many, and some of the Methodists were not interested in trying all of the holy-living exercises. But on the other hand, Ingham and his friends occasionally extended the Wesleyan design into new areas—Ingham and James Hervey opened up the work in the Gloucester Green Workhouse and tried to start a ministry to the "Bartlemas men" (the poor at St. Bartholomew's Hospital). Ingham more than any other of the Methodists spent much time and energy ministering to the poor in the Hamel, a section of St. Thomas' parish. Ingham also convinced two of his friends to "watch" with him (pray, meditate, and study) on Saturday evenings until midnight, a practice which Wesley advised him was perhaps useful for some but "not necessary for all" (Wesley did not follow the practice at that time).

As the Methodist scheme spread in the University through 1733 and 1734, Wesley himself was becoming more and more singular in his pursuit of holiness. This trend is reflected in his diary, which in January 1734 takes on a new format, the **"exacter" diary,** indicating every hour in minute detail the resolutions broken and kept, his temper of devotion (on a rating scale from 1 to 9), his level of "simplicity" and "recollection," in addition to the usual record of his reading, visiting, writing, conversing, and other activities, often evaluated as to his "degree of attention." This increased level of introspection comes in part from his immersion in the writings of the mystics, to whom he was introduced by William Law, who gave him a copy of the medieval mystical treatise *Theologia Germanica* in the latter half of 1732. Madame Guyon, Antoinette Bourignon, Bishop Fénelon, the Marquis de Renty, and other mystics soon became prominent in his reading lists. Wesley resonated with the spirituality of these writers, and was able to look beyond some of what he felt were their theological inadequacies in order to share their concern for holy living.

Wesley's increased level of self-examination resulted in a degree

A page from Wesley's diary in early 1735 after he had begun using the "exacter" format. On this particular day, he also cast lots to test his resolutions on early rising every day and fasting on Fridays (both were supported by the lots).

of spiritual pulse-keeping that appears obsessive. Eventually, the basic impulse of the mystical method began to cause Wesley to raise questions about his various rules and methods: if he was trying to become more holy, what he needed was to transcend the evil of this world. His many rules, combined with his conviction that no actions were morally indifferent, were having just the opposite effect, fastening his mind and attention on those things he was trying to move beyond. The realization that his method might just be counterproductive began to weaken what slim assurance he had that he was on the right track—the increased introspection, rather than giving him more hope and assurance, was making him even more aware of his shortcomings and failures. But he was equally aware of the dangers of laxity and antinomianism—there were examples aplenty all around him.

His dilemma and the answer to which he still clings after at least half a decade are spelled out in the front of his diary for late 1734: "How steer between scrupulosity as to particular instances of self-denial, and self-indulgence? *Fac quod in te est, et Deus aderit bonae tuae voluntati*" ("Do what lieth in thy power, and God will assist thy good will," Wesley's own translation in *The Christian's Pattern*, 1735). He was still trying to do his best in all things, trusting his own sincerity to be the basis for his assurance. But he understood the mystics to say that the religion of Christ and the Apostles provided him "a plenary dispensation from all the commands of God" (*J&D*, 18:213).

The tension between law and gospel was beginning to take its toll on Wesley, who was trying to see how the Pauline concept of Christian liberty could be understood within the demands of the holy living tradition (*Letters*, 25:411–13). In his confusion, he fluctuated between obedience and disobedience. His diary indicates that his intention to live by rule and method was losing its firm grip on his mind. He began testing the necessity of some of his rules by means of **casting lots**, using this practice in particular instances to determine whether God would have him rise early, omit breakfast on fast days, and maintain other aspects of the Methodist regimen of self-denial. The lot was authoritative for Wesley and others because they felt it operated under the guidance of divine providence.

Although recourse to casting lots generally overruled his occasional inclination toward relaxing his rules, Wesley's first use of the lot with regard to early rising in January 1735 resulted in forty minutes more sleep for him that day. And surprisingly, by mid-February this new inclination to test his practices led him to consider one of his regular practices, the Wednesday fasts, to be non-obligatory. The actual results of casting lots were often not in keeping with his expectations.

In the midst of his continuing search for "the more excellent way," Wesley was confronted with yet another major decision. Samuel Wesley, faced with advancing age and declining health, had hoped that one of his sons would succeed him in the Epworth parish. John had declined the suggestion as early as January 1733, but Samuel engaged his oldest son and namesake in the cause of persuading John, and the pressure to please his father by accepting the idea increased over the following months. Samuel, Jr., placed the matter directly in the category of fulfilling the obligations of ordination: "It is not a College, it is not an University, it is the *order of the Church* according to which you were called."

In December 1734, Samuel, Sr., wrote a very "pressing letter" on the subject, to which John gave a seemingly definitive reply. In trying to determine between a college life or that of rector of a parish, he presented his argument very logically: "The glory of God and the different degrees of promoting it are to be our sole consideration. . . . That course of life tends most to the glory of God wherein we can most promote holiness in ourselves and others." The previous month, he had been very clear in stating his objectives: "The question is not whether I could do more good to others there or here, but whether I could do more good to myself; seeing wherever I can be most holy myself, there, I am assured, I can most promote holiness in others." In twenty-six numbered paragraphs, John now outlined for his father the reasons why he felt that Oxford was "the best place under heaven" to promote his own, and therefore others', holiness. And responding to the observation that he had received a great deal of contempt at Oxford, he unabashedly repeats a principle that will provide some solace for years to come: "Till he is thus despised, no man is in a state of salvation."

Brother Samuel continued to press the issue on the basis of the obligations implicit in the ordination vows. The continuing exchange of letters led John to note in his diary at the end of February 1735, "almost convinced of duty to go to Epworth." A consultation with the bishop who had ordained him, however, solved his problem. John sent word to his brother that Bishop Potter had advised him that his vows had not put him under obligation to take the care of a parish, provided he could "as a clergyman better serve God and his Church in [his] present or some other station." No other word was needed;

Time Line 3		
The First Rise of Methodism		
1725	1730	1735
George I	George II	
JW deacon / Graduates M.A. / JW prebyter	Colony of Georgia chartered	Samuel Wesley dies
JW reads Taylor's *Holy Living*	JW in Wroot and Epworth / JW back to Oxford	JW joins SPCK	JW & CW to Georgia
JW begins keeping diary	CW has religious reformation	JW preaches "Circumcision of the Heart"
Influence of English Pietists	WESLEYAN GROUP BEGINS AT OXFORD	Interest in Early Church	Influence of Mystics
		Clayton joins	Proliferation of groups
Quest for holiness	Begin visiting prisons and poor	"Methodists" attacked in print

John sent a copy of the bishop's words to his brother, with the observation that he could of course better serve God and his Church "in my present situation."

All these logical arguments lost their power in April, however, when John Wesley faced his father on his deathbed. In order to allow his father to "end his days in peace," John agreed to pursue the matter of succeeding his father at Epworth, using Sir John Phillips' acquaintance with the Bishop of London as a means to that end. Sir John "declined intermeddling," in spite of encouragement from **James Oglethorpe**, and Wesley consequently laid aside all hopes (or fears, as Charles observed) of succeeding.

For two months after his father's death on April 25, John remained in Epworth to help the parish and his family during the period of transition. In the meantime, his Oxford friends were scattering, George Whitefield to Gloucester, James Hervey to Northamptonshire, Thomas Broughton to London, Benjamin Ingham to Matching. Wesley finished his own duties at Epworth as the summer began. In his farewell sermon to the people there, he spoke "with utmost clearness of having *one design, one desire, one love*, and of pursuing the *one end* of our life in *all* our words and actions," that is, the renewal of our fallen nature "in the image of God" (*Sermons*, 4:351–59). Leaving them with this distinctively Methodist proclamation, he headed south to resume his chosen way of life at Oxford.

Wesley resumed his duties at Oxford no doubt expecting to live out his days there in pursuit of holiness, in spite of the jarring events of the previous months. Within a week of his arrival at the University in July, however, he was called to London by the publisher of his father's book on Job. And while in London to assist Charles Rivington in the final stages of publication, Wesley was contacted by John Burton about the possibility of him and his friends going to Georgia, the new colony about which Samuel Wesley had written Oglethorpe the previous fall, "had it been but ten years ago, I would gladly have devoted the remainder of my life and labours to that place" (*Memorials*, 142). Here then was an alternative to the Epworth living that would still provide a chance for Wesley to fulfill his father's dreams. At the same time, it would provide a unique opportunity to withdraw from "the world" in his attempt to implement his singular design of pursuing Christian perfection.

The manner of Wesley's decision on this matter is revealing, both of its importance to him and of his method of discerning God's will for him. As to the latter, Wesley held "that a man had no other way of knowing God's will but by consulting his own reason, and his friends, and by observing the order of God's providence" (*OM*, 64). In this matter Wesley consulted most of his friends, travelling from London to Oxford, Berkswell, Manchester, and Epworth. He received encouragement from all sides, but his mother's was perhaps the most convincing: "Had I twenty sons, I should rejoice that they were all so employed, though I should never see them more" (Moore, 1:234).

Arrangements for the Georgia venture entailed gathering a group of friends to accompany him and going through the proper procedures of the SPCK and SPG. In the first matter, he had a willing companion in his student, Westley Hall, who had ended his simultaneous courtship of two Wesley sisters—he had married one of them (Patty) and planned to take her with him to Georgia. Charles Wesley was less excited about the prospect of the American wilderness, but John overruled his doubts about the journey and (with John Burton) also pressed him to take holy orders. Charles was ordained deacon in Oxford on September 21 and priest in London on September 29. Two other friends, Matthew Salmon and Hall, also received ordination in anticipation of their mission to the colony, the Trustees of the colony expecting that the latter would succeed Samuel Quincy as priest at Savannah. Ingham, encouraged by Wesley and his friends to go along, said he was waiting for a call from God in this matter, and felt that he should go only if Hall and Salmon should happen to back out.

The SPCK provided special assistance. In late September, they provided John with a £13 packet of "such books as he shall desire" since he was going to Savannah. Charles was named Oglethorpe's Secretary for Indian Affairs, with authority to officiate occasionally in the church at Frederica until they could get "a settled minister." In early October, Mr. Quincy's authority as priest in Georgia was revoked, and Hall was recommended to be appointed in his place.

But just as the plan was falling into place, it began falling apart. Salmon decided not to go, and at almost literally the last minute, Westley Hall gave up his plans also, leaving the Wesley brothers to be accompanied by Ingham (who saw these developments as the sign he was looking for) and his friend, **Charles Delamotte**, who "had a mind to leave the world and give himself up entirely to God" (*OM*, 68). As the four friends made their way down the river to the ship, the SPCK sent a notice to the papers indicating that the ships taking the Georgia settlers also carried "three clergymen, two of whom intend (after some stay at Savannah to learn the Indian languages) to devote themselves to preaching the Gospel of our Saviour Jesus Christ to the Indian nations bordering upon that colony." The notice ends on a note of hope: "they seem to be extraordinarily qualified for so glorious an undertaking, and there is great reason to hope that God will in a peculiar manner assist the zealous endeavors of these pious persons."

John Wesley was headed to Georgia as a volunteer missionary, without pay or specific appointment. In the face of Hall's last minute withdrawal from the scheme (apparently due to family pressures), the secretary of the SPCK, Henry Newman, wrote a note to Quincy encouraging him in his work: "The method you have taken to form a Religious Society [we] hope will be attended with good effects." To this end, Newman introduced the "volunteer missionaries" who were coming and who would "undoubtedly be always ready to assist you in your labours to cultivate a sense of religion among the Europeans in your settlement, and if possible among the natives who for many ages have lived in the utmost darkness."

At the same time, Wesley himself was writing a letter to answer John Burton (*Letters*, 25:439–41), who had seen the motive of this "pious undertaking" as "the desire of doing good to the souls of others, and in consequence of that, to your own." Wesley reversed the order again as he pointed to his continuing objective, now transferred from the Oxford scene to a new field of endeavor: "My chief motive . . . is the hope of saving my own soul." Now he had found a setting in which this process could be advanced in a more nearly perfect manner; his secondary motive, then, was "the hope of doing more good in America." Wesley set out for the New World fully convinced that his call to Georgia was of God and would promote that grand end which was the motivating goal behind the whole design of Methodism at Oxford: "I am assured if I be once (fully) converted myself, He will then employ me, both to strengthen my brethren and to preach His name to the Gentiles, that the very ends of the earth may see the salvation of our God." This was not a desperate attempt to work out his salvation simply by his own efforts. Even at this point he recognized that ultimately God's grace is the effective force in the story: "Nothing so convinces us of our own impotence as a zealous attempt to convert our neighbor; nor indeed, till he does all he can for God, will any man feel that he can himself do nothing."

The Second Rise of Methodism—Georgia

Setting sail for the New World in the eighteenth century was not for the weak at heart. John Wesley had never been on a ship; he had abhorred and feared the sea from his youth (*J&D*, 18:222). The almost certain prospect of a rough winter crossing was not one of the attractions of his call to Georgia. Burton had suggested that Wesley's first opportunity of doing good to the souls of others would be on shipboard: "Your private as well as public address to them will then most probably have the best effect on their minds while they see the wonders of the Lord in the deep; thus will they come better disposed for religious habits from such impressions." In fact, it was Wesley himself who was deeply influenced by the powerful Atlantic storms.

The stark reality of death staring him in the face exposed the frailty of Wesley's sense of assurance; the question of salvation now took on a new sense of immediacy and urgency. He was afraid to die, he was unwilling to die, and he was ashamed to admit it: "O how pure in heart must he be who would rejoice to appear before God at a moment's warning!" (*J&D*, 18:141). Wesley's anxiety was compounded by his growing tendency to see his fear of death as a testimony to his lack of faith.

The third and worst storm, just a week before sighting land, brought Wesley to "submission to the wise, holy, gracious will of God"; it also opened his eyes to the depth of faith of the German Moravians on board. While he attended their evening service (as was his custom), the

Seal of the Society for the Propagation of the Gospel in Foreign Parts, under whose auspices the Wesleys were appointed as missionaries to the colony of Georgia in 1735.

sea spilled over the ship, split the mainsail, and poured between the decks "as if the great deep had already swallowed us up." The English passengers screamed in fright; the Germans calmly continued singing the psalm "without intermission." Wesley was tremendously impressed by the Moravians' faith in the face of death. Such calm assurance he had never witnessed. From this experience, he found himself enabled to speak to his friends "in boldness" and to point out to them the difference, in the hour of trial, between those who fear God and those who do not. The significance of this trauma for Wesley is evident in his reaction noted in the Journal: "This was the most glorious day which I have hitherto seen."

Wesley set foot in Georgia on February 6, 1736. He did not know then that he would remain in the colony for less than two years. But this period was important enough for Wesley later to call it "the second rise of Methodism." Such terminology refers primarily to the establishment of a Wesleyan group in Georgia similar to the Oxford Methodists. But the Georgia experience also was an important episode in Wesley's spiritual pilgrimage and thus had a significant role in his theological development. And the Wesleyan mission to Georgia, although only modestly successful at best, did present an opportunity for implementing specific aspects of Wesley's developing concept of the church in mission to the world.

One of the first crises in his new parish might have been a sign of troubles to come—on returning to the *Simmonds* that first evening, he found everyone drunk. The next day before leaving the ship, he watched the casks of rum being destroyed in accordance with the colony's laws: slavery and rum were both outlawed, much to the chagrin of many colonists. Wesley himself would have neither the inclination nor ability to act as a daily watchdog over the whole parish, two hundred miles in length.

One immediate result of the trying events in mid-Atlantic was that Wesley submitted himself to the spiritual tutelage of the German pietists, who had the faith and assurance he coveted for himself. One of his first conversations when he arrived in Georgia was with **August Spangenberg**. The Moravian leader introduced Wesley to the differences between the two groups of German pietists represented in Georgia. On the one hand the **Salzburgers,** settled at New Ebenezer, followed the teachings of August Hermann Francke and Samuel Urlsperger, grounded in the tradition of Philipp Jacob Spener and the University of Halle. On the other hand the **Moravians**, settled at Savannah, followed the teachings of Spangenberg and Nicholas Ludwig von Zinzendorf, who had provided a haven for the separatist Moravian community at Herrnhut in central Germany. Although the former were perhaps a bit less solifidian in their maintenance of a basically German Lutheran tradition than the latter, the tension between the groups seems to have been caused primarily by peculiar differences in polity, practice, and personality. Wesley came into contact more often with the Moravians, who he thought manifested in their faith and discipline the vestiges of primitive Christianity.

Spangenberg also counseled Wesley as to his personal state of salvation, pressing especially the question that was at the heart of Wesley's dilemma: "Does the Spirit of God bear witness with your spirit that you are a child of God?" Wesley answered the various questions as best he could, and although he recorded dejectedly in his journal, "I fear they were vain words," he seems to have satisfied the German leader, who wrote in his own journal, "I observe that grace really dwells and reigns in him" (Schmidt, 153). Wesley's diary records

Tomochichi, a Mico or Chief of the Yamacraw (part of the Creek nation), was reputed to be 90 when he first met Wesley on a tour of England in 1734.

his distress that Spangenberg denied the Apostolic Succession, but the observation, "he a mystic," does not seem to be bothersome at that point. Wesley continued his close association with the Germans (especially in Savannah) throughout his stay in Georgia, not only living in their house for several weeks until the previous minister, Samuel Quincy, vacated the parsonage, but also meeting with them regularly in the evening for their public service, where he was particularly moved by the singing.

Wesley's design of ministering to the Indians began to materialize during February, before the missionaries moved permanently from ship to shore. His first contact with the Indians of Georgia, on board the *Simmonds*, clearly exposed the misconceptions upon which his proposed mission to these "noble savages" was based. He was quickly disabused of the notion that they were without preconceived notions or party interest and ready as little children, eager and fit "to receive the gospel in its simplicity." Although Tomochichi, a chief of the Creeks, expressed his hope to hear "the Great Word" (if the wise men of his nation would allow it), he warned the Wesleys and their friends that the French, the Spanish, and the English traders had caused great confusion and had turned many of the people against hearing the Word. Tomochichi made it clear that he did not want them to evangelize in the Spanish manner; he would rather they instruct first and then baptize. The chief had strong feelings about Christianity; his own father had been killed by the Spanish because he refused to be baptized. Tomochichi and Sinauky, the king of the Savannah nation, invited the Wesleys to visit their village, but five days later, when John and Charles went up the river past Savannah to visit them, they found neither of the Indian leaders at home. Wesley's summary comment in his diary for the day is telling: "Beware America—be not as England!" The mission to the Indians had gotten off to a rather shaky start and would not improve markedly in the months ahead.

Wesley's ministry to the people of Savannah also began with a portent of both promise and problems. Among the persons he saw March 4 on his first day of parish visitation was **Robert Hows**, the parish clerk, who would play an important role in Wesley's Methodist designs before the year was out. The following Sunday, a serious congregation crowded into temporary quarters to hear Wesley preach on the Epistle for the day, 1 Corinthians 13, which he related to the second lesson for the day, Luke 18, showing that the demands of love and commitment were balanced by the divine promise of eternal life to those who were content, *nudi nudum Christum sequi*—"naked to follow a naked Christ." Wesley then read a paper that (as he later said) apprised them "that offences would come" (*J&D*, 18:365), forewarning them of his intention to abide by the ecclesiastical regulations in all things as a faithful servant of the Church of England. No one should have been surprised that Wesley held to this stated intention with resolution.

Such an approach to church life was perhaps more suitable for Wesley's German pietist friends than for his largely apathetic, unchurched English parishioners. Nevertheless, there was a small group in Savannah that would provide the nucleus for a typically Methodist program of spiritual enrichment. A small **religious society** had been formed the previous summer in Savannah by Robert Hows. Ingham discovered this group in early April 1736 while John and Charles were in Frederica. Their design was to read, pray, and sing psalms together, meeting on Wednesday, Friday, and Sunday nights. Ingham encouraged them and promised to meet with them on occasion, which he did on Sunday evenings that spring.

On John Wesley's return to Savannah at the end of the month, Ingham must have described to him the work of this little society.

Wesley's *Journal*, published four years later, indicates that he and Ingham then agreed to promote such a design among the "more serious" in their "little flock" in order that they might "reprove, instruct, and exhort one another." His recollection was that they advised these folks "to form themselves into a sort of little society," though it appears that in fact the society was already formed. Wesley's later published account also says that they then encouraged a select number of the group to gather on Sunday afternoons for a "more intimate union with each other." Wesley's diary indicates that he "agreed" with Ingham on May 9, but there is no indication in Wesley's diary, letters, or manuscript journal of his involvement in any such meetings of either kind of group in the spring or summer of 1736 in Savannah. As a matter of fact, in mid-May, he left Savannah for Frederica and, before September, was in his home parish for barely four weeks—in July when his only regular evening activity was to attend the German public service.

The design was, however, attempted by Wesley in **Frederica**. The *Journal* account of the beginnings of a Methodist society there is clear:

Thursday, June 10. We began to *execute* at Frederica what we had before *agreed* to do at Savannah [ed. ital.]. Our design was, on Sundays in the afternoon, and every evening after public service, to spend some time with the most serious of the communicants in singing, reading, and conversation. This evening we had only Mark Hird. But on Sunday, Mr. Hird and two more desired to be admitted. After a psalm and a little conversation, I read Mr. Law's *Christian Perfection* and concluded with another psalm.

The diary corroborates this account in nearly every detail; the only additions would be the names of the new participants that Sunday with Mark Hird—Betty Hassel, Phoebe Hird, and *Mrs.* Hird (not Mr. Hird as in the published account). Mr. Hird did join them the following evening after prayers, and the group met faithfully until Wesley left, just a week or so later. One might note in passing that Mark, Betty, and Phoebe were 21, 18, and 17 years old respectively— the Methodists were by and large a young lot, as had been the case at Oxford. On June 16, another combination of friends also agreed to meet at noon on the fast days, Wednesdays and Fridays, but there is no evidence that this group continued beyond its initial week.

On Wesley's next visit to Frederica in August, he again records in his diary the regular evening meetings, usually noted as some variation of the pattern begun in the Oxford diaries: "Mr. Hird, etc., sang, prayed, sang, read, religious talk, sang." Of the nine or ten people who attended the meetings during the following days, five or six people agreed to continue meeting after John left at the end of the month. Mr. Reed, a lay assistant, promised to read evening prayers in his absence. Before leaving Frederica, John marked a copy of the *Psalms and Hymns*, perhaps for Mr. Reed to use.

In Savannah, the familiar diary entry that indicates Wesley's involvement in a society meeting begins to appear in September— once on a Sunday afternoon and twice on Wednesday evenings. In addition, Wesley has begun to have a group of communicants meet with him every Saturday evening. With Charles Wesley and Benjamin Ingham gone back to England, the name mentioned most prominently in Wesley's diary notations of these meetings in Savannah over the next few months (beginning more regularly in November) is Robert Hows.

NEXT PAGE: This map of the colony of Georgia in 1740 shows the coastline from Charleston, South Carolina, to St. Augustine, Florida. The grid of Savannah's streets is clearly visible, and the inset shows the location of Frederica on Great St. Simons Isle.

November 1736 seems to be a critical point in the group's development. Up to that point, Wesley always visited the German public service after reading Evening Prayers himself; in November, the pattern shifts so that he visits the Germans earlier in the evening, then reads Evening Prayers and meets either with individuals (such as Sophy Hopkey and Miss Bovey) or with the little Methodist society. Wesley's more constant attention to the Savannah society seems to have helped it thrive. The communicants met with him every Saturday night he was in Savannah from mid-September 1736 until his diary breaks off a year later. The Sunday afternoon group became regular in mid-November 1736, and Wesley's weekday sessions with Miss Bovey and Sophy Hopkey enlarged in December 1736 to include "Mr. Hows, etc."

By February 1737, the little society had settled into a regular pattern of meeting with Wesley after Evening Prayers on Wednesday and Saturday evenings and Sunday afternoons, Mr. Hows and Mrs. Gilbert seeming to be two of the more regular participants. The meeting format evident in his diary entries is reported to the SPCK in February 1737:

> Some time after the Evening Service [on Sunday afternoon], as many of my parishioners as desire it meet at my house (as they do likewise on Wednesday evening) and spend about an hour in prayer, singing, reading a practical book, and mutual exhortation. A smaller number (mostly those who desire to communicate the next day) meet here on Saturday evening; and a few of these come to me on the other evenings, and pass half an hour in the same employments (*J&D*, 18:476).

The society in Savannah seemed to thrive throughout the remainder of Wesley's stay in the colony, and the attendance at public services continued to increase.

The little society in Frederica, however, did not have the same success. When John visited for a week in October 1736, he found that the public prayer services had been discontinued. He attempted to infuse some life into the group by having regular evening meetings at which they read Ephrem Syrus. But his next (and last) visit to the little village in January 1737 bears all the marks of final despair; his diary indicates no evening meetings of the Methodist group. He later recalled his departure in his *Journal*: "After having 'beaten the air' in this unhappy place for twenty days, [at noon] I took my final leave of Frederica. It was . . . an utter despair of doing good there which made me content with the thought of seeing it no more."

Wesley had hoped to pursue his contacts with the Indians, particularly the Choctaws, whom he saw as "the least polished, that is, the least corrupted, of all the Indian nations." This purpose was continually frustrated by Oglethorpe's concern that Wesley's absence would leave Savannah "destitute of a minister." The few conversations he did have with the native Americans left Wesley with a very unfavorable impression, describing them in his *Journal* in such derogatory terms as "gluttons, drunkards, thieves, dissemblers, liars," and worse. The heart of his criticism becomes evident in his concluding remarks about the Creeks: "They show no inclination to learn anything, but least of all Christianity, being full as opinionated of their own parts and wisdom as either modern Chinese or ancient Roman" (*J&D*, 18:204). For his part, Ingham had spent much of his time at **Irene**, a house built on a mound near the Creek Indian settlement; he had not only learned to speak the Creek language but had also begun to develop a written form, using Greek letters (Schmidt, 185). Patrick Tailfer reported that the Wesleyans soon abandoned Irene, having "soon wearied of that undertaking."

Wesley seems to have had better feelings about his mission to the black inhabitants in America. John Burton had told him that one purpose of the SPG was "the conversion of Negro slaves" and that a door was open to this end in Purrysburg. His contact with several slaves at a church in Charleston in August 1736 left him somewhat disheartened at their lack of Christian instruction and understanding in the basics of the faith. A similar experience in Ponpon the following April resulted in his catechizing a young black girl, whose attention to his instruction he described as "inexpressible." The girl was particularly intrigued with Wesley's comment that if she were good, her soul would leave her body at death and go to live with God "above the sky" where no one would beat or hurt her. The next day she remembered all, and told Wesley she would ask God her creator to show her "how to be good" (*J&D*, 18:180). His success in this venture was duplicated shortly thereafter with a young lad in Purrysburg, whom he found "both very desirous and very capable of instruction." These incidents led him to propose a program of itinerant instruction for the American Negroes:

> First, to inquire after and find out some of the most serious of the planters. Then, having inquired of them which of their slaves *were best inclined* and understood English, to go to them from plantation to plantation, staying as long as appeared necessary at each (*J&D*, 18:181).

Though he mentions the willingness of some gentlemen in Carolina to pursue this goal, there is no indication that the plan was ever put into effect. He was constantly reminded of the truth of his earlier comment to the Georgia Trustees: "A parish of above two hundred miles in length laughs at the labor of one man" (*Letters*, 25:474). Wesley's opposition to inhuman treatment, however, was persistent and extended also to the many instances of white enslavement that came to his intention, including the sad cases of Rachel Uré and David Jones, the latter's suicide resulting from mistreatment at the hands of Captain Williams, a notorious plantation owner (*J&D*, 18:177, 445–46).

Wesley's interest in educating the young, evident in the work of the Oxford Methodists, continued in Georgia with the Methodist involvement in the school at Savannah. Charles Delamotte was the instructor, maintained in part by the SPG. He not only taught the children "to read, write, and cast accounts," but also gave catechistic instruction to the younger ones before school in the morning, to the older ones after school. Wesley then catechized them all on Saturdays and before Evening Prayers on Sunday afternoons. Wesley himself also took a special interest in the education of Miss Hopkey and Miss Bovey, two young women whom he tutored in languages and divinity and for whom he developed a special fondness.

Other particular individuals and groups received special attention from John Wesley in Georgia. He had learned German to converse with the Moravians and Salzburgers. In order to talk with some Spanish Jews in his parish (such as Dr. Núñez and his family), he learned their language as well. In May 1737 he had bemoaned the fact that some German and French settlers who knew no English lived a good distance from any minister who knew their own tongue, and they were therefore compelled (until they learned English) to be without public worship and "in effect to be without God in the world." In the late fall of 1737, he began to read public prayers in German and French on Saturday afternoons to the settlers at Hampstead and Highgate. When some of the non-English-speaking settlers in Savannah heard of this, they also asked for services in their own language, which Wesley began on the following Sunday, reading the Prayer service in Italian "to a few Vaudois" at nine in the morning and in French at one in the afternoon, in between services in English at five, ten-thirty, and three (*J&D*, 18:194). This ministry to non-English colonists was short-lived, however, since Wesley's days in Georgia were numbered.

The parish at Savannah was none the worse for Wesley's ministry. The attendance at public worship had grown steadily since his coming.

The Sunday afternoon service regularly attracted sixty to eighty persons by the fall of 1737; even the daily "short prayers" at five in the morning were then regularly attended by two to three dozen. Public criticism did not seem to have a devastating effect on the life of the parish; Wesley had been criticized more than once for preaching sermons that were "satires upon particular persons," and although some people did not appreciate such personal abuse, others must have been attracted by such a method (even Patrick Tailfer, often a critic of Wesley, had positive comments on his sermons).

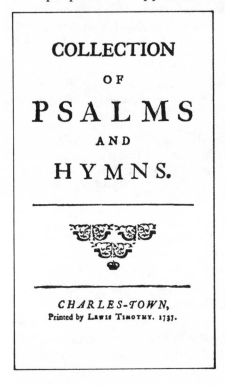

COLLECTION

OF

PSALMS

AND

HYMNS.

CHARLES-TOWN,
Printed by LEWIS TIMOTHY. 1737.

One attractive, unique feature of the worship services in Georgia was their use of **hymns**, facilitated by the Wesleys' publication of *A Collection of Psalms and Hymns* in 1737, the first English hymnbook published in America. These texts, many translated from the German, express the heart of a pietism grounded in Scripture and elucidate the themes that are central to Wesley's spiritual quest—utter dependency upon grace, the centrality of love, and the desire for genuine fire to inflame his cold heart (see Zinzendorf's bridal song of the soul). The hymnbook itself is organized in such a way as to facilitate its use at Methodist meetings: section 2 contains "Psalms and Hymns for Wednesday or Friday" and section 3 for Saturday.

Although Wesley's ecclesiastical fastidiousness (as seen in a diary note of February 1737: "Observe every circumstance of the rubrics and canons") was apparently not a problem for a sizeable contingent of colonists, in the end it contributed to the most serious challenge he faced. Wesley had earlier despaired over some settlers' attempts to have private baptisms and to omit publishing the marriage banns, crying "O discipline! Where art thou to be found? Not in England, or (as yet) in America" (*J&D*, 18:419). Sophy Hopkey's hasty marriage to William Williamson was not only personally devastating to Wesley as a suitor, but also was ecclesiastically improper in the eyes of Wesley, the parish priest. His subsequent discovery of her secretly duplicitous behavior and her lack of penance led him to bar her from Communion, a public affront which led her new husband to bring a series of charges to the grand jury in Savannah. In combination with the divisions in the community caused by his unfortunate actions regarding Sophy Hopkey, his manner of ministry provided the grounds for most of the charges levelled against him. The Chief Magistrate (Sophy's guardian, Thomas Causton) brought together a rigged grand jury that indicted Wesley on ten counts. Wesley claimed that Causton spread rumors that he was

> "a sly hypocrite, a seducer, a betrayer of my trust, an egregious liar and dissembler, an endeavourer to alienate the affections of married women from their husbands, a drunkard, the keeper of a bawdy-house, an admitter of whores, whoremongers, drunkards, ay, and of murderers and spillers of blood to the Lord's Table, a repeller of others out of mere spite and malice, a refuser of Christian burial to Christians, a murderer of poor infants by plunging them into cold water, a Papist, if not a Jesuit, or rather, an introducer of a new religion, such as nobody ever heard of; a proud priest, whose view it was to be a bishop, a spiritual tyrant, an arbitrary usurper of illegal power; a false teacher enjoining others under peril of damnation to do what I would omit myself, to serve a turn; a denier of the King's supremacy, an enemy to the colony, a sower of sedition, a public incendiary, a disturber of the peace of families, a raiser of uproars, a ringleader of mutiny"—in a word, such a monster "that the people would rather die than suffer him to go on thus" (*J&D*, 18:540–41).

The actual charges brought to the grand jury did not have quite the same ring to them, but they did spell out many of the same charges in more technical language, showing how Wesley had "deviated from the principles and regulations of the Established Church, in many particulars inconsistent with the happiness and prosperity of this Colony," such as by introducing unauthorized innovations and novelties into the public services and sacraments of the Church, by restricting the Lord's Supper only to a small number of persons who would "conform to a grievous set of penances, confessions, mortifications, and constant attendance of early and late hours of prayer," by using servants and spies to meddle into the affairs of families. Some of the charges were eventually drawn up into ten "true bills" of indictment, which Wesley summarized as follows:

1. By writing and speaking to Mrs. [Sophy] Williamson against her husband's consent.

2. By repelling her from the Holy Communion.
3. By dividing the Morning Service on Sunday.
4. By not declaring my adherence to the Church of England.
5. By refusing to baptize Mr. Parker's child by sprinkling unless the parents would certify it was weak.
6. By repelling Mr. Gough from the Holy Communion.
7. By refusing to read the Burial Service over Nathanael Polhill, an Anabaptist.
8. By calling myself Ordinary of Savannah.
9. By refusing to receive William Aglionby as a godfather, because he was not a communicant.
10. By refusing Jacob Matthews for the same reason (*J&D*, 18:561–62).

These would have provided the basis of a trial, had Wesley not slipped out of the colony before the matter came to court. The charges, even if not presenting a strong legal case against him (a minority report of the grand jury pointed out that the accusations presented nothing "contrary to any known laws"), do give a fairly accurate picture of the kind of actions which raised some opposition among Wesley's parishioners in his first (and only) parish assignment. His enemies never enjoyed the pleasure of his conviction, however, since Wesley jumped bail and abruptly departed from the colony in December 1737 before any trial could be held.

Time Line 4				
The Second Rise of Methodism				
1736		1737		1738
		George II		
JW & CW depart for Georgia	Land in America	CW back to England	Ingham back to England	JW back to England
JW meets Moravians on ship		JW reads Beveridge's *Synodicon*	JW meets with Salzburgers	
R. Hows leads Savannah religious society		FREDERICA METHODIST SOCIETY FORMED	JW reports to Ga. Trustees	Charleston hymnbook published
			Sophy Hopkey marries Williamson	JW bars Sophy from communion
	JW meets with Indians	Ingham works with Indians		JW indicted

Wesley had landed in Georgia with high expectations; he left with some measure of bitterness and disappointment: "I shook off the dust of my feet and left Georgia, after having preached the gospel there, . . . not as I ought, but as I was able." And yet he had grown immeasurably in self-understanding. After a long voyage back to England, during which he was once again confronted by the peril of a great storm at sea, he was able to see some positive values in his Georgia ministry, even though the design he went upon "did not take effect." He felt that God had humbled him, proved him, and showed him what was in his heart (cf. Deut. 8:2). He had learned to be cautious; he had learned to acknowledge God's direction; he had overcome his fear of the sea. In addition, he had come to know many of God's servants, "particularly those of the church of Herrnhut." All in Georgia had heard the Word of God and some had responded in both faith and love. Many children had learned how to serve God, and he had taken steps toward "publishing the glad tidings both to the African and American heathens" (*J&D*, 18:222).

Perhaps most importantly, Wesley had moved significantly along the path of his spiritual pilgrimage. His long quest for assurance of salvation had been accompanied by a succession of theological influences which he outlined in a reflective memorandum on his way back from Georgia (*J&D*, 18:212–13). His beginnings in a parish rectory, catechized by his priestly father and tutored by his pietist mother, left him grounded in a high-Church Anglican perspective, bent noticeably toward a certain Puritan practicality, a position that avoided too much stress on outward works on the one hand, or on a faith without works on the other. During his early years of schooling, Wesley came into contact with some Lutheran and Calvinist authors whose writings he now recognized were marked by "an overgrown fear of popery" and had magnified faith at the expense of the commandments. The English pietists, Beveridge, Nelson, Taylor, Law, whom Wesley had begun reading in the mid- to late 1720s, seemed more consistent with reason and Scripture, although their different interpretations of Scripture caused some confusion. Beginning in 1732, Clayton and his friends, the Manchester non-jurors, had provided him a "sure rule of interpreting Scripture," namely the consensus of the ages; the primitive age of Christianity became his measure for understanding the Oracles of God and provided the pristine model for Christian thought and action. Hardly had he begun to understand the implications of such an approach when he met William Law personally, who had by mid-1732 become more mystically inclined. Law introduced Wesley to the medieval mystical treatise *Theologia Germanica*, which marked the beginning of Wesley's contact with a wide range of continental Catholic mystic writings.

The tension between the latter two influences, one presenting a model of disciplined Christian life and thought, the other suggesting that true religion transcended the bonds of obedience, presented the perimeters of the arena within which Wesley's personal spiritual struggle took place in Georgia. The tension began to be resolved when, after a careful study of Beveridge's *Pandectae* in September 1736, he came to understand that the canons of the Early Church were not as authentic, universal, or authoritative as he had once thought. And then within two months, he also largely abandoned the essential perspective of the mystics, those whom he understood to slight any of the means of grace and whose writings, he told his older brother, were "the rock on which I had the nearest made shipwreck of the faith" (*Letters*, 25:487). In both instances, Wesley shifted his concern away from their theological methodology toward their manner of Christian living. One of the charges brought against him by the colonists included the comment that "he endeavored to imitate the primitive fathers, who were strict imitators of the life of Christ." And on the ship back to England, Wesley spent a great deal of time finishing an abridgement of *The Holy Life of Monsr. de Renty*, a French mystic whose life of piety and faith continued to inspire Wesley in his search for assurance.

But above all, the German pietists had now taken center stage in his search for a meaningful faith. The central teachings and imagery of the Moravians' "heart theology" were clearly imprinted on his mind and spirit in Georgia. The fire metaphor that had developed special meaning in the light of his childhood rescue from the burning rectory now began to take on additional spiritual meaning. Not only was he "preserved from the burning" on more than one occasion with Miss Sophy, his increasing desire was to avoid those "strange fires" that the Psalmist associated with earthly passions. The mystics' message he came to realize was "set on fire of hell." But his translation from Count Zinzendorf in the *Collection of Psalms and Hymns* reveals the positive heat image that the Moravian theology had fixed as one goal of his spiritual quest:

> O shine upon my frozen breast;
> With sacred warmth my heart inspire.

The Third Rise of Methodism—London

Wesley's ship sailed into Deal harbor just as George Whitefield's ship was about to set sail for Georgia. John, by now long accustomed to exercising his role as spiritual director for his friends, cast lots on the matter of Whitefield's travels. The lot indicated that George should "return to London" rather than go to the colony and Wesley sent Whitefield a note to that effect before setting out for London himself. Whitefield, however (as his diary indicates), had begun to grow accustomed to his role as leader of the Methodists in England in John's absence. He took notice of (and offence at) Wesley's note but proceeded to fulfill what he felt was his "call to Georgia." In the colony, Whitefield would discover and report in his journal (with typical effusiveness) that "the good [that] Mr. John Wesley has done in America, under God, is inexpressible" (Whitefield, 157). Wesley, on the other hand, was about to discover that Whitefield (now ordained and an increasingly popular preacher) had been actively working among the religious societies, not only at Oxford and back home at Gloucester, but also at London.

John's return was not only unexpected by those who had sent Wesley to Georgia but also a surprise to brother Charles as well. John's own intentions at the time seem to have been somewhat ambiguous. He was not immediately ready, for instance, to resign his position as parish priest of Savannah; whether he intended to return soon is not clear. For the first few weeks he was back in England, his attention would be divided between old interests and new directions—on the one hand, reporting to the Georgia Trustees on the status of things in Georgia, drumming up support, as Charles and Ingham had done before him, and checking with his old friends on the state of affairs at Oxford and London; on the other hand, becoming active in new groups and making new friendships, especially among the German Moravians who were newly arrived in London.

Rumors of his abrupt return preceded Wesley to the Georgia Trustees, who felt that he should not have returned without their leave, and before whom he reported on three occasions in February. He gave them a depressing report on the state of affairs in the colony and, complaining of the "usage he had received at Georgia," delivered to them "several papers and certificates for his justification" (Egmont, 2:467). His account of Causton "was enough to make all [the Trustees] quit," according to one of the Trustees, the Earl of Egmont, who felt Wesley was certainly guilty of "indiscretion" but that Causton was "much more to blame," being guilty of "gross mis-administration."

When Wesley finally resigned his license for Savannah on April 26, Egmont remarked more candidly that Wesley appeared to be "a very odd mixture of a man: an enthusiast and at the same time a hypocrite."

As for the Methodists in England, Wesley found their work not only managing to survive at Oxford, but also beginning to spread to other areas. In Oxford, Charles had, upon his return in 1737, tried to encourage several of the Methodists to "resume all their rules of holy living" and meet together as had been their custom (*CWJ*, 1:115, 127). John now discovered that most of his former associates were scattered abroad but did find "three gentlemen who trod in their steps." On his first visits back to Oxford, Wesley fell into part of his old routine, preaching once again at Carfax, the Castle, and Lincoln College chapel, and meeting with some religious societies in the town (notably at the home of Mr. Fox, a former prisoner at the Bocardo jail).

Wesley was also to discover that many of his former friends were busy in other parts of the kingdom. A dozen or so "London and Oxford Methodists" were gathering together at James Hutton's home in London to "sing Psalms audibly, against the peace and quiet of the neighborhood." One of this group was **George Whitefield**, who had, during Wesley's absence, begun to preach a zealous evangelical gospel among the religious societies in London and beyond. Upon hearing of Wesley's return, James Hervey sent him word of Whitefield's activities: "You cannot but have heard, and hearing, you cannot but rejoice at the successful zeal of our friend Whitefield. All London, and the whole nation ring of 'the wonderful works of God' done by his ministry." John had had little contact at Oxford with Whitefield, who had joined their activities just before the Wesleys left the university in 1735. Whitefield in the meantime had experienced a spiritual awakening and was preaching his evangelical gospel throughout London and in many parts of the kingdom.

Benjamin Ingham, upon his return from Georgia, had begun to preach in many of the parishes around Leeds in Yorkshire, and through his contact with the Delamotte family at Blendon in Kent, brought Charles Delamotte's brother, William, into the movement. Will, a student at **Cambridge**, had in that university "raised a party for God" that had by the beginning of 1738 already been "stigmatized" as Methodists (see *Cambridge*, 251–83). In a letter to John (written to Georgia after John's departure), Charles Wesley exuberantly announced, "We see all about us in an amazing ferment. Surely Christianity is once more lifting up its head" (*Letters*, 25:526). But this wider renewal was not all directly of Wesleyan origin. Around the kingdom, other sparks of spiritual revival were beginning to take hold. **Griffith Jones** and **Howell Harris** had pioneered a Welsh evangelical movement in the early 1730s that featured educational reform and itinerant preaching. Jones, Harris, Whitefield, and Ingham had all experienced some form of evangelical conversion by 1737 and were actively working in the church, among the religious societies (still fostered by the SPCK), and throughout the countryside to promote revival across the land. In this continuing movement for spiritual renewal, in which John Wesley had been an early pioneer, he was conscious that he lagged behind the vitality and zeal of many of his old and new friends.

The arrival of several Moravians from Germany provided for the continuance of his spiritual apprenticeship to them, begun in Georgia. **James Hutton**, son of a London bookseller and an important link in this connection, had met the Wesleys earlier at Oxford and had been a neighbor to Samuel in Westminster. James and his sister had been "earnestly awakened" by John Wesley's solemn preaching on "The One Thing Needful" just prior to the Wesleys' departure for Georgia. Hutton subsequently attended more than one of the old religious societies in London (including one in Aldersgate Street) and had formed a new one in his parent's home, in which he frequently read Wesley's journal letters from Georgia, wherein he learned of the Moravians (Hutton, 181–82). Hutton had also befriended many of the Oxford Methodists and found pulpits for them in London (especially the Tower and St. Helen's, Bishopsgate, on Tuesdays). Hutton's society benefited from the preaching of Whitefield and other Oxford students, who not only preached "in a more than ordinarily earnest way" but also continued "on the Methodist plan" in such things as visiting the sick and much praying (Hutton, 183). John fit easily back into this pattern, and he attended Hutton's groups frequently and preached at St. Helen's three or four Tuesdays during the spring of 1738, with some success.

Charles Wesley's return from the colony, Hutton's involvement, Whitefield's preaching, John Wesley's journal letters from Georgia, and now his return from Georgia and the arrival of the new Moravians from Germany helped encourage the new societies as well as breathe new life into some of the old societies. Wesley began to press his own quest for spiritual assurance by cultivating these several new friendships and by sharing in the ministries of numerous societies in London.

Peter Böhler and the Quest for Faith

Within a week of Wesley's return to England, he met **Peter Böhler**, a Lutheran minister (subsequently ordained by Zinzendorf into the Moravian ministry) newly arrived from Germany and on his way to America. Wesley's contact with Böhler over the next four months would furnish models for both personal spiritual renewal and corporate organizational developments in Methodism.

John's continuing concern was a lack of **assurance of faith**, which had become starkly evident in his brush with death during two ocean crossings. In the face of drowning in the midst of an Atlantic tempest, Wesley realized that he was not ready to meet his Maker. His first reaction was to assume that his faith was deficient, not strong enough to overcome such fear. He fell back upon his finely-honed Oxford methods and renewed his former resolutions.

By the beginning of March, however, Peter Böhler had convinced him that the deficiency was not one of degree—Wesley's problem was not weakness of faith but plain unbelief. According to Böhler, Wesley totally lacked "that faith whereby alone we are saved." The problem was not weak faith, but of no proper faith at all—there were no **"degrees" of faith**; either you have it or you don't. And true faith is always accompanied by a sense of assurance and evidenced by freedom from sin, fear, and doubt, three fruits which inseparably attend assurance and attest to a proper faith. Any doubt or fear, therefore, is a sign of unbelief. Thus convinced that he had no faith, Wesley felt it was inappropriate to continue preaching. Böhler's reaction and advice was memorable: "Preach faith *till* you have it, and then, *because* you have it, you *will* preach faith" (*J&D*, 18:228).

On March 6, Wesley began to preach this "new doctrine" of **salvation by faith alone**, starting at the Castle with a prisoner, William Clifford, on death row for assault, burglary, and desertion from the foot guards. John's enthusiastic preaching had already caused him to be barred from some London churches. He was not discouraged by such reactions; the signs of persecution always reinforced his conviction of truth and spurred him on to open defiance of the churchly status quo. He now perceived that God's special blessing was upon those sermons that "gave most offense" (*J&D*, 18:226).

Wesley was moving more and more toward a Moravian view of salvation, which Wesley tried to understand in terms of his own tradition. The Book of Homilies defined faith as "a sure trust and confidence in God." Böhler highlighted the experiential aspect of the rest of the definition: "that through the merits of Christ *my* sins are

St. Andrew's Church, Holborn, was just one of the many London churches that barred Wesley from its pulpit in 1738 as he began following Peter Böhler's advice to "preach faith." John's father, Samuel, had been ordained in this church in 1689.

forgiven and *I* am reconciled to the favor of God." On April 23, he was finally convinced by five Moravians, including Böhler, that "faith converts at once," and that such **instantaneous conversion** was not only scripturally grounded but presently possible (*J&D*, 18:234, 576). Not all Methodists were so convinced, however. Upon hearing John expound "this new faith" of sinners "believing in a moment," Charles Wesley and Thomas Broughton were "much offended at his worse than unedifying discourse."

Now the list of barred pulpits began to grow more rapidly. More of his old Oxford friends, such as John Clayton, tried to convince Wesley that he needed to control his zeal, leave off extempore preaching, curb his "vehement emphasis," and even cut his hair. But such criticisms from friends did not leave Wesley without encouragement and company on his quest for personal assurance. Wesley continued to meet with Henry Washington and other students at Oxford University, several of whom were encouraged by Böhler to meet thrice weekly. In the town of Oxford, Wesley also met occasionally with two or three societies that totalled about a hundred persons. In London,

Wesley associated with Hutton's group of about seventy persons who met for prayer, singing, and Bible study, but who apparently, as Wesley told Böhler, had little organization or supervision (Böhler, 5, 8).

Peter Böhler took steps to rectify that situation on the first of May, 1738. He invited several persons "who were of the same mind and who seek closer fellowship with each other" to organize a band. Meeting at John Hutton's, a small handful of persons (including Hutton and John Wesley, who had unexpectedly returned to London that day to visit his ill brother Charles at Hutton's) accepted two rules, by which a small society was established:

> 1. That they will meet together once in a week to confess their faults one to another and to pray for one another that they may be healed [cf. James 5:16].
> 2. That any others, of whose sincerity they are well assured, may, if they desire it, meet with them for that purpose (Watson, 197).

These simple rules provided the original framework for the group that soon became known as the **Fetter Lane Society**, whose organization Wesley would later call "the third rise of Methodism." Although its only stated requirement was sincerity of intention, the group seems to have been made up of persons well-disposed toward Methodist and Moravian views, neither of which required separation from the doctrine and discipline of the Church of England, to which they all subscribed. Their explicit agenda, however, was soteriological—the spiritual health (*salus*) of the participants. At this point, it seems that all the members were male, for Böhler projected that as the group added members, the married and unmarried men would form two groups for regular meetings, coming together for a meeting once a month.

Peter Böhler left London three days later to embark for the New World, which left John Wesley as the predominant leader of the little society. Though Böhler was gone, his influence continued. Within days, several more persons (including Charles Wesley and George Stonehouse, vicar of Islington and an Oxford Methodist) became convinced of the Moravian perspective. Some also experienced the assurance of faith. Among these was Charles Wesley, who, in the midst of continuing spiritual struggles and while sick in bed on Whitsunday, felt "a strange palpitation of heart," was able to say, "I believe, I believe!" and found himself at peace with God (*CWJ*, 1:146–47).

The "surprising news" of his brother's experience put John into a state of "continual sorrow" and heaviness of heart. The Pentecost season seems to have heightened his desire to experience the witness of the Holy Spirit, but his own quest for this perceptible assurance had only led him to recognize, as he wrote to a friend at that time, "God is a consuming fire; I am altogether a sinner, meet to be consumed." His anxiety was only amplified by the testimonies of a growing number of friends who had experienced assurance. Even his younger brother could now testify of a conversion and, with John present, would join with other friends in praying for him.

John's own experience of **assurance** followed his brother's by three days. His account of the events on May 24 reflects his view of God's providential guidance in this crucial development, from the scripture reading in the morning, to the anthem at St. Paul's in the afternoon, and the society meeting later in the day (after the church bells had rung to announce the birth of the royal child who would become George III):

> In the evening I went very unwillingly to a society in Aldersgate Street, where one was reading Luther's Preface to the Epistle to the Romans. About a quarter before nine, while he was describing the change which God works in the heart through faith in Christ, I felt my heart strangely warmed. I felt I did trust in Christ, Christ alone for salvation, and an assurance was given me that he had taken away *my* sins, even *mine*, and saved *me* from the law of sin and death (*J&D*, 18:249–50).

Wesley celebrated the exuberance of the moment with an immediate testimony to those present; later that night the celebration continued in Charles's rooms with the singing of a hymn, probably "Where shall my wondering soul begin?" Faith as trust and confidence was no longer just a propositional truth but rather an experiential reality. The teaching of his Moravian mentors now became a confession that he could claim for himself—*Christus pro me*. Wesley felt that now he was truly a Christian. Now he could say, in keeping with the Moravian perspective, that previous to this experience of assurance he had not been a Christian.

The real test, however, of the authenticity of this experience was to be found, not in terms of whether or not he felt his heart "strangely warmed," but whether or not the expected and necessary fruits of faith and assurance (as he was taught by the Moravians to expect) would be in evidence: freedom from sin, doubt, and fear, and the fullness of peace, love, and joy in the Holy Ghost (otherwise called "holiness and happiness").

Questions began to develop almost immediately, raised by Wesley's continued quest for positive evidence of the fruits of faith and assurance. The "enemy" soon suggested that what he had experienced

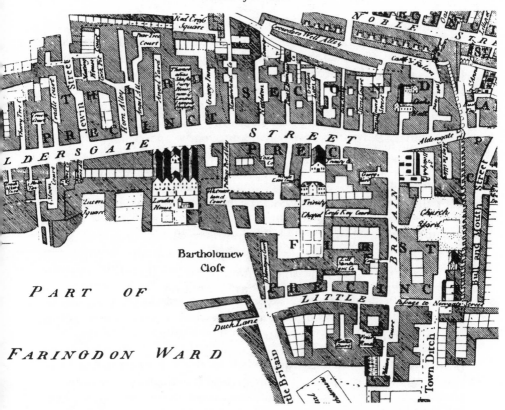

Nettleton Court, the apparent location of the society meeting on May 24, 1738, was the eighth opening to the north (left on this map) on Aldersgate Street, not far from the gate itself (which still stood at that time). Little Britain, the location of Charles's experience of assurance, is directly west from Nettleton Court and is noted at the bottom of this map.

could not be faith: "for where is thy joy?" He was at least comforted by the awareness that, although still buffeted with temptations, he had the sense that he was now "always conqueror." The following day, Wesley's empiricism got the better of him: "If thou dost believe, why is there not a more sensible change?" Again, comfort came in the form of a measure of "peace with God." The matter of fears (which he had been taught to equate with unbelief) was pushed aside for the moment by a text from St. Paul—"Without were fightings, within were fears." He resolved to go on and simply try to tread them under his feet. The same was true concerning "heaviness because of manifold temptations"—the Moravians advised not fighting them but fleeing from them. Four days after Aldersgate, he was still bothered by waking "in peace, but not in joy."

During the following days, he was constantly troubled by one problem after another relating to his only partially fulfilled expectations. This did not keep him from proclaiming his "new gospel," though some of his friends doubted his view of it all. At the Huttons', he was "roughly attacked" for being an enthusiast and seducer for putting forth "new doctrines." Mrs. Hutton, for one, took exception to John's new claims and wrote his brother, Samuel:

> Confine or convert Mr. John when he is with you. For after his behavior on Sunday, May 28, when you hear it, you will think him a not quite right man. . . . John got up [at our house] and told the people that five days before he was not a Christian. . . . He made the same speech again [at supper], to which I made answer, "If you was not a Christian ever since I knew you, you was a great hypocrite, for you made us all believe you was one" (*JWJ*, 1:480n).

John continued to press his close friends as he did everyone else, telling them that until they had renounced everything but faith and then "got into Christ," they could have no reason to believe that they were Christians. He also continued to preach his sermon, "Salvation by Faith," which he had been using as the nucleus of his pulpit proclamations since early March.

Privately, however, Wesley was still plagued with doubts, especially on the matter of "degrees of faith." Although his Moravian friends continued to stress the point that "no doubting could consist with the least degree of true faith," Wesley's own experience seemed to confirm for him that although he did not have a constant abiding joy, he did at that point have constant peace and freedom from sin and therefore some measure of faith.

Wesley decided to visit the Moravian community in Germany to converse with "those holy men who were themselves living witnesses of the full power of faith and yet able to bear with those that are weak." What he discovered, however, was that they were not all willing to tolerate Wesley's lack of full confidence and joy. On one occasion they barred him from participating in the Lord's Supper with them because it was evident to them that he was still *homo perturbatis*, a perturbed person not clearly evidencing the marks of full assurance. The confusion of that occasion was compounded by his discovery that some of the Moravian views in **Herrnhut** differed remarkably from those of Böhler and the English Moravians on crucial points.

Nicholas von Zinzendorf, the head of the community, claimed that assurance could be separate in time from the moment of justification—one might not *know* or be assured of one's justification until long afterward. This notion countered Böhler's argument that one could not have forgiveness of sins without experiencing an immediate sensation of it. Zinzendorf also presented a more moderate view of other evidences of justification: peace *may* be evident, but joy is frequently *not* present. For Wesley, this view of salvation seemed closer to his earlier experience and understanding of Scripture: a view that would allow for degrees of faith and growth in piety.

The German Moravians made several distinctions that Wesley would soon find crucial: distinguishing between justification and assurance (both theologically and chronologically), between faith and assurance, and between the beginning and the fullness of salvation (see below, pp, 85, 87f.). Wesley noticed especially four sermons by Christian David, who repeatedly spoke of "those who are 'weak in faith,' who are justified but have not yet a new, clean heart; who have received forgiveness through the blood of Christ but have not received the indwelling of the Holy Ghost." Since his discussions with Böhler in the spring, Wesley had spoken generally in terms of "salvation by faith," as in his sermon of that title. From this point, Wesley begins to use the more precise concept of "**justification**" much more frequently.

While he was in Germany, Wesley met and interviewed several persons who could testify that their experience matched their doctrines. Wesley wrote careful notes on these interviews and later published them in his *Journal* as evidence of the true doctrines of the Moravian Church in order to clear the Moravians from any aspersion arising from the teachings of the English brethren.

The conflict between the German and English Moravian positions represented the nub of the problem for Wesley at this point. He had been taught by the English Moravians of the necessity of an experience of the type Böhler described, with its absolute requirements and necessary evidences and allowing for no doubt or fear. Wesley's confusion in his attempt to understand his own experience in the light of those expectations was caused in part by the difficulties inherent in the Moravian position. The English Moravians had, in Lutheran fashion, collapsed sanctification into justification and, in Pietist fashion, extended forgiveness of sins (**imputed righteousness**) into freedom from sin (**infused righteousness**). This approach resulted in the expectation of a sinless perfection (including a full measure of the fruits of the Spirit) as the necessary mark or evidence of salvation (genuine conversion).

This tendency to equate faith with assurance and correlate sanctification with justification did not match Wesley's own theological background: he was trying to understand (and experience) a Lutheran theology in the context of his own Anglican and Arminian

Herrnhut, established by Count Nicholas Ludwig von Zinzendorf and home of the *Unitas Fratrum*, was the center of the Moravian movement in Europe in the eighteenth century.

assumptions. The English Moravians looked for marks of salvation that Wesley would more naturally understand (within his own tradition) as evidence of sanctification. They were propounding a view that essentially equated conversion with perfection, an understanding of salvation as sanctification that Wesley was never able to accept fully, even in the light of his own experience under Moravian tutelage. Wesley had not yet worked out some of the finer distinctions between justification and sanctification, much less the various nuances of his own doctrines of faith and Christian perfection. For the time being, he maintained his ties with the Moravians and tried to work out his spiritual quandary and theological problems in fellowship with them.

During his travels about the countryside in Germany, Wesley kept journal notes that reveal a fascination with the schools, cathedrals, churches, and synagogues. He made a special trip to **Halle**, the home of the late August Hermann Francke, whose books he had read and used with the Methodists at Oxford. His journal records his particular interest in the famous **Orphan-house**, which housed 650 children and taught three thousand. He was especially interested in its means of support, including revenue from its printing house, the sale of books, and the apothecary's shop.

Wesley also took careful notes on the **Moravian organization**. The division of Herrnhut into neighborhood divisions called choirs provided the basis for eleven geographical "classes." In addition, there were ten classes determined by gender and age which provided the basis for daily spiritual oversight and regular religious conference. At the heart of their program of spiritual nurture stood ninety "bands" which met two or three times a week to follow the strictures of James 5:16, the pattern of Böhler's rules for the Fetter Lane group in London. Although Wesley records no sharing of the Eucharist with his Moravian friends, he did participate in many facets of their communal spiritual discipline, including religious conferences and love-feasts.

In Rotterdam, as Wesley waited at his inn for the delayed ship that was to carry him home, he redeemed the time by exhorting several English travellers "to pursue inward religion, the renewal of their souls in righteousness and true holiness." These are long-familiar terms for Wesley, but during these crucial months of 1738 they are beginning to take on some new meaning.

Wesley carried many impressions with him as he left the continent. Some newly-gained insights provided grist for his continuing debates with the English Moravians. Other notions furnished practical methods for the structure and function of Christian fellowship in order to provide effective spiritual nurture. All his reactions were not positive, however. In some observations noted at the time, he listed several faults in their community: the neglect of fasting, the magnification of their church and their leader, a tendency toward levity, a spirit of secrecy, the use of cunning, guile, or dissimulation—thereby falling short of the apostolic Christianity he had expected to find in Herrnhut.

Returning to England in September 1738, Wesley began immediately to work on clearing up several matters of confusion in his own mind and experience. On some points, he began to qualify his views and found himself increasingly in conflict with the Moravians. Wesley was put in a quandary by the Moravians *requiring* the plerophory (fullness) of faith (assurance) evidenced by the *full* measure of fruits thereof (love, joy, peace) as the *necessary* expectation of the *true* (i.e., the only "real") Christian. It is interesting to note that during the several months Wesley was working on these issues (in growing conflict with the Moravians), although he personally dealt quietly with the questions of degrees of faith, the presence of doubt, and using the means of grace, he publicly continued by and large to preach the necessity of full assurance of faith and actual freedom from sin as the true ground of a Christian's happiness.

In the midst of Wesley's attempts to work out these questions in the autumn of 1738, two important discoveries helped shed some light on his developing ideas. On October 10, he read **Jonathan Edwards'** "surprising" narrative of the conversions in New England. In this work he could plainly see the influence of the Holy Spirit in the revivals in New England. This reading confirmed for him the significance of the spiritual dynamic in the story and the pneumatological dimension in the theological explanation; it set the stage for his understanding of the movement of the Spirit among the people.

Then a month later, during the week of November 12, Wesley rediscovered the **Book of Homilies** on that "much controverted point of justification by faith." In the homilies on salvation, faith, and good works (numbers 3, 4, and 5), Wesley discovered within the authoritative doctrinal statements of his own tradition the sum of what he had been putting together on his own and the answer to some of the problems raised by the Moravians. Although he could not then sense how close he would eventually come to reiterating the doctrine of the Church of England, he immediately recognized that the answer to most of his theological problems with the English Moravians were contained in those homilies, of which he hastened to publish an extract.

In the meantime, Wesley continued to circulate among a dozen or so religious societies in London and Oxford. Hutton had continued to develop the "new society" while Wesley and Ingham were in Germany. During the summer, it had grown to more than thirty persons. By mid-October the group, which Wesley also refers to as "our little society," consisted of eight bands of men (56) and two bands of women (8) totalling sixty-four. Wesley also continued to preach in many different churches around the city, especially in those areas where he had some influence in the societies. As might be expected by now, in a few more of these places, it was (as he proudly noted in his Journal) for the last time. While he was publicly proclaiming the message of salvation by faith according to the Moravian model during the last few months of 1738, Wesley was also experiencing a period of intense self-scrutiny and questioning.

Questions were raised by his own experience (and the experience of others), his own church's tradition, and Scripture. The tension can be seen clearly in several memoranda of **self-examination** Wesley wrote between October 1738 and January 1739. The first came shortly after reaching Oxford in October, when he measured his spiritual state according to the guideline provided by St. Paul: "If any man be in Christ, he is a new creature: old things are passed away; behold, all things are become new." Wesley saw five requirements that provided the test:

> First, his judgments are new: his judgment of *himself*, of *happiness*, of *holiness*. . . . Secondly, his designs are new. . . . Thirdly, his desires are new. . . . Fourthly, his conversation is new. . . . Fifthly, his actions are new (*J&D*, 19:17).

Based on the evidence of his experience, Wesley judges that he is indeed a new creature in regard to the first four criteria. But on the final criterion he falls short. On the matter of the "fruits of the Spirit," Wesley's evidence is somewhat disheartening: he does find some measure of peace, long-suffering, gentleness, meekness, temperance; yet in other areas he is definitely lacking but still full of hope and with some confidence that he is a child of God:

> I cannot find in myself the love of God, or of Christ. . . . I have not that joy in the Holy Ghost; no settled, lasting joy. Nor have I such a peace as excludes the possibility either of fear or doubt. . . . Yet upon the whole, although I have not yet that joy in the Holy Ghost, nor the full assurance of faith, much less am I, in the full sense of the words, "in Christ a new creature"; I nevertheless trust that I have a measure of faith, and am "accepted in the Beloved"; I trust . . . that I am "reconciled to God" through his Son (*J&D*, 19:18).

The absolute demands of the Moravians were beginning to crumble in Wesley's mind. He was beginning to accept the idea that there were degrees of both faith and assurance. And he began to sense that full assurance of faith (which he now felt he had never experienced) was not necessary to the new birth, but a "measure of faith" was adequate for reconciliation through Christ.

In the matter of assurance, Wesley began to distinguish further between **assurance** and **faith** as two distinct realities. The Moravians had related these so closely as practically to correlate them. Wesley's own post-Aldersgate experiences continued to raise variations of the question of degrees of faith first posed in conversation with Spangenberg in Georgia—whether one could speak of weak faith and strong faith, and whether faith could admit any doubt or fear. As long as faith was equated with full assurance (as in the Böhler/English Moravian understanding), doubts and fears plainly indicated a lack of faith, which was to say, no true faith at all but rather the sin of unbelief. But faith must surely be able in many cases to subsist with doubt and fear.

Wesley recognized that "some measure of this faith" had resulted in "peace and trust in God through Christ" in his own life. And he also was convinced that freedom from sin, which he had claimed since 24

May, surely must be understood as freedom from the *reign* of sin rather than from the *remains* of sin. And although he now realized that he had yet to experience what he had seen many others receive, full assurance through the witness of the Spirit (evidenced by the fruits of the Spirit), he could see himself (since 24 May) and others in his condition as being Christians, even though in an "imperfect sense." His brother Samuel continued firmly to deny John's claim of not being a Christian before 24 May and also expressed serious doubts that John was even now free from the dominion of sin.

Continuing to press the whole matter of assurance, Wesley also distinguished between the assurance of *faith* and assurance of *salvation*. The former, a conviction of present pardon, he still felt was important and perhaps necessary as a normal expectation for the Christian, but the latter, based on the expectation of perseverance and the promise of final salvation, was rare and not necessarily to be expected, much less required. The "plerophory of faith," he pointed out to Arthur Bedford, is "nothing more nor less than hope: a conviction, wrought in us by the Holy Ghost, that we have a measure of the true faith in Christ, and that as he is already made justification unto us, so *if* we continue to watch and strive and pray, he will gradually become 'our sanctification here, and our full redemption hereafter'" (*Letters*, 25:564).

Time Line 5			
The Third Rise of Methodism			
1738		1739	1740
George II			
JW back in England	JW visits Moravians in Germany	Whitefield starts revival in Bristol	Wesleys barred from parish pulpits
Short visits to Oxford		JW doubts his salvation	
			JW to Bristol
JW meets Böhler	CW & JW experience assurance	JW reads Edwards' *Narrative*	Molther arrives in London JW splits with Moravians
			"United Societies"
JW & BÖHLER START FETTER LANE SOCIETY	Bands organized		New Room built in Bristol Foundery Society London
JW preaches "Salvation by Faith"	JW publishes extract from the Homilies	JW begins field-preaching	Kingswood School near Bristol

He goes on to point out that "this assurance . . . is given to some in a smaller, to others in a larger degree." Assurance, then, for Wesley was also a matter of degrees and not to be confused with final perseverance; assurance was a daily confidence (more or less) that one is a child of God. The real possibility of backsliding never left Wesley's frame of thinking.

On 29 October, Wesley noted that he was again "doubtful of my own state," especially concerning faith. Some relief, in keeping with developing inclinations, was provided by his method of bibliomancy, for he opened his Bible upon James's description of Abraham (in 2:22): "Seest thou not how faith wrought together with his works? And by works was faith made perfect."

Whatever comfort he might obtain from such self-examination, however, was tested by his friends, especially those associated with the Moravians. Charles Delamotte, who had accompanied him to Georgia but was now back in England and under Moravian influence, told Wesley in November that Wesley was now better off than when he was in Savannah because Wesley now recognized that he was wrong in Georgia. But, Delamotte went on, "You are not right yet; you know that you was then blind, but you do not see now." Delamotte tried to convince Wesley that he was still trusting in his own works and did not believe in Christ; that his freedom from sin was only a temporary suspension of it, not a deliverance from it; and that his peace was not a true peace—"if death were to approach, you would find all your fears return" (*J&D*, 19:363).

Pressed on the matter of his own spiritual pilgrimage, Wesley wrote from Oxford to four friends in London inquiring as to "the state of their souls." His continuing fascination with this sort of spiritual autobiography led him to include two of the responses in his published journal (*J&D*, 19:23–26).

In December 1738, Wesley wrote some notes that provide a sequel to the memorandum of October 14, and in which he measures himself on some of the same evidences as before. As for happiness, "I still hanker after creature-happiness," which he explains in terms that are again reminiscent of his sentiments in 1726—"I have more pleasure in eating and drinking, and in the company of those I love, than I have in God." He refers to the degree of his progress with a scriptural phrase that is telling and will become a familiar metaphor: "The eyes of my understanding are not yet fully opened." On the second point, as to the design of his life, his eye is not yet single. And on the third point, his desires are not all new; his affections in general are mixed between spiritual and natural.

Others were continuing to see the light, nevertheless. Thousands were gathering to hear Whitefield preach; the clergy responded by closing their churches to him as well. Whitefield simply moved to the open air. Encouraged and enlarged by such developments, the "new society" grew beyond the capacity of Hutton's home and on December 26 moved its meetings to a room in Fetter Lane, from which the group now took its name. Each society and band had its own set of rules, which were continually updated. The Islington religious society, for instance, had its own Rules, which Wesley helped to develop. Wesley's diary indicates that several times during the early weeks of 1739 he "writ our orders," producing copies or revisions of the rules for the societies and bands, including "rules for the women." The "**Rules of the Band Societies**" which Wesley later dated 25 December 1738 (actually 1739?) was a revised version of the Fetter Lane Society rules, which themselves had been revised twice since the organizing meeting (*Societies*, 9:79).

At the turn of the new year, during a watch-night celebration of the love-feast, the power of God came "mightily" upon the Fetter Lane group, "insomuch that many cried out in exceeding joy and many fell to the ground." Such demonstrations of the work of the Spirit caused Wesley to reflect upon his own condition, and within days, he again took an opportunity for writing notes of self-reflection. This memo, however, reveals more serious self-critical doubt on the questions of love, peace, and joy; in it, he holds himself up to the strict definition of Christian that admits no degrees of perfection in measuring the evidence:

> My friends affirm I am mad, because I said I was not a Christian a year ago. I affirm I am not a Christian now. Indeed, what I might have been I know not, had I been faithful to the grace then given [on May 24], when, expecting nothing less, I received such a sense of the forgiveness of my sins as till then I never knew. But that I am not a Christian at this day I as assuredly know as that Jesus is the Christ.

He then goes on in very logical fashion to explain the criteria by which he measures a true Christian at that point:

> For a Christian is one who has the fruits of the Spirit of Christ, which (to mention no more) are love, peace, joy. But these I have not. I have not any love of God. . . . I feel this moment I do not love God; which therefore I *know* because I *feel* it. . . . Again, joy in the Holy Ghost I have not. . . . Yet again, I have not "the peace of God." . . . From hence I conclude . . . , though I have given, and do give,

all my goods to feed the poor, I am not a Christian. Though I have
endured hardship, though I have in all things denied myself and
taken up my cross, I am not a Christian. . . . My works are nothing,
my sufferings are nothing; I have not the fruits of the Spirit of Christ.
Though I have constantly used all the means of grace for twenty
years, I am not a Christian (*J&D*, 19:29–31).

Wesley seems here again to assume the necessity of full assurance
of faith, which not only excludes all doubt and fear concerning present
salvation but also excludes all sin as shown by the full presence of
peace, love, and joy as the fruits of the Spirit. He now understands
the explicit role of the **Holy Spirit** as central, both as a source of
self-knowledge (direct internal evidence—witness of the Spirit, the
basis for claiming assurance) and as a source of the fruits (indirect
external evidence—fruits of the Spirit, the basis for confirming assurance). The genuine Christian is the perfect Christian, and Wesley is
not hesitant during this period to define the character of a Methodist
(i.e., a "genuine Christian") in these same terms, namely as one "who
has the love of God shed abroad in his heart by the Holy Spirit."

Although Wesley is beginning at times to allow for some qualitative
distinctions and levels within the definition of **Christian**, the general
sense of his preaching is that the "altogether Christian" is the "real"
Christian and the "almost" Christian is not really a Christian at all. To
put it differently (in terms he was not yet using), the hard question
still is whether the only "true" Christian is the fully sanctified Christian. Wesley still had not worked out the full implications of his ideas
in this regard nor the careful use of his terminology.

In January 1739, he makes a crucial distinction between being
born again "in the lower sense" and in "the full sense of the word."
What he describes, without using the terminology, is the difference
between justification and sanctification: remission of sins as distinguished from a thorough, inward change by the love of God shed
abroad in the heart. The implication is that the latter, being born again
in the higher sense, is the genuine Christian. But it is significant that
Wesley is beginning again to allow for gradations ("the lower sense")
rather than to hold a simple either/or position. His mature theology
will come to rest upon the "both/and" of justification and sanctification, which he is here only beginning to sense and develop.

Wesley nevertheless continued to preach the central significance
of the "**witness of the Spirit**" in the societies at London and Oxford.
In fact, he developed an increased measure of confidence in its truth
through what he will come to call "living arguments." Reading Edwards' account of the work of God in New England had shown him

the possibilities of divine action among the people. Now the work of the Spirit was beginning to be evident in the lives of his own hearers. He mentions several women in particular who responded to the work of the Spirit in consequence of his preaching at Oxford. In December 1738, one at St. Thomas's Workhouse was delivered from her raving madness, and another woman at Mr. Fox's society "received a witness that she was a child of God." In March 1739, Mrs. Compton, who was "above measure enraged at this new way and zealous in opposing it," was further inflamed by Wesley's arguments, but when he began praying with her, she soon experienced the witness of the Spirit and cried out, "Now I know I am forgiven for Christ's sake."

Spiritual inspiration of this sort, however, brought controversy. Wesley was not simply credulous in every case but was inclined to "**try the spirits**" in the scriptural manner, testing "to see whether they be of God." In January 1739 he visited a meeting led by one of the "French prophets." But after over two hours of observation, he felt the evidence was inconclusive and pointed out that "anyone of a good understanding and well-versed in the Scriptures" might have said the same things and the motions could easily have been "hysterical or artificial." His advice in such situations was that "they were not to judge of the spirit whereby anyone spoke either by appearances, or by common report, or by their own inward feelings . . . all these were, in themselves, of a doubtful, disputable nature . . . and were therefore not simply to be relied on . . . but to be tried by a farther rule to be brought to the only certain test—the Law and the Testimony." And Wesley concludes with a quotation from the Acts of the Apostles that exemplifies his own tendency toward acting as though he were indeed living in those apostolic times: "I let the matter alone, knowing this; that 'if it be not of God, it will come to nought.'"

This advice would become increasingly more important as Wesley continued to emphasize the work of the Holy Spirit in the lives of true believers while trying at the same time to determine whether the outward signs were authentic, how the inward signs could be discerned, and just what these both signified. These questions were all soon to be magnified as the Methodist movement began to leave the society room and took to the streets and fields. Whitefield, who had set the pattern in this regard, encouraged Wesley with typical overstatement: "I rejoice sincerely in your indefatigable zeal and great success in the gospel of our dear Redeemer." Toward the end of March, he sent John another word of praise from Bristol, with a request attached: "I rejoice at the success God has given you at Oxford and elsewhere. . . . I wish you would be here the latter end of next

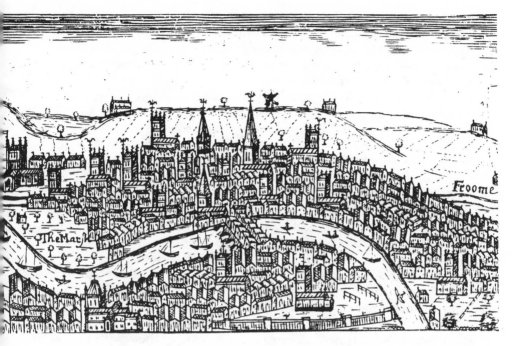

Bristol, although one of the largest urban centers in England in 1739, was still a relatively small city. It was, nevertheless, a major port for trade with North America and was in the center of a coal-mining district that was becoming more important with industrialization.

week." To strengthen his point, he adds in a postscript, "It is advertised in this day's journal" (*Letters*, 25:604, 611–12).

As Wesley set out for Bristol, he could have had no idea of the significance of what lay in store for him there. But his mind was becoming clear as to his calling and his role within the Church. In a letter written about this time to a close but critical friend, he answered again the charge that he should settle into a collegiate or parish living and stop invading other clergymen's parishes by his circulating among the various religious societies in Oxford and London. His answer, was plain and memorable: "I look upon all the world as my parish; thus far I mean, that, in whatever part of it I am, I judge it meet, right, and my bounden duty to declare unto all that are willing to hear the glad tidings of salvation" (*Letters*, 25:616). Bristol would put that principle to the real test.

Whitefield had taken up the reins from Wesley in England when the latter went to Georgia. The first rise of Methodism, at Oxford, had presented the world with a group of conscientious students, bent upon developing a disciplined approach to the Christian life, a meditative piety that tried to implant inward and outward holiness; a theology that exhibited the eclectic tendencies of the holy living tradition; an organization that was based on a connected system of small groups that shared rules and resolutions by which to implement their scriptural theology in everyday life. It was solidly within the religious society tradition of the Church of England. Whitefield came into this group rather late and oversaw its dispersion from Oxford.

Whitefield also had taken up the reins from Wesley in America when John went back to England. The second rise of Methodism, in Georgia, though marked by some interesting innovations, had seen only limited success in a situation wrought with political and personal tensions. The efforts to plant a version of high-Church meditative piety within a colony struggling to maintain basic civility and order did not gain a large following among a population not inclined toward matters religious. The stigma of troublesome fanatics attached to the followers of Wesley in the colony was not relieved at all by Whitefield, who seemed more interested in his personal project, the orphan-house, than the development of the religious community in the colony. Whitefield also seems to have supervised the dispersion of the Methodists from the colony of Georgia, taking some of them with him as he worked his way up the Atlantic seaboard through Virginia to Pennsylvania.

On the other hand, Wesley had taken up the reins to some extent from Whitefield in London when the latter went to America. The third rise of Methodism, the Fetter Lane Society, was the result of a combination of influences—Anglican, Methodist, and Moravian. The spirit of renewal that began to spread among the religious societies was encouraged greatly by Whitefield's preaching and the societies started by Hutton, Böhler, and Wesley, benefited from Whitefield's work. Whitefield was the fiery speaker, and the public reaction to his evangelical fervor made him the focus of public attention, both inside and outside of the Church. When the bishops addressed their attacks to the Methodists, it was Whitefield they had in mind at this point. Wesley's involvement in the societies was much quieter and he received much less public attention, but his organizational interests and abilities had more concrete results. Wesley helped consolidate the work of the Methodists and Moravians within the structures provided by the Church of England. But his own spiritual quandaries did not allow him to have the same exuberance or confidence as Whitefield. Wesley was quietly hammering out his theology in the context of his own spiritual pilgrimage and within the mutual nurturing of small fellowships of believers. Now Whitefield was asking Wesley to move out into yet another area of mission—Bristol.

Chapter 2—Suggested Additional Reading

Böhler, Peter, "Diary," translated by W. N. Schwarze and S. H. Gapp, in "Peter Böhler and the Wesleys," *World Parish* 2 (Nov. 1949), 5.

Cambridge — Walsh, John, "The Cambridge Methodists," in *Christian Spirituality* (London: SCM Press, 1975).

CWJ — Wesley, Charles, *The Journal of the Rev. Charles Wesley*, ed. Thomas Jackson, 2 vols. (London: Conference Office, 1849).

Egmont — John Percival, Earl of Egmont, *Diary*, 3 vols. (London: HMC, 1923).

EMW — Heitzenrater, Richard P., *The Elusive Mr. Wesley*, 2 vols. (Nashville: Abingdon Press, 1984).

Hutton, James, "James Hutton's Account of 'The Beginning of the Lord's Work in England to 1741'," *WHS* 15 (1926).

Ingham — Ingham, Benjamin, *Diary of an Oxford Methodist: Benjamin Ingham, 1733–1734*, ed. Richard P. Heitzenrater (Durham: Duke University Press, 1985).

J&D — Wesley, John, *Journal and Diaries*, ed. W. Reginald Ward and Richard P. Heitzenrater (Nashville: Abingdon Press, 1988—); vols. 18–24 of the Bicentennial Edition of *The Works of John Wesley*.

JWJ — Wesley, John, *The Journal of the Rev. John Wesley*, ed. Nehemiah Curnock, 8 vols. (London: Epworth Press, 1909–16).

Letters — Wesley, John, *Letters*, ed. Frank Baker (Oxford: Oxford University Press, 1980–82; Nashville: Abingdon Press, forthcoming); vols. 25–31 of the *Works*.

Memorials — Stevenson, George J., *Memorials of the Wesley Family* (London: Partridge, 1876).

Moore, Henry, *The Life of the Rev. John Wesley*, 2 vols. (London: John Kershaw, 1824).

OM — Tyerman, Luke, *The Oxford Methodists* (New York: Harper, 1873).

Schmidt, Martin, *John Wesley; A Theological Biography*, 2 vols. (London: Epworth Press, 1963–73).

Sermons — Wesley, John, *Sermons*, ed. by Albert C. Outler (Nashville: Abingdon Press, 1984–87); vols. 1–4 of the *Works*.

Societies — Davies, Rupert, ed., *The Methodist Societies: History, Nature, and Design* (Nashville: Abingdon Press, 1989); vol. 9 of the *Works*.

Watson, David L., *The Early Methodist Class Meeting* (Nashville: Discipleship Resources, 1985).

Whitefield, George, *George Whitefield's Journals* (London: Banner of Truth Trust, 1960).

George Whitefield

CHAPTER 3

The Revival Begins (1739–1744)

The Evangelical Revival in England was part of a larger world-wide movement of the Spirit. German Pietism of the late seventeenth century and the American Great Awakening of the early eighteenth century were among the precursors of the English revival. They were variously marked by strong preaching, evangelical conversions, and assorted manifestations of spiritual vitality, ranging from increased individual piety to enthusiastic group frenzy.

In the British Isles, there were antecedents to several of the chief characteristics of the Wesleyan revival. Since the 1670s, the religious societies had made serious attempts at religious renewal through small groups within the Church of England, establishing local and national programs of Christian education, publication, and missions. Itinerant field preaching had been evident in Wales before the 1720s with the work of Griffith Jones, whom Wesley first met while at Oxford and who became a close friend of Whitefield and the Wesleys. The revival in Wales began in earnest in the mid-1730s with the conversions of Howell Harris and Daniel Rowland. And spiritual revival preceded Wesley into both Cornwall and Scotland.

John Wesley himself, of course, was not the first among the Methodists to have an evangelical experience or conversion—White-field, Ingham, and even his younger brother, Charles, had a typical evangelical experience before John. And Whitefield also preceded him into the "fields," preaching in the open air near Bristol (to the coal miners at Kingswood) in February 1739. Even though John Wesley was active among the various religious societies in London and Oxford at this point and was still preaching in many of the churches in London and the surrounding countryside, it was Whitefield who was the more flamboyant preacher and therefore the more public figure, becoming the predominant target of the literature aimed against the Methodists. In the meantime, Wesley was widening his contacts with religious societies in southern England, including new groups started by persons such as John Cennick in Reading, who had been influenced by the Methodists at Oxford in 1738.

This map of Bristol in the seventeenth century shows Nicholas and Baldwin Streets (in St. Nicholas' parish) forming two arcs just southwest of the city center, and the Horsefair extending eastward from the gate at the northeast corner of the city wall (in St. James').

Wesley and Whitefield had already experienced some tensions between them over their methods and theology, but the ever effusive Whitefield tended to gloss over John's rebukes with words of thanks and praise. Late in March 1739, Whitefield (who was moving on to Wales) requested that Wesley come to Bristol to take his place in the societies there, noting that "many are ripe for bands." George realized his own limitations at organization but could lay his own subtle claim to some priority: "Though you come after, I heartily wish that you may be preferred before me" (*Letters*, 25:612).

The Revival in Bristol

John set out for Bristol in March 1739. This small city was the growing commercial center of southwestern England; it was emerging as the leading provincial city in the kingdom and the chief port for trade with North America and the West Indies. Its merchants imported tobacco and sugar while exporting manufactured goods and African slaves. The city of nearly 50,000 people, about one-tenth the size of London and the site of a magnificent cathedral, was surrounded by coal mines that helped to fuel the growing industrial revolution, with all its attendant problems and possibilities.

As it turned out, pride of place was not so much of a concern for Wesley in Bristol as propriety of method. When he discovered that Whitefield had been holding services in the open air, Wesley could "scarce reconcile [himself] at first to this strange way of preaching in the fields" (*J&D*, 18:612). He noted in his *Journal* that nearly all his life he had been "so tenacious of every point relating to decency and order that I should have thought the saving of souls almost a sin if it had not been done in a church." Outdoor preaching was not illegal in England, but it was irregular and was associated with the heretic Lollard "poor priests" of the pre-Reformation time and some itinerant dissenters of later days. Wesley's own text for Sunday, April 1, from the Sermon on the Mount, brought to his attention "one pretty remarkable precedent of field preaching." That afternoon, he saw Whitefield preach from "a little mount" on Rose Green to about thirty thousand people! The following afternoon, he himself "submitted to 'be more vile'" by preaching outdoors.

Wesley's diary records that "three or four thousand" attended his outdoor preaching at "the glasshouse" (which he began calling "the brickyard" the following week). Over the next few days, the scene was repeated at several sites in and around Bristol: Baptist Mills, Hanham Mount and Two Mile Hill at Kingswood, Rose Green, Bath, and Pensford. The numbers ranged from one to seven thousand ("by computation," Wesley noted) at the open-air meetings in April (though the formula is not revealed). Interspersed with these large meetings, Wesley continued to meet with the Bristol societies at Baldwin Street, Nicholas Street, Castle Street (where he met Griffith Jones again), Gloucester Lane, Back Lane, and Weavers' Hall. In addition, he continued to preach in some parish churches in the area, as well as the chapel at Newgate prison and the poorhouse at Lawford's Gate.

The open-air preaching was called "**field preaching**," even though it did not necessarily take place in the fields. Any open-air site sufficed, as long as people could gather and the preacher could be heard. By this method, the gospel could be brought to the people where they were, to people who could not or would not go to a church at the appointed hour for services. Wesley soon discovered that graveyards were a good location, with a tomb as a pedestal and the church as a backdrop and sounding board. Market squares were an even better amphitheater, surrounded by buildings and often provided with a market cross, from whose steps Wesley could be seen and heard. Some trees were shaped so as to amplify the sound coming from under the branches, and mine pits were at times nearly custommade to accommodate an audience. On one occasion, Charles reports preaching at Evesham from "Whitefield's pulpit, the wall."

In his *Journal*, Wesley records the attendance at his field preaching during that first month in the Bristol area as totalling 47,500 and averaging about 3,000 per occasion (by his estimation). The following month saw even more attend the open-air preaching—just about one year after Aldersgate, Wesley preached to ten thousand people at Rose Green. By the next month, traveling back and forth to London, he was preaching to crowds as large as fifteen thousand at Blackheath and Kennington Common. Whitefield's crowds were even larger: in July there were seventeen thousand on one occasion at Rose Green when Whitefield preached. Charles Wesley felt some skepticism about these mass meetings, especially the numbers of listeners being reported, until he himself preached at Moorfields on June 24 to a crowd that he calculated at ten thousand. That removed all his scruples; such a work was indeed God's will (*CWJ*, 1:155). By September, Wesley was preaching to crowds in and around London that ranged from twelve to twenty thousand, not as many as came to hear Whitefield (by then preaching to crowds of thirty thousand), but still a remarkable number when one considers that Wesley was not as well-known or lively a preacher as Whitefield.

The size of these crowds is not as startling as the relatively small numbers of persons who actually were associated with the societies at this point. During this period, Wesley was also organizing and attending band meetings daily and circulating among the several society meetings in the evening. Although his description of some of the meetings indicates that the homes they met in could not hold the crowds, the typical society consisted of a few dozen people at the most. In typical fashion, Wesley was quick to provide "orders" for the bands on his third day in Bristol, probably using the form he had adapted for the bands in London three months earlier.

Contrary to some impressions, most of the occasions when persons "received" remission of sins or were "comforted" were those small group meetings, not the large open-air preaching services. Wesley notes many occasions when persons were "thunderstruck," "wounded by the sword of the Spirit," "seized with strong pain," "cut to the heart," or "sunk to the earth." Word soon circulated that the people were "falling into strange fits" at the society meetings; the same also began

Kennington Common, southwest from London Bridge, was one of several outdoor sites at which tens of thousands of people gathered to hear Whitefield and the Wesleys preach.

happening occasionally in the public services at Newgate and elsewhere. Wesley heard that many were offended at these outward manifestations of God's power, but explained that in most cases, the stricken persons were relieved through prayer and were brought to peace and joy. Charles was inclined to describe such a person with the familiar phrase, "a brand plucked out of the burning" (*CWJ*, 1:149, 157)

The local clergy, quite naturally, looked upon these activities of the visiting clergy as unwarranted if not illegal incursions into the parish life of the city. Josiah Tucker, rector of All Saints in Bristol, was one of the first to attack Whitefield and Wesley in print. He attacked their methods as well as their theology. It was difficult to hit them both with the same theological volley since Wesley had diverged sharply from Whitefield's Calvinism. John believed in universal atonement and Christian perfection, frequently preaching (and finally publishing) a sermon on "Free Grace" (on Rom. 8:32), to which he appended Charles's hymn on "Universal Redemption." Wesley's response to Tucker and later to the Bishop of Bristol, Joseph Butler, followed the reasoning of a letter he had previously written to a likewise critical friend: God has called me to preach the gospel, and as a Fellow of a College my ordination is not to any particular parish but to any part of the Church of England; therefore my ministry is not limited by parish boundaries, but "I look upon all the world as my parish."

The implication is clear. Wesley felt that his calling as well as his ordination made it necessary for him to disregard parish boundaries and normal parish protocol in his attempts to fulfill God's commission to him to preach the gospel. It was the basic rationale that would undergird Methodist **itinerancy**: God determines the scope of mission and preaching. At this time, the phrase, "I look upon all the world as my parish" had a particular application to the question of parochial boundaries and proprietorship, but such captivating terminology would naturally take on much wider connotations (*EMW*, 2:107). As for his theology, Wesley not only defends his Arminianism and disclaims any responsibility for what Whitefield preaches, but also counterattacks by charging Tucker before the bishop with preaching incorrect doctrine, namely justification by good works, though not in so many words(*J&D*, 19:473).

In his *Journal*, Wesley refers to this Bristol episode as a "new period" in his life, and so it was. This scholarly don whose search for a meaningful faith had rallied a few students around the rigors of meditative piety in Oxford, this Anglican priest who struggled to implement religious discipline among the ragamuffin colonists of a remote parish in Georgia, this searching Christian who received the assurance of faith nearly a year earlier at Aldersgate, had spent the previous months trying to gain some spiritual certainty himself amid continuing doubts, while still encouraging a few small bands of friends in the religious societies of Oxford and London. Now at Bristol, John Wesley saw the movement of the Spirit in ways that he had only read about in Jonathan Edwards' description of the revival in New England. Now in the response of the people to his preaching, especially to the message of salvation by faith, he sensed the confirmation of his own faith and hope in God's grace. His brother Charles celebrated the first anniversary of his own conversion in May by writing a seventeen-stanza poem, the seventh of which began, "O for a thousand tongues to sing my dear Redeemer's praise!" Charles also had a poetic way of expressing the public response to their preaching: "God had set his seal to my ministry" (*CWJ*, 1:129). Now among the thousands of listeners, the seeds of the Methodist revival were beginning to sprout in ways that the Wesleys had not previously experienced or expected. The Wesley brothers certainly continued to have moments of doubt and despair, as expressed also by Charles: "God continues to work *by* me, but not *in* me" (*CWJ*, 1:159). Having a Job-like reluctance, however, did not seem to diminish the fruits of their labors.

The United Societies

The societies in Bristol began to outgrow the homes in which they met. In May, the two largest societies (Nicholas Street and Baldwin Street) bought ground to construct a building large enough to house them both. Wesley decided to step in with financial assistance when the subscriptions from the members fell far short of the costs. He also took a crucial step by assuming managing control (as well as financial responsibility) from the feofees of the societies, heeding Whitefield's warning that if he didn't, such trustees could turn him out of the building if they didn't like his preaching (*J&D*, 19:56). The arrangement was accepted, and the edifice John called "our Room" (later the "**New Room**") was built in the Horsefair at the northeast edge of town.

These societies in Bristol, as also those in London and Oxford, did not conceive of themselves at this time as part of a distinctively "Methodist" movement, even though they had a connection with well-known Methodists such as the Wesleys and Whitefield. The many

The New Room, Bristol, was built back from the street in accordance with regulations for dissenter meeting places, although it was not at first registered as such.

societies that the Wesleys nurtured or simply attended at this point generally were not yet distinguished as "Methodist" but rather shared most of the traditional characteristics of the religious societies within the Church of England. The term "Methodist" was not yet adopted by or applied to any particular society or confederation of societies, but was used primarily by opponents to designate (disparagingly) a particular type of fanatical evangelical person. And simply having the Wesleys or Whitefield associated with a particular society would not make it necessarily "Methodist" at this point. Charles Wesley, for one, was not ready to accept the designation. In December 1738 when "Methodists" were prohibited from preaching in St. Antholin's Church, London, Charles had responded to the Clerk's question, "Do you call yourself a Methodist?" by saying, "I do not; the world may call me what they please" (*CWJ*, 1:139). He was allowed to preach.

The **bands** proliferated as the societies grew. The bands, in this context, were somewhat more distinctively Wesleyan than the societies as a whole. Similar to some of the smaller subdivisions of Oxford Methodism, they bore the marks of Moravian influence as well. They were small groups of five to ten persons who voluntarily banded together for intense spiritual nurture and support. Their primary activities were confession and prayer; their goal was spiritual growth. The membership of each band was homogeneous, in the Moravian pattern: there were women's bands, men's bands, even boys' bands mentioned in Bristol. In addition to gender distinctions, they were grouped by marital status—single men, married women, etc. The purpose of this careful sorting was to allow for the highest possible degree of openness and candor within the bands.

The three or four societies most closely related to the Wesleys in London, Oxford, and Bristol were characterized by their focus on the development of the bands, which constituted the heart of the societies. Not everyone who attended society meetings belonged to a band, but everyone in the bands attended the society.

Wesley's bands had a slightly different shape from the Moravian model, which assumed that the members' experience of assurance had resulted in continuing freedom from sin, fear, and doubt. Wesley's theology, based on his own experience as well as scriptural teachings, allowed for continuing doubts among the justified, resulting in an allowance for "degrees of faith" and being in a "wilderness state" beset by manifold temptations. Wesley was beginning to understand that justification was not simply a one-time formal change by which Christ's righteousness was imputed to the believer. Rather, he was realizing that holding and embodying the gift of righteousness (holiness) in the midst of a turbulent world was difficult for most people. Wesley was beginning to work out the relationship between justification (what God does *for* us, forgiveness of sin) and **sanctification** (what God does *in* us, holiness of life). The substantive change that could result from Christ's righteousness being imparted to the believer was not a one-time experience, but a matter of daily concern and (hopefully) growth for everyone.

The Wesleyan bands, therefore, were not so much spiritual elitist groups in which the leader monitored the perseverance of the saints, as they were more collegial groups that stressed nurture by means of mutual accountability, confession, and growth in grace through Christian fellowship and religious conference. Wesley's rules for the band societies were a modification of the Fetter Lane Society rules; they had more specificity in the questions asked of band members as to their state, sins, and temptations. The point was to encourage faith working through love, that the love of God might be shed abroad in their hearts and lives. To this end, the bands met regularly (at least once a week) for intense spiritual intercourse.

Wesley began meeting with the societies in the unfinished shell of the new "room" in the Horsefair at the beginning of June 1739. About a month later, according to Whitefield, the Baldwin Street and Nicholas Street societies were united. Wesley, however, continued to call the group the "Baldwin Street Society" but began to use the terminology **"United Society"** about three months later, with a note in his diary on October 30 (the same day he first referred to the building as the "New Room").

In June, Wesley also undertook to meet another need in the Bristol area. In the Wesleyan scheme of things, knowledge was a crucial counterpart to vital piety. And at this point, learning was without a home in the collieries of Kingswood. He therefore carried through a plan that Whitefield had originally conceived: he built a school near Two-Mile Hill, with a large hall for preaching, facilities for two schoolmasters, and an invitation to scholars of all ages, including grey-headed ones. He was especially concerned that poor children not only learn "to

Early listing of band members in John Wesley's hand, noting the time of their weekly meetings.

read, write, and cast accounts, but more especially (by God's assistance) to 'know God and Jesus Christ whom he hath sent'" (*J&D*, 19:124–25). Wesley's parish was not only without boundaries and his congregation without pedigree, but his concept of ministry was without limits so long as the activities fit into his vision of scriptural Christianity by helping a person receive the wholeness that God's salvation could bring to humanity.

Disputes with Calvinists and Moravians

Not everyone associated with the Wesleys (much less in the broader revival) agreed on the extent to which humanity itself was responsibly involved in this quest for holiness. In London at that time, the Fetter Lane Society, with the encouragement of James Hutton, was beginning to come under more direct Moravian influence. Late in the fall of 1739, on one of Wesley's frequent trips back to London, he discovered that **Philip Henry Molther**, recently arrived from Germany, had convinced many in the society that they did not have true religion and, therefore, should discontinue all the means of grace and all works of piety and, instead, remain "still" before the Lord (see Ps. 46:10). Molther's argument was that there are no "means of grace" but Christ and that therefore, until persons have true faith in Christ, they should refrain from the so-called means of grace, especially the Lord's Supper.

The conclusions reached by this line of reasoning ("sublime divinity," according to Wesley) ran counter to everything Wesley had long believed and practiced, even after his Aldersgate experience. Now he faced a serious threat to his basic theological stance from within the very society that he thought of as his spiritual home. The tensions engendered by this "**stillness**" controversy with the Moravians pushed Wesley once again to clarify his understanding of the nature of true religion.

In a turnabout of the quietists' favorite terminology, which included the Psalmist's phrase "wait upon the Lord," Wesley countered by exhorting the societies to wait upon God "in all his ordinances, and in doing so to be still and suffer God to carry on his whole work in their souls." Wesley was still convinced of the primary necessity of faith for salvation but could not abide a *sola fide* that cancelled out works of piety and mercy as if they were attempts to earn salvation by doing good works. For Wesley, such anti-legalism, or **antinomianism**, was as serious a challenge to vital Christian living as was the doctrine of predestination, with its corollary belief in the perseverance of the saints ("once saved, always saved"). Although Wesley often tended to deprecate the generally held idea that religion was simply doing no harm, doing good, using the means of grace (he realized that one could do all this and still not have true religion; *J&D*, 19:123), he soon came to appreciate the value of this three-fold pattern as a corrective to the antinomianism of both the Calvinists and Moravians (the proponents of predestination and of stillness). At the same time, Wesley could agree with these spiritual compatriots that the heart of the religious experience is righteousness, peace, and joy in the Holy Ghost. The true "Methodist," he would write in *The Character of a Methodist* (1741), is one who has "the love of God shed abroad in his heart by the Holy Ghost given unto him." This emphasis was the basis of Wesley's doctrine of **Christian perfection**: to love God with all one's heart, soul, and mind, and to love one's neighbor as oneself.

Wesley's theological dispute with Whitefield encompassed two foci: the doctrines associated with predestination and the question of imputed righteousness. Whitefield held the Calvinist belief that one who was truly justified by God would persevere in the faith unto the end—there was no such thing as backsliding among true believers. As to the matter of justification, Whitefield asserted the Calvinist view that Christ's righteousness alone is imputed to us for our salvation and that we have no righteousness but Christ's. Wesley was becoming convinced that God's activity in Christ, although the *cause* of our salvation, was only half of the picture; God's activity in us was also important, so that the faith that we have in us by the grace of God ("a sure trust which a man hath that Christ hath loved him and died for him") was the required *condition* of our salvation. And this faith would result in a real change in the believer where, by the grace of God, Christ's righteousness would be imparted to the person, who would thus not only be *accounted* righteous but would *become* righteous (sanctified or holy).

Wesley was challenged on this point of holiness or Christian perfection by many fellow clergy besides Whitefield. They viewed with alarm yet another exhibition of a doctrine that promoted "perfection." Although the terminology was different, they saw Wesley's position as being not far removed from the Moravian view that he had tried to accept in 1738, that a justified person was free from fear, doubt, and sin. And in spite of the many qualifiers and disclaimers that Wesley began to attach to the concept, those who read "perfect" as entailing a finished state (made possible in part by human effort) could not abide such a doctrine. Whitefield was in America from August 1739 to March 1741, but the two protagonists continued their dispute by correspondence, as the controversies over predestination and perfection broadened into a wider pamphlet war in England.

Wesley's dispute with the Moravians encompassed more than "stillness." Wesley was also bothered by the fact that a small contingent of about a dozen members of the Fetter Lane Society had formed around Molther and were making decisions "as if they were the whole body." This closed approach was contrary to Wesley's expressed desire for open decision-making ("Christian openness and plainness of speech"; *J&D*, 2:139). These conflicts were dividing the society right down the middle.

Wesley also increasingly realized that the Moravian concept of band societies (carefully monitored groups within a closed religious community) was not well-suited to the needs of working-class English people who faced the hardships of changing social and economic conditions of the workaday world. Preaching to the colliers of Kingswood was nothing like preaching to the Moravians of Herrnhut, the former being famous "for neither fearing God nor regarding man."

John fought these battles not only with new German friends and old Oxford compatriots, but also with members of his own family. Charles, though often following John's lead in many areas (even preaching some of John's sermons), continued to differ with him on some points of emphasis and method. John's ongoing controversy with his brother Samuel over the questions of field preaching and the assurance of faith, however, came to a close in November 1739 with Samuel's death. This sad occasion was accompanied, for John, by yet another confirmation of his theological position, since it was reported to him that God had given Samuel "a calm and full assurance" several days before his death. John's *Journal* entry pleads with the reader: "Oh may every one who opposes it be thus convinced that this doctrine is of God!"

About this time (Nov. 12, 1739), a "connectional" pattern of organization begins to appear in the Wesley's activities, starting with a chance (or providential) meeting of three Johns—Wesley, John Gambold, and John Robson, all part of Oxford Methodism (*Letters*, 25:700). They agreed to gather yearly at London on the eve of Ascension Day (usually in April or May). In addition, as many as possible were also to meet quarterly there, on the second Tuesday in July, October, and January. In the meantime, they would circulate monthly accounts of what each was doing in his own particular station. They also developed a list of possible recruits, mostly former Oxford Methodists: Westley Hall, Benjamin Ingham, John Hutchings, Kinchin, Stonehouse, John Sympson, as well as Jacob Rogers, John

The Foundery became Wesley's headquarters in London. The rebuilt facility included (A) Mr. Wesley's apartments, (B) his study, (C) a bell, rung daily at 5 a.m. for morning service and 4 p.m. for evening prayers, (D) the main entrance, (E) the entrance to the preaching-house, (F) a dwelling home for family, preachers, etc., (G) the school-room, band-room, etc., (H) the stable, (I) the coach house and yard.

Cennick, William Oxlee, and John Browne, and perhaps other "spiritual friends who are able and willing" to join with them. The concept of annual and quarterly conferences of this sort was not new, but reveals the direction that Wesley's mind and method was already beginning to take during the first year of his involvement in the revival.

Divisions and the United Society in London

On November 11, 1739, John Wesley preached ("to seven or eight thousand") on the site of a former royal foundry for cannon (*Letters,* 25:699). His introduction to this location by two new acquaintances, Messrs. Ball and Watkins, was propitiously timed. During the winter, a period of heightening tension with the Moravians, he was pressed by the two gentlemen to take the place into his own hands. These two friends proved their earnestness by lending him the necessary £115, which was repaid by subscribers who paid from four to ten shillings a year to pay for and put the building into good repair (£200 first year, £140 after that). The rebuilding of what Wesley called "that vast, uncouth heap of ruins" cost nearly £700 (*Appeals*, 85). When finished, however, the Foundery provided rooms for band meetings, a school, Wesley's living quarters, guest rooms (for his mother and visiting preachers), a stable, and coach house. Silas Told described it in less than glowing terms, as "as ruinous place, with an old pantile covering, a few rough deal boards put together to constitute a temporary pulpit, and several other decayed timbers which composed the whole structure" (*People*, 111). Most importantly, however, it had a large room with plain benches that would hold fifteen hundred people (with separate galleries for men and women), thus making it the first Wesleyan preaching-house in London.

Wesley was out of London through most of the winter, but during two weeks' stay in December, he became increasingly distressed at the disputing in the Fetter Lane Society. On Christmas eve, after meeting with the Society (which was in "utmost confusion, biting and devouring one another"), he met with a small company for hymns, spiritual songs, and exhortation. Back in town again for the month of February, he was still meeting with the Fetter Lane group. On the last day of the month, he met with "many who were in heaviness" and came to him for advice. This seems to be a group of like-minded people within the Fetter Lane Society that was beginning to associate with Wesley, although there is no mention in his *Journal* of any meetings at the Foundery yet. He had in January still been negotiating to acquire the building, which needed extensive renovation. A United Society seems to have started at the Foundery shortly after the buildings were repaired (*City Road*, 22). Charles preached there as early as Thursday, April 3, and remarked in his Journal, "My heart was enlarged in prayer for the infant Society" (*CWJ*, 1:205). By mid-April, the **Foundery Society** was organized to the point that they had agreed upon two rules that showed clear lines of demarcation between them and the Fetter Lane group (although there appears to be some overlap in attendance, if not membership): "(1) That no order shall be valid, unless the Minister be present at the making of it; (2) That whosoever denies the ordinances to be commands, shall be expelled the Society."

When John Wesley returned to London again for a fortnight at the end of April, he attended "our Society" at Fetter Lane with Charles, who noted that the group parted as they met, "with little of singing, less of prayer, and nothing of love." But the following night John noted in his diary a meeting of "The United Society," his first actual notation of the new group that was gathering on Thursdays at the Foundery. His sermon to the society confirmed Charles in the belief that they preached the same gospel.

The Foundery also became the site for regular preaching services twice daily, most days in the mornings at 6 or 7 a.m. and the evenings at 6 or 6:30 p.m. Charles and John seem to be the most regular preachers. Charles had preached to an overflowing crowd at 7 a.m. on Easter Sunday. The Wesleys' preaching services usually consisted of a short opening prayer, a hymn, a half-hour sermon, another hymn, and a concluding prayer (*Societies*, 528). Silas Told, an ex-slaver, described his attendance at an early morning preaching service at the Foundery about this time, expressing some astonishment that Wesley, when he arrived at 5 a.m. in his robe, started the service by singing a hymn, with which the visitor was "almost enraptured." The extempore prayer, however, Silas found to be "quite unpleasant." The sermon on forgiveness of sins led him at first to suspect that Wesley was a papist, but he was soon moved by a still small voice in his heart that said, "This is the truth," upon which Silas felt forgiveness in his own soul (*People*, 111–12).

These preaching services were not society meetings. Although the society meetings frequently included preaching, along with other religious conversation, that was not always the case. The Fetter Lane Society, in particular, was a case in point: the "stillness" perspective increasingly led them to have long periods of silence (Charles refers to the "dumb show") rather than speaking of any sort.

Before leaving town again, John Wesley tried unsuccessfully both in public and in private to convince Molther and his followers of what he considered to be their errors. Upon his return in June, Wesley's relationship with the Fetter Lane Society worsened. Some of the Fetter Lane people began to associate more closely with the Wesleys, who gathered a large group together on Friday, May 9, to attend to two of the ordinances, prayer and fasting (*CWJ*, 1:227). Charles was worried that some of the Fetter Lane members would corrupt the Foundery Society, and warned that anyone wanting to join the Foundery group must come to him and announce such an intention; such a rule, he hoped, would exclude the worst of the "disputatious fraternity." In the meantime, John again pressed his objections with the Fetter Lane Society, telling "the poor, confused, shattered society wherein they had erred from the faith." The leaders of the Fetter Lane Society were intransigent. But having delivered his soul at that point, Wesley felt he was now "clear from the blood of these men," even though he still continued to meet with them, still called them "our society," and still (with Ingham's help) argued his points in sermons every morning at the Foundery, with barbs aimed directly at their points of contention.

The estrangement that Charles had seen as inevitable in early May and that had since become increasingly apparent, reached a peak at the beginning of July. James Hutton had acquired a chapel for the Fetter Lane Society to use, and they promptly voted not to let Wesley preach there. Two days later (on Friday, a fast day), Wesley gathered with a few of those "who still stand in the old paths," took the Sacrament (with his mother in attendance), and made a unanimous decision as to the appropriate action to take. The following Sunday, after a love-feast in Fetter Lane, Wesley read a paper to the group reasserting his position against their views, which he felt were "flatly contrary to the Word of God." He concluded by saying, "I have borne with you long, hoping you would return. But as I find you more and more confirmed in the error of your ways, nothing now remains but that I should give you up to God. You that are of the same judgment, follow me." He then withdrew, followed by eighteen or nineteen of the society. The final breach was made; for Wesley, Fetter Lane was no longer "our society."

The group of dissidents grew. The following Wednesday (the day before the regular weekly meeting of the United Society), Wesley met at the Foundery with this "little company" of followers from Fetter Lane, now numbering about a third (twenty-five) of the men who had been in bands and most (forty-eight) of the women. Charles had written from Bristol the previous week, asking that no new members be allowed until he returned to town, warning that "we shall be overlaid" (*Letters*, 26:20). Nevertheless, these seceders from Fetter Lane were soon amalgamated into the United Society, which was already larger than the Fetter Lane group.

The split in the Fetter Lane Society highlighted the issues that were causing larger divisions among the Methodists. In April, Gambold had written John to say "I am none of your people"; Sympson, Oxlee, and Stonehouse also sided with the Moravians against Wesley's position on ordinances and degrees of faith. The annual conference that the Oxford group had proposed for June 1740 never materialized as the group began to diverge theologically, and the quarterly conferences appear to have been called off as well. After July 1740, Wesley concentrated his energies in London on meetings with the United Society at the Foundery, and although he still met with several other groups (Savoy, Bowes', Whitechapel, Islington, Long Lane, Wapping, etc.), he never mentions meeting in Fetter Lane again. The "infant society" that Charles had met at the Foundery in April had by

June increased from twelve to three hundred members (*CWJ*, 1:241). In addition to meeting on Thursday evening, they also met frequently on Tuesdays and Saturdays. Although Wesley continued the public preaching services early every morning (before people had to be at work) and in the evening, he noticed that the real work was being carried on in the societies. Those who had begun to "fear God and work righteousness" but were not participating in the society grew faint and fell back, while those who were united together grew stronger in the faith (*Societies*, 257–58).

The growth of the societies also brought on other problems and opportunities. Like many other aspects of early Methodism, **lay preaching** evolved more out of necessity than design. The growing United Societies in London and Bristol, and the associated groups at Kingswood and Oxford, required almost constant attention in the face of potentially destructive disputes from within and criticism from without. Although the Wesleys had hoped to have enough compatriots among the clergy to manage the societies (as was the tradition within the religious society movement in England), most of the solid group of six or eight clerics associated with the Wesleys in 1738, by and large former Oxford Methodists, had become alienated from the brothers as the revival began to split into Calvinist, Moravian, and Wesleyan segments. Many of the religious societies continued to be locally autonomous, not affiliated with any of the regional or national leaders. Nevertheless, John and Charles began itinerating among many of the societies in order to encourage them and provide needed leadership. In their developing confederation of societies, the Wesleys relied on local leaders among the bands to keep the societies going in their absence, using various lists of rules to provide some standards of activity and organization.

If the Wesleys were losing clergy allies, they were gaining lay assistance. When the scattered and growing but potentially disputatious societies required closer attention, John began appointing specific (reliable) lay persons to be in charge. One of the earliest, John Cennick, was of Quaker lineage, an aspiring teacher from Reading who shortly after his conversion in 1737 had been influenced by the Methodists (especially John Kinchin) in Oxford, while John was still in Georgia. Recognizing Cennick's leadership within a religious society in Reading, John asked him to go to Bristol and Kingswood in the summer of 1739 to help the societies there in the Wesleys' absence. Wesley expected that he would lead the people in prayer and Bible study, perhaps exhorting occasionally (as distinguished from preaching or exposition, which the Wesleys would have reserved for clergy).

The Methodist preacher, shown here in a portable pulpit, carries on a long tradition of itinerant field preaching. Many Church of England clergy disapproved of the practice itself, as well as the growing Methodist use of lay preachers in the movement.

Cennick was excited at the prospect; he had earlier heard from George Whitefield of plans for the school at Kingswood and had hoped to become a schoolmaster there.

Samuel Wathen, a band-leader in the Baldwin Street Society, was also helping to lead the Kingswood Society, but on one occasion (June 14) was late, and one of the women pressed Cennick, who was in the crowd, to read a sermon or expound to them. Cennick cast lots to find out God's will in the matter, and then stood under a sycamore tree and spoke to the people "with boldness and particular freedom in my heart." In his diary he noted that his preaching was well accepted, not only there but also in Bristol and in a dozen or more other locations in the area. In every instance, however, he tried very hard not to "appear like a minister," especially in his manner of dress.

Another early lay preacher was Joseph Humphreys, a Moravian who was attending the Dissenters Academy in Deptford when he began a society for Whitefield converts in August 1739. Wesley visited the new society within its first month, and soon asked Humphreys to help him at the Foundery. Humphreys had begun preaching in June of 1738 and four months after setting up the society in Deptford, was expelled from the Academy for preaching before he was ordained. Humphreys began preaching at the Foundery in September 1740.

When John Cennick began to stray into Calvinistic thinking later that fall, Wesley asked Humphreys to go to Bristol to keep that flock in line. But Humphreys' long ties to Whitefield made it impossible in the end for him to preach against final perseverance or for Christian perfection (much less "sinless" perfection), and he soon left the Wesleys (*Letters*, 26:62).

In the meantime, Thomas Maxfield, who had had a violent religious experience under John Wesley's preaching in Bristol in April 1739, had been travelling with Charles Wesley to the societies. During a stay in London during the summer of 1739, Charles reported in a journal letter to John that the Moravians considered Brother Maxfield the only hindrance to Charles's conversion to stillness. This stalwart leader among the bands was on occasion left in charge of the Foundery Society. At some point, probably in 1740, Maxfield began to preach to the society in the Wesleys' absence, being "insensibly led" by his earnest listeners to "go further than he at first designed." Henry Moore later reported the story that upon discovering that Maxfield was preaching, John protested this irregularity to his mother Susanna (who was living in the Foundery at the time): "Thomas Maxfield has turned Preacher, I find." Susanna's response, while not countenancing lay preaching in general, was, "Take care what you do with respect to that young man, for he is as surely called of God to preach, as you are. Examine what have been the fruits of his preaching, and hear him also yourself." Moore reports that Wesley "bowed before the force of truth, and could only say, 'It is the Lord: let him do what seemeth him good.'" (*WHS*, 27:8).

During the summer of 1740, Thomas Richards and Thomas Westall also began assisting the Wesleys, at times writing or copying correspondence and perhaps preaching as well. John later referred to them as being among his first "**sons in the gospel**," a term applied to those lay preachers who had agreed to labor full-time at Wesley's behest, going where and when he directed (*J&D*, 19:186).

Although Maxfield and Richards assisted Charles Wesley during this period, Charles did not develop the same tolerance, much less enthusiasm, for lay preaching that John did. In the spring of 1739, Charles had sided with George Whitefield against two Moravians in the Fetter Lane Society, Shaw and Wolf, who claimed that there was no Christian priesthood as such, and that they could administer the Sacrament as well as anyone. Charles did all he could to oppose Shaw, whom he calls the "self-ordained priest," and when Shaw and his friends declared themselves no longer members of the Church of England, that was enough for Charles. He sided with Howell Harris and George Whitefield, and favored expelling Shaw and Wolf from the Fetter Lane Society. Charles found such threats to church order even more serious than did John, and laity acting in pastoral capacities approached a form of ecclesiastical irregularity that Charles found difficult to accept. In the case of William Seward (thought by many to be an enthusiast), Charles had to admit that upon hearing him, he was not convinced of the man's call to preach (*CWJ*, 1:250). A month later, Seward was beaten to death by a mob and became the first Methodist martyr (*WHS*, 39:2–5).

Charles himself was as prone to speak out against lay preaching as to preach against predestination. He was still hoping for a different means of spreading the revival, more in line with William Law's projection that clergy with Methodist inclinations would disperse among the Church and act as leaven in the whole (*CWJ*, 1:159).

In order to maintain good relationships with the Church, the Wesleys found it necessary to guard against excesses, and Charles was always the more ready in this regard. The spiritual exercises that broke out among the societies in the spring of 1739 had brought them a great deal of bad publicity. A year later in Bristol, therefore, John was quick to note "in how different a manner God works now from what he did last spring." With perhaps only slight exaggeration, he described the difference: "He then poured along like a rapid flood, overwhelming all before him; whereas now, 'He deigns his influence

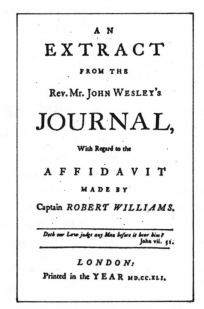

A N

EXTRACT

FROM THE

Rev. Mr. JOHN WESLEY's

JOURNAL,

With Regard to the

AFFIDAVIT

MADE BY

Captain ROBERT WILLIAMS.

Doth our Law judge any Man before it hear him?
John vii. 51.

LONDON:
Printed in the YEAR MD.CC.XLI.

Title page of Wesley's 1741 pamphlet answering Captain Williams' repeated charges against him. Wesley had already published a fuller "extract" of his Georgia *Journal.*

to infuse / Secret, refreshing as the silent dews.' Convictions sink deeper. Love and joy are more calm, even, and steady" (*J&D*, 19:140).

The opposition did not disappear, however. And a challenge from a new, howbeit old, quarter appeared on the scene that same spring in the form of a printed broadside being hawked on the streets of Bristol (*J&D*, 18:81). Robert Williams, a sea captain who had returned from Georgia during the winter, published an affidavit (sworn before the mayor) outlining Wesley's romantic escapades and ensuing legal problems in Georgia.

Wesley decided to respond by publishing his own account of his activities in Georgia. For some time, the Wesleys had circulated handwritten extracts from their journals to be read in the society and band meetings as a means of explaining and defending their activities. Whitefield had begun publishing his own journals the previous year. Now John decided to expand his own audience and publish his autobiographical recollections.

The first "Extract" of his *Journal*, printed in May or June 1740, covered the Georgia episode; it combined versions of material that he had previously written (portions of manuscript journals, letters, and memoranda), recollections based upon his private diary notes, and editorial reflections that bracketed the narrative and gave it some direction. The result was an intriguing combination of missionary adventure, theological explication, ecclesiastical defense, and colonial travelogue. This defense of Methodism took the form of an historical narrative, just as it had earlier in Oxford. It is perhaps no accident that Wesley decided at the last minute to add his "Letter to Mr. Morgan" (the Oxford apologia from October 1732) as part of the preface to this published journal.

The first extract was followed five months later by a second that took the story nearly to the end of 1739. The direction was becoming clear. The material comprised a form of Wesleyan (if not Methodist) propaganda. Although Charles decided not to publish his own journal, John's became a fixture in the literature used by the movement, not only to be read by the members but also to be distributed to the public.

Classes and Leaders

With the building of the New Room in Bristol and the remodeling of the Foundery in London, Wesley had provided for two "united societies" that were, in turn, under his direct control. Up to this point, the organization consisted primarily of small bands of five to ten people, who also made up the core of the larger societies. Wesley's problems with the Moravians over doctrine and discipline had also spilled over into a concern for the way the bands operated within the society. One new adaptation was to institute (as noted in his diary on May 21, 1741) the **select bands** for those who had received remission of sins and were leading an exemplary life. But one gap in the society structure was that persons who were not in a band had no small group in which to seek encouragement and guidance. An unlikely set of circumstances soon solved this problem.

The debt that Wesley had assumed for the buildings in Bristol and London was heavy. He was still receiving the annual income from his fellowship, generally £25 to £35 (which, he said, "supplies me with all I want"), but it would not adequately allow for paying off the loans on his buildings. Moreover, solicitations of contributions from individuals were not amply successful.

In February 1742, he met with several leading persons from the society in Bristol to consider ways of paying the debt on the New Room. Captain Foy proposed that everyone in the society contribute a penny a week, a common method of subscription used in the religious societies and already implemented in the Foundery society to assist the poor. But someone protested that many of the members of their society were very poor and could not afford to give that much, a shilling per year being equivalent to the cost of a small bag of sugar or three pencils. Foy's innovative solution was simple: divide the society into groups of twelve, each with a leader who would be responsible for turning in twelve pence a week, making up themselves whatever they could not collect. He also volunteered to take as his group the eleven poorest of the lot. His offer was accepted; others fell in line; it was done.

The whole society was thus divided into **classes** (from the Latin *classis*, or "division"), neighborhood subdivisions of about twelve persons, each class having an assigned leader. Two months later, the same plan was implemented at London in the Foundery Society.

The importance of these groups soon superseded their original design. As the leaders began their weekly rounds, contacting every member of the society, they soon discovered problems: domestic disputes, drunkenness, and other sorts of behavior not indicative of the pursuit of holiness. Wesley saw the pastoral opportunity presented by the practical structure of the class: the **leaders** of the classes (appointed by Wesley as "those in whom I could most confide") became the spiritual overseers of their group. Wesley met with the leaders weekly when possible. The London society had over a thousand members by this time, but this method helped Wesley overcome the difficulty of coming to know each person in the rapidly increasing societies and extended the personal touch of his pastoral oversight (and discipline). For a variety of reasons, it became advantageous to bring the class members together, rather than visit each in his or her own home. By this means, as Wesley said, "a more full inquiry was made into the behaviour of every person . . . advice or reproof was given as need required, quarrels made up, misunderstandings removed; and after an hour or two spent in this labour of love, they concluded with prayer and thanksgiving" (*Societies*, 262).

The classes were different from the bands in several ways: they were generally a bit larger; they were geographically oriented rather than divided by age, sex, or marital status; they contained everyone in the society, not just those who voluntarily banded together. They allowed for exercising discipline among the whole society, whereas most of the bands fostered nurturing among the more spiritually mature. In both instances, however, the groups were small, and the leaders were laity hand-picked by Wesley.

Besides the band-leaders and class-leaders, another important lay leadership position was necessitated by these developments. The subscriptions to the paying for and rebuilding of the Foundery were put into the hands of a society member, who received the money and paid it out accordingly. This was the first **steward** among the Methodists, soon joined by others, who handled the financial transactions and accounts for each of the societies. Thus, when Wesley began special collections for the needy, the organization was in place to handle the contributions (*J&D*, 19:193–94). By this means, none of the money or goods thus collected passed through the hands of the Wesleys, who were beginning to face charges of becoming rich at the expense of the poor.

Continuing Disputes

Several of the new forms of renewal within the Church recognized that disputation was counterproductive. The religious societies had rules against "discoursing of any controverted point of divinity" (Watson, 188). Spener had urged the German pietist preachers to convert rather than convince, edify rather than dispute. Wesley had discouraged disputing among the Methodists at Oxford.

Although many of the evangelicals in eighteenth-century England shared the same goals, their theological differences of opinion resulted in shaky alliances. In such an uneasy state, Wesley was willing to overlook some differences so long as the disputing person did not cause trouble. The Moravians had incurred Wesley's wrath as much by their divisiveness as by their opinions. When John Acourt wanted to join the United Society in London, it appeared that he was being refused because of his predestinarian principles, even though some in the society also held these views. Having been chided the previous year by George Whitefield for not acting "with a catholic spirit" on these matters, Wesley now made it clear that he did not ask what particular opinions prospective members held, only that they "not trouble others by disputing about it." The clear expectation was that members would not trouble one another with "doubtful disputations" (Rom. 14:1) but simply "follow after holiness and the things that make for peace" (*J&D*, 19:153).

The impetus for the revival and the bond of the societies was the quest for salvation, and the expressed and evidenced sincerity of that search became the guidelines for receiving and maintaining membership. There was no creedal test for entrance, although Wesley's experience with the Moravians had shown that on some basic issues, he had set certain perimeters for an understanding of scriptural truths. Contrary to the case of Acourt, who meant to press his view on every occasion, Joseph Humphreys had been able to assist Wesley under these conditions as a lay preacher. He held quite different views in some areas, but for some time was not inclined to press them. One of the continuing tensions between the Wesleys and John Cennick was on the question of whether Cennick would openly oppose the Wesleys' teaching on universal redemption; for some time, he restrained himself. And even Charles and John felt constrained to challenge each other on many points in their correspondence but generally kept their disputes private.

Whitefield was another case. As the leading Calvinist proponent among the evangelical revivalists, he was not hesitant to take on the Wesleys. Wesley had preached his sermon on "Free Grace" in April 1739, at the very outset of the revival in Bristol (*Sermons*, 3:544–63). It was aimed directly at his basic point of difference with George Whitefield, the doctrine of irresistible grace and all the corollaries of predestination: limited atonement, unconditional election, reprobation (the "horrible" decree), and perseverance of the saints. Shortly afterward, he published it, with Charles Wesley's poem on "Universal Redemption" appended.

Whitefield professed shock at the very idea, recognizing that publication meant open controversy, and that silence on both sides would be better (*Letters*, 25:662). An uneasy peace followed while

Whitefield was in America from November of 1739 to March of 1741. While there, Whitefield published and sold an edition of the Wesleys' *Hymns and Sacred Poems*, in order to raise money for his orphanage in Georgia.

Wesley continued to press rather firmly against predestination, in his preaching, his publishing, and in his correspondence with his young colleague in the colonies. The real danger, in Wesley's eyes, was not so much doctrinal as practical—the implicit danger of antinomianism. Just prior to returning to England, Whitefield, who said he was now "ten thousand times more convinced" of election and final perseverance, sent a contentious letter to Wesley, attacking him for holding that sinless perfection was possible in this life: "What a fond conceit is it to cry up perfection and yet cry down the doctrine of final perseverance!" (*Letters*, 26:32). He also criticized Wesley's doctrine of sin and poked fun at his practice of casting lots.

During the winter of 1741, Whitefield's letter was published in England. On February 1, it was distributed surreptitiously at the door of the Foundery. When Wesley discovered this, he procured a copy, told the congregation what he thought of it, and tore up the broadside before their eyes, asking others to do the same. According to Wesley, they did, so that "there was not a whole copy left" (*J&D*, 19:180).

The battle was engaged. The warring parties had set their course in public. Even though Whitefield had said that he was not going to preach against Wesley, in the heat of the controversy he began to do so. In addition, he published another broadside in the form of a letter answering Wesley. Wesley responded by publishing large editions (perhaps totalling 6,000 copies) of two or three tracts against predestination.

This flare-up, in addition to other instances of notoriety, apparently caught the attention of the Bishop of London, Edmund Gibson, who on several occasions called Whitefield and the Wesleys on the carpet to explain their ideas and actions in these matters. With regard to the question of perfection, John says he did so "without any reserve or disguise," and the Bishop's response was, "Mr. Wesley, if this be all you mean, publish it to all the world." Wesley did so in his sermon, *Christian Perfection*, which spelled out what he did and did not mean by the term. Wesley's view was simple: "A Christian is so far perfect as not to commit sin." Whitefield's response was predictable: "I cannot agree that the inbeing of sin is to be destroyed in this life" (*Letters*, 26:66). Just as he had preached "true stillness" against the Moravians (wait on the Lord through his ordinances), so he also preached "the *great* decree" against the Calvinists—"He that believeth shall be saved;

Class tickets were held by members who continued "to evidence their sincere desire of salvation" at quarterly examinations. Early examples typically contain a verse of Scripture in addition to the date (and later the letter) of the quarter for which the ticket is valid.

he that believeth not shall be damned" (*J&D*, 19:196).

This whole episode, of course, did not end the controversy between the two, which lasted beyond Whitefield's death thirty years later. Whitefield continued to hope for a union, saying that his method was essentially the same as the Wesleys—to "offer Jesus freely to every individual" (*Letters*, 26:66). But the events of the spring of 1741 clearly signalled the division of the revival in England between its Calvinistic and Arminian branches, with Whitefield going on to lead the Calvinistic Methodist connection under the patronage of Lady Huntingdon. John's comment to his brother Charles seems to have both a positive and negative implication: "I must go round and glean after George Whitefield" (*Letters*, 26:55).

With this clear division, Wesley also lost two of his lay preachers to Whitefield. John Cennick had been at odds with the Wesleys for some time, and the winter of 1740–41 saw him nearly tear apart the Kingswood Society by preaching contrary to the Wesleys. John Wesley tried to get another lay assistant, Joseph Humphreys, to go to Kingswood and bring the society under control. Humphreys, however, was inclined to agree with Cennick's theology and became increasingly distressed at the Wesleys' tendency to preach against predestination (in spite of their protestations against controversy and disputes). With the tearing up of Whitefield's letter and the public rebuke of Cennick,

Humphreys joined the latter in leaving the Wesleyan fold. Together they publicly burned a copy of John Wesley's "Treatise on Predestination," which the Wesleys had circulated among Whitefield's congregation as well as at the Foundery. The breach was widened.

In the spring of 1741, then, John Wesley felt increasingly alone in his theological position. He had broken in turn with both the Moravians and the Calvinists, though continuing to dispute with both sides. Within his own diminishing circle of friends and helpers, many had sided early with the Moravians. Even his brother Charles seemed to have been tainted by their doctrines. In April 1741, he wrote to Charles: "Five of us did still stand together a few months since, but two are gone to the right hand (poor Humphreys and Cennick), and two more to the left (Mr. Hall and you)." Both Wesley brothers were still being sought by the Moravians, who were hoping for their conversion and the recapture of the Foundery Society. John was still attracted to them in some ways—it is not unwarranted that he uses warmed heart imagery in describing his feelings: "I scarce ever see any of them but my heart burns within me. I long to be with them; and yet I am kept from them" (*J&D*, 19:190). On May 1, 1741, John even went to a love-feast organized by Peter Böhler for the ten original members of the Fetter Lane Society, which had started exactly three years earlier. The following week, the bands of the United Society met to consider reunion with Fetter Lane but decided that the time was not right. It did not look like it would ever be right.

In the midst of Wesley's trials with Cennick at Bristol, he began to tighten up the membership requirements in the societies. In February 1741, Wesley began to use **tickets**, being "determined that no disorderly walker should remain" within the society. By careful examination before the bands, Wesley took an account of persons for whom "any reasonable objection" was made or those who were not recommended by a reliable person "on whose veracity I could depend." Upon examining members of the bands, Wesley issued membership tickets to those who were recommended; the others faced their accusers—the innocent and the contrite were received into the society and given tickets. The tickets were small slips of paper or cardboard, probably handwritten at first, with a verse of Scripture and the person's name on them. Those who did not receive tickets were put "on trial" again (as they often were at entrance), unless they "voluntarily expelled" themselves, which forty did in this first instance (*J&D*, 19:183–84).

In March, John put some of the Bristol women "who were grown slack" into bands by themselves. These groups became known as

penitential bands and were comprised of backsliding members of the bands. In this way, the use of quarterly examination, giving or withholding tickets, and the configuration of bands became a primary means of discipline as well as nurture within the United Societies. The penitential band was the organizational manifestation of the Wesleyan theology that is expressed strongly by Charles at this point in a letter to John:

> Suppose a justified person settled again upon his lees [sank to the dregs]; ... he is now in a far worse state than if he never had tasted the graces of God from which he is fallen.... He never can recover till he comes to Christ as he did at first, a poor damned unjustified sinner, stripped of all! But while he rests in his former comforts, he is worse than a publican, worse than even a gross Pharisee, inasmuch as he is now a subtle, inward spiritual pharisee and trusts in the abuse of mercy (MS letter, 10/24/40).

If anyone had any doubts about the serious consequences of backsliding, it certainly was not Charles.

The Wesleys also began to incorporate new practices into the societies to further their spiritual goals. About this time, several persons in the Kingswood Society began to meet together on Saturday nights for prayer, praise, and thanksgiving, following the apostolic command to "watch and pray." A decade earlier (with John Wesley's hesitant encouragement), Benjamin Ingham and some of the Oxford Methodists had regularly employed this method of preparing for Sunday (*Ingham*, 205). Charles Wesley also had "watched" with John at Kingswood in May of 1741, reflecting in his journal, "I would this primitive custom were revived among all our brethren" (*CWJ*, 1:278).

John Wesley could find no cause to forbid such a practice in the societies. He felt that the "novelty" of this ancient custom might be an effective means to save a soul from death, or "snatch that brand out of the burning." Indeed, many of the colliers who formerly had spent that night at the alehouse now spent their time in prayer. Not only was there precedent in the Early Church for these "midnight assemblies" that went beyond "the noon of night," but such a practice was in keeping with the "vigils" of the Church of England (*Societies*, 264, 305). These **watch-night services,** generally three or four hours long, were then instituted in London on April 9, 1742. The practical side of Wesley is evident in assigning Friday night nearest the full moon as the regularly monthly time for such "solemn services" so that those who lived some distance away could have the light of the moon to find their way home after midnight (*J&D*, 19:258).

The Mission of Methodism

The Oxford Methodists in the early 1730s, nearly all university men, had spent a good deal of their time, money, and energy in a ministry of mercy to the poor—educating the children in the workhouses, taking food to the needy, providing wool and other materials from which people could make clothes and other durable goods to wear or sell. This particular emphasis on "love of neighbor" and following Christ's example ("who went about doing good," Acts 10:38) continued to characterize Methodism as it entered the revival.

Charles and John continued to carry on an extensive ministry to the prisons, especially Newgate and the Marshalsea in London, the Castle in Oxford, and Newgate in Bristol. They saw their primary task as preaching the gospel, especially to those who were facing the death penalty. Charles had some reluctance about this practice for a time, holding a prejudice against death-bed repentance.

The prison wardens did not always welcome these visitors—Charles tells of having his permit cancelled on one occasion, but getting a new one from the sheriff, much to the consternation of the prison keeper. On that occasion, he also found it necessary to contradict the counsel of Thomas Broughton (a former Oxford Methodist), who had told the prisoners that they could not expect to know that their sins were forgiven (*CWJ*, 1:305). He and John pursued their quarries right down to the hangman's scaffold at Tyburn, at times even getting into the cart with the condemned prisoners to sing and pray with them. John also took the opportunity on at least one occasion to preach to the mob that had gathered to watch the hangings at Tyburn (*J&D*, 19:362).

Experiences of prisoners often provided the Wesleys with opportunities to exhort their listeners or readers. Such was the case with John recounting in his *Journal* the story of his attempted visit to Robert Ramsey, who was sentenced to death. Ramsey, destitute and in distress, had been taken in by the United Society in Bristol. He and an accomplice were soon suspected of taking money from the Kingswood School fund, but in spite of many suspicions, had never been proved guilty or confessed to any wrongdoing. But, as Wesley said, "they did not deceive God, nor escape his hand." Upon returning to London, they were apprehended for robbery and condemned to die. The accomplice confessed the robbery to Wesley the day before his execution. Ramsey then requested a visit from Wesley, who was refused admittance by the keeper. John summarizes the story in homiletic fashion: "So that he who before would not receive the word of God

A Methodist preacher is shown in this Hogarth print reading from "Wesley's Sermons" as he rides in the cart with a condemned prisoner to be hung at Tyburn near Marble Arch.

from my mouth, now desired what he could not obtain. And on Wednesday he fell a sacrifice to the justice of a long-offended God. O consider this, ye that now forget God and know not the day of your visitation!" (*J&D*, 19:245).

The Wesleys hoped that a solid Christian education would turn youths away from such a life and "know the things that make for their peace." (*J&D*, 11/27/39). The rooms he had built at Bristol and Kingswood provided facilities both to house masters and mistresses and to teach scholars of all ages. In part, this arrangement fulfilled the original design of Whitefield, whose interests in this direction had now largely turned toward his Orphan-house in Georgia. Wesley discovered that the expenses of such an operation outstripped the original design, which soon had to be trimmed back. Even though the masters were unpaid volunteers, there was not enough money to keep as large a staff as originally planned (*Letters*, 25:702). Whitefield complained at one point that the buildings were "adorned" too finely and that the children were being clothed as well as taught. During the tensions with Wesley in 1741, Whitefield tried to claim the Kingswood operation for his own, but Wesley pointed out that by that time, he himself had twice the financial investment in the school as Whitefield. Wesley had, nevertheless, drawn up a will in which he named George as successor, along with brother Charles (*Letters*, 26:59).

One way of raising money was to preach **charity sermons**. The most familiar examples are perhaps the annual sermons on behalf of the SPCK for the support of the charity schools. Whitefield was a master at moving congregations; he could easily inspire almost any group to give generously to a special offering collected for a particular cause. He had done so for Kingswood; he was now doing it for the Orphan-house in Georgia. The Wesleys used this method also, to good purpose, in combination with raising money within the societies, even at times making special solicitations to the classes.

There were many needs among the people that the Methodists served, and financial support was sought from every possible source. Even the developing publication program of the Wesleys was in part designed to raise money for the use of the societies. Some critics estimated that this money, which they assumed was Wesley's, was £1300, roughly equivalent to a bishop's income. Wesley admitted that he had food, raiment, and a place to lay his head, but also noted that most of the money was under the control of the stewards in the society, and that if he died with more than £10 to his name, they could call him "a thief and a robber" (*Appeals*, 83–88). His private financial accounts verify the fact that he gave away most of the money that passed through his own hands.

Over the years, the religious societies, consisting mostly of affluent members, had considered assistance to the poor as a part of their mission. In Oxford in the early 1730s, the Methodists (mostly university men) had collected money and goods for the poor in the town. As the Methodist revival spread into the poor suburbs of the English cities in the early 1740s, the new Methodist societies began to fill with colliers, servants, and many other working class people who lived on the edge of hardship if not disaster.

In January 1740, a severe frost in the Bristol area caused hardship for many people. Wesley made some special collections for the poor who, having neither work nor assistance from their parish, "were reduced to the last extremity." By this means, up to a hundred and fifty people a day were fed ("those whom we found to need it most") (*J&D*, 19:135–36).

In 1741, Wesley noticed that the United Society in London

contained a large number of persons who likewise lacked the necessities of life. In May, he called upon the Society to contribute, if they were able, a penny each (more or less) weekly to a fund for the relief of the poor and sick, and to bring what clothes they could spare to be distributed among the needy by the stewards. He also set up a small cottage industry in knitting for the women who desired work and established a method for visiting the sick. Twelve persons were appointed **visitors of the sick** for their area and were asked to gather on Tuesday evenings for consultation with Wesley.

During two months in 1744, he raised £196 in the United Society in London (which numbered about two thousand by then), enough to provide about 360 poor with "needful clothing" (Curnock, 3:125). In this way, the society began its mission at home with taking care of its own ("them whom I knew to be diligent and yet in want") (Curnock, 3:117). The members discovered the neighbor that they were to love was often sitting right next to them on the bench in the Foundery.

Widespread poverty and hardship also meant that death was an ever-present reality. The art of dying (*ars moriendi*) was for the pietist a testimony to the art of Christian living. The death-bed scene was one last opportunity for the faithful to witness his or her faith to gathered friends, and for them to witness "the change" from this life to the eternal. Among the earliest devotional books mentioned in Wesley's Oxford diary were Jeremy Taylor's *Holy Living* and *Holy Dying*. It is no surprise that accounts of death experiences became a standard fixture in the Methodist literature and were often read at society meetings. The Wesleys' journals for this period contain a number of such accounts, including the exemplary death of Jane Muncy (one of the first women in the Fetter Lane Society), the faithful demise of Sarah Whiskin (a young woman of Cambridge), and the long account of John Woolley's death (a thirteen-year-old repentant delinquent). Wesley's account of his mother's death in July 1742 is remarkably restrained but appropriately appreciative, recognizing her important role (in her measure and degree) as "a preacher of righteousness."

Defense and Apology

The theological disputes in which Wesley became embroiled during the first few years of the revival were over large issues—election or universal atonement, stillness or good works, imputed righteousness or Christian perfection. They were the basic issues that defined the shape of whole movements. Over the previous century, the Church of England had developed latitudinarian tendencies that allowed many of these views to coexist within its scope. The turmoil of the Revolution, the tension and turmoil of trying to implement varieties of Puritan orthodoxy, and the relief of the Restoration with its relative sense of toleration if not comprehension, all combined to keep the clergy and their congregations from getting excited over theological issues. In fact, Wesley could claim with some justification that he was simply preaching the "old religion" of the Church of England, which for most people (clergy included) had disappeared in the dust of the Restoration.

Wesley's argument in *The Character of a Methodist* (1742) was that the distinguishing marks of a Methodist were not some special scheme of religion or particular set of notions. He correctly pointed out that most Methodist beliefs and practices were held in common with large segments of Christianity. The distinguishing marks of a Methodist are simply love of God and love of neighbor (*Societies*, 9:35). To the reaction that these are only the "common, fundamental principles of Christianity," Wesley responds, "Thou hast said. So I mean." He wanted Methodists to be distinguished from the unbelieving world, but not from "real Christians." Methodism, then, is simply "genuine Christianity." This is not so much an apology for Methodism but a demonstration that Methodists are interested in unity. In an ecclesiastical world where theological debates can only be divisive, Wesley says the Methodists are interested in one basic question: "Do you love and serve God?" This is the basis of Wesley's practical divinity.

A Collection of Tunes (1742) provided music for many of the Wesleyan hymns sung at the Foundery, referenced by the volume and page to *Hymns and Sacred Poems* (1740).

But Wesley was also not hesitant to spell out his theology in more detail; he published two more treatises in the following few months that dealt with more specific details. His response to Josiah Tucker's *Brief History of the Principles of Methodism* was his own outline of *The*

Principles of a Methodist (1742). In it, Wesley argues for "sound divinity," agreeable to Scripture and experience, and consistent with itself (*Societies*, 9:64). He rebuts Tucker's claim that the Methodists have relied upon William Law and the Moravians for their ideas. In the process of explaining his views, Wesley argues that he does not believe in sinless perfection (in a certain sense) but that he does believe in justification by faith alone (in a certain sense). To correct Tucker on some matters, Wesley quotes his own *Journal*; to some issues of theological concern, he writes an outline of his beliefs (on the assurances, conditions, and effects of justification). Under pressure of time and duties, Wesley leaves for the time being a response to Tucker's idea that "gospel holiness is a necessary qualification, antecedent to justification," noting for the time being that this idea "is directly opposite to the gospel of Christ." In all these matters, he claims that his brother Charles "is as my own soul."

Wesley had claimed to have neither the time nor the inclination to enter into controversy with anyone (*J&D*, 19:90). But in 1743, he decided again to rebut his critics, hoping to quell the rumors that were in part behind the public attacks, literary and physical, upon the Methodist movement. Wesley published *An Earnest Appeal to Men of Reason and Religion*, a "plain account" of the Methodists' principles and actions. Wesley reiterates a familiar base in an opening "rude sketch" of the doctrine he teaches: Methodism moves beyond a lifeless, formal religion to one worthy of God, and that is love—love of God and love of neighbor, seated in the heart and showing its fruits in virtue and happiness.

The argument of the treatise is aimed at any reasonable person. Part of its strength is the constant address to the reader. To the non-Christian, he says: "What evil have we done to you, that you should join the common cry against us?" He goes on to play on a popular theme in the age of reason: "You, at least, will not plead for robbing us of what you so strongly claim for yourselves: I mean, the right of private judgment, which is indeed inalienable from reasonable creatures. . . . Upon your own principles, therefore, you must allow us to be at least *innocent*."

After setting the stage with general principles, Wesley begins a tutorial on faith. In this context, it is natural for him to develop his religious epistemology and draw out the relationship between faith and reason. In empirical fashion, he points out that true judgments of natural things are based on the perception of the "natural senses." So also, clear apprehension of spiritual things is made possible by the "spiritual senses," which can perceive "the evidence of things not seen"

(Heb. 11:1). Until these internal senses are brought alive by regeneration ("the new birth"), there can be no apprehension of things divine.

Wesley then speaks to those who consider themselves Christian, pressing hard on the question of holy living. To the immoral, he says, "Either *profess* you are an infidel, or *be* a Christian." To the moral (who avoids evil, does good, and uses the means of grace), he says, "You may go thus far, and yet have no religion at all—no such religion as avails before God . . . You have not the faith that worketh by love." Wesley goes on to describe this inward religion, outlining doctrines such as Christian perfection and asking, "Now is it possible for any who believe the Scripture to deny one tittle of this?" Feeling that he has convinced the Christian reader that all vital religion has this common base, he says, "No difference between us (if thou art a child of God) can be so considerable as our agreement is. . . . How is it possible, then, that you should be induced to think or speak evil of us?"

Wesley also defends his movement against charges that Methodists were undermining and dividing the Church. He claims to follow the rubrics and canons of the Church with a more "scrupulous exactness" than most of his clergy compatriots. To make his point, Wesley quotes selections of both, asking the reader which of them has followed these more closely. And how can we be splitting the Church, he says, when no person who divides from or leaves the Church has any place among the Methodists.

Wesley's concluding final recommendation to the rational "men of the world" was the advice of Gamaliel in the book of Acts: "Refrain from these men, and let them alone; for if this work be of men it well come to nought, but if it be of God, ye cannot overthrow it, lest haply ye be found even to fight against God."

Not everyone was convinced that the Wesleyan movement was the work of God. Thomas Herring (Archbishop of York) expressed surprise that Wesley could claim "enthusiastic ardour" as "the true and only Christianity." Also the author of *Observations Upon the Conduct and Behaviour of a Certain Sect usually Distinguished by the Name of Methodists* (probably Edmund Gibson, Bishop of London) outlined the manner in which he felt the practices of the Methodists were disruptive of parish life. Among other things, the bishop contradicted his earlier advice to Charles and John Wesley, and now claimed that what had begun as evening meetings in private houses had now gone public and, since the participants had not registered as dissenters, the meetings were illegal conventicles under the Act of Toleration. He thereby tried to differentiate Methodism from some religious societies that continued to further spiritual fellowship in a private inoffensive way.

Some people took stronger steps to oppose the Methodists. In a land where "risings" were not uncommon, it was not hard to raise a mob to protest any number of disruptions to the public peace. Charles had tried to keep the colliers in Kingswood from joining a riot against high corn prices in 1740 (*CWJ*, 1:249). Three years later, he was the object of rioters in Sheffield, who not only pelted him with stones, but also (supposedly at the instigation of the parish priest and certainly with the encouragement of the constable) literally tore down the society-house and nearly destroyed the house of John Bennet, where Charles was staying. Charles preached to the rioters and then actually read the Riot Act to them (*CWJ*, 1:309–10).

John had also faced mobs in Bristol and violent disruptions in London (including an ox being driven through his outdoor congregation at Charles Square). But these incidents did not prepare him for the violence of the opposition that had been aroused by the once-friendly vicar of Wednesbury when Wesley arrived there in October 1743. The story of that riot, told in great detail in Wesley's *Journal*, became the epitome of God's providential protection in the face of brutal opposition (*J&D*, 19:344–49). Dragging the Oxford don (at times by the hair) through the countryside at night through a heavy rain, the mob soon was confronted by a rival gang from a neighboring

This old print depicts Wesley being attacked by a mob. The lack of violence seems to be in keeping with Wesley's own claim of the protection afforded by his guardian angel.

village. The custody of Wesley was their common excuse for the fighting that ensued. Through it all, Wesley observed, many had intended him harm, but none were able to effect it, the two blows he did receive causing him no pain whatsoever. When Charles heard the story from his brother the next day, including John's comment that he now knew how the early Christian martyrs could face the flames with no pain and that he was protected through all by his guardian angel, the younger brother's reaction was more practical than theological: "Many blows he escaped through his lowness of stature" (*CWJ*, 1:338). John closed his own account of the incident by reproducing a curious declaration circulated by the justices of the peace in the area:

> Several disorderly persons, styling themselves Methodist preachers, go about raising routs and riots, to the great damage of his Majesty's liege people and against the peace of our Sovereign Lord the King: [We command you] to make diligent search after the said Methodist preachers, and to bring him or them before some of us . . . to be examined concerning their unlawful doings.

It is not surprising that four months later, hundreds of rioters in that area gathered to "plunder all the Methodists in Wednesbury." Over a period of four or five days, roving mobs destroyed and looted many homes of purported Methodists in the area. And the opposition to the Methodists was further incited by the published notice in the *London Evening Post* that this insurrection was *by*, rather than *against*, the people called Methodists. It was not a totally incredible possibility—the tinners of Cornwall who supported the Wesleys, let it be known that "If any man speak against us, he deserves to be stoned" (*CWJ*, 1:326).

The variety of accusations against the Methodists continued to mount. Added to the longtime charge that they were separatists came the even more treacherous charge that they were papists. This indictment had political overtones in view of the impending threat posed by Bonnie Prince Charlie, the Stuart claimant to the throne who had allied himself with Catholic France and was thought to be poised to invade England. Consequently in March 1744, Wesley wrote a letter to the king, George II, calling it "The humble address of the Societies in England and Wales, in derision called Methodists." In it, Wesley declares that they are a faithful part ("however mean") of the Church of England, and that they "detest and abhor the fundamental doctrines of the Church of Rome, and are steadily attached to your Majesty's royal persons and illustrious house . . . ready to obey your Majesty to the uttermost in all things which we conceive to be agreeable [to the Word of God]" (*Letters*, 26:105). Brother Charles objected

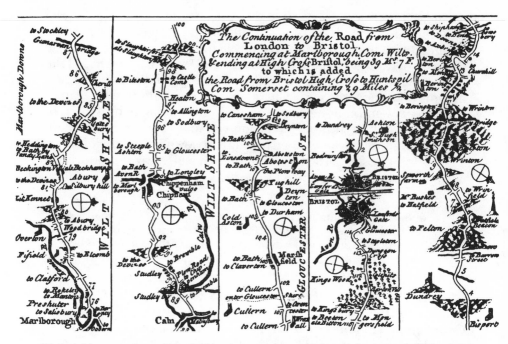

Wesley's itinerancy throughout the kingdom took him on many roads, many of which were listed in contemporary guides, the "traveler's companion." Some road directories contained strip maps such as this section of the "London road" from Marlborough to Bristol.

to sending the letter in the name of the Methodists, since that would imply that they considered themselves a distinct sect. Wesley withheld the letter for the time being. When war was declared on France the following month, many other opportunities arose in which he could declare his allegiance to the crown.

The Widening Parish

Wesley had told Bishop Butler that he had an "indeterminate commission" to preach the Word of God throughout the land (*J&D*, 19:472). The boundaries of his unlimited parish were extended beyond the London/Bristol axis when at the "pressing insistence" of Howell Harris in October 1739, he went to Wales. John's five-day preaching tour saw him preach three times a day. His texts were different, but his aim was the same—to describe the way of salvation. His perspective is evident in his *Journal*, where he says that he "simply described the plain old religion of the Church of England which is now almost everywhere spoken against, under the new name of

Methodism" (*J&D*, 19:106). He goes on to say that he found the people to be "ripe for the gospel, . . . and as utterly ignorant of it they are as any Creek or Cherokee Indians." The reader is then asked if "these poor creatures should perish for lack of knowledge" rather than be saved, even by the exhortations of an itinerant preacher?

In June 1741, John's itinerancy was extended northward. He was invited to visit the Midlands by the Countess of Huntingdon, whose home in Donington Park was becoming the focal point of many societies organized in that area by Ingham, David Taylor, and others. He had known the Countess through her association with the Fetter Lane Society, and some of the leaders of societies in that area were acquaintances of the Wesleys. The Moravians had also recently visited the area, and Wesley found their literature and their influence pervading many of the societies (*J&D*, 19:271). Nevertheless, John preached in the usual variety of venues (churches, homes, marketplaces, under trees) on his usual themes: repentance, justification, faith, and backsliding. He also tried an interesting experiment, speaking to no one about religion unless his heart was "free to it." The result was that he spoke to no one at all for the eighty miles from London to Leicester (not even to a fellow-traveller in the chaise) and was shown much respect as a "civil, good-natured gentleman" wherever he went. In the end, this reaction ("pleasing to flesh and blood") served to confirm him in, rather than dissuade him from, his normal patterns of personal evangelism (*J&D*, 19:197–98).

On the return trip to London, Wesley read Luther's commentary on Galatians, finding it muddy, shallow, confused, and tinctured with mysticism. Wesley makes what might seem to be a rather obvious connection: the Moravians follow Luther! And that, he says, is "the real spring" of their grand error (*J&D*, 19:201). It is not surprising that Wesley follows the typical Anglican assessment of his day by claiming that the root of the Moravian problems reached deep into Luther, who (from his point of view) consistently spoke ill of good works, the law, the commands of God, and decried reason (which, Wesley says, is but the power of apprehending, judging, and discoursing; *Sermons*, 2:590).

To many persons at that point, the revival may have seemed to be cooling off and fragmenting. There was still an interest in unity among some of the various leaders, but the differences cast a large shadow over such hopes. John Gambold told Wesley he was "ashamed of his company" (*J&D*, 19:203). These tensions had devastating results in some of the societies. The Wesleys found the Oxford society in a shambles in the summer of 1741—"torn asunder and scattered

Wesley's first occasion for preaching in Newcastle-upon-Tyne, in the streets of Sandgate. This portrayal does not depict a crowd that reached beyond the range of his voice.

abroad" as John described it. Of the previous twenty-five to thirty members, only two were still weekly communicants and none attended daily prayers of the Church. Two years earlier, Charles had considered settling at Oxford, taking a parish at Cowley. The Wesley brothers had then also enquired at the University about the requirements for the B.D. degree, usually taken by collegiate fellows who were interested in preferment in the Church or leadership in the University. In the summer of 1741, John actually began the exercises required for the degree, writing the requisite *geneses* (on predestination, on the means of grace, and on justification), and a Latin sermon to preach before the University (*Sermons*, 4:408–19). The text for the latter—"How hath the city become an harlot"—was obviously not chosen to placate the officials at Oxford, considering that he developed the theme upon the hypocrisy and apostasy of Oxford. He was apparently dissuaded from using this sermon, and a month later preached before the University on "The Almost Christian." He also either failed to satisfy the degree requirements or discontinued the attempt. In either case, this short interlude, largely spent in the Bodleian Library allowed him to garner scholarly support for some of his favorite theological ideas and did not in the end divert him from pressing on with the United Societies.

The Orphan-house at Newcastle was the first Wesleyan building in the north country.

The following year, Wesley's travels took him beyond Wales and the Midlands. Lady Huntingdon, familiar with the Methodists' work in Kingswood, suggested that the Wesleys visit the colliers in the north, and John Nelson had invited him several times to come to Birstall. Nelson, a young stone mason who had met Wesley in London, had begun preaching "like an owl in the desert," and continued his efforts, despite warnings, because "a few were bruised by the hand of God . . . and received the doctrine of *conscious pardon*" (*People*, 32).

John therefore visited Yorkshire in the spring of 1742, circulating among the societies in the area, many of them led by friends and acquaintances. On May 30, he began his ministry in Newcastle by going to Sandgate, "the poorest and most contemptible part of the town." Standing at the end of the street with John Taylor, he began singing the doxology, whereupon three or four curious souls came out to see what was going on. Soon there were four or five hundred, and before long, Wesley was preaching to twelve or fifteen hundred people on the text, "He was wounded for our transgressions." He gave them his name and announced that he would preach again that evening, whereupon more people came than he had ever seen at Moorfields or Kennington—so many, he noted in his Journal, that he knew more than half could not hear him preach his sermon on backsliding, "although my voice was then strong and clear" (*J&D*, 19:269).

Before the year was out, Wesley laid the first stone for a preaching-house in Newcastle, the largest of the four now under his control. Once again, he had launched a venture in faith, starting the building with only £1.6s. in his pocket. He solicited contributions, preached charity sermons, accepted gifts (such as £100 from a Quaker who had a dream that Wesley could use the funds), and generally trusted that the money would come in. He was following the method that August Hermann Francke had used with the Orphan-house at Halle. Following Francke and Whitefield, Wesley also called his building in New-castle the "Orphan-house" and used the facility for a number of uses, including a school and an infirmary, in addition to a preaching-house.

After a quick trip south, partly to raise funds, Wesley returned to Newcastle in February 1743 and found that discipline was lax in the society. Three months earlier, he had examined some of the people who had "cried out" in the congregation (Charles became adept at exposing the "counterfeits" of this sort). In this case, however, upon examining the members, Wesley found it necessary to "put away above fifty persons" who did not "walk according to the gospel." Before he was finished, sixty-four persons were expelled from the society. The list of their offences is enlightening:

> 2 for cursing and swearing
> 2 for habitual Sabbath-breaking
> 17 for drunkenness
> 2 for retailing spirituous liquors
> 3 for quarrelling and brawling
> 1 for beating his wife
> 3 for habitual, willful lying
> 4 for railing and evil-speaking
> 1 for idleness and laziness, and
> 29 for lightness and carelessness (cf. *J&D*, 19:318).

Two days later, Wesley codified the examination process by writing *The Nature, Design, and General Rules of the United Societies*. In a brief history and description of the societies, Wesley spelled out the rules for membership. In order to *join* a society, persons were required to demonstrate only one condition: "a desire to flee from the wrath to come, to be saved from their sins." Those who desired to *continue* in the societies, however, were expected "to evidence their desire of salvation, First, By doing no harm, . . . Secondly, By doing good, . . . Thirdly, By attending upon all the ordinances of God." These three rules, simple in outline, were fleshed out by Wesley with specific examples (*Societies*, 70–73, 79). Understandably, the list of avoidable evils bears a striking resemblance to the list of reasons why people had been expelled from the society. And the list of ordinances is a precise enumeration of the means of grace that the quietist Moravians would have people omit.

Although Wesley had often said that these three prerequisites were not the whole of true religion, they now became the minimum expectations for a person to manifest the sincerity of his or her desire for salvation. They represented the antithesis to antinomianism, which represented one of the biggest threats to the Wesleyan program at this point. The **General Rules**, then, became one basis for renewing class tickets in the societies. Even though seventy-six people had left the society voluntarily, about eight hundred of the Newcastle society remained in good standing after the February purge. Nevertheless, the next week, Wesley confronted the remaining members with these "rules which all our members are to observe," knowing full well that this expectation would shake many of them. For good measure, he examined the classes again the following week. Charles seems to have been an even tougher examiner than John, at least in some instances ferreting out "counterfeits and slackers" among those who had passed John's inspection (*CWJ*, 1:305).

Some Methodists were rather open with the Wesleys about their inability to keep all the various rules. Thomas Willis wrote a long letter to John in November 1744 in which he explained the manner of his conformity or nonconformity to each of the rules for the band-leaders, to which John had applied some specific directions selected from the General Rules. His plain admission to Wesley was that although he could follow the Savior's Golden Rule "very near to perfection," he could not follow Wesley's directions for the band-leaders "in the strict sense as they are penned." Willis had special problems with the prohibition against buying and selling on the Lord's Day and used the trade in milk as an illustration: cows must be milked; children must be fed; the milk will not last from Sunday morning to Monday. Wesley's simple notation was, "Quite right" (*Letters*, 26:116–18).

The Network Grows

Throughout his preaching tours to the west and north, John Wesley came into contact with a host of persons who were involved in organized religious activities and friendly to the Wesleyan movement: former associates (like Benjamin Ingham in the Leeds area), clergy allies (like John Hodges in Wenvoe, Wales), friends whom he had met in London and with whom he had kept in touch (like John Nelson at Birstall), and new acquaintances (like John Bennet in Derbyshire, who

West Street Chapel pro-
vided the Wesleys a place
to administer the Lord's
Supper to the Methodists
in London.

would form societies and become a "son in the gospel"). He took every
opportunity to speak to their societies, occasionally also preaching in
local churches or in the countryside. Not every church would accept
him, of course. Even in his home town of Epworth the previous year,
John Romley the curate would not permit him to preach in St.
Andrew's Church, so he preached in the adjacent graveyard, using
his father's tomb as a pulpit (*J&D*, 19:273).

It was just this sort of itinerancy on the Wesleys' part that spread
the movement and began to consolidate a network of acquaintances
into a "**connection**" of societies scattered in pockets across the land
(see Rack, 214–37). John Wesley himself was becoming a link between
these various local societies; he also tried to represent to them a firm
commitment (if not connection) to the Church of England.

The Methodists were encouraged to attend their parish church
for the Sacrament as frequently as possible. Recognizing that this
attendance was not always possible, John and Charles at times
stretched the rubrics in order to provide the Sacrament for their
followers. When the poor colliers of Kingswood were repelled from
the Table by the clergy in Bristol, Charles (in spite of his churchly
inclinations) proceeded to administer the Sacrament to them in the
unecclesiastical setting of Kingswood (*CWJ*, 1:267). For years, John
had broadened the administration of the Sacrament to the sick to
include many Methodist friends, claiming that this was not the sort of
"private administration" that was prohibited by the Church.

In 1743, an opportunity arose that helped meet the needs of those Methodists in London who could or would not attend their own Church for the Lord's Supper. In May, John leased an unused Huguenot chapel in West Street. He had preached there in August 1741 and for five Sundays had administered the Sacrament to the members (with a couple hundred Methodist visitors each time). Since it was a consecrated building, he felt comfortable acquiring it specifically for the administration of the Sacrament to Methodists from the London area. The large number of communicants that appeared at West Street Chapel on the first few occasions in 1743 (there were over two thousand members of the United Societies in London) required a service five or six hours long, so Wesley began to divide the group into three parts so as not to have more than six hundred at once (*J&D*, 19:326). Although the rector of St. James' complained to the authorities about the incursions of the Methodists into his parish, Wesley had already cleared this procedure with John Potter, who had been Bishop of Oxford when Wesley was there but was now Archbishop of Canterbury. Yet another means used by Wesley to revive the Church through the Methodist movement left him vulnerable to charges that he was establishing a new sect with a self-consciously separate identity.

The large numbers in the society in London also presented a need for more preaching-houses. In August 1743, Wesley was offered "a convenient chapel" at Snowsfields on the south bank of the Thames. It was not a pleasant area: as one person remarked, "There is not such another place in all the town; the people there are not men but devils" (*J&D*, 19:330). Charles had preached there in 1740 and the Methodists were increasing in that part of town. The Snowsfield chapel was the third building used by the Wesleys in London (*WHS*, 43:59–61). As the revival spread in other parts of the country, similar needs arose, as at Newcastle. A number of the local societies that became associated with the Wesleys, however, had previously settled their meeting places.

Controversy and the Conference

Wesley's Arminian theology and loyal churchmanship differentiated him from many of the local revivals that had begun to spot the British landscape. The Calvinist bent of the Puritan heritage was strong in many evangelical preachers, and the tendency toward dissent made them less worried about separation from the Church of England. And Wesley's doctrine of perfection also differentiated him from many of the evangelical clergy within the Church, who saw this teaching as a form of enthusiasm. However, with Whitefield spending a great deal of time in America, Wesley was now reassuming and consolidating his leadership role within the revival.

One attempt to exercise this leadership appears in John's attempt to hold a **conference** in London in August 1743 "to confer with the heads of the Moravians and predestinarians." The leaders of the revival had maintained contact through the course of events, and some of them had gotten together on more than one occasion since 1739. As we have seen, Wesley had in fact been part of an agreement to begin holding annual conferences in London in 1740. That plan had collapsed with the increasing fragmentation of the revival. Now in 1743 John decided to call a conference of leaders in order to overcome the tensions that were splitting the revival.

Charles was "summoned" (as he said) from Land's End; John Nelson came from Yorkshire. When John Wesley arrived from Newcastle, he found the Moravians and predestinarians missing. Spangenberg said he would come to represent the Moravians, but had left the country. James Hutton claimed the Moravian brethren would not allow him to come. Whitefield did not appear. Although the original design was not fully carried out, Charles indicates that on August 12, the three of them who did turn up met at the Foundery "to good purpose" in any case (*CWJ*, 1:333–34).

The uniting conference had failed to materialize, but the occasion still had a definable effect on the direction of the revival. Wesley had no doubt outlined the issues in his mind in preparation for the conference. The following week, before going to Cornwall, he laid out in writing some of these sentiments about his problems with Whitefield. He outlined his position on three issues: unconditional election, irresistible grace, and final perseverance. In this memorandum, he grants as much as possible in order to reduce the debate, as well as to show that he is purportedly still desirous of union with Whitefield. In fact, however, his allowances in the first two categories are negated by his firm denial of reprobation and his strong assertion of free will, and his allowances in the third category are couched in the code language of sanctification that could be defined a number of ways. Although designed to be an olive branch to the predestinarians such as Whitefield and Lady Huntingdon, this *credo* in fact defined a final line of demarcation (*J&D*, 19:332–33).

The following year, Wesley again decided to hold a conference. Again there were persons invited who were of a Moravian and Calvinist bent of mind. But they were not the leaders of those parties; they were persons who had committed themselves to Wesley's leadership, such as Richard Viney, a Moravian layman from Oxford who had questions about Christian perfection, and Thomas Meriton, a clergyman from the Isle of Man who was seeking to escape "out of the hands of Calvin" (*CWJ*, 1:365). Not all the clergy and lay preachers associated with the Wesleys were invited or came to this conference in June 1744 (*Polity*, 231). Viney, for one, did not come, but four lay preachers did: Thomas Richards, Thomas Maxfield, John Bennet, and John Downes. Four clergy also joined the two Wesleys at this occasion: Meriton, Samuel Taylor (of Quinton, near Evesham), Henry Piers (of Bexley, Kent), and John Hodges (of Wenvoe, Wales). Most of the major areas into which the Wesleys had travelled were represented.

Wesley again prepared for the conference by sorting through some theological problems, this time regarding especially the Moravians. On the eve of the gathering, he wrote a letter to the Moravian Church in England. As with his memorandum on predestination the previous year, this letter outlines the points on which he can agree with his disputants and the traits that he admires in them. He then says, "Some of you will say, 'If you allow all this, what more can you desire?'" In this case, however, the differences are not spelled out in the letter, which he had designed as a preface to an extract of his Journal which was then in the press: "The following extract will answer you at large." At the end of the extract, Wesley then outlined

Time Line 6
Early Period of the Revival

1740		1745		1750		1755
			George II			
Richardson's *Pamela*	Susanna Wesley dies	Prince Charles invades	CW married	JW married		Johnson's *Dictionary*
		Francis Asbury born	Thomas Coke born	Handel's *Messiah*	Wesley's *Dictionary*	
Disputes with Whitefield	*Earnest Appeal*	Sermons, vol. 1	*Primitive Physick*	Christian Library		*Notes upon N.T.*
Split with Moravians	Classes start in Bristol	Early Conferences & *Minutes*		Circuits established	First Irish Conference	"Ought we to Separate"
"Sons in the Gospel"	*General Rules*	Medical dispensary	Kingswood school reopens		separation	Disputes over separation
JW to Newcastle		JW first visit to Ireland		JW first visit to Scotland	London preaching plan	

his problems with the Moravians, especially in three categories: universal salvation, antinomianism, and quietism. He concluded by pressing them to change in three areas: doctrine, discipline, and practice (*J&D*, 19:220–24). Having thus dealt with the Moravians as he had the previous year with Whitefield, Wesley had now laid down the final lines of demarcation with both of the other major wings of the revival with which he had associated.

The stage was set then for the conference of 1744 to become an important benchmark in the development of Wesleyan doctrine and discipline. Wesley had drawn the line; the main efforts to overcome divisions were behind him, and he was ready to move forcefully ahead in his own domain.

The first order of business at the conference was for the clergy to decide whether the lay preachers should be included in the discussions. The question was a logical one in the light of the prejudices against lay preaching. The six priests gathered there could not have known at that point just how many clergy might be attracted into the Wesleyan side of the revival. The choice to include the lay preachers may have been a foregone conclusion in the light of John's attitudes; it was, nevertheless, a momentous decision for the nature of future conferences and the shape of Methodism.

The purpose of this conference was outlined in some basic questions: "What to teach; how to teach; and what to do." Wesley had drawn up a corresponding three-part agenda, raising particular questions on how to regulate doctrine, discipline, and practice. It was made clear from the start that everyone might speak freely and that every question would be fully debated ("bolted to the bran"). The aim was to arrive at a consensus that all could follow "without wounding [their] consciences," but it is clear from the answers spelled out in the minutes not only that John Wesley had written the questions, but also that his perspective dominated the conversation.

The discussions for the first two days were on doctrinal questions. The lay preachers in particular tended not to be deeply grounded in theological concepts. For Wesley, preaching at its root (biblical exposition) was more than witnessing to one's spiritual experience, which was the basis of much of the lay exhortation that took place in the Methodist class meetings. Over the previous few years, Wesley had been made keenly aware that the attempt to correlate experience and Scripture required some basic interpretive choices. Just because Whitefield could say he offered Christ to everyone did not mean that he had no basic differences with Wesley's Arminian theology. For Wesley, the consequences of these differences and the choices they entailed were crucial to the very heart of religion itself, holy living.

Wesley was prepared to clarify several doctrinal issues that had become settled in his mind over the previous months. The minutes of this meeting indicate that justification by faith was strongly asserted, but repentance and works meet for repentance (defined in terms reminiscent of the *General Rules*) preceding faith were also accepted. Assurance was affirmed as being received by all true Christians, but degrees of faith (with doubts and fears) were acknowledged as common experiences shortly following the "first joy." Antinomianism was decried and sanctification was defined.

As for discipline, dealt with on the third and fourth days of the conference, the first concern was to outline the nature of the Church of England and define the Methodists' role as members thereof. They strongly asserted that they had no intention of separating; their purpose, short of being thrust out, was to leaven the whole. They discussed the logistics of the revival, and decided that they should spread out little by little from the societies already established, so that "a little leaven would spread with more effect and less noise," and help would always be at hand. They examined the structure of the United Societies, described all the parts and read out the rules for each. The societies consist of awakened persons; from the larger group, those "who seem to have remission of sins" are united in the bands; those "who seem to walk in the light of God" make up the select societies; those "who have made shipwreck of the faith" meet apart in the penitential bands. The various offices in the society were then described, with the rules for each: assistants, stewards, leaders of bands and classes, visitors of the sick, schoolmasters, and housekeepers. Field preaching was allowed, but discouraged when a church or an indoor place might be available. Lay assistants were allowed "only in cases of necessity." The best general method of preaching (in every sermon) was outlined: to invite, to convince, to offer Christ, and to build up.

On the last day, the question of union with the Moravians and Whitefield was discussed. The former was given up as a lost cause; the latter was allowed if he should make any overtures. They had also decided that Wesley should publish an address to the clergy (who did not hear their preaching), write a "Farther Appeal," and publish sixteen sermons, along with some other useful treatises and abridgements.

The ten Methodists also agreed that quarterly meetings would be held at the three corners of the Methodist itinerancy for those who could attend: Newcastle in November, Bristol in February, and London in May (cf. *Letters*, 25:700). The fourth quarter would then be another yearly meeting on August 1. In the meantime, they also set the schedule for the special monthly meetings during the first quarter: watch-nights, love-feasts, and **letter-days**, which were occasions, common among the Moravians, when letters containing news or accounts of religious experiences were read to the society (*Cambridge*, 271). Before the participants left, they decided to "fix where each labourer shall be," with Wesley no doubt having a primary role in making these appointments.

Minutes of these discussions were organized in the fashion of Wesley's notes in the front of his Oxford diaries: brief questions with cryptic answers, often carefully outlined in numbered paragraphs. His penchant for logic and his training in writing scholastic *geneses* were being put to good use.

The length of this conference, the seriousness and thoroughness of its discussions, and the broad representation of the participants indicates that this meeting was not just another gathering of friends. This conference was an organizational watershed for Wesley and the Methodists—a gathering of their forces, a recapitulation of their ideas, a sorting out of their structure and methods, and a plan for their growth. The Methodist movement had come of age, and the Wesleys had taken a firm hold on their future.

Chapter 3—Suggested Additional Reading

Appeals — Cragg, Gerald R., ed., *The Appeals to Men of Reason and Religion* (Nashville: Abingdon Press, 1976), vol. 11 of the Bicentennial Edition of *The Works of John Wesley*.

City Road — Stevenson, George J., *City Road Chapel, London, and its Associations, Historical, Biographical, and Memorial* (London: Stevenson, 1872).

People — Church, Leslie F., *The Early Methodist People* (London: Epworth Press, 1948).

Polity — Baker, Frank, "The People Called Methodists: Polity," in *A History of the Methodist Church in Great Britain*, ed. Rupert Davies and Gordon Rupp (London: Epworth Press, 1965), 1:213–55.

Rack, Henry, *Reasonable Enthusiast: John Wesley and the Rise of Methodism*, 2nd edition (Nashville: Abingdon Press, 1992).

Walsh, John, "The Cambridge Methodists," in *Christian Spirituality*, ed. Peter Brooks (London: SCM Press, 1975), pp. 251–83.

WHS — *Proceedings of the Wesley Historical Society* (Burnley and Chester, 1898–).

CHAPTER 4

Consolidation of the Movement (1744–1758)

At the Conference of 1744, Wesley had begun to regulate more precisely the doctrine, discipline, and practice of those preachers who were "in connection" with him. While acting in concert with other revivalists, such as Howell Harris, Benjamin Ingham, and George Whitefield, the Wesleys at the same time had begun to define a movement that was becoming increasingly distinctive, both from other forms of the revival and to some extent from the Church as well. John's threefold agenda for the 1744 Conference ("What to teach? How to teach? What to do?") reveals the main concerns of the emerging leader, who sought to consolidate and unify his connection. The Minutes of that occasion demonstrate both the specific nature of those concerns and the emerging shape of the Wesleyan method.

The rise of the United Societies was not simply the result of Wesleyan evangelization, as we have seen. The spread of the movement beyond London and Bristol entailed the networking, in scattered localities, of societies frequently begun by local evangelical leaders, both clergy and lay (Rack, 214–18). Many of these groups were led by persons who previously had some association with the Wesleys, such as John Nelson in Birstall. Other groups, such as societies led by William Darney in Todmorden and John Bennet in Derbyshire, were the result of independent local revivals that began spontaneously or were part of another leader's movement, such as Lady Huntingdon's or David Taylor's.

As the extent of the Wesleyan societies expanded, in part by absorbing various local leaders and their groups, a somewhat disparate array of theological positions and organizational patterns appeared in the Methodist movement, and some discord among the preachers and people ensued. Some Calvinists had wavered between loyalty to Whitefield and to the Wesleys as competing leaders; some Moravians felt a degree of kinship with the Wesleys on certain issues but disagreed with them on others. Baptists and Quakers, bringing their own sense of organizational identity into the revival, moved in and out of the Methodist societies regularly (see *J&D*, 20:41–42).

A detail from "Credulity, Superstition, and Fanaticism," by William Hogarth (1762), satirizing a Methodist service. Despite the combination of spiritual and sexual emotions exhibited, the religious thermometer registers only "luke warm."

The Wesleys' insistence that the Methodists remain within the Church of England and adhere to its standards did little to solve specific problems. No good precedents existed for either Wesley or the Church to follow in every circumstance that arose. The Church had for years tolerated certain varieties of expression within its general rubrics of organization and belief. The Puritans had long expressed a strain of Calvinist reform within the Church, and the English

Moravian strain of Lutheranism allowed dual membership with the Church of England. For over half a century, the religious societies had flourished as an organized renewal movement within the Church. Despite all the varied religious settlements of the previous two centuries, some difficulty still remained in defining precisely the line between acceptable and unacceptable perspectives within the Established Church. The Act of Toleration (1689) had drawn the basic line of demarcation between establishment and dissent, but the practical implications of recognition, interpretation, and enforcement were sometimes vague.

Nevertheless, many Church people thought that the Methodists' distinctly evangelical emphases presented a brand of enthusiasm and fanaticism that marked them as dissenters, even though the Wesleyan doctrinal framework was self-avowedly orthodox. Moreover, the mission and organization of their movement had begun to move beyond the patterns of the religious society movement in ways that suggested independent ecclesiastical self-identity. By the mid-eighteenth century, the Wesleyan movement in fact no longer matched the configuration of any current model of conformity.

It was left to the Wesleys, therefore, to establish more particular guidelines for the United Societies of the people called Methodists within the broader framework of ecclesiastical "uniformity" and evangelical variety. Of particular import were those issues of doctrinal emphasis that stretched the Church's position and those matters of organizational structure that required innovations beyond the patterns of the traditional religious societies within the Church.

The Evolution of Connectionalism

Having begun at the 1744 Conference to set the foundation of doctrine and discipline for those in connection with him, Wesley then continued to sort through the implications of various decisions that he had enumerated in the Minutes. His obvious intent was to hold the spread of Methodism to a consciously measured pace that would not outstrip his ability to manage its design and to prevent undue criticism. There was no "wildfire" spread here. Wesley had even cautioned against excessive field preaching: "To avoid giving needless offense, we never preach *without* doors when we can with any conveniency preach *within*." He intended to expand gradually, to "go a little and a little" from the established societies "so a little leaven would spread with more effect and less noise, and help would always be at hand" (*Minutes,* 23).

Shortly after the Conference, on St. Bartholomew's Day (August 24), John Wesley preached his turn at St. Mary's, Oxford, and delivered a scathing attack on the hypocrisies of the university in his sermon, "Scriptural Christianity." Having described the nature and spread of true, scriptural Christianity (in terms of his characteristic scheme of inward and outward holiness), he came to the main point:

"Where does this Christianity now exist? . . . Is this city a *Christian* city?" By that point in the sermon, the answer, of course, was clearly "no," and Wesley wasted no charity in rehearsing the failures of the university in some detail. He found not one real Christian among the heads of the colleges, he felt the general character of the fellows ranged from "peevishness" to "proverbial uselessness," and he described the younger students as, for the most part, "a generation of triflers."

Some in attendance had expected a display of enthusiasm from Wesley, who, with Whitefield's frequent absence in America, was fast becoming known as *the* "Methodist" in the country. But no one anticipated what Benjamin Kennicott called the "flaming sacred censure" (*Sermons*, 1:112) that Wesley laid upon even the "shining lights" of the university. It was not an alumni sermon to be received gladly, and Wesley realized that it would probably be his last ser-

St. Mary's Church, Oxford.

mon there. He recorded his sentiments in his *Journal*: "Be it so. I am now clear of the blood of these men. I have fully delivered my own soul." Although still a Fellow (with stipend and perquisites), Wesley had effectively put his university career behind him and proceeded now to concentrate fully on the revival. Just as the initiation of his field preaching in Bristol had marked "a new period" in his life, so this sermon at Oxford signalled a new spirit of independence and intensity in his vocation as revivalist.

Itinerancy and Preaching

Through constant travelling and preaching, John and Charles Wesley not only spread but also connected the work of the Methodist movement among the people. John's itinerary over the following year covered almost every area of the kingdom marked by Methodist societies, including Wales, Cornwall, the Midlands, and the North country, to which he traveled in February through wind, hail, rain, ice, snow, driving sleet, and piercing cold (see map, p. 180). The work was not only demanding but also replete with special challenges; the "war against the Methodists" was still being fought in all parts (*J&D*, 20:40). John records several occasions where attempts were made to drown out his preaching—by yelling, bell-ringing, organ-playing, or in one remarkable instance by a miller who let the water fall out of his nearby pond "with a great noise" while Wesley spoke. Wesley also reports many physical attacks upon him, typically by persons throwing eggs, tomatoes, stones, or clods of dirt (e.g., *J&D*, 20:64–65).

One particularly vexing problem was prompted by the alleged connection between Wesley and the Stuart Pretender, "Bonnie Prince Charlie," who, at this time, was expected to invade England and attempt to regain the English crown. The Stuart sympathizers had hoped that Prince Charles could gather local support as he moved southward from Scotland onto English soil. In some minds, Wesley's Oxford reputation as a Jacobite (well-founded or not), in conjunction with his growing network of followers in the North, represented a potentially subversive threat to the public order. Thus, Wesley found himself in an awkward position. Persistent rumors in Cornwall had linked John with the Pretender in France (*J&D*, 20:22). About the same time, Charles Wesley had been charged in Yorkshire with speaking "treasonable words or exhortations, as praying for the banished, or for the Pretender." The witness who spoke against Charles eventually admitted to the Justice of the Peace that he had simply heard Charles pray "that the Lord would call home his banished," that it had occurred before the first news of the threatened invasion, and that these words might certainly apply in a scriptural sense to spiritual pilgrims who are seeking to be with their Lord. The Justice cleared Charles, who took the opportunity to speak strongly for the loyalty of all Methodists to the crown (*CWJ*, 1:358–61). With these troubles in their past and the threat of war with France on the horizon, John Wesley thought it best, on behalf of the Methodists, to write to the king an address of loyalty, which he did over Charles's protest that such an action made them look like a sect, distinct from the Church (*J&D*, 20:16; *CWJ*, 1:354)

The challenges to Methodism, however, were not all external. Continuing questions of polity and doctrine confronted the Wesleys at every turn in their attempt to weave together a cohesive body of followers. In the late summer of 1745, Wesley called another Conference of preachers, this time in Bristol. The Minutes of the previous Conference specified that, in order to monitor developments during the year, Wesley had intended to institute a regional conference every three months on a rotating schedule at the three corners of his national circuit. The quarterly pattern had first been an abortive proposal in 1739 (see pp. 108–9 above); there is little evidence to suggest that it fared any better in 1744–45. Charles was in Newcastle and London at the proposed times in November and May, and John was in Bristol in February, but neither of them mentions in their journals or letters any conferences on these occasions.

The Conference in August 1745, however, was a significant occasion. At the very least, it established the practice of an **annual Conference**, a regular opportunity for Wesley to consult with his preachers on matters of polity and doctrine. The three clergy and six lay preachers (of a possible twelve) who gathered in Bristol spent much of their time discussing "What to preach." The previous Conference had suggested that lay preachers ("helpers" or "assistants") were only allowable "in cases of necessity." This general necessity appeared now to have presented itself, and this Conference continued to refine both the methods and the content of Methodist preaching.

The conferees devoted much of their time to a discussion of the basic doctrines that defined their mission. Some of the preachers expressed some concern that they had abandoned their original design and perhaps had changed their doctrines. Wesley pointed out that at first they had been preaching almost entirely to unbelievers and had therefore emphasized justification. Now, there was more need to exhort those in the society "in whom the foundation is already laid" to go on to perfection, a necessity the earlier Methodists "did not see so clearly at first." Nevertheless, Wesley warned that justification should not be deprecated in order to "exalt the state of full sanctification." At the same time, an emphasis on *sola fide* should not exclude the need to press for repentance and "works meet for repentance" prior to justification.

Several parts of the discussion focused also on continuing concerns of John Wesley and the preachers. Again, the question of the absolute necessity of assurance arose; again, they dared not exclude the possibility of "exempt cases." The conversation continued through a variety of issues: the loss of faith, the presence of visions, the problem of persecution, the relation of faith to doubt and fear, and the proximity of the truth of the Gospel to Calvinism and antinomianism ("within a hair's breadth").

Matters of polity, both theoretical and practical, also came before the Conference. A rather lengthy discussion of the nature of church government revealed a developing flexibility in Wesley's mind on this matter. Wesley was perhaps influenced by his reading of Edward Stillingfleet's *Irenicum*, which argued that no particular polity is wholly right or wholly wrong and that the proper focus of concern should not be upon polity but upon spiritual fruit (*Church*, 145).

Society attendance by non-members also came under scrutiny. Wesley advised that not every "serious person" should be allowed to be present, and certainly not the same person very frequently. On the other hand, the question arose about how to deal with those who left the society. The answer was to avoid bitterness and resentment, to try to talk with them, and if they persist, to "consider them as dead." These were more than passing concerns, given the strict expectations of the *General Rules* among the Methodists, the transience among various arms of the revival in general, and the problems of proselytizing and "sheep-stealing" in some areas.

The dearth of assistants and the wealth of opportunities for mission forced Wesley to suggest an untypical Methodist experiment in Wales and Cornwall—to preach **without forming societies**. According to Wesley's perspective, such a trial would also entail more emphasis on preaching justification, which he feared might have been neglected. It is also perhaps no accident that, since Wesley was preparing his first volume of collected sermons at about this time, many of the items chosen for inclusion dealt with justification and assurance, which coincided nicely with the renewed emphasis on field preaching.

The Minutes of this Conference also note an expressed concern that perhaps the lay preachers were emphasizing "too much of the wrath and too little of the love of God." A related concern, the desire to institute a "seminary for laborers," was postponed until God would "provide a proper tutor." One explicit addition, however, was made to the "Rules of a Helper" to reinforce their full-time status and expectations—"You have nothing to do but to save souls. Therefore spend and be spent in this work. And go always, not only to those who want [i.e. "need"] you, but to those who want you most."

Recognizing that the needs of the people were more than simply spiritual, Wesley asked the preachers to keep "a little stock of medicines" at the preaching-houses in London, Bristol, and Newcastle, to support the remedies prescribed in Wesley's recently published *Collection of Receipts*. Wesley was also concerned that the preachers' minds be richly furnished; therefore the preaching-houses would also house a basic store of literary resources. The inventory of books to be supplied at London, Newcastle, and Bristol (especially for Wesley's use) includes not only a solid core of doctrinal and practical divinity, but an even longer list of physic, natural philosophy, astronomy, history, poetry, Latin and Greek prose and verse, and Hebrew works (*Minutes*, 29). The innocuous item, "Our Tracts" (an inclusive entry for Wesleyan writings) would no doubt have included the several volumes of poems, psalms, and hymns that they had published, as well as *A Collection of Tunes set to Music, as They are Commonly Sung at the Foundery* (1742). By this time, the Wesleys themselves had published over seven dozen works for their people, through a handful of trusted publishers, especially in London, Bristol, and Newcastle. The publishing endeavor was becoming one of the main features of Methodism.

The Growing Publishing Enterprise

At this Conference of 1745, Wesley asked whether he could "travel less in order to write more." The answer was, "As yet it does not seem advisable." Nevertheless, the Minutes list several specific topics for Wesley's attention, and he continued to find time to publish at a rate of over a dozen items a year. The previous year, the preachers had requested a "farther Appeal," referring to his 1743 work. In fact, he used the phrase in the title and produced *A Farther Appeal to Men of Reason and Religion* as a "postscript" to his earlier *apologia* for Methodism. In this sequel, he replied to several recently published attacks on Methodism and promised at the end to continue to rebut the latest attacks as they appeared.

Shortly thereafter, he put forth *An Answer to the Rev. Mr. Church's Remarks on the Rev. Mr. Wesley's Last Journal*, in which he answered Church's charge that Wesley shared many of the very problems that he had laid at the Moravians' feet in the *Journal*, such as denying any value to good works. Although John had split from the Moravians three or four years earlier and although their antinomian influence continued to infect the societies, he could not help but appreciate the depth of piety that characterized many of the Brethren. So that while the possible dangers of their influence inspired him to publish *A Short View of the Difference between the Moravian Brethren . . . and the Reverend Mr. John and Charles Wesley* and *A Dialogue between an Antinomian and his Friend* (followed by a sequel of the same title), the strength of their devotion had also prompted him to abridge and print an edition of Zinzendorf's *Sixteen Discourses.* In keeping with his typical manner of "extracting," Wesley purged Zinzendorf's writings of the "three grand errors" that he found

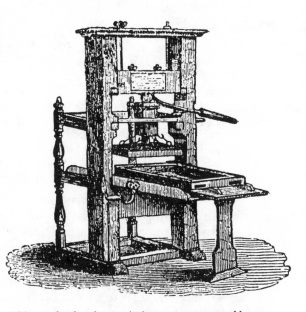

This wooden box hose printing press, once used by Benjamin Franklin, was typical of those used by English printers in the eighteenth-century.

therein: universal salvation, antinomianism, and quietism. He did manage to delete most of the offensive material, but one of the very passages that he had chosen specifically to criticize in his *Journal* slipped past his blue pencil (cf. *J&D, 19:222–23*).

With an eye toward providing his preachers and people with a constant flow of useful treatises, Wesley also abridged and published several other substantial **tracts** during this busy period, works by Jonathan Edwards, William Law, Henry Scougal, Daniel Brevint, Abbé Fleury, and Richard Baxter. He also added *A Word to a Sabbath Breaker* and *A Word to a Swearer* to a series of small tracts he had begun earlier, the target audience usually specified in the titles that would be produced over the next few years, such as *A Word to a Drunkard, A Word to a Streetwalker, A Word to a Condemned Malefactor,* and *A Word to a Smuggler.* Brief and inexpensive, these handouts were direct and forceful calls to repentance and holiness. The rhetoric evident in the plea to the prisoner on death row is no doubt typical of the message the Wesleys brought into the prisons:

> What a condition you are in! The sentence is passed; you are condemned to die; and this sentence is to be executed shortly! You

have no way to escape; these fetters, these walls, these gates and bars, these keepers, cut off all hope. Therefore, die you must. But must you die like a beast, without thinking what it is to die? . . . But, O, how will you stand before God; the great, the holy, the just, the terrible God? Is it not his own word, "Without holiness no man shall see the Lord?" . . . How then can you escape the damnation of hell—the lake of fire burning with brimstone, "where the worm dieth not and the fire is not quenched?" You can never redeem your own soul; you cannot atone for the sins that are past. . . . One thing is needful: "Believe in the Lord Jesus Christ, and thou shalt be saved!" . . . Trust him alone; love him alone; fear him alone; and cleave to him alone, till he shall say to you (as to the dying malefactor of old), "This day shalt thou be with me in paradise."

The Wesleys also produced several hymn pamphlets at this time, including an important collection of *Hymns on the Lord's Supper*, with a treatise on the Sacrament by Daniel Brevint appended. They also published more devotional and catechetical materials, such as *A Collection of Prayers for Families* and *Lessons for Children* (the first in a series of four). The Conference in 1745 also asked that John finish the *Farther Appeal* and write a word of *Advice to the People Called Methodists*, in addition to reiterating their desire for a published collection of his sermons. Before the next Conference, another critique by Thomas Church appeared in print, charging Wesley with irregularities that exhibited separation from the Church and obligated him to resign from the priesthood. Wesley's response in *The Principles of a Methodist Farther Explained* laid forth his basic understanding of what was entailed in separation from the Church, as summed up in his comment: "Nothing can prove I am no member of the Church till I either am excommunicated or renounce her communion" (*Societies*, 195). This principle was the foundation of Wesley's consistent assertion that the Methodists did not and would not separate from the Church. This publication also contains Wesley's capsulation of the main doctrines of the Methodists, which he says include all the rest and which he sees as basic to Christianity: repentance, faith, and holiness. "The first of these we account, as it were, the porch of religion; the next, the door; the third, religion itself" (*Societies*, 227).

In 1746, the Wesleys advertised a collection of *Tracts Published by the Rev. Mr. John and Charles Wesley*. The fifteen volumes consisted of sixty three items they had already published separately, now gathered into groups (biography, controversial and devotional writings, hymns, journals, etc.) and bound together with a new title page for each volume. It was, in effect, the first offering of the Wesleys' **Works.** Besides providing an opportunity to defend the movement from

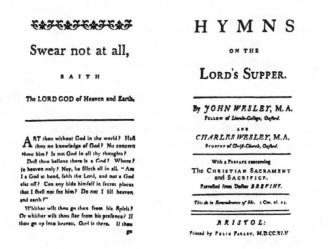

Title pages of two of sixty-three items included in the Wesleys' fifteen-volume collected *Tracts,* one a four-page leaflet, the other a 141-page collection of hymns.

attack, these Wesleyan publications represented a practical extension of the Methodists' ministry and mission. The wide variety represented in their own tracts, as well as their collected libraries, is a good indication of the breadth of their concern for the mind, body, and soul of the people. It was, however, only one facet of an emerging organizational network that could offer spiritual nurture, physical assistance, leadership training, and other support services for those in connection with the Wesleys.

Continuing Controversies

Refinements in the design of the connection of the people called Methodists continued year to year in response to needs as they arose. The range of particular developments for 1745–46 furnishes an example of the process of conferring, itinerating, corresponding, and publishing that continued throughout the century. The most conspicuous disputes appeared in print, the most obvious developments were recorded in the Minutes of the annual Conferences. But a significant part of the process took place in the day to day contact between the Wesleys and the preachers, the members, the critics, and the Establishment. Some of the conversations that were most influential were not a part of the public record, such as the correspondence in 1745–48 between John Wesley and "**John Smith**," a clergyman who wrote under a pseudonym.

Smith claimed to share Wesley's intention to spread "solid, inward, vital religion" to all the world. But he challenged Wesley's claim in the *Appeals* that his Methodist views were in keeping with Scripture and the Church of England. As the letters between the two multiplied, the main points of contention became Wesley's understanding of faith and his emphasis on the "witness of the Spirit," especially in terms of assurance. Most of the issues dealt with doctrine, although quite often the differences were simply problems of phraseology and definition. Smith had difficulty with some of the ideas that he saw in Wesley: that faith is a "supernatural illapse [i.e., infusion] from heaven, the immediate gift of God"; that pardon is evident by a "perceptible attestation"; that the person who receives salvation is made perfect with a perfection "admitting of degrees, yet such a perfection that he cannot sin." Smith strongly affirmed his own faith but saw little correlation between his experience and the Wesleyan way of salvation.

Through a correspondence of at least twelve lengthy letters, Smith pressed Wesley especially hard on what he called Wesley's doctrines of "momentaneous illapse," "perceptible inspiration," and "sinless perfection." He also pointed out several self-contradictions in Wesley's arguments. For instance, at one point, Wesley claimed that after 1738, "salvation by faith" was his only preaching theme, but at another point, Wesley says that he preached "the love of God and man" as his favorite tenet, ten to one over any other subject.

Wesley's by now typical responses to these doctrinal challenges did not satisfy the scholarly inquisitor. To say, as Wesley did, that something is "instantaneous" because it begins in a particular instant and then increases at a gradual pace is to misuse the term, according to Smith. And to require assurance as a prerequisite for salvation raised several questions in Smith's mind, not least of which is whether or not the Wesleys themselves would have gone to hell if they had died while at Oxford, and whether or not their father Samuel also faced the same predicament.

John's answers relied heavily on references to previous publications, repetitions of earlier arguments, rationalization of "seeming contradictions," and some intellectual tap-dancing. He most often held the line against Smith, such as on perceptible inspiration: "For this I earnestly contend, and so do all who are called Methodist preachers." And after reiterating that "none is a *true Christian*" without experiencing assurance, Wesley explained that, if they had faced death at Oxford, the Holy Spirit certainly would have first "wrought

in our hearts that holy love without which none can enter into glory."
And Wesley later explained to Smith that such was the case with his
father, who during his last illness "enjoyed a clear sense of his acceptance with God" and told John more than once, "The inward witness,
son, the inward witness; that is the proof, the strongest proof of
Christianity" (*Letters*, 26:289).

The definition of faith that Wesley relied upon was a combination
of Hebrews and the Homilies that he had begun to reiterate often:
"Justifying faith implies, not only a divine *evidence* or conviction that
'God was in Christ, reconciling the world unto himself,' but a sure *trust
and confidence* that Christ died for *my* sins, that he loved *me*, and gave
himself for *me*" (*Sermons*, 1:194). Smith had more difficulty with
Wesley's explanation of backsliding related to assurance: how could
one experience a clear sense of assurance of salvation and then
subsequently experience doubt and fear? If the previous sense was
mere fancy, says Smith, the argument might hold; but if assurance
were taken as a fact, then "what was a matter of fact yesterday will
continue a matter of fact to all eternity" (*Letters*, 26:210).

In spite of having met his match in logic and theology, Wesley
would hardly admit any modifications of his position to Smith. But
the impact of Smith's influence upon Wesley is evident in the Minutes
of the Conferences that took place during this period. Several of the
same topics appeared, with some alterations. In 1746, the Minutes
record Wesley's comment concerning "the nature of faith itself, im-
plying consciousness of pardon" (i.e., assurance). In July 1747, John
asked his brother Charles, "Is justifying faith a sense of pardon?" The
clear answer was no—there is such an explicit assurance, which is the
common privilege of real Christians, Wesley says, "but I cannot allow
that justifying faith is such an assurance, or necessarily connected
therewith." And yet, the Minutes of that year present another confusing picture in the answer to the question, "But does not matter of fact
prove, that justifying faith does not necessarily imply assurance?" With
particular people in mind, Wesley is tempted to admit of "exempt
cases" (which he had allowed at the 1745 Conference) but finally
concludes, "But this we know, If Christ is not revealed in them, they
are not yet Christian believers."

The problems pointed out by John Smith, apparent also in these
indecisive Minutes, soon began to appear more clearly in Wesley's own
thinking, as he stated the case in a letter to his brother a month after
the Conference: "It is flatly absurd. For how can a sense of our having
received pardon be the condition of our receiving it?" The difficulties
that this issue presented prompted John to observe, in this letter to

Charles, that the two of them needed to develop "a *genesis problematica* on justifying faith" (*Letters*, 26:254–55). In the midst of the revival and on a point that was central to the evangelical message, the Wesleys fell back upon their Oxford scholastic methodology and prepared an academic theme on the question of justification. John's continuing tutorial mind set is also evident in his advice that the assistants should consider themselves as "young students at the University" in need of "a method of study." The daily schedule, strict discipline, and broad reading that John prescribes is strongly reminiscent of his own Oxford method (*Minutes*, 32). And at this point, several years after Aldersgate, he was even willing to grant some concessions to the value of "sincerity" which sound very much like his Oxford stance, *Fac quod in te est* ("Do all you can"). Sincerity, he says, is important *before* justification to bring forth "works meet for repentance," and *after* justification to bring forth "good works." But Wesley is now quick to point out that, although sincerity is a "condition" of a person's acceptance by God, it can never take the place of faith, which is the direct requirement for salvation (*Minutes*, 12–13).

One difficulty for Wesley at this time, of course, was the need to prescribe definitive guidelines on specific issues for the preachers while he was still in the process of developing his own views. The particular issue of justification, however, was becoming increasingly clear to him: although faith was the only *necessary* condition for salvation, "works meet for repentance" were also expected prior to justification, and "assurance" was the normal expectation after justification (with the possibility of "exempt cases" in both instances).

In the public arena, Wesley also responded to attacks on the theology and methods of the Methodists (and their leaders), as he had parried the earlier assault by Edmund Gibson, Bishop of London, in his anonymously published *Observations* (1744). When Gibson published further accusations, Wesley replied in an open *Letter to the Right Reverend the Lord Bishop of London* (1747), which responded item by item to the bishop's critique of six "doctrines big with pernicious influences upon practice." Resisting the temptation to return in kind Gibson's personal attack on "the wild and indigested effusions of enthusiastical teachers," Wesley wrote in a tone that combined candor with courtesy. The work illustrates Wesley's controversial writing at its best (*Appeals*, 330).

Political issues in some ways challenged Wesley as much as theological ones during this time. The troubles in the North had continued to put the Methodists in an awkward position. When Prince Charles, the Young Pretender, invaded Scotland in September 1745, Wesley went to Newcastle, the site of much anxious furor, to be with his people. He immediately contacted the mayor and pledged his loyal support, stating clearly, "I exhort all that hear me to do the same, and in their several stations to exert themselves as loyal subjects, who so long as they fear God cannot but honor the king" (*Letters*, 26:152). If anyone had suspected that Wesley would attempt to influence the restless working people to support rebellion for whatever reason, this strong expression of loyalty would continually counter that suspicion. Wesley thought that even persecution of the Methodists by mobs supported by the establishment was no reason for them to be disloyal to the crown.

Charles Edward Stuart,
"Bonnie Prince Charlie"

After many false alarms, the expected invasion of England came in November 1745, but was pushed westward and bypassed Newcastle. Wesley, with the rest of the country, followed the events with concern as Prince Charles and his allies from the Scottish clans moved as far south as Derby before being turned back in December. The threat finally ended when Prince Charles was defeated at Culloden near Inverness, Scotland, in April 1746 and escaped from the country five months later. Charles Wesley was inspired to write a set of hymns for the public thanksgiving that celebrated the event in the fall.

The Revival Spreads

During the time of these particular theological and political developments, the mission of Methodism was proceeding apace. Charles was busy preaching in the fields, a method urged at the Conference in 1746 and strongly reinforced the following year: "Have we not limited field preaching too much? . . . We cannot expect the wanderers from God to seek us. It is our part to go and seek them" (*Minutes*, 37). John Wesley pointed out to John Smith his conviction that he "did far more good to [the parishioners in Epworth] by preaching three days on my father's tomb than I did by preaching three years in his pulpit" (*Letters*, 26:237).

In order to coordinate this program of widespread field preaching, Wesley established seven **circuits**, which were regional preaching "rounds" comparable to the groupings of societies that some of the independent revivalists had established. The Methodist circuits were listed in the Minutes of 1746: London, Bristol, Cornwall, Evesham, Yorkshire, Newcastle, and Wales. Preachers were assigned, usually in groups of two or three, for a month's itinerancy in one of these seven regions and then moved the following month to another circuit.

Charles also entered into the spirit of this new emphasis on widespread preaching. On one occasion in Redruth, he went to the church, then "drew the congregation after me to the field" (*CWJ*, 1:421). When visiting Plymouth during the summer of 1746, Charles had "designed to preach only in the streets or fields." This method of preaching brought its own set of dangers. Although the gentry "occasionally listened as well as the poor," and the poor received the gospel "with tears of joy," field preaching often brought out "the wild beasts," as Charles called them. Even when preaching in churches, such as at Shoreham, he noted "the wild beasts began roaring, stamping, blaspheming, ringing the bells, and turning the church into a bear-garden." On that occasion, he continued to preach for half an hour, "though only the nearest could hear" (*CWJ*, 1:428).

First entries under "E" in John Wesley's MS sermon register, listing his preaching for 1747–57, the last line in his own hand.

Suspicion and persecution did not necessarily diminish the growth or vigor of the revival. In fact, Charles Wesley noted that the opposite was often the case: "For one preacher they cut off, twenty spring up. Neither persuasions nor threatening, flattery nor violence, dungeons or sufferings of various kinds, can conquer them. Many waters cannot quench this little spark which the Lord hath kindled, neither shall the floods of persecution drown it" (*CWJ*, 1:423; cf. Song of Solomon 8:7). One of Charles's favorite preaching texts at this time was, "I will bring the third part through the fire" (Zech. 13:9).

The emphasis during this period on widespread preaching rather than forming societies may account in part for the spread of Methodism into Ireland during 1747. The 1746 Minutes had defined "a sufficient call of Providence" to new places, such as Dublin or Edinburgh: "1. An invitation from . . . a serious man, fearing God, who has a house to receive us. 2. A probability of doing more good by going thither, than by staying longer where we are."

The work in Dublin apparently started before the summer of 1747, at which time two veteran preachers, Jonathan Reeves and John Trembath, were assigned to take their "journeys" in Ireland. The pioneering Methodist work there had involved leaders who were not in connection with the Wesleys. Benjamin LaTrobe, a Baptist turned Moravian, had established a religious society the previous year "on the plan of the Methodists." This society, meeting in a house on Marlborough Street, soon invited John Cennick, an early Methodist preacher who was still known as a Methodist although, as a friend of Whitefield, he had parted with the Wesleys a decade earlier and was now inclined toward the Moravians. His preaching about Christ, "the babe that lay in swaddling clothes," gave the Methodists in Ireland the nickname "Swaddlers."

In the summer of 1747, a new Methodist society in Dublin seems to have been started by Thomas Williams, whom the Wesleys had severed from the London society three years earlier, but who apparently resolved his problems with the Wesleys shortly thereafter. It was Williams who wrote the Wesleys asking for help. The call of Providence was evidently being heard, and the Wesleys responded.

The Conference had met in June; John Wesley set out with Trembath for **Ireland** several weeks later. When they arrived at Dublin in August, they found a society that numbered nearly three hundred, mostly quite "teachable" and several having "found peace with God." At the same time, Wesley found the local clergy to share the typical prejudice against lay preachers and field preaching, and an Archbishop "resolved to suffer no such irregularities in his diocese." In typical fashion, Wesley faced the challenge head on, meeting with the Archbishop for two or three hours, during which, he says, he "answered abundance of objections" (*J&D*, 20:188–90). After a fortnight

---

1747 Rules for Preaching

1. Be sure to begin and end precisely at the time appointed.
2. Sing no hymns of your own composing.
3. Endeavour to be serious, weighty, and solemn in your whole deportment before the congregation.
4. Choose the plainest texts you can.
5. Take care not to ramble from your text, but to keep close to it, and make out what you undertake.
6. Always suit your subject to your audience.
7. Beware of allegorizing or spiritualizing too much.
8. Take care of anything awkward or affected, either in your gesture or pronunciation.
9. Tell each other, if you observe anything of this kind.

(*Minutes* [1747], 38)

---

in Dublin, John returned home through Wales, crossing paths with Charles, who was en route to Ireland.

Charles remained in and about Dublin for some four months, examining the classes, negotiating for land, soliciting subscriptions for a new building (turning down a surreptitious offer to take over the lease on Mr. Cennick's preaching-house), and facing several unruly mobs. Even during this first round of revival in Ireland, Charles showed some hesitance to establish or enlarge societies too quickly. In one instance, he noted taking in new members, but also dismissed others "who had been admitted too hastily by our helpers" (*CWJ*, 1:463). His own conversations with the local clergy were somewhat successful in convincing them that Methodism represented "no schism or new religion, but the faith once delivered to the saints" (*CWJ*, 1:465).

The spread of Methodism into Ireland thus appears to follow the typical spread of the revival. Local revival activity and the resultant societies were initiated by persons who either had been associated with the Wesleys or had followed a general pattern similar to the Methodists. These groups were then incorporated into the connectional network, provided with Wesleyan preachers, and "regularized" by inclusion in the Wesleys' own itinerary and correspondence.

This process sometimes required the Wesleys to pursue the preachers around the country in an attempt to keep the connection under control. Such was the case when Charles discovered in 1748 that the preachers had abandoned some of the societies west of Dublin in favor of going a hundred and sixty miles south to Cork, which was then "the widest door." Within days, he was on the spot in Cork, attempting to regularize the Methodist activities. Two hundred had signed up to start a society, but such a multitude showed up that the resulting confusion led Charles to conclude that it was impracticable to start a "regular society." Nevertheless, two days later he began examining the candidates and the following week began meeting with the "infant society." A week later, Charles also found hundreds of people a few miles further southwest in Bandon who were "impatient to have a Society and to take the kingdom of heaven by violence" (*CWJ*, 2:18–29).

Nurture and Mission

One of Wesley's rules for preaching, enumerated at the 1747 Conference, was to "always suit your subject to your audience." Field preaching, aimed at "a mixed, unawakened multitude," entailed a heavy emphasis upon repentance, faith, justification, and assurance. The Wesleys' own problems in defining the full implications of the doctrine of justification, as seen in the Smith correspondence and the Conference Minutes, may have been one reason that the focus of the 1748 Conference once again turned to the formation of societies. In any case, the need for a change was clear. They had tried preaching without forming societies in the west and then the north for well over two years, and the results were disastrous, as Wesley noted in the *Minutes*: "Almost all the seed has fallen by the wayside; there is scarce any fruit of it remaining." The preacher had little opportunity for instructions, the awakened souls could not "watch over one another in love," and the believers could not "build up one another and bear one another's burdens." The experiment had frayed the threads of connectionalism.

Caring for Body, Mind, and Soul

The renewed concern for establishing and nurturing the societies led the Conference to consider anew the means by which the societies could be "more firmly and closely united together." To this end, on Christmas day 1747, Wesley began to use the language of **covenant renewal** as a means of engaging his people together in the pursuit of more serious religion, a method that he had encountered at Oxford in *The Country Parson's Advice*.

And in order to ensure future continuity within the local societies, the Methodists organized the children together into "**little societies**" for the purpose of instruction and exhortation. Wesley had just published the third annual installment of *Lessons for Children*, which presented in lesson form "the plainest and most useful portions of Scripture" (Old Testament), with an occasional explanatory note. The networking of societies still presented a problem, however.

Although the length of preachers' assignments on the circuits had been extended to two months in 1747, something more was needed to create greater unity and cohesion among the Methodist societies. Consequently, some Methodists began in October 1748 to hold **quarterly circuit meetings** at which stewards and other leaders of the local societies within the circuit gathered to coordinate accounts, activities, and spiritual oversight (*Polity*, 239).

The activities of each society and the problems of coordinating the work of the societies became more complicated as the movement grew. One of Wesley's earlier attempts at economic reform had led him in 1744 to include a stipulation in the rules of the select societies that had specified, "until we can have all things common," each member would weekly bring "*bona fide*, all he can spare towards a **common stock**" (*Minutes*, 23; also Walsh, 40–50). In 1746 he tried a different approach to economic assistance, namely, to make a collection in London for a specific **lending stock**. The fifty pounds thereby collected from his friends was given to two stewards of the society, who came to the Foundery on Tuesday mornings and dispensed loans of up to twenty shillings (one pound) to those who needed "a present supply of money" for such purposes as "to carry on their business." The borrowers, whose membership in a particular class was entered on the note, pledged (with the cosigner) to repay the money within three months. This short-term small-business loan program assisted two hundred and fifty persons in the first year (*WHS*, 2:197).

During that same period, Wesley expanded the medical assistance program among his people. Fascinated by diseases and cures since his days at Oxford, Wesley had been long since convinced "from numberless proofs that regular physicians do exceeding little good" (*Letters*, 26:235). He had stocked medicine in the three main preaching-houses for about a year and had published a small collection of medical recipes. Now he engaged a surgeon and apothecary to help him in "a kind of desperate expedient," the regular dispensing of medicine.

In December 1746, Wesley announced to the London society his intention of "giving physic to the poor" on Fridays at the Foundery, which thereby became a **medical dispensary**. About thirty came the following day, and a steady stream of about a hundred per month followed, at a cost of less than ten pounds per month (*J&D*, 20:177).

Not wanting to "go out of my depth" (his phrase), Wesley said his intention was to help those with chronic rather than acute illnesses, and to send all difficult and complicated cases to physicians.

Among his first cases was a true test of his method: seventy-one-year-old William Kirkman, a weaver who had experienced "a very sore cough" since he was eleven. Wesley's fear that failure in this case would discourage others from coming was short-lived. The prescribed decoction cured the cough in two or three days, for which Wesley was careful to take no credit, ascribing all to God's power (*Societies*, 276).

Wesley did not limit these services to members of the Foundery Society; of the five or six hundred who received his attention in the first five months or so, "several"

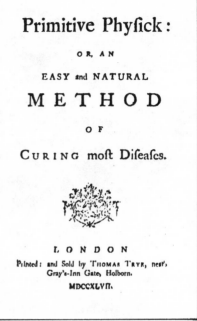

Title-page of *Primitive Physick* (1747), Wesley's collection of folk remedies.

were strangers. Wesley also extended this medical ministry to the preaching-houses in Bristol and Newcastle. Although the latter was initially successful, a shortage of desirable medicines and competition from a free dispensary at the Bristol Infirmary led to the demise of that Methodist enterprise. Nevertheless, for those beyond the reach of these Methodist medical dispensaries, Wesley published an expanded version of his collection of medical recipes under the new title, *Primitive Physick* (1747).

Another experiment in Christian charity, "The **Poorhouse**," consisted of two small leased houses near the Foundery. In these, Wesley provided warm and clean accommodations for "feeble, aged widows." The dozen or so tenants, with whom Wesley and the preachers occasionally visited and ate, also included a blind woman and two poor children (*Societies*, 277).

Wesley also began to provide at the Foundery for many other children who roamed the streets like "wild ass's colts," their poor parents unable to send them to school. He hired two school-masters to teach reading, writing, and casting accounts. Voluntary contribu-

Kingswood School near Bristol, originally established by Whitefield and Wesley, was reorganized in 1748 with a new set of rules and curriculum.

tions also covered the costs of this venture. Two stewards of the society managed the whole operation. They held a weekly Wednesday meeting with the parents, Wednesday being the day after the children were examined for conformity to the stated rules. By the end of 1748, the school served sixty children (*Societies*, 277–79).

By this time, Wesley had also built a new **Kingswood School** outside Bristol, with a revised set of rules. Three weeks before the school reopened on June 24, 1748, the Conference spent considerable time settling the rules and curriculum of the school, which was designed to instruct children "in every branch of useful learning," from the alphabet to those qualifications that would fit one for "the work of the ministry." The list of subjects is imposing: Reading, Writing, Arithmetic, French, Latin, Greek, Hebrew, Rhetoric, Geography, Chronology, History, Logic, Ethics, Physics, Geometry, Algebra, Music. For the English classes and the five other languages, Wesley wrote and published grammars. Beginning in the first class, with students aged between six and ten, the scheme included work in the languages, the children translating in both directions such books as *Instructions for Children* and *Praelectiones Pueriles*. By the third class the students read Augustine's *Confessions;* by the fourth, Caesar. The seventh class is the top level, at which point they are expected to repeat Homer's *Iliad*, make Greek verses, and read the Hebrew Bible. Wesley was convinced that any student who completed the Kingswood curriculum would be a better scholar than ninety percent of the graduates at Oxford and Cambridge.

The severity of the daily schedule matched the rigor of the academic discipline. As originally proposed, the routine began with private prayer and singing at 4 a.m. and moved through various academic subjects, devotional practices, meals, and bedtime at 8 p.m. The morning and afternoon were each concluded with a brief respite for "walk or work." The absence of play time was explained simply: "He that plays when he is a child, will play when he is a man" (*Documents*, 4:104–6). The school's menu was carefully outlined by Wesley in the 1748 Conference Minutes, including a note that a Friday fast would be observed until three o'clock by all who were "in health."

Wesley's analysis of the result of this program, after a few months, was that "some of the wildest children were struck with deep conviction; all appeared to have good desires; and two or three began to taste the love of God." However, a growing laxity of discipline and the wickedness of some of the boys resulted in a gradual loss of scholars and a necessary "purging" of the house, which was soon reduced to eighteen scholars and eventually down to eleven (*J&D*, 20:393–94).

The regulating of the Kingswood School by the Conference is yet another part of the ordering of the connection during this important period. The movement, somewhat informal in many ways, found an increasing need to provide various rules and standards and to acknowledge the legal implications of the management of property. With the renewed attention to the development of societies came the necessity of leasing or building preaching-houses.

When the Methodists first began erecting buildings in 1739, Wesley had taken Whitefield's advice to avoid challenges from trustees by financing the buildings himself. As the movement spread, however, Wesley found it more difficult to finance and manage increasing numbers of widespread properties. Therefore, in May 1746, he executed legal arrangements to turn over the preaching-houses in Bristol, Kingswood, and Newcastle to seven carefully selected trustees, into whose care the management and oversight of the properties was finally entrusted the following year (*Polity*, 229). The deeds upon which the houses were thus settled stipulated that the trustees would permit John Wesley "and such other person and persons as he shall for that purpose from time to time nominate . . . to have and enjoy the house and benefit of the said premises . . . and may therein preach and expound God's Holy word." Upon John's death, Charles would assume his powers (*Documents*, 4:148–49). Although the stipulations seem minimal, they gave the Wesleys firm control. And the guidelines

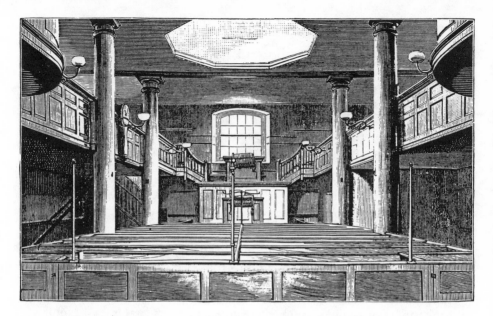

Interior of the New Room, Bristol, remodeled and registered in 1748, with its three-tier pulpit, octagonal skylight, and clock hanging on the left balcony.

for preaching, though stated in very general terms, are reminiscent of the code language of the Protestant Reformation (such as "preaching the Word"), which carried specific implicit expectations.

In 1748, the New Room in Bristol was remodeled, being only a "shell" when Charles preached there in July, but finished when John was there in September. In spite of Wesley's strong statement in his *Farther Appeal* (1745) that the Methodists were not dissenters and therefore they could not use and did not need the Act of Toleration (*Appeals*, 183), the remodeling of the New Room prompted one of the trustees to **register** the property under the protection of the Act as a meeting house for dissenters from the Church. On the back of the document was subsequently scribbled, by an unknown hand, what surely must have been John Wesley's own sentiments on the matter: "Needless, useless, and senseless" (Perkins, 15). The danger to the Methodists was not simply theoretical, however, as the persecutions continued to prove. The Bishop of Durham, Edward Chandler, had commented the previous year that the Methodists, "this mission of exhorters under age and purely laics," might be "of dangerous consequence." He suggested at first that they should be punished by justices of the peace under the Act of Uniformity, then later proposed that they be dispersed under the terms of the Riot Act (*WHS*, 28:47).

The opposition in Ireland escalated during John's second visit there in 1748. In Dublin, he encountered people "hallooing and calling names." In Birr, a small riot broke out while he was preaching in the streets to a "dull, rude, senseless multitude" when a Carmelite friar cried, "You lie! You lie!" Some zealous Protestants then knocked him down and hustled him away (*J&D*, 20:223).

Questions of Unity and Uniformity

Despite a continuing variety of attacks, by 1748 the United Societies of the people called Methodists had established societies in over seventy localities, clustered into nine "divisions" or circuits (Staffordshire and Cheshire now being added to the evolving pattern begun two years previous). The desire to unite the work of the societies, "both in things spiritual and temporal," which had

Howell Harris

given rise to the quarterly circuit meetings, also had wider implications. Wesley continued to envision a **union** of the various branches of the revival. In 1747, he had attended a conference of the Welsh Association, led by Howell Harris. Harris not only supported "several rules toward an union" but also attended Wesleyan Conferences during the next three years. The Wesleys also hoped to work closely with George Whitefield, whom Selina, Countess of Huntingdon, had appointed as one of her chaplains in 1748.

The Wesleys, Harris, and Whitefield held a special conference in August 1748, at which the main question was "How far can we unite with each other?" They made only small steps toward union, though their intentions were noble. At the least, they agreed not to speak ill of each other. In addition, they reached some mutual understanding on the issues of justification, predestination, and perfection, and agreed that they would not "preach controversially" either for or against absolute election, irresistible grace, final perseverance, or perfection. They would use scriptural language as much as possible, avoid terms such as "sinless," and even make use of each other's expressions to some extent. They laid their suspicions squarely on the table: Harris feared closer union lest Wesley should consider himself the "head" of it all; Whitefield objected to Wesley's "monopolizing the name of Methodist to himself only" (Beynon, 230). In the end, it seems, the tensions strained the attempted spirit of unity—Charles Wesley felt that the conference "came to nought," and John's copy of the minutes is endorsed "Vain agreement." Nevertheless, Whitefield was given full rein to roam through the Wesleyan societies, and Charles was able two months later to refer to himself, his brother, and Whitefield as "a threefold cord which shall no more be broken."

In the spring of 1749, John Wesley set out again for Ireland, accompanied by Charles through Wales until they reached Garth. There, on April 8, John officiated at the wedding of brother Charles and Sarah Gwynne, a match he had earlier approved with reluctance because he feared that Charles would no longer seek happiness primarily from God. The bride's mother was also a bit reluctant to have her daughter married to an itinerant preacher with no obvious income, although Vincent Perronet, a longtime clergy friend of the Wesleys, convinced her that the equity in their publishing enterprise, worth probably twice the appraised £2500, would more than guarantee a marital annuity of £100 a year (*CWJ*, 2:50–55). John set off for Ireland two days after the wedding; Charles waited two weeks before resuming his itinerancy for a month on his own.

John found the society in Dublin flourishing. It had increased by over ten percent since the previous year, in spite of some trouble caused by the Moravians. John preached in fields and churches around the country, and also took time to examine the classes and establish new societies. Sizable societies now met at Mountmellick and Cork, despite rumors that Methodists (thought to be persons who "placed all religion in wearing long whiskers") had been rooted out by the government in Ireland, were dying out in England, and were Jesuits at the root! (*J&D*, 20:279). The confusion was not uncommon. While visiting the Cork area the previous year, Charles had discovered that people thought he was "of every religion": "The Presbyterians say I am a Presbyterian; the church-goers that I am a minister of theirs; and the Catholics are sure I am a good Catholic in my heart" (*CWJ*, 2:31).

Although John's published *Journal* of this period gives no hint of any companion, he was accompanied throughout this half-year (including the Irish voyage) by **Grace Murray**, a widow who had previously served as housekeeper at his Newcastle "Orphan-house," and with whom he now (in Dublin) became engaged to be married. He considered her to be "a fellow-laborer in the gospel" who exhibited an incomparable measure of "grace and gifts and fruit." Considering also her work with the women and her care for him personally, Wesley was ready to cast aside all his previous objections to marriage, although some of his preachers (including his brother Charles) felt the match with a servant-woman would not only be scandalous but would also reduce his authority among the preachers and break up the societies (*Letters*, 26:381–87). Before the year was out, Charles managed to put an end to the relationship by fanning the flame between Grace and John Bennet (another suitor) and marrying them in John's absence (*JWJ*, 3:435-39).

Though John Wesley expected trouble in 1749 from the mob in Dublin on the festival anniversary of the Battle of Aughrim (1691), he was not molested at all. Such had not been the case a month or two earlier when Nicholas Butler ("a worthless ballad-singer") raised up daily mobs in Cork to attack the people called Methodists in their preaching-houses, in their businesses, in their private homes, and on the streets, calling them "heretic bitches" and attacking them with clubs, swords, stones, and clods of dirt (*J&D*, 20:285–87). Wesley had intended to go to Cork, where Charles had previously encouraged the work, in spite of the opposition of hostile clergy such as the Rev. John Baily. But upon approaching the city (which he had never visited), he was advised by one of his preachers that rioters filled the streets and that he would not be able to appear there, much less preach, without "immediate hazard" to his life (*Letters*, 26:365). Never one to back down fully from a challenge, Wesley proceeded to Bandon, going straight through Cork, where the mob did not have time to organize before he had left the city limits. Upon returning to Dublin in July, Wesley wrote and published *A Short Address to the Inhabitants of Ireland Occasioned by some late Occurrences* (which were in fact still proceeding), in which he explained the nature and design of Methodism and called upon every lover of "God, mankind, and country" to be more tolerant of those who promote virtue, holiness, love, sobriety, and patriotism, i.e., the Methodists. The coming months also saw Wesley write and publish his open *Letter to a Roman Catholic* and his sermon, "**Catholic Spirit**," both of which emphasized the need to stress the "essentials" of the Christian gospel (as expressed earlier in his sermon, "The Way to the Kingdom") and to be more tolerant on matters of "opinion" (toleration being most often the cause and cry of the persecuted). True religion, Wesley asserts, does not consist of "orthodox opinions" on matters such as forms of worship or modes of baptism. Rather, true religion, the "right heart," is found in the person who believes in God, who knows "Christ and him crucified," whose faith is "filled with the energy of love"—love of God and love of neighbor, evidenced by works of piety and mercy. This is the faith that cuts across the boundaries of denominations, the catholic love that found expression in Charles Wesley's poetry:

Weary of all this wordy strife,
  These notions, forms and modes, and names,
To Thee, the Way, the Truth, the Life,
  Whose love my simple heart inflames
Divinely taught, at last I fly,
With Thee, and Thine, to live, and die.

The plans for wider cooperation among various branches of the revival in England and Wales having stalled after the attempted alliance in 1748, Wesley decided to promote union among his own societies. At the 1749 Conference of preachers, held in London in November, the main concern was for "a general union of our societies throughout England . . . firmly united together by one spirit of love and heavenly mindedness." With an untypical slip into ecclesiastical terminology, he proposed that the London society be seen as "the mother church" of the connection (*Minutes*, 44). Everything would be coordinated through the London society. Information that had begun to be collected the previous year at the various quarterly circuit meetings would now be transmitted to London. This data included lists of members drawn up every Easter (usually noting four categories: awakened, seeker, justified, sanctified) and accounts "of every remarkable conversion" and "of everyone who dies in the triumph of faith." This material was to be gathered by the "**Assistant**," a term formerly applied to all Wesley's preachers, which was now limited to distinguish the head of each circuit who was in charge of the societies and the other preachers on that circuit. The "Rules for Assistants" were consequently modified to include an appropriate duty: "To hold Quarterly Meetings, and therein diligently to inquire both into the spiritual and temporal state of each Society."

Important in this centralized unity was the enhanced role of the stewards in the London society, who were now expected to coordinate and regularize temporal matters throughout the connection. The various quarterly circuit meetings would take care of their own local debts and report their condition to the stewards in London, sending along (if possible) some contribution toward the common debt. The hope was, that after payment of the local debts, there would remain a small connectional **Fund**, "out of which a Society under persecution, or in real distress, . . . might speedily be relieved" (*Minutes*, 708).

This Conference in 1749 was also the first at which printed **Minutes** were available from the previous Conferences. Published in Dublin earlier that year as two small pamphlets with the same basic title, the *Minutes of Some Late Conversations between the Rev. Mr. Wesleys and Others* contained the doctrinal Minutes from 1744–47 and the disciplinary Minutes from 1744–48. Bound together, they made a booklet of sixty-two pages. The availability of these basic guidelines allowed for the development of more "form and solemnity" in receiving new preachers ("**helpers**") into the connection, a desire expressed in 1746 but left to the gradual opening of providence. A new five-step process was instituted at this Conference: (1) The candidate must be recommended by the Assistant and (2) must read and agree to the doctrine and discipline recorded in the previous Minutes. (3) Upon acceptance as a **probationer**, the helper would receive a copy of the *Minutes* inscribed with the note, "You think it is your duty to call sinners to repentance. Make full proof that God has called you hereto, and we shall then be glad to act in concert with you." (4) After a year of probation, the helper would be given a new copy of the *Minutes* with the inscription, "So long as you freely consent and earnestly endeavour to walk according to the following rules, we shall rejoice to go on with you hand in hand," signed by John Wesley. (5) Full acceptance was renewable yearly. The Minutes of this Conference indicate that the nine circuits in the connection now had, besides the Wesleys, twenty-one preachers (eight Assistants and thirteen helpers) and fifteen probationers.

1746 Examination of Preachers

1. Do they know in whom they have believed?
    Have they the love of God in their hearts?
    Do they desire and seek nothing but God?
    And are they holy in all manner of conversation?
2. Have they gifts (as well as grace) for the work?
    Have they (in some tolerable degree) a clear, sound understanding?
    Have they a right judgment in the things of God?
    Have they a just conception of salvation by faith?
    And has God given them any degree of utterance?
    Do they speak justly, readily, clearly?
3. Have they success?
    Do they not only so speak as generally either to convince or affect the hearers?
    But have any received remission of sins by their preaching?
    A clear and lasting sense of the love of God?

    As long as these three marks undeniably concur in any, we allow [i.e., acknowledge] him to be called of God to preach. These we receive as sufficient reasonable evidence, that he is moved thereto by the Holy Ghost. (*Minutes* [1746], 30–31.)

Initial and **annual review** of the helpers was not a new procedure in the Methodist connection. The examination of preachers had begun in 1746 with a concern to "try those who believe they are called to preach." The prospects were asked a list of questions that inquired into their religious life and experience, and that tested their "gifts (as well as grace) for the work"—whether they had a "just conception of justification," a "clear sound understanding," and "a right judgment in the things of God." Such an examination occurred with the interrogation of Jonathan Reeves that year at the Conference itself, during which he was asked questions about his understanding of conviction of sin, faith, and assurance as they related to his own experience. The Wesleys and an Assistant would also listen to each of the helpers preach, after which each candidate would write down the reasons why he believed he was called of God to preach. The preachers, considered to be "as young students at the University," were also required to follow a strict method of study and keep a "journal of every hour," the explicit model of which was the diary method which the Wesleys had used at Oxford (*Minutes*, 31–32).

In 1748, Wesley extended the examination process to the class-leaders, so as to scrutinize "their grace, their gifts, and their manner of meeting their several classes" (*Minutes*, 40). Discipline was becoming the hallmark of the Methodist movement, with accountability at every level: quarterly ticket-renewal of all members and yearly examination of all preachers and leaders. Charles Wesley was designated as the primary examiner of the preachers, a task which he approached with some rigor and with special attention to the matter of "gifts."

Educating the Preachers

The preachers, generally lacking formal education, received many resources in their training. The early Minutes of Conference had listed specific publications that Wesley had written for doctrinal guidance. In 1746, he had published the first volume of a projected three-volume series of **Sermons on Several Occasions**. The preface indicates clearly Wesley's intentions: the reader will see "what those doctrines are which I embrace and teach as the essentials of true religion" (*Sermons*, 1:103). His hope was to reach "the bulk of mankind," to design "plain truth for plain people," to be a *homo unius libri*—a person of one book, the Bible, wherein one could find "the way to heaven."

The tone of the preface and the contents of the first volume were fully in keeping with his design in 1746 and 1747 to emphasize field preaching more broadly. The emphasis of this first group of sermons is primarily upon faith, justification, and assurance—the main themes of sermons directed to "mixed" crowds that included large numbers of unbelievers. They are not, however, written versions of sermons that Wesley had preached to such multitudes. The first four are sermons that he and Charles had preached before the University of Oxford, thus presenting at the outset of the collection an effective notice of their having severed any relationship with their *Alma mater*, which John claimed had "become an harlot" (*Sermons*, 4:393). Of the other eight sermons, only three are on texts that Wesley recorded as having used more than five times for preaching. The published sermons were, nevertheless, written summaries of the ideas that were central to all of his preaching, spelled out carefully for his preachers to read, to understand, and to use as a guide for their own preaching. Wesley no doubt had the function of the Book of Homilies in mind as he designed these volumes—homiletical material that provided a solid doctrinal basis and boundary for homiletical proclamation by uneducated preachers.

SERMONS

O N

Several Occasions:

I N

THREE VOLUMES.

B Y

JOHN WESLEY, M. A.
Fellow of *Lincoln-College*, Oxford.

VOL. I.

LONDON:

Printed by W. STRAHAN: And fold by T. TRYE, near Gray's-Inn Gate, Holbourn; and at the Foundery, near Upper Moorfields. MDCCXLVI.

Title-page of the first volume of Wesley's collected *Sermons* (1746).

In 1748, Wesley published a second volume of *Sermons* that has a distinctly different tone from the first. The Conference that year rescinded the somewhat exclusive emphasis on field preaching and reemphasized the formation of societies, in which the Christian life could be nurtured. It is therefore fitting that the sermons in the second volume focus on regeneration and sanctification, themes befitting the nurturing context of the societies. Wesley was producing these homiletical treatises for the theological guidance of his preachers at the same time that he was endeavoring to sort out his own position on several issues. This dual function becomes evident to the reader in the first item in the volume, John's earliest sermon on Christian perfection, "Circumcision of the Heart" (1733), which here he revised by adding a paragraph that affirms his more recent view of faith and assurance. The bulk of the volume contains the first part of a series of thirteen discourses "Upon our Lord's Sermon on the Mount," one of the traditional texts for an exposition of evangelical ethics.

Wesley concluded this series on the Sermon on the Mount in 1750 in volume three of the *Sermons*, which also has three sermons on the relationship between the "law" and "faith," his well-known sermon on "Christian Perfection," and an interesting trio of sermons that developed in part out of his experiences in Ireland: "The Nature of Enthusiasm," "A Caution against Bigotry," and "Catholic Spirit." In this three-volume set, then, Wesley set forth the basic spiritual themes and doctrinal emphases that were emerging in his own life and thought—a focus on "the way of salvation" (*via salutis*) that mirrors the spiritual pilgrimage: prevenient grace, conviction of sin, repentance, justification, assurance, regeneration, sanctification, Christian perfection, and final salvation. Each step along the way is made possible by the gift of God's **grace** accepted by the believer through faith and evidenced in love of God and neighbor.

In these homiletical treatises, then, Wesley carefully delineated his own developing understanding of essential contemporary emphases for preaching. He felt that these were not novel in any way; they were not only completely scriptural, but also fully in keeping with the doctrinal standards of the Church of England (the Thirty-nine Articles, the Homilies, and the Book of Common Prayer). That Wesley crafted these thirty-six sermons especially for this project is evident by the texts he chose—over half of the sermons are based on specific texts that he never noted as preaching texts in his diaries, journals, or sermon register. In fact, of his favorite thirty-six preaching texts, only one is represented in these three volumes: Mark 1:15 ("The Way to the Kingdom").

The three volumes of sermons were only part of Wesley's educational effort for his preachers and people at this time. In March 1749, John undertook his most grandiose publishing project, *A Christian Library*, which, as the title page noted, contained "extracts from, and abridgments of, the choicest pieces of practical divinity which have been published in the English tongue." The ambitious plan would comprise fifty volumes, including not only some material that he had abridged ("collected") in his earlier days at Oxford, but also a great deal that he had more recently extracted. His interest in this sort of compendium of literature for preachers probably went back to his father's "Advice to a Young Clergyman" and could be seen more recently in his request of Philip Doddridge, D.D., for advice on compiling such a collection (*Letters*, 26:190).

Wesley intended to help the readers sort through the voluminous literature of eminent authors and occasionally to add whatever he thought necessary "to clear their sense or to correct their mistakes." But he especially hoped to separate the grain from the chaff, extrapolate truth from falsehood, avoid controversial and unintelligible styles, and leave out that which was either too superficial or too mystical. He arranged the contents chronologically, starting with the Early Church and continuing to his own day, so that the readers could see the unity of "the genuine religion of Jesus Christ," and so that a successor could pick up the project should Wesley not live to complete it.

Wesley always considered the present as well as the future to be in God's hands. And when he looked back over the development of Methodism, he interpreted specific aspects of its history (and his role in it) in terms of God's providential activity, whether it was his own decision to go to Georgia, the process of opening of the work in Ireland, or the development of a procedure for accepting new helpers in the connection. Charles frequently displays this same approach by comments such as "I quickly saw God's design" (*CWJ*, 2:17).

As the middle of the century approached, John Wesley wrote an account of the history and "economy" of the "people commonly called Methodists" in a letter to his friend Vincent Perronet, vicar of Shoreham. The overarching historical hermeneutic is predictable: "they had no previous design or plan at all, but everything arose just as the occasion offered." But he certainly did not mean that fate or historical accident or simple utilitarianism was at work, to be sure. He makes his position clear at the very beginning: "we knew God could work by whomsoever it pleased him." When this letter was printed in London (and reprinted in three other cities within months) as a thirty-two page pamphlet, *A Plain Account of the People Called Methodists*, it broadcast a lively picture of the development of the Wesleyan connection in England, Wales, and Ireland. It described the field preaching, the message of faith and forgiveness, the rise of the societies, the development of Christian fellowship in bands and classes, the concern to "live the gospel," the need to "fear God and work righteousness." It documented the implementation of watch-nights, love-feasts, and class tickets, the formation of rules for various types of leaders (e.g., Assistants, stewards, visitors, schoolmasters), and the establishment of schools, poorhouses, medical clinics, and the lending society. It presented the story of the people called Methodists fighting evil, pursuing good, and using the means of grace, all in an effort to spread "true Christianity."

The subject of Wesley's portrayal is not simply the emergence of an organization with certain structures, leaders, and rules; it is not merely the implementation of an increasingly complex charitable mission to a needy society; it is not only the outline of an unfolding theology that is squeezed out of Scripture, attested in antiquity, hammered out in debate, and confirmed in human experience. The tapestry is all of a piece, interwoven in such a way as to show the theology, organization, and mission developing out of a common concern to renew and revitalize the Church through a fresh understanding and implementation of God's forgiving and empowering love in the lives of believers.

What is particularly ironic is the fact that almost every method that was employed by the Wesleys in this growing revival movement—a movement intended explicitly to revive the Church from within—could be seen as a step towards increased self-conscious identity among the United Societies as a separate organization with a strong if not intended potential for separation from the Church. By 1750, the Methodists had a specific doctrinal identity expressed in the *Minutes* and the *Sermons*; a national organizational network featuring circuits of societies (using membership tickets) with some centralized

Methodist circuits in 1749–50 in England and Ireland.

financing, led by set-apart preachers who met yearly in Conference; and a characteristic missional program that consisted of benevolent institutions as well as charitable activities. It was not just the opponents of Methodism that perceived their inherent problem of explicit or implicit separation from the Church—Charles Wesley was the first to keep reminding his brother John of this persistent danger.

Discipline in the Connection

By 1750, the Methodist revival under the Wesleys was a recognizable feature on the British landscape. Even Whitefield recognized somewhat begrudgingly that "Methodist" was now a term most often associated with the Wesleys. The movement was now centralized in London, where the societies in that area comprised over two thousand members. Though a sizable group, the Methodists still represented less than one-half of one percent of the population in the growing metropolis. On the national scene, the Methodists were only a tiny group of about 10,000 among a total population of some ten million in Great Britain, and were concentrated only in certain areas (see map). Nearly three dozen preachers in England, Wales, and Ireland were preaching on nine circuits, which served almost one hundred societies. There were no societies along the Channel coast, in East Anglia, the eastern Midlands, Scotland, and most of Wales, Yorkshire, and Ireland. But three strong southern circuits, containing nearly half the Methodists, nearly linked up in an arc extending from the Thames region westward to both sides of the Bristol channel and on to St. Ives. Two circuits in the northern Midlands formed a belt of Methodists from Grimsby through Leeds to Cheshire. And in the north country, the circuit that hung southward from Newcastle now also included a society in Berwick-upon-Tweed. In addition, two circuits were developing in Ireland around Dublin and Cork.

Still facing occasional persecution, Methodism was considered fanatical by many and was not well understood by most people in the country. Nevertheless, while the shape of its theology had been subjected to public and private scrutiny, it had more or less withstood several significant challenges with only minor adjustments. The mission of Methodism had diversified and expanded in keeping with its vision of the Christian life and responsibility; it had taken into account both the spiritual and physical health of God's children. The Wesleyan organization had developed into an intricate network of classes, societies, and circuits, all coordinated by leaders who were given direction by Wesley at the annual Conferences.

In each of these areas—theology, mission, and organization—John Wesley stood ready to defend the nature, design, and activities of the movement, though he was always open to continued refinements in the light of emerging needs. The regulation of the United Societies of the people called Methodists had resulted in an intricate set of standards defined by lists of rules, which furnished uniform procedures for the increasing number of laity who were providing leadership at every level in the movement. As the movement continued to grow, it became more difficult to assume that every leader would comply. From the beginning, Wesley faced the occasional problem of dealing with recalcitrant helpers. Now more than ever the Wesleys faced the challenge of providing leadership that was spiritually alive, doctrinally sound, and missionally active. At the same time, they relied more and more heavily upon lay persons without theological education or training in religious leadership.

Examining the Preachers

In March 1751, Wesley called the first major Conference since implementing the plan for examining preachers eighteen months earlier. John may have been a bit more sensitive than usual to the matter of his preachers' diligence, having felt the heat of his brother's displeasure over John's marriage during the previous month. Leaving his new wife, the former Molly Vazeille, at home in London, John travelled to Bristol for his "conversation" with the preachers. He expressed the concern that the preachers hold "the truth as it is in Jesus," and he expected many objections to their "first doctrines." But all went well on this occasion, and he returned home to his bride for a week before departing to the north country for his annual rounds, noting in his *Journal*, "I cannot understand how a Methodist preacher can answer it to God to preach one sermon or travel one day less in a married than in a single state" (*J&D*, 20:380).

Over the next six months, the Wesleys continued to **examine preachers**, individually and in groups. John apparently entrusted Charles with primary responsibility in this area, and his brother was clearly more severe than John in this regard. John counselled him "not to check the young ones without strong necessity." He was worried about having have a sufficient supply of preachers and made it clear to Charles that "of the two, I prefer grace before gifts." John ordered the expulsion of all disorderly walkers, effeminate men, busybodies, and triflers, but cautioned Charles that they must either have forty preachers or "drop some of our societies." Charles, however, was very anxious over the problem of insufficient gifts, which he had seen in the preachers in Ireland (*Letters*, 26:472–73). And of course, immorality was cause for automatic suspension, as in the case of "that wonderful self-deceiver and hypocrite," James Wheatley. His "obstinate wickedness" in his behavior with seven women, which he defended as "little imprudences," the Wesleys saw as a scandal on the gospel and on Methodism (*J&D*, 20:394).

William Grimshaw

John and Charles met in conference with groups of preachers on three more occasions in 1751, twice in Leeds and once in Newcastle, with the expressed purpose of examining them as to "their grace, gifts, and fruit." On these occasions, two new ones were admitted and two were dismissed on the spot. One particular problem was William Darney, whose round of societies in the Todmorden area had been absorbed into the Methodist connection in 1747 at the recommendation of William Grimshaw, incumbent of Haworth, who by 1750 had become the Wesleys' designated successor as leader of the movement. At Leeds in September, Charles was determined "to bend or break" Darney, who in his "stiff-neckedness" had been examined and continued by his "patient (too patient!) brother" John at the previous Conference. At Leeds, Charles extracted a promise from Darney that he would not preach any doctrines contrary to what the Wesleys believed and preached. After several hours of private and public hearings, Darney was given the opportunity to continue again for half a year if he would also refrain from "railing, from begging, [and] from printing any more of his nonsense" (i.e., some of his doggerel poetry that he claimed was divinely inspired) without the Wesleys' *imprimatur*. Charles agreed to his being a probationer on these conditions but would not allow Darney to sit with them in Conference, so as to emphasize his not being in full connection.

At the end of the year, John and Charles met at Vincent Perronet's house in Shoreham to survey the situation. They agreed to "lay aside" nine preachers, including Darney. They also agreed to allow **local preachers** who exhibited the "grace and gifts"; these should not desist from their trade, however. Charles was beginning to chafe under John's control in the matter of examining the preachers. He therefore pressed that no person was to be received as a **traveling preacher** or taken from his trade by either of the Wesleys alone, but "by both of us conjointly, giving him a note under both our hands." Any difference of opinion they would settle by appeal to Mr. Perronet (*Documents*, 4:109).

In one instance, Charles had discerned Robert Gillespie's "unworthiness to preach the gospel," in spite of his brother John's approval. He therefore had sent Gillespie back to his old business and wrote a note to John Bennet explaining the situation: "A friend of ours (without God's counsel) made a preacher of a tailor; I, with God's help, shall make a tailor of him again." Charles wanted to spread the word that he was both doing the Lord's business and attending to his own "most important concern: to purge the Church, beginning with the laborers" (*CW*, 86).

Charles also had personally set up one of the expelled preachers, Michael Fenwick, in his old business of barbering. His intentions in this regard were not always altruistic, however. To some extent, Charles shared the preachers' complaint that John ruled "with a rod of iron." Therefore his handling of Fenwick had an additional rationale, which he had disclosed in a letter to Lady Huntingdon: if the preachers kept themselves and did not depend upon John "for bread," it would "break his power . . . and reduce his authority within due bounds." Charles added that such financial independence would also serve to "guard against that rashness and credulity of his, which has kept me in continual awe and bondage for many years." Unfortunately, this letter was intercepted and diverted to John Wesley, who replied to Charles with a nasty note in which he in return raised a question about Charles taking additional funds from the quarterly circuit fund for preachers' expenses, when he has already been provided an allowance of fifty pounds plus a healthy annuity of one hundred pounds from the book funds to maintain his wife in the manner to which she had been accustomed. John again suggested Mr. Perronet as a mediator for any difference of judgment on these matters (*Letters*, 26:479–80). John must certainly have had in mind the spirit of the principle laid down in the Minutes for 1744: "Let there be no pretense to say we grow rich by the Gospel," even though that rule had by now been dropped from the Rules of a Helper. The tension between the brothers was increasing daily.

At this time, partially in explanation of the "purge" of the preachers, John wrote down his thoughts on a long-debated problem: what it meant "to preach Christ" (*Letters*, 26:482–89). Failure on this point, he thought, was the problem with about half of the preachers who had been expelled, they having been influenced by James Wheatley, whose "unconnected rhapsody of unmeaning words" became a popular style (especially in Ireland) that threatened to infect the connection. This so-called "gospel-preaching," Wesley held, was only a "new" method of spreading a perverse antinomianism that sapped their preaching of all sound doctrine and spiritual nourishment. The "old" (proper) way of preaching, according to Wesley, was to preach both the law *and* the gospel—"this is the scriptural way, the *Methodist* way, the true way." It was a consistent theme: his earliest field preaching in Bristol, on the Sermon on the

Covenant among thirteen Methodist preachers, signed in January 1752.

Mount, had stressed this theme; his latest published volume of *Sermons* the previous year had reinforced precisely the same point.

The Wesleys, their own feelings about each other notwithstanding, were acutely aware of the dreadful consequences that such "intestine divisions" could have, both from inside and outside the connection. One solid preacher on a circuit, John claimed, could not prevent the damage of three such "gospel preachers," as he had discovered in the Newcastle round, where most of the societies had lost a third of their members during the previous year (*Letters*, 26:488).

In the light of these problems among the preachers, the Wesleys decided in January 1752 to draw up a covenant that would cement the loyalty of the faithful preachers. Eleven preachers, promising thereby not to speak or believe ill of each other, joined with John and Charles in signing the document. As an afterthought, they also agreed to have weekly Monday morning conferences whenever practicable (*Letters*, 26:490). Here again, John and Charles did not see eye to eye.

Charles expressed his main concern in a similar covenant that he drew up in March of that year, signed by the Wesley brothers and four others who thereby promised not only "to abide in the closest union with each other," but also (except by common consent) "never to leave the communion of the Church of England" (*Letters*, 26:491). Charles was becoming acutely aware of the increasing threat posed by many of John's decisions in terms of potential separation from the Church.

Problems of doctrine and discipline were not unique to English Methodists. In mid-August of 1752, John met at Limerick, Ireland, with nine of the preachers for two days. The Minutes of this first **Irish Conference** display a pattern of concerns typical of Methodist organization: six circuits were established, quarterly conferences were fixed, preachers were stationed, and new preachers were received. But the records of the meeting also indicate a resolve to take steps in the connection to tighten up both the doctrine and discipline, which had exhibited some decay in recent months (Crookshank, 1:91–93; *Documents*, 4:113–14).

Back home in England in early 1753, Wesley decided to regularize another important feature of the Methodist scheme. By now, the Wesleys had published over a hundred separate works, including the monumental *Christian Library* in fifty volumes, their fifteen volumes of collected *Tracts*, and such separate works as *The Complete English Dictionary*, which John claimed was not only "the shortest and cheapest" dictionary, but also "the most correct which is extant at this day" (*JWW*, 14:234). In April, therefore, John announced his decision to appoint Thomas Butts and William Briggs, two honest and capable businessmen, as special stewards in the London society—**book stewards** in charge of the printing, distribution, and sale of the many Methodist publications. The circular letter (signed by Butts and Briggs) that announced this method also declared that the stewards in the provincial societies were to keep careful accounts, to be punctual in making payments each quarter, to disperse none of the book monies themselves, to give none of the money to any of the preachers directly, and to order books only from the book stewards in London. In an increasingly complex organizational network, with myriad potential difficulties, yet another feature had come under centralized control under the watchful eye of Wesley.

The annual Conference of preachers at Leeds in May 1753 presented an opportunity to settle several other matters. Doctrinal problems were the first order of the day, especially the continuing tensions with the "corruptions of the Germans" (i.e., Moravians) and the "taint" of both predestination and antinomianism (i.e., Whitefieldites). On the one hand, Wesley informed the Conference that a union with Benjamin Ingham, whose societies were closely allied with the Moravians, might be effected "when he returns to the old Methodist doctrine." On the other hand, John had just published *Serious Thoughts upon the Perseverance of the Saints* and *Predestination Calmly Considered* in the previous six months to counteract those two ideas. He and Charles had, for a time, granted the possibility of an unconditional election of *some* people, along with a conditional election of *all*, but by this time had dropped the scheme since it seemed to support the idea of perseverance, which leads to antinomianism (*Letters*, 26:499). John had come to recognize even more clearly that backsliding was a persistent reality and that assurance was never final. And as for the challenge represented by the dilute manner in which the gospel-preachers "preached Christ," Wesley again reinforced what he called practical religion and practical preaching: the Methodists were instructed to preach Christ "in all his offices and to declare his law as well as gospel both to believers and unbelievers" (*Minutes*, 718).

As for discipline, the life and doctrine of the traveling preachers was also examined, their names being called before the Conference one by one. About thirty preachers served England and another nine or ten were in Ireland. In spite of the purge of the preachers, John had managed to keep nearly the forty he had said he needed to keep the connection intact.

Leadership and Unity

Before the end of the year, however, another threat to the well-being of the Methodist connection made its first appearance. John Wesley's health deteriorated badly in November 1753, prompting him to retire to the country for several weeks to treat his "consumption." During this time, he composed his own epitaph: "Here lieth the body of John Wesley, a brand, not once only, plucked out of the fire; he died of a consumption in the fifty-first year of his age, leaving (after his debts were paid) not ten pounds behind him, praying—God be merciful to me an unprofitable servant" (*CWJ*, 2:26). Not only is this text (in Charles's record of it) notable for its recognition of the multiple applicability of the "brand" metaphor, by that time frequently applied to new converts, but also for its reiteration of John's claim, nearly a decade earlier in *An Earnest Appeal*, that if he died with more than ten pounds in his pocket, he should be considered a thief and a robber (*Appeals*, 83–88; above, p. 130). After the New Year, he went to the Hot

Well near Bristol to drink the mineral waters as part of his convalescence.

Unable to travel or preach, but well enough to read and write, John began a project he had long envisioned—a commentary on the Bible. In the preface to *Explanatory Notes Upon the New Testament*, penned on January 4, 1754, just as John was starting this major task, he points out that the work is not designed for the learned but written chiefly for the "plain, unlettered" people who understood only English. The biblical text (placed at the top of each page) was basically the Authorized ("King James") Version, somewhat altered by the Wesleys so as to bring it "nearer to the original." Charles helped John in this task at the end of February. The notes were to be brief; the intent was to avoid critical inquiries, learned languages, and polemical arguments. In fact, the notes were largely a collation of material from John Heylyn's *Theological Lectures*, John Guyse's *Practical Expositor*, Philip Doddridge's *Family Expositor*, and Johannes Bengel's *Gnomen Novi Testamenti*. The latter was one of the first works of modern critical biblical scholarship, and Wesley adopted many of Bengel's principles of textual criticism. Although the predominance of material in the notes comes from these sources, Wesley wove them together in such an editorial way that he could own the combined whole. Having acknowledged his debt to these authors in the preface, Wesley chose not to document particular borrowings, so as not to "divert the mind of the reader from keeping close to the point in view" (*JWW*, 14:235–39).

John's serious illness transformed the question of the succession of leadership within Methodism from a theoretical to a practical one. The obvious candidate to succeed John was Charles, who quickly squelched the suggestion. He announced to the London society in December that "I neither could nor would stand in my brother's place (if God took him to himself) for I had neither a body nor a mind, nor talents, nor grace for it." The next likely candidate would have been William Grimshaw, rector of Haworth, who was named in some of the early deeds to Methodist property as being third in line after the Wesleys. John, however, regained his health by early spring, and the question of succession once again receded to become only a small cloud on the horizon.

The matter of unity within the connection, however, persisted as a major concern. The covenantal agreement of 1752, in which the signees attested mutual confidence and pledged loyalty to the Church and each other, was reaffirmed annually. Such an agreement was again signed by the Wesleys and two dozen others early in May 1754, and

Ch. xxiii. 38—49. ST. LUKE. *Jis.* 2/

38 save thyself. * And a superscription also was written over him in Greek, and Latin, and Hebrew letters, THIS IS THE KING OF THE JEWS.

39 And one of the malefactors, who were hanging on the cross, reviled
40 him, saying, If thou be the Christ, save thyself and us. But the other answering, rebuked him, saying, Dost not thou fear God, seeing thou
41 art in the same condemnation? And we indeed justly; for we receive the due reward of our deeds: but this person hath done nothing amiss.
42 And he said to Jesus, Lord, remember me, when thou comest in thy
43 kingdom. And Jesus said to him, Verily I say unto thee, To-day shalt thou be with me in paradise.
44 And it was about the sixth hour; and there was darkness over all the
45 earth till the ninth hour. And the sun was darkened, and the veil of
46 the temple was rent in the midst. And Jesus crying with a loud voice, said, Father, into thy hands I commend my spirit. And having said thus,
47 he expired. And the centurion seeing what was done, glorified
48 God, saying, Certainly this was a righteous man. And all the people who had come together to that sight, beholding the things which were
49 done, returned, smiting their breasts. And all his acquaintance and the women who had followed him from Galilee, stood afar off, beholding these things.

V. 39. *And one of the malefactors reviled him:* St. Matthew says, *The thieves;* St. Mark, *They that were crucified with him, reviled him.* Either therefore St. Matthew and Mark put the Plural for the Singular (as the best Authors sometimes do:) or both reviled him at first, till one of them suddenly felt "the overwhelming Power of saving Grace."

V. 40. *The other rebuked him*—What a surprising degree was here, of Repentance, Faith, and other Graces! And what abundance of Good Works, in his public Confession of his Sin, Reproof of his Fellow-criminal, his honourable Testimony to *Christ,* and Profession of Faith in Him, while he was in so disgraceful Circumstances, as were stumbling even to his disciples. This shews the Power of Divine Grace. But it incourages none to put off their Repentance to the last Hour; since as far as appears, this was the first time this Criminal had an Opportunity of knowing any thing of *Christ.* And his Conversion was designed, to put a peculiar Glory on our Saviour in his lowest State, while his Enemies derided him, and his own disciples either denied, or forsook him.

* Matt. xxvi. 37. Mark xv. 36. John xix. 19.

V. 42. *Remember me, when thou comest*—From heaven, in thy kingdom. He acknowledges him a king, and such a king, as after he is dead, can profit the dead. Not the Apostles themselves had then so clear Conceptions of the Kingdom of *Christ.*

V. 43. *In paradise*—The Place where the Souls of the Righteous remain, from Death till the Resurrection. (a.)

V. 44. *There was darkness over all the earth.* The noon-tide Darkness, covering the Sun, obscured all the upper Hemisphere. And the lower was equally darkened, the Moon being in Opposition to the Sun, and receiving no Light from him.

V. 46. *Father, into thy hands*—The Father receives the Spirit of *Jesus;* *Jesus* himself the Spirits of the Faithful.

V. 47. *Certainly this was a righteous man:* Which implies an Approbation of all he had done and taught.

V. 48. *All the people*—who had not been Actors therein, *returned, smiting their breasts*—in testimony of sorrow.

V. 1. Cr-

(a) As if he had said, I will not only remember thee then, but this very day.

Proof page of Wesley's *Explanatory Notes Upon the New Testament*, with his revised scripture text at the top, commentary below, showing his corrections and additions.

their intention not to act independently of each other was reaffirmed at the Conference later that month. The amalgamated nature of the Methodist movement made this agreement increasingly important in order to foster unity and discipline. In keeping with this spirit, the Conference made final the severing of relationship with William Darney and his societies. Darney had promised not to preach any doctrines contrary to what the Methodists believed and preached, but in fact he had persisted in his Calvinistic emphasis on final perseverance—that a believer cannot make a shipwreck of his faith and cannot fall. He was therefore declared out of the connection. Another preacher, John Green, severed relations with the Wesleys under pressure; he literally walked out after being rebuked for preaching against John Wesley (*JWJ*, 20:486).

Of the two dozen or so preachers who attended the 1754 Conference, some fourteen were given preaching assignments around London during late April and into the early summer. Wesley himself drew up a plan (the first **circuit plan**) that charted the who, where, and when of their daily preaching among the seven locations on the circuit—columns for the Foundery, Spitalfields, Snowsfield, Wapping, Wells, West Street Chapel, and Westminster, and lines listing morning and evening assignments (by initials) for every day of the week. The chart eventually extended over eighteen pages in one of Wesley's notebooks. By this means, the regular circulation of traveling preachers among the local preachers in the societies was established in an orderly fashion from mid-May to mid-August. Among the forty-five preachers noted at some point on that particular plan, only four or five of them remained on the London circuit with the Wesleys beyond the time of Conference.

In spite of the tight discipline, both among leaders and members, the societies continued to spread and grow, howbeit at a measured pace. As Methodism moved into East Anglia, Charles Wesley exhibited the same caution towards such growth that he had shown earlier in Ireland. After preaching near Norwich in July, Charles noted several people following him to his host's home; they desired admission into

Wesley's first manuscript circuit plan, listing the assignments for April 15–21, 1754. Two of these preachers left the connection prior to the Conference in May.

a Society there. Charles's reaction was circumspect: "I told them (as others before) to come among us first for some time and see how they like it. . . . I am in no haste for a society. First let us see how the candidates live" (*CWJ* [MS], 7/27/54).

One casualty of success, in a sense, was the Methodist medical clinic in London. Wesley had started providing free medical services at the end of 1746. The clinic at the New Room, Bristol, had been short-lived. But from the beginning, the clinic at the Foundery in London served an average of over two dozen patients a week and continued to grow for several years. But by the time he published the seventh extract of his *Journal* in 1754, the expanded services had increased the expenses to the point where the society, which included most of the poor it was serving, could no longer bear the financial burden (*J&D*, 151). The Poorhouse project had also suffered the same fate (*Societies*, 277n).

Pressure for Separation

As the expanding revival continued to consolidate and the preaching-houses became the locus of the Methodists' religious self-identity, there was increasing pressure from the preachers and people to receive the Sacrament from Methodist hands. Thomas Walsh, a convert from Irish Catholicism, had put the case before Wesley: the people must have the ordinances of Christ, but they will not go to the Church because of the ungodly priests; they would, however, "joyfully communicate with those by whom they have been brought to God" (*Church*, 132). This fact was evident at such occasions as when Whitefield assisted Grimshaw administer Communion at Haworth in 1753—the crowd filled the church four times over and "sipped away thirty-five bottles of wine within a gill" (*Grimshaw*, 183).

Some Methodists had difficulty finding opportunities to receive Communion. The vicar of Devlin had described the Methodists' complaint to his bishop in 1751, saying that on the previous Christmas, fifty faces that he had scarce seen before appeared at the Sacrament. One of these told him "it was a great trouble to the Society that they had not more frequent opportunities of receiving the Communion. . . . Some had come that morning . . . very near ten miles on foot, though the weather was very severe." The vicar added that in the several parishes in his vicinity, fully ninety percent of those who attended the Sacrament were Methodists (*People*, 5).

Wesley was clear, however, that unordained Methodist preachers should not administer the Sacrament. An alternative, of course, would have been to ordain the preachers. Wesley had been convinced in 1745 by Lord Peter King's *Enquiry into the Constitution, Discipline, Unity, and Worship of the Primitive Church* that bishops and presbyters were, from the beginning, of the same order and that therefore the episcopacy was only a functional distinction. Although he held fast to the idea that deacons could preach but not administer the Sacrament, he was coming to the conclusion that presbyters had a sacerdotal office that could, in cases of necessity, include the function of ordaining others. He was not yet ready, however, to take that step.

Even the matter of lay preaching was a point of continuing tension, not only between the brothers Wesley but also within the Church of England itself. The Act of Toleration required preachers to be licensed; most of the Methodists were not. John would not have them be dissenters. The issue of dissent and/or separation, however, was given added urgency in June 1754, when Thomas Sherlock, Bishop of London, excommunicated a Mr. Gardiner for preaching without a license. John's reaction was succinct: "It is probable the point will now speedily be determined concerning the Church. For if we must either *dissent* or be *silent, Actum est*" ("It is all over"; *Letters*, 26:563).

In the fall of 1754, when Charles complained to John that two of their preachers, Charles Perronet and Thomas Walsh, had administered the Lord's Supper, John's response was, "We have in effect ordained already," that is, by setting them apart to preach. Apparently, as the preachers knelt during their commissioning, John sometimes handed them a New Testament and charged them, "Take thou authority to preach the gospel" (*EMP*, 2:7). Charles was furious over this blatant simulation of and disregard for the order of the Church, especially John's inclination both "to lay on hands and to let the preachers administer" (*Church*, 162–63). Although this was a wavering inclination on John's part at that time, Charles perceived the direct threat to the Methodists' good relations with the Church and began mustering the opposition.

Charles tried to induce his clergy friends (such as William Grimshaw, Walter Sellon, and Samuel Walker) to write and persuade John not to ordain or separate. Several of the more ambitious Methodist preachers, the would-be priests whom Charles called "Melchisedeckians" (see Heb. 7:15), were pushing John in that direction. Charles was convinced that "ordination is separation," and in this he was supported by Lord Chief Justice Mansfield, an old schoolmate from Charles's Westminster days. Grimshaw also let it be known that if John moved further toward making priests of the preachers, he would retreat from Methodism back into the Church.

Charles, the examiner of preachers, wanted to enforce the last clause of the preachers' covenant: to exclude those who were "irreclaimable" in their desire to separate, and never to accept another who was inclined in that direction. But at this time, Charles had been excluded from his brother's inner circle, the "cabinet council." Nevertheless, his friends' letters seemed to work. By December, John was reasserting his intention never to leave the Church, although Charles feared the decision was based more on the expediency than either conviction or the legality of the situation.

At the Leeds Conference of May 1755, John Wesley presented a treatise to the gathered preachers on "Ought We to Separate from the Church of England?" One by one, the arguments for separation were laid aside: they would not renounce the Church's doctrine, nor refrain from its public service, much less fail to submit to the governors and laws of the Church—to do so would neither be legal nor expedient. John specifically countered the argument that such Methodists "set apart" to preach had thereby been given authority to administer the sacrament: a person was "permitted" to preach in the connection without ordination once the Wesleys were convinced that God had appointed him as "an extraordinary preacher of repentance." Using biblical precedents, Wesley pointed out that "extraordinary prophets" existed in the Jewish church, but not "extraordinary priests." In early Christianity, evangelists, deacons, and even women preached "when under extraordinary inspiration," but none of them administered the Lord's Supper, even in those circumstances. Otherwise, the different orders of Christian ministers would be reduced to one, which John saw as "contrary both to the New Testament and to all antiquity" (*Societies*, 569–73). This traditional stance by Wesley does represent a slight difference from seven years earlier, when he argued against the Quaker practice of allowing women to preach by saying that biblical references to women "prophesying" should not be taken as "preaching" (*JWL*, 2:119–20).

Charles, always concerned about the preachers' "gifts," was upset by the proceedings at Conference, afraid that they were about to give up everything. He left early and vowed, "I have done with Conferences for ever." John, typically concerned about the preachers' "grace," gave them another lecture (perhaps playing off his brother's hymn, "And Are we Yet Alive?") before they departed from Leeds:

> It has been affirmed that none of our Itinerant Preachers are so much alive as they were seven years ago. I fear many are not. But if so, they are unfit for the work, which requires much life: otherwise your labour will be tiresome to yourself, and of little use to others.

Tiresome because you will no longer serve Christ and the people willingly and cheerfully. Of little use because you will no longer serve them diligently, doing it with your might.

He then asked them specific questions: Which of you is exemplarily alive to God, so as to carry fire with him wherever he goes? Which of you is a pattern of self-denial, even in little things? Which of you drinks water? Why not? Who rises at four? Why not? Who fasts on Friday? Why not? And so on, for twenty-two more questions. The message was clear: a tightening of discipline was in effect across the board. Fifteen persons were noted in the *Minutes* as the main "local preachers," and twelve other preachers were listed as "**half-itinerant**," meaning that they were in one way or another only half-time (a status first listed in 1753). William Shent, for instance, who was also a barber in Leeds, travelled only half the year; Matthew Lowes augmented his preacher's stipend by selling veterinary medicine.

Full-time itinerancy was still the expectation for the Methodist preacher, however. There had long been a great need for persons "to comfort, exhort, and instruct those who were athirst for God," but the need was so great and the number of qualified persons so small that most of the preachers "were obliged to travel continually from place to place" around the circuits. There was also another reason for the preachers changing circuits nearly every year, as John explained:

> I know, were I myself to preach one whole year in one place, I should preach both myself and most of my congregation asleep. . . . Frequent change of preachers is best. This preacher has one talent, that another. No one whom I ever yet knew has all the talents which are needful for beginning, continuing, and perfecting the work of grace in an whole congregation (*JWL*, 3:195).

John Wesley had earlier reaffirmed his opinion, in a letter to Samuel Walker, that separation on their part must entail a conscious renunciation of the Church's doctrines or a refusal to join in its services. There were, however, four points of the Methodist program that he would sooner separate from the Church than give up: lay preaching, field preaching, extempore preaching, and forming societies (*Letters*, 26:595). None of these, we might note, was either illegal or a likely cause for excommunication, from the Church's point of view.

In the meantime, nevertheless, Charles was anticipating the worst. He still preached frequently from the text, "I will bring the third part through the fire," but his earlier imagery that "many waters could not quench" the spark that became the revival now took a new twist. He wrote his brother John: "The short remains of my life are devoted to this very thing, to follow our sons (as C[harles] P[erronet] told me we should you) with buckets of water, to quench the flame of strife and division, which they have or may kindle" (*CWJ*, 2:131). Charles was particularly disturbed at the preachers who railed and laughed at the Church, and he suggested to John that they should use "much greater deliberation and care in admitting preachers"; they should make sure that the preachers were grounded in the doctrine and discipline of the Methodists and in the communion of the Church. Writing from the "shattered society" in Manchester, Charles warned Grimshaw, "Nothing but grace can keep our children, after our departure, from running into a thousand sects, a thousand errors." To the Methodists at Leeds he wrote: "Continue in the old ship. Jesus hath a favour for our Church, and is wonderfully visiting and reviving his work in her" (*CWJ*, 2:135–36). To the society at Rotherham, which was on the brink of separation, Charles had proclaimed "that 'there was no salvation out of the church'." He then noticed that they not only "suffered" the exhortation, but were even glad when he said to them, "Let us go into the house of the Lord" (*CWJ*, 2:116).

As part of his campaign to influence his brother, Charles published a poem, *An Epistle to the Reverend Mr. John Wesley*, which includes the stanza:

> When first sent forth to minister the word,
> Say, did we preach ourselves, or Christ the Lord?
> Was it our aim disciples to collect,
> To raise a party, or to found a sect?

Charles's pressure on John began to show. At the end of the 1756 Conference, Charles was able to say, "My brother and I ended the Conference with a strong declaration of our resolution to live and die in the communion of the Church of England. We all unanimously agreed that whilst it is lawful or possible to continue in it, it is unlawful for us to leave it." The unanimity of the preachers in this regard was confirmed by their signing yet another covenant of unity on August 30, 1756, based on the 1752 model.

In order to help alleviate the predicament concerning ordination and the sacraments, Charles tried to recruit "sound" preachers who might qualify for ordination in the Church. He had long complained about the great evil done by "unsound" preachers among the Methodists, such as John Tooker, who did more harm than good "by talking in his witty way against the Church and clergy." Roger Ball, an infamous self-proclaimed antinomian, continued to raise his voice among the Methodist societies, "picking up their pences and persons"

Charles Wesley

while spreading his gospel of free grace and free love. And there was
still some sheep-stealing going on, some by former Methodist preachers, such as John Edwards in Leeds, who turned independent, "robbing" the Methodists of their "children," and some by Baptists, who
were always watching to steal away some Methodists "and make them
as dead as themselves." Charles noted that the Manchester society had
been hard hit: their "itching ears" had reduced their number by half.
Some Baptist meetings in the area were wholly made up of former
Methodists (*CWJ*, 2:128–30).

The amalgamated nature of the Methodist revival and the eagerness of preachers such as Whitefield, Edwards, and others, to preach among the Wesleyan societies caused innumerable problems for the Wesley brothers. These interlopers also did much good. Whitefield, for instance, was a powerful preacher. On one occasion, after remarking that "brother George . . . spoke with a voice that raised the dead," Charles noted approvingly that Whitefield did "great good" in the societies, even preaching the necessity of holiness after justification (*CWJ*, 2:133). However, Charles felt that no one would be drawn away if able discreet preachers were stationed in the right places, and that, in fact, many of the departed would be happy to return.

The growing network of societies and leaders that made up the Methodist connection had become more organized and more disciplined during the 1740s and 1750s. Wesley was trying to be open to the providential work of the Holy Spirit in the revival, but his adherence to a model of "scriptural Christianity" and his traditional ties to the Church of England resulted in the fixing of certain guidelines and boundaries within which he felt that the diversity of the movement could and should develop. The various sets of rules (of the Society, of the Bands, of the various leaders, of Kingswood School, etc.) were often reviewed at the annual Conferences and, as in 1756, usually reaffirmed with little change. The growing interdependence of the various societies had been bolstered by the creation of a connectional fund in 1749. Now a connectional drive was also begun to support Kingswood School, either by subscription or annual collections in every society (*J&D*, 21:77). Kingswood was designed first and foremost to educate preacher's sons, and the opportunity to provide needed leadership for the future of the movement was not lost on the Wesleys.

Wesley's training program also included a continuing education program for his leaders through a steady stream of publications. The *Christian Library* was completed in 1755, a project that cost him hundreds of pounds of his own money that was never fully recovered. The 759-page *Explanatory Notes* had finally appeared at the end of the same year, with one complaint from a friend that John had been a bit too sparse in his comments. The book list appended to the Wesleyan publications in 1757 included one hundred fifty-three items. Sensitive to the charge that he was "growing rich by the Gospel," John included a note in his *Journal* for September 1756 pointing out that during the previous eighteen years, he "had gained by printing and preaching together, a debt of twelve hundred and thirty-six pounds" (*J&D*, 21:77).

Despite the cost, Wesley felt compelled to provide his people with these resources, even though the material may at times have over-reached their capabilities. In some cases, he adapted the marrow of certain works into other forms. In August 1755, he recast portions of Richard Alleine's *Vindiciae Pietatis* (included in the *Christian Library*) into a **covenant renewal service** for his people at Spitalfields, expand-ing upon a practice he had encouraged eight years earlier. When Wesley recited the covenant, featuring the words, "I will be no longer mine own, but give up myself to thy will in all things," eighteen hundred Methodists stood up "in testimony of assent." Wesley was sure that he had come upon another useful instrument of God's grace: "Such a night I scarce ever saw before. Surely the fruit of it shall remain for ever" (*J&D*, 21:23).

Chapter 4—Suggested Additional Reading

Beynon, Tom, *Howell Harris, Reformer and Soldier* (Caenarvon: Calvinistic Methodist Bookroom, 1958).

CW — Baker, Frank, *Charles Wesley as Revealed by his Letters* (London: Epworth Press, 1948).

Church — Baker, Frank, *John Wesley and the Church of England* (Nashville: Abingdon, 1970).

Crookshank, C. H., *History of Methodism in Ireland*, 3 vols. (Belfast: Allen, 1885).

Documents — Vickers, John A., "Documents and Source Material," Part 1 of Vol. 4, *A History of the Methodist Church in Great Britain*, ed. Rupert Davies, A. Raymond George, and Gordon Rupp, 4 vols. (London: Epworth Press, 1988).

EMP — Jackson, Thomas, ed., *Lives of Early Methodist Preachers*, 6 vols. (London: Wesleyan Conference Office, 1872).

Grimshaw — Baker, Frank, *William Grimshaw, 1708–1763* (London: Ep-worth Press, 1963).

JWL — Telford, John, *The Letters of John Wesley*, 8 vols. (London: Epworth Press, 1931).

JWW — Wesley, John, *The Works of John Wesley*, ed. Thomas Jackson, 14 vols. (Grand Rapids: Zondervan, 1959–62).

Minutes — *Minutes of the Methodist Conferences, from the first, held in London*, vol. 1 (London: Mason, 1862).

Perkins, E. Benson, *Methodist Preaching Houses and the Law; The Story of the Model Deed* (London: Epworth Press, 1952).

CHAPTER 5

The Maturing of Methodism (1758–1775)

Several times during the decade of the 1750s, the Methodist revival appeared to be on the verge of disintegration. Disputes over lay preaching and the sacraments, a notable defection of preachers, and a loss of members to proselytizers led to a purge of the preachers and an extraction of repeated pledges of unity and loyalty from those who remained. A period of turmoil within Methodism generally, it was heightened by increased tensions between the Wesley brothers themselves. Most of the points of contention seemed to pertain to the matter of separation from the Church of England. Charles, the "Church Methodist," continued to press for stronger ties to the Church of England and its clergy. He was clear in his priorities: God, Church, and Methodism. John was not so clear. Having retreated from the ideas of ordaining his preachers and allowing them to administer the sacraments, however, John was now hard pressed to maintain unity within Methodism as well as with the Church.

Standards of Doctrine and Discipline

At the 1758 Conference in Ireland, held in the summer at Limerick, charges of doctrinal unorthodoxy were levied against one of the preachers, Mark Davis, who had recently become Methodist. Thomas Walsh, a convert from Catholicism, defended his comrade by saying that "these objections to his phraseology will soon be done away when he becomes more acquainted with the writings of the Methodists." And indeed, the Wesleys had produced a host of publications for just that purpose.

That spring (1758), John had published *A Preservative Against Unsettled Notions in Religion*, a collection of treatises that spoke to many of the diverse sources of friction within the movement. The book included materials that dealt with the Deists, Roman Catholics, Quakers, Predestinarians, and Moravians. Some items were aimed at individuals: William Law (on mysticism), Micaiah Towgood (on dissent), and James Hervey (on antinomianism); others addressed topics such as baptism, the Godhead of Jesus Christ, and godfathers and godmothers. Most of these treatises had been published previously. The collection featured Wesley's "Reasons against a Separation from the Church of England," which consisted of the last half of his Conference paper on "Ought We to Separate" that enumerated twelve reasons why it was not expedient for Methodists to leave the Church.

Not surprisingly, then, Wesley's expressed views on **baptism** are essentially in agreement with those of the Church. John's "Treatise on Baptism" was actually an abridgement of a work his father Samuel had written as an appendix to *The Pious Communicant* (1700). John was not hesitant to repeat his father's orthodox Anglican views on baptism; he even quotes the ordinal, that the person to be baptized may be "washed and sanctified by the Holy Ghost, and, being delivered from God's wrath, receive remission of sins and enjoy the everlasting benediction of his heavenly washing." He points out that by baptism, persons are not only incorporated into the Body of Christ and made members of the Church, but also are infused by a principle of grace by which children of wrath become children of God by adoption. He not only reiterates the traditional arguments for infant baptism, but also answers many of the typical criticisms. Even the traditional evangelical argument against baptismal regeneration, that repentance and faith are necessary before justification and new birth, he answers by drawing a parallel between baptism and circumcision (which had similar prerequisites), thereby showing that God commanded that it be done to infants on the eighth day (*JWW*, 10:188–201). Most people in England had been baptized as infants, of course, but there were

Page proof of Wesley's treatise on *Original Sin* (1757), showing manuscript corrections for the printer.

also occasions for adult baptism, such as in December 1758 when Wesley baptized two African servants of Nathaniel Gilbert, a recent convert from Antigua who soon returned to pioneer Methodist work in the West Indies (*J&D*, 21:172). Nevertheless, this treatise on baptism, in conjunction with others in this same collection, gives clear evidence of Wesley's longtime claim that he is a faithful son of the Church.

Diversity and Debate

Such claims by Wesley, of course, did not always satisfy those with whom he differed, inside and outside of the revival. He continued to address a number of such controversies through private correspondence. For instance, the flurry of opposition caused by his earlier views on assurance, about which he had carried on a long correspondence with "John Smith" the previous decade, was easily stirred up by others. Both Richard Tompson and Samuel Walker found occasion to challenge him on this issue during the 1750s.

Given Wesley's volume of publication over a period of three decades, along with some modification of his views in the meantime, critics could easily quote Wesley against himself. Tompson, for instance, points to Wesley's claims, on the one hand, that a person may be a believer without having received assurance, but on the other hand, that a person cannot be justified without knowing that he is so (i.e., without assurance; *Sermons,* 1:154). Wesley had already worked through many of these issues, especially the matter of assurance, and was able to answer Tompson very succinctly: "I know that I am accepted; and yet that knowledge is sometimes shaken, though not destroyed, by doubt or fear.... I agree with you that justifying faith cannot be a conviction that I am justified" (*Letters,* 26:575).

To Samuel Walker, Wesley showed his tendency to divert attention from the controversial to the essential: "*Assurance* is a word I *do not use* because it is *not scriptural.* But I hold a divine evidence or conviction that Christ loved *me* and gave Himself for *me* is essential to if not the very essence of justifying faith" (*JWL*, 3:222). But even a constant flow of such tenuous diversions could not have helped Wesley avoid all the controversies that continued to erupt.

The fluctuating internal boundaries between divisions of the revival had caused some of the problems the Wesleys faced, with dissenters of various sorts (Quakers, Baptists, Catholics, and the unchurched) wandering among and in and out of the societies. Benjamin Ingham had tried again to join with the Methodists in 1755.

But the Wesleys had again refused to take their old friend into the Methodist connection because of his separatist tendencies. A year later, the Inghamite connection consisted of a thousand persons in a four-hundred-mile circuit that was served by Ingham and six preachers, two of whom he had just ordained (*CWJ*, 2:122; *Church*, 250). In 1756, Charles also refused to hear the petitions of John Edwards of Leeds, a preacher who had defected the previous year but had many times expressed his readiness to preach in the Wesleyan societies. However, the Wesleys remained on friendly terms with Whitefield, Harris, and others, following the rule, "If it be possible, as much as lieth in you, live peaceably with all men" (Rom. 12:18; see *CWJ*, 2:121).

In some cases, the Wesleys' working relationship with others was rather close. James Wheatley, an expelled preacher turned repentant and befriended by Whitefield and William Cudworth, had built in Norwich a strong following and a sizable building, the Tabernacle, to which he invited a hesitant Wesley. John eventually accepted the invitation. Subsequently, when Wesley divided the Norwich society into classes in the spring of 1759, he noted that no distinction was made between those who had belonged to the Foundery or to the Tabernacle societies (Wesleyan and Whitefieldite respectively). At the same time, however, if people joined the Methodist society—about twenty percent of the 570 Norwich members had never belonged to any society—they were expected to follow its rules and standards and be subject to its discipline. Wesley once again made them show their class tickets, required the men and women to sit apart, and allowed no spectators at the Lord's Supper. When he visited Norwich five months later and found disorder and chaos, he told them, as he said, "in plain terms that they were the most ignorant, self-conceited, self-willed, fickle, intractable, disorderly, disjointed society that I knew in the three kingdoms." His *Journal* records that "many were profited" by such chastisement, and not one was offended. In fact, many stubborn hearts were melted down (*J&D*, 21:181, 227).

Opposition continued in many forms, including the familiar mobs of hecklers and stone-throwers. Occasionally, the church people would amplify their displeasure by other means. For example, the church wardens in Pocklington hired men to ring the church bells while Wesley was preaching in the nearby street. Publications attacking the Methodists still poured forth, such as *Methodism Examined and Exposed; or, The Clergy's Duty of Guarding their Flocks against False Teachers*, by John Downes, a rector in London. Referring to the Methodists as "grievous wolves," and the Wesleys as "beardless divines" who speak perverse things among the faithful flock, Downes presents a particu-

larly virulent attack that Wesley answered in kind, point by point
(*Societies*, 351–66). In a long *apologia* to the Earl of Dartmouth, Wesley
pointed out that the Methodists were not subversive and did not
renounce the established constitution: "Not so; their fundamental
principles are the very principles of the Established Church." Wesley
did admit, however, that their practice was basically that of the Church
"save in a few points wherein they are constrained to deviate." Any
deviation, of course, was no more than a "hair's breadth." Once again,
Wesley uses the fire and water imagery, with a new twist: "A fire is
kindled in the church, the house of the living God, the fire of love of
the world, ambition, covetousness, envy, anger, malice, bitter zeal—in
one word, of ungodliness and unrighteousness! O who will come and
help to quench it?" (*JWL*, 4:149–51).

Attempts at Unity with the Clergy

To Methodist friends, Wesley was quick to point out the "unspeak-
able advantages" that they enjoyed in their own services as compared
with those of the Church: the Methodists' services were not "inter-
rupted either by the formal drawl of a parish clerk, the screaming of
boys who bawl out what they neither feel nor understand, or the
unseasonable and unmeaning impertinence of a voluntary on the
organ" (*JWL*, 3:227). The Wesleys, however, in trying to maintain
good relations with the Church, were still hoping that the evangelical
clergy would form an alliance with them. John had published an
Address to the Clergy in 1756 in which he outlined the specific "gifts and
grace" that he perceived necessary to effective ministry. He had
spelled out the curriculum of a well-furnished mind in a fashion not
unlike his father's *Advice to a Young Clergyman*, which John had published posthumously for his father in 1735. Nevertheless, John also
made it clear that the higher consideration was the grace of God, in
comparison with which "all intellectual endowments vanish into nothing" (*JWW*, 10:493). As he told Samuel Furley, insofar as the qualifications of a gospel minister were concerned, "grace is necessary,
learning is expedient" (*JWL*, 3:175).

At this point, the Wesleys were in contact with several evangelicals,
some of whom were associated with the Methodists during this period:
Vincent Perronet (Shoreham), James Hervey (Northampton), Samuel
Walker (Truro), John Baddiley (Hayfield), John Berridge (Everton),
and William Grimshaw (Haworth). In a letter to Walker, Wesley
indicated that he had asked at the 1757 Conference, "What can be
done in order to a closer union with the clergy who preach the truth?"

William Hogarth's "The Sleeping Congregation" (1762 edition), satirizing the Church of England.

Walker himself had long since begun a "Parsons' Club" for sympathetic clergy in Cornwall. John Fletcher, Wesley's Assistant who was soon to become vicar of Madeley, would also design for Worcestershire a "Society of Ministers of the Gospel in the Church of England" (*Church*, 183). Wesley, however, was thinking more in terms of a national union of evangelical clergy.

John Wesley wanted the clergy to preach "the three grand scriptural doctrines—original sin, justification by faith, and holiness consequent thereon" (*JWL*, 4:146). These emphases incidentally coincided with his earlier capsulation of the three main Methodist doctrines (see above, p. 156). At the end of the decade, the Wesleys were in contact with an increasing number of clergy, some of whom they met at the London home of Selina, Countess of Huntingdon. The Countess had also been "seized by a powerful urge to wrestle with the soul of the nation" and was recruiting clerical help for the task (*Church*, 185). John appreciated her help, but pointed out to her his disappointment in many of the friendly clergy, most of whom focused simply on "justification and the other first principles of the doctrine of Christ." Wesley thought it appropriate to thirst after something farther—actual holiness, a knowledge of God that would result in coming "to the measure of the stature of the fullness of Christ" (*JWL*, 4:57–58). In the midst of it all, Charles wrote his wife with confidence: "the number of converted clergy will be multiplied by the time my brother and I finish."

Problems with the Preachers

The Wesleys' emphasis on holiness, especially in terms of Christian perfection, was one of the main barriers to successful *rapprochement* with the clergy. Perfection also presented difficulties of a different sort with some of the Methodist preachers. In August 1758, the Conference in Bristol had discussed the matter at some length. Wesley suggested special caution for those "who think they have attained," so that they speak of their experience "with the deepest humility and self-abasement before God." No one, it was pointed out, ever gets beyond making mistakes, and even the perfect have the continual need for the merits of Christ. In the Minutes, Wesley again defined Christian perfection as "the loving God with all the heart, so that every evil temper is destroyed, and every thought and word and work springs from and is conducted to that end by the pure love of God and our neighbor" (*Minutes*, 713). A year later, much of the time at the Conference was spent "examining whether the spirit and lives of our preachers were suitable to their profession." In particular, there was a danger of "diversity of sentiments" among the preachers on the matter of Christian perfection, which they again reviewed. Wesley could not afford to have the preachers exhibit such a multiplicity of views on this crucial doctrine at a time when he was trying to unify the clergy of the Church, many of whom were dubious of the whole idea of perfection.

The examination of the preachers at Conference also inquired into their reading habits. In particular, the preachers who gathered in 1758 agreed to read over "our Works" (that is, the collected fifteen volumes of *Tracts*) and to "bring in what remarks occurred." When asked how many had done so already, the answer was telling: "None yet. We will begin without delay, and bring in our remarks at the next Conference" (*Minutes*, 712). Some of the Wesleys' frustration with the preachers is vented in the question that followed: "Are not many of us still wanting in seriousness!"

At the end of 1759, John prepared another volume of *Sermons on*

Several Occasions (publishing date 1760) in which he incorporated seven sermons and four treatises. In one of the treatises, *Thoughts on Christian Perfection*, he summarized again the notions reiterated at the Conferences as to what the doctrine did and did not include. Although this volume was his fourth publication of collected sermons, it bore no such number on its title page, and successive editions of the previous volumes continued to be published as a three-volume unit. Nevertheless, the sermons in this volume were of the same type and importance as those in previous volumes.

Two of the sermons summarized key soteriological doctrines, original sin and regeneration. The sermon on the New Birth gave Wesley an opportunity to present an interesting supplement to the earlier treatise on Baptism. He had preached on this text (John 3:7, "Ye must be born again") nearly fifty times in the previous five years. In this published version, he again recognizes the Church's position that new birth (regeneration) is associated with baptism, but here he points out that new birth does not *always* accompany the sacrament—a person may be born of water but not of the Spirit. And Wesley goes on to point out that, baptismal regeneration notwithstanding, most adults have sinned away the grace given them in baptism and need to be born yet again. Outward holiness will not suffice: doing good, avoiding evil, and attending the ordinances of God will not replace the need for inward holiness that results from the new creation. Without rejecting the Church's position on baptism, Wesley in these two sermons on Original Sin and New Birth presents part of the rationale for the revival's characteristic view of conversion.

When John Wesley preached in the remodeled West Street Chapel in January 1760, he reflected, "When I took this [building], eighteen years ago, I little thought the world would have borne us till now." He had an explanation, of course: "the right hand of the Lord hath pre-eminence" (*J&D*, 21:239). Within months, however, controversies over the sacraments and perfection again threatened to tear the movement apart.

Norwich was again one of the centers of discord. In February, the Wesleys discovered that three of the preachers there had begun administering the Lord's Supper. In some local circumstances, John had looked aside as preachers were licensed as "Protestants," so long as it was clear that they should not administer the Sacrament without proper ordination. Charles had made his opposition to licensing very clear; to John Nelson he wrote, "Rather than see thee a dissenting minister, I wish to see thee smiling in thy coffin" (*Church*, 134).

Some of the preachers continued to argue that their pastoral role

West Street Chapel, first leased in 1743, renovated by the Methodists in the 1750s.

in the societies would be enhanced if they could administer the Sacrament. Although Wesley stressed that the people should attend Communion regularly, many of the Methodists would not go to their parish church for it, for one reason or another, and were therefore missing the benefits of one of the primary means of grace. The Norwich society, which intermingled with dissenters from the Tabernacle society, apparently had pressed their preachers to give them the Sacrament just as William Cudworth, a registered dissenting minister, administered it at the Tabernacle (during Church hours on a Sunday morning). Charles bristled at the news, especially when he discovered that John had put the matter off until the upcoming Conference, five months away.

Charles again began mustering support to avoid what he saw as certain separation from the Church. He republished his brother's *Reasons Against a Separation* and appended a paragraph of his own, along with seven hymns intended to end any suspicion of the Methodists "having any design of ever separating from the Church" (*Societies*, 341–49):

> And ne'er from England's Church will move,
> Till torn away—to that above.

William Grimshaw, once again coming to Charles's aid, wrote a letter in which he said enough is enough: "To your tents, O Israel! It's time for me to shift for myself—to disown all connection with the Methodists" (*Grimshaw*, 256). When Charles read Grimshaw's letter to the London society, it "put them in a flame," which was just the effect he wanted. They cried out against licensed preachers and said they would all live and die in the Church.

At the Conference of 1760 in Bristol, John reiterated the position he had first laid out in "Ought We to Separate" (1755), that administering the ordinances was part of the ministerial office, quite distinct from preaching, prophesying, or evangelizing. When some of the preachers pressed him to ordain them, he reasserted a position that Charles had held for years, that to do so would in effect be to renounce the Church and its bishops, thereby causing separation. Some of the preachers persisted, claiming that they were already *de facto* dissenters, and that this step would assist their ministry to other dissenters. The Wesleys, however, with the help of Howell Harris (who attended this Conference by Charles's invitation), held firm in their opposition to ordination and their opinion of the unlawfulness of lay administration of the sacraments. Although John had begun as the more reticent opponent to the recalcitrant preachers, he finished strong, as Harris reported the next day: "John . . . said he would not ordain, and said if he was not ordained, he would look upon it as murder if he gave the ordinances. He struck dumb the reasoners by saying he would renounce them in a quarter of an hour, that they were the most foolish and ignorant in the whole Conference" (Beynon, 79–83).

This strong stand ended the overt pressure for ordination among the Methodist preachers. Although some preachers and preaching-houses continued to be registered under the Act of Toleration (over Charles's protests), the preachers did not administer the sacraments. And Grimshaw did not abandon the Methodists.

On an interesting related issue, sixteen Methodists in Rolvenden, Kent, were charged with holding a conventicle in the farmhouse of Thomas Osborne. They were fined forty-three pounds, including twenty each for the owner and the preacher, John Morley. They appealed unsuccessfully to the Quarter Sessions, but the Court of the King's Bench quashed the convictions (*People*, 47). John Wesley realized the significance of the decision: "If we do not exert ourselves, it may drive us to that bad dilemma—Leave preaching, or leave the Church. We have reason to thank God it is not come to this yet. Perhaps it never may" (*JWL*, 4:99).

Perfection Controversy

If Wesley was concerned that "a diversity of sentiments would steal in" among them in 1759, he had cause to worry even more a year or two later. Rumblings over the matter of the Sacrament continued. To his brother Charles in 1761, he reported from the Conference (a gathering at which Charles by that time was not very regular in attendance): "I told you before, with regard to Norwich, *dixi* ['I have spoken']. I have done at the last Conference all I can or dare do. Allow me liberty of conscience, as I allow you."

The issue of Christian perfection also continued to cause a stir. It became a regular topic at the annual Conferences. One of the preachers, Peter Jaco, also wrote Charles an account of the September 1761 Conference in London, including the decision: "It is determined that there are no texts of Scripture which will absolutely support instantaneous perfection; that there is no state in this world which will absolutely exempt the person in it from sin, and that therefore they have need of caution, etc."

The need for such directives arose from the increasing number of claims by Methodists beginning around 1760 that they had received the gift of Christian perfection. Wesley was fascinated by these spiritual assertions that seemed to attest to his long-held teaching that one could be cleansed from all sin (though the "infirmities" might remain) and experience pure love before death (*J&D*, 21:240–41). This "glorious work of sanctification" spread throughout the connection and had, by Wesley's testimony, a powerful effect: "wherever the work of sanctification increased, the whole work of God increased in all its branches. Many were convinced of sin, many justified, many backsliders healed." The London society itself grew from 2300 to 2800 in two years. Services like the annual covenant renewal at Spitalfields on New Year's day were attended by nearly two thousand society members in 1762, according to Wesley's count.

Problems began, however, with the excessive claims and extremist teachings of certain of the preachers. Some had been claiming that until perfected, a person was under the curse and damnation of God (*JWL*, 4:10). Thomas Maxfield, one of Wesley's first lay preachers, and George Bell, a soldier in the King's Life Guards, caused some of the more serious problems. Both men had taken the doctrine to its furthest limits, claiming that the perfected Christian was without sin and, once perfected, would persist in this angelic-like state. Their view led to a dangerous combination of assertive infallibility and blatant antinomianism; people began to imagine that they would not die or that they were immune from temptation. Some, like Bell, also began to practice faith-healing and speaking in tongues. When Wesley heard George Bell speaking "as from God what I knew God had not spoken," he asked him to stop. Wesley realized that, despite the good that had occurred during this period, he had experienced more "care and trouble" in those few short months than he had for several years preceding.

Wesley's letter to Maxfield in November 1762 had little if any subtlety. The message was clear:

> 1. I like your doctrine of perfection, or pure love; . . . but I dislike your supposing man may be as perfect as an angel. . . .
> 2. As to your spirit, I like your confidence in God and your zeal for the salvation of souls. But I dislike something which has the appearance of pride, of overvaluing yourselves and undervaluing others, particularly the preachers. . . .
> 3. As to your outward behavior, I like the general tenor of your life, devoted to God, and spent in doing good. But I dislike your slighting any, the very least rules of the bands or Society, and your doing anything that tends to hinder others from exactly observing them.

Maxfield and his friends, however, unimpeded by Wesley's comments, moved even further into fanaticism. By January 1763, George Bell was proclaiming that the end of the world would come the following month, on February 28. Wesley's attempts to convince Bell of his mistakes left him "as unmoved as a rock." Maxfield's response was to pray for Wesley's heart to be "set at full liberty" that he might then see everything in a new light (presumably in the same light then as Maxfield). Matters reached a crisis point on the 25th of January when a member of the Foundery society, Mrs. Coventry, came to Wesley and, throwing down her class ticket and those of her family, declared they would no longer hear two doctrines. Wesley wrote Maxfield and laid the breach at his feet, for contradicting what Wesley had taught about perfection from the beginning, especially the need for continual growth in grace. Within days, Maxfield began meeting with his followers separately from the Wesleys.

This period of turmoil was also the occa-

Charles Wesley's note expelling Michael Fenwick, read at the Foundery on February 22, 1760.

sion for one of John Wesley's more subtle attempts at humor. Michael Fenwick, who had travelled with Wesley in the 1750s, often complained that he was never mentioned in any of Wesley's published *Journal* extracts, which appeared every three or four years. Fenwick, as it happened, was expelled from the Foundery Society in February 1760; the following year, Wesley published his extract for the years 1755–58 and made his first mention of Fenwick: "[July 25, 1757] I left Epworth with great satisfaction, and about one preached at Clayworth. I think none was unmoved but Michael Fenwick, who fell fast asleep under an adjoining hayrick." Not exactly the type of notice the young man was coveting!

Setting Standards of Conformity

The turmoil over Christian perfection and the ferment generated by the exodus of Maxfield guaranteed that the Conference of 1763 would be lively and important. Although no official minutes have survived, accounts by two or three participants paint part of the picture. On the first day, Wesley, never one to back down from a challenge, preached (as might have been anticipated) on Christian perfection. Some of the preachers were apparently still chafing under his strict control. Howell Harris, who was visiting, stifled the swell of discontent by commenting publicly, "If Mr. Wesley should at any time abuse his power, who will weep for him if his own children will not!" According to John Pawson, who was present, those simple words had an astonishing effect on the preachers, who "were all in tears, on every side, and gave up the matter entirely."

On one important matter, the preachers prevailed over Wesley's natural prejudices against pensions. By this time, several special funds, at the circuit and the connectional level, supported Kingswood School, provided for emergency expenses of needy societies, helped with building costs, and paid for preachers' traveling expenses. A yearly collection had been instigated in 1761, "to which every Methodist in England" was "to contribute something" (with a reminder about the widow's two mites). This **General Fund** was used primarily for paying debts incurred in the building of preaching-houses, which had accrued to about 4,000 pounds. At this Conference two years later, a new fund, called the **Preachers' Fund**, was established to provide pensions for "worn out" preachers, their widows and children. Pawson noted that Wesley "thought it worldly and not Christian prudence to provide for a rainy day, yet he consented to it."

In spite of the chaos leading up to this Conference, the meeting proceeded "with love and simplicity" (to use Howell Harris's evaluation). Wesley himself noted that "it was a great blessing that we had peace among ourselves, while so many were making themselves ready for battle" (*J&D*, 21:421). Wesley also seems to have decided that this was a good time to produce another revision of the published *Minutes*. The first issue in 1749, appearing in two pamphlets, both entitled *Minutes of Some Late Conversations,* comprised doctrinal and disciplinary matters from the early Conferences. These were combined and revised into a sixteen-page pamphlet around 1753 entitled *Minutes of Several Conversations* and contained an updated selection of the main points of doctrine and polity for the connection. Now in 1763, Wesley again revised and enlarged this document to include many of the issues that had been discussed in the Conferences during the previous decade (the Minutes of each annual Conference had not been published). This new handbook, inscribed copies of which were given to the preachers upon their successful examination at Conference, became known as the **"Large"** *Minutes*, since it incorporated the more significant Minutes of "several conversations" (i.e., Conferences). That this publication appeared at an important moment in the development of the movement was, like many other developments in Wesley's Methodism, not simply accidental.

The question of doctrinal conformity on essential issues had been a matter of concern for most of the nearly twenty-five years of the revival. The Wesleys had tried to encourage doctrinal uniformity through personal contact with detractors, public arguments with critics, discussions at annual Conferences, and yearly examinations of the preachers. John had provided tutorials and publications, encouragement and reprimands. The very nature of the revival with its somewhat tolerant interplay of different persons and diverse ideas had created complex sets of tensions, not least of which were doctrinal. This situation had led to the examining and purging of the preachers. Several preachers now had been barred from the Methodist societies because they preached doctrines contrary to the Wesleyan teachings. The continuing turmoil over the sacraments and perfection now led Wesley to consider specific ways of protecting the Methodist preaching-houses from being used by persons who contradicted his teachings.

During the previous decade, John had hoped the publication of his Bible commentary, *Explanatory Notes Upon the New Testament*, would provide doctrinal help for his preachers. The first edition, in 1755, had been prepared more hastily than Wesley had hoped. The second edition the following year was essentially a reprint, though with the *errata* incorporated. In 1760, however, he and Charles had embarked on a major revision of the work, further refining the biblical text and expanding the notes. They finished this new edition in 1762 and, combined with the collected *Sermons on Several Occasions* John had published (four volumes by 1760), it provided basic doctrinal guidelines for the preachers.

By the late summer of 1763, Wesley had firmly fixed these two resources as the measure of proper Methodist preaching. The vehicle for such a step was the legal form they used for settling the property associated with the preaching-houses, a "**Model Deed**." The "Large" *Minutes* of that year contain the stipulated form of the deed that was to be used by the societies (the dates, names of local trustees, etc., to be inserted in each local instance). One crucial designation among the provisions of the deed was that the trustees should permit John Wesley "and such other persons as he shall from time to time appoint, and at all times, during his natural life, *and no other persons,* to have and enjoy the free use and benefit of the said premises," that they may "therein preach and expound God's holy Word." This limited the Methodist pulpits to preachers approved by John Wesley. A special proviso specifically defined the boundaries of their preaching: "Provided always, that the said persons preach no other doctrine than is contained in Mr. Wesley's *Notes Upon the New Testament,* and four volumes of *Sermons.*" By this stipulation, the *Sermons* and *Notes* became the **doctrinal standards** for the Methodist preachers.

Understandably, Wesley chose to limit the homiletical boundaries for his lay preachers (uneducated, unordained) in a manner similar to the way the Church of England restricted the uneducated, unordained curates to reading from the Book of Homilies (without gloss or omission). This method served to protect the people from unorthodox doctrines. The doctrinal standards of the Church of England were the Thirty-nine Articles, which provided the basis for the preaching by the educated, ordained priests, who were allowed to write their own homilies. Priests were expected, of course, not to preach doctrines contrary to the Articles, but they (unlike curates) could treat the Book of Homilies simply as a model for their own preaching, not a boundary.

Wesley constantly claimed that the Methodists taught nothing but what was in the Thirty-nine Articles, the Homilies, and the Book of Common Prayer, and would "unwillingly vary from it in any instance." But those documents still allowed a great deal of leeway for various emphases and interpretations. For his own movement, Wesley decided to restrict his preachers to the doctrines exposited in a set body of material (the *Sermons* and *Notes*) in order to sanction the proper emphases and assure a distinctive Methodist perspective.

The Methodist Mission and the Church

One of the earliest questions in these "Large" *Minutes* encapsulated Wesley's view of the mission of Methodism: "Q. What may we reasonably believe to be God's design in raising up the Preachers called Methodists? A. To reform the nation and, in particular, the Church; to spread scriptural holiness over the land." And one of the last questions gave Wesley an opportunity to summarize his advice on how to maintain good relations with the Church of England, which he was trying to reform:

> (1) Let all our Preachers go to church. (2) Let all our people go constantly. (3) Receive the sacrament at every opportunity. (4) Warn all against niceness in hearing, a great and prevailing evil. (5) Warn them likewise against despising the prayers of the Church. (6) Against calling our Society a Church, or the Church. (7) Against calling our Preachers Ministers, our houses meeting-houses (call them plain preaching-houses). (9) Do not license them as such.

In spite of Wesley's attempts to engage the clergy in his movement, the controversy over Christian perfection seems to have driven away some who had been close to the movement, such as Martin Madan, Thomas Haweis, and John Berridge. And the fray also drove a wedge between Whitefield and Wesley. Whitefield's tendency to downplay the necessity of sanctification and nurture in the Christian life provoked thinly veiled attacks in Wesley's *Journal*, such as his note in August 1763 of the conditions in Pembrokeshire, one of Whitefield's territories: "How much preaching has there been for these twenty years all over Pembrokeshire! But no regular societies, no discipline, no order or connection; and the consequence is that nine in ten of the once-awakened are now faster asleep than ever."

Wesley clung to his vision of Methodism working hand in hand with the clergy in reviving the Church. In 1762, he had invited several clergymen to attend his annual Conference at Leeds, and three or four did. On the last day of the Conference in 1763, the Wesleys agreed to meet with some of the clergy and two of the Moravian bishops in order to promote a union of their efforts (Howell Harris pushed the Moravian connection). There is no record of any success in this regard. In March 1764, again meeting with several "serious" clergymen, he tried again to promote a union between all who preach "those fundamental truths, original sin and justification by faith, producing inward and outward holiness." He had earlier referred to these three "grand scriptural truths" as the main doctrines of Methodism; he continued to use them as the framework for his ecumenical call to revival. In April 1764, he wrote a circular letter to some three dozen evangelical clergy of the Church who he thought might agree on a union based upon these three "essentials." His proposal generated a resounding silence. Three responses trickled in, the tone of which was mostly skeptical, if not hostile. Wesley's evaluation from the previous month was sustained: "God's time is not fully come" (*J&D*, 21:444). With the accession of George III to the throne in 1760, some had anticipated changes on the religious scene that might be favorable to the evangelicals in the Church, but no major changes seemed to be forthcoming.

Undaunted, Wesley again invited the evangelical clergy to his Conference in August 1764, in an attempt to create a "good understanding with all our brethren of the clergy who are heartily engaged in propagating vital religion" (*J&D*, 21:485). Twelve clergy attended. The lively issue that emerged was whether or not Methodist preachers should be removed from parishes of the evangelical clergy. The Conference in 1760 had agreed that the Methodists would focus their efforts on setting up societies where there was no "gospel ministry." Huddersfield became a test case for the inevitable complication when Henry Venn, an evangelical clergyman, came there as parish priest in 1761. Wesley then restricted his preachers to visiting the society in that parish but once a month, and finally withdrew them altogether in 1762. Now, in 1764, Charles Wesley supported the clergymen who requested that the Methodists not preach in such places at all. John Hampson, sounding very much like the young Mr. Wesley, said that he, having an equal right, would preach there and never ask. John Fletcher said he was not uneasy with Methodist preachers in his parish. John Wesley sided more or less with the latter position, since he did not want to abandon societies that were already established in a parish where a friendly clergyman might then move. Nevertheless, he made one exception and extended the prohibition at Huddersfield for one more year.

One complication in this picture of Church and revival is that the term Methodist was applied to a wide variety of persons and groups. Some of the sympathetic clergy were at times called Methodists; Whitefield and his followers were Methodists; some dissenters who reflected similar interests were called Methodists. In 1765, Wesley published a *Short History of Methodism* in an attempt to "reckon up the various accounts" that had been given of "the people called Method-

The preaching-house at Heptonstall, an octagon building touted by Wesley as a model.

ists." He pointed out that some accounts were rather far-fetched, such as the rumor among the Irish that Methodists are "the people who place all religion in wearing long beards." After a short description of Methodist origins at Oxford and Georgia, Wesley describes the manner by which Whitefield "entirely separated" from them over the matter of predestination. Then Cudworth and James Relly separated from Whitefield as antinomians. Soon there were other clergy of the Church that preached "salvation by faith." But some preachers, like Bell and Maxfield, separated from the Wesleys over the question of perfection. The picture Wesley paints in this history is clear: not all who call themselves Methodists, or are called Methodists, are in connection with Wesley. At that time, he points out, most of those who remain with him are "Church of England men" who "love her Articles, her Homilies, her Liturgy, her discipline." They preach salvation by faith and "endeavor to *live* according to what they preach, to be plain, Bible-Christians."

Nearly two-thirds through the century, Methodism was quite a different phenomenon from what it had been two decades earlier. There were now over thirty circuits in England, Wales, Ireland, and Scotland. The traveling preachers, their numbers approaching a hundred, had been drawn through the fire of public protest by the mobs and had survived the yearly examination by the Wesleys. Over twenty thousand people were members of the societies, still a relatively small number (barely one fifth of one percent of the population), but the number was growing by about a thousand members per year. And they differed quite markedly from their early predecessors, in many cases. Their disciplined efforts to live the Christian life had resulted in a cleaner, more educated, upwardly mobile congregation in many of the Methodist preaching-houses. Wesley found himself in the unusual predicament of having Methodists accumulating wealth and wearing fine clothes. Even their preaching-houses were beginning to hint at a more affluent clientele, such as the stone edifice built in Heptonstall in 1764, the octagonal shape of which provided an unusual architectural model. Two of his treatises in the 1760 collection of *Sermons* had addressed the problems associated with these developments: wealth and ostentation.

In his sermon "On the Use of Money," Wesley propounded the basis of his own financial practice as a Christian economic principle. He had long preached against surplus accumulation of wealth. But here he lays out the whole formula: gain all you can, save all you can, and (most importantly) give all you can, that is, give all you have to God. While this principle allowed for the adequate provision of the "necessaries" of life, everything else should be applied to helping one's neighbor.

Wesley's treatise "Advice to the People Called Methodists with Regard to Dress" was a natural outgrowth of this same concern (*JWW*, 11:466–77). He points out that he had cautioned against "adorning the body" as early as his ministry in Georgia. He advises neatness, plainness, and modesty in apparel, similar to that of the Quakers. One corollary is that even the poor should try to be as clean as possible, "because cleanliness is one great branch of frugality." In the end, he says it would be better to burn or throw away costly apparel rather than to wear it at peril of the soul. But those who would be faithful stewards would more likely sell it and give the money to those who are in need. The closing sentiments are typically Wesleyan:

> After providing for those of thine own household things needful for life and godliness, feed the hungry, clothe the naked, relieve the sick, the prisoner, the stranger, with all that thou hast. Then shall God clothe thee with glory and honor in the presence of men and angels.

As we have seen, the growth and development of Methodism to this point was not without tensions and problems. When Wesley visited the Norwich society in 1763, he found it necessary to put an immediate halt to their preaching on Sunday mornings during the

John Wesley (1765),
by Nathaniel Hone.

time of Church services. They once again felt the force of his blunt comments: "For many years I have had more trouble with this society than with half the societies in England put together. With God's help, I will try you one year longer, and I hope you will bring forth better fruit" (*J&D*, 21:434). He was almost always willing to give his people another chance.

Now in his sixties, an age at which many of his earlier companions were dead, Wesley found himself trying to give shape, direction, and discipline to a lively and diverse group of enthusiastic Christians. He had given them a message of hope, a fellowship of nurture, and a pattern of spiritual discipline. To implement his program, he had developed practical guidelines in the form of rules, standards, and structures. Many Methodists shared much of his spirit without always appreciating the nature and limits of his commitment to a mission that would "reform the nation, especially the Church."

John himself either failed to recognize or refused to admit what was obvious to many others, including Charles: the characteristic features of Methodism that embodied his method of reform were also the features that gave the people called Methodists a distinctive identity and were most likely to bring pressure for separation from the Church. During this period, which had seen the development of many of those features, the Wesleys faced tremendous pressure on the matter of separation. Although many of the specific crises had been successfully overcome, they knew that the future was likely to bring similar challenges.

Forging a Theology

Wesley reflected his priorities in life with the comment in his mid-sixties, "I have always thought there is something venerable in persons worn out with age, especially when they retain their understanding and walk in the ways of God" (*J&D*, 22:157). Even as his Oxford days receded farther into the distance, Wesley was never able to discard completely his academic gown. He continued to nurture a love of learning and at the same time to focus on the need for holiness. This dual emphasis is perhaps best remembered in the words that Charles Wesley had recently published in his hymn for children ("At the Opening of a School in Kingswood"): "Unite the pair so long disjoined, / Knowledge and vital piety" (*Collection*, 644). John's personal phrasing and Charles's poetic expression of this essential connection was "writ large" upon the whole movement in terms of the intertwining of doctrine and discipline. No matter how simple the Methodist people, no matter how untaught the Methodist preachers, the Wesleys constantly found ways to combine the teaching of doctrine with the fostering of discipline.

At the Conference of 1765, John Wesley read into the Minutes a brief history of Methodism, which summarized the *Short History* he had published that year. The sketch opens with John and Charles reading the Bible in 1729. They "saw inward and outward holiness therein, followed after it, and incited others so to do." But the story of the early spread of the movement also continues with the challenges of Calvinism, antinomianism, and worldliness, which result in the gross neglect of duties, especially the education of children. He goes on: "This is not cured by the Preachers. Either they have not light or not weight enough. But the want of these may be in some measure supplied by publicly reading the Sermons everywhere, especially the fourth volume, which supplies them with remedies suited to the disease" (*Minutes*, 51–52). This reinforcement of the doctrinal role of the Sermons, fixed in the Model Deed, also includes a somewhat uncommon emphasis on the educational treatises in the fourth volume.

At the same time, Wesley was writing new sermons that spoke to some of the issues raised by both his followers and his challengers. One of the hallmark sermons in the Wesleyan repertoire was published in 1765. "**The Scripture Way of Salvation**" signals the maturation of his theology, hammered out during the years of contention and controversy. It stands as perhaps the single best homiletical summary of his soteriology, or doctrine of salvation (*Sermons*, 2:153–69). He had preached on this text, Ephesians 2:8, over forty times already, and had also published an early sermon on it, "Salvation by Faith." But the previous decade had witnessed the exceptionally unsettling controversies generated by Maxfield, Bell, and other Calvinists and antinomians who had challenged Wesley's view of the nature of justification and sanctification. Now, in this examination of faith and the "way of salvation," Wesley succinctly reiterates his emphasis on grace—prevenient, convincing, justifying, sanctifying—and strongly underscores his correlative stress on the necessity of good works.

An outline of this published sermon furnishes, in effect, a profile of Wesley's main preaching points, all drawn out within an understanding that salvation is not "going to heaven" or eternal blessedness, but is the whole work of God in the individual, "from the first dawning of grace in the soul till it is consummated in glory." Prevenient grace leads to conviction of sin, which brings repentance and fruits meet for repentance. Faith is the only condition directly necessary for God's forgiveness or justification, which is the work of Christ that results in a *relative* change in the individual, who is then "accounted as righteous." At the same time, regeneration (new birth) takes place. It is the beginning of sanctification, the work of the Holy Spirit that brings a *real* change in the individual, who thereby begins this process of actually becoming righteous or holy. As the believer goes on "from grace to grace," entire sanctification is the goal—"full salvation from all our sins." This Christian perfection, or perfect love, "takes up the whole capacity of the soul" and thereby excludes all sin: "For as long as love takes up the whole heart, what room is there for sin therein?" This goal of being perfected in love is still precisely the same as that expressed in the meditative piety of the Oxford Methodists, thirty five years earlier (*M&M*, 100–104). The details, however, have undergone some adjustments.

In the process of explaining this *via salutis*, his understanding of the spiritual pilgrimage, John touches again on some of the controversies of the previous three decades by reiterating the conclusions that have emerged in his own understanding. He dispenses with a simplistic view of the "faith of adherence," held by many Anglicans, by claiming that faith necessarily implies an assurance, or evidence, that "Christ loved *me* and gave himself for *me*." The Holy Spirit witnesses with the spirit of the believer that he or she is a child of God. Wesley challenges the view that repentant faith is all that is necessary for justification by showing that "fruits meet for repentance are in some sense necessary to justification." Not in the same sense or in the same degree as faith, but, nonetheless, necessary if the believer has time and opportunity. Faith is the only immediate and direct necessity; good works are, however, a conditional and remote necessity. Wesley takes further aim at the Calvinists by stating not only that it is incumbent upon all who have been justified to be "zealous in good works" of mercy and piety, but also that repentance is necessary after as well as before justification—no "once saved, always saved" in this scheme! The conviction of any sin still remaining in a heart "bent to backsliding" or cleaving to the words and actions of the believer brings a constant, daily reliance upon the grace of God. And the release from sin can be either gradual or instantaneous, depending upon the will of God. This theme leads rather naturally into the climax of this landmark sermon on salvation, a strong appeal to the reader (somewhat unusual in his published sermons): "look for it then every day, every hour, every moment. Why not this hour, this moment? Certainly you may look for it now, if you believe it is by faith."

Another crucial Wesley sermon, **"The Lord Our Righteousness,"** clarifies even further the Wesleyan view of justification and sanctification in terms of imputed and imparted righteousness. Wesley's dispute with the Calvinists on this point goes back at least to his conflicts with George Whitefield in 1739. The occasion of this particular sermon, however, was a longtime dispute with James Hervey, a former Oxford Methodist (since turned Calvinist), whose letters of response to Wesley's criticisms in the 1750s (though never actually sent to Wesley) were published after Hervey's death in 1758 by William Cudworth. Wesley responded by publishing a lengthy extract of John Goodwin's work in *A Treatise on Justification* (1765). Then he preached this sermon at West Street Chapel, London, in November 1765 as a summary homiletical rejoinder.

The issue in question, the **imputation** and **impartation** of Christ's righteousness, seems to come down to a theological technicality: is Christ's atoning death the "formal" cause or the "meritorious" cause of justification? Wesley's emphasis on holiness, Christ's righteousness infused in the heart of the believer, led many to claim that he did not hold the traditional doctrine of imputed righteousness. Wesley looked more closely, however, and saw a seemingly minor issue as the nub of the problem. He therefore challenges those who attempt to disjoin Christ's passive and active obedience (righteousness) and who thereby see the former (Christ's passive obedience or righteousness in his suffering and death) as the formal cause of justification. The Calvinists and others who held such a position were thus compelled to accept predestination and irresistible grace as implied in this understanding of formal cause. For Wesley, an understanding of both Christ's passive *and* active obedience or righteousness (as a man "who went about doing good") as the meritorious cause of justification was more adequate and allowed a place for prevenient grace, free will, and universal atonement. Wesley did not want to separate the active and passive righteousness ("what Christ hath done and suffered for us") and therefore claimed that it was with regard to these two conjointly that Jesus is called "the Lord our righteousness."

This approach, if accepted, effectively undercut the basis of the Calvinists' argument. Wesley knew that the Calvinists would claim that he was using the term "imputed righteousness" but filling it with his own meaning, and he therefore asks for tolerance in the difference of expressions. Wesley argues that he has always held the doctrine of imputed righteousness (rightly understood), but that he knows there is more : "God *implants* righteousness in every one to whom he has *imputed* it." Wesley proceeds with an explication of the imputation and impartation of Christ's righteousness in such a way as to emphasize the necessary but subsidiary role of the former and the necessary priority of holiness of heart and mind as the essence of real religion. True believers should never use Christ's imputed righteousness as a cover for their own unrighteousness (a possible consequence of a "wrong" understanding of imputation). Wesley also points out, further, that one may be ignorant of the correct doctrine of imputation and still have a heart that is "right toward God" and therefore "effectually know 'the Lord our righteousness'." This position is a variant of another basic Wesleyan presupposition—wrong opinions may be destructive of true religion, but right opinions do not guarantee it.

This sermon not only outlines Wesley's position on a crucial theological point but also illustrates one of Wesley's emerging techniques of handling controversial theological questions. His underlying presupposition here is that theological disputes are often over simple matters of opinion (i.e., not really essential) or may simply result from the different ways those opinions are expressed. He suggests that if contending parties really understood each other, there would often be no dispute: "Different persons may use different expressions and yet mean the same thing." He then goes on to explain, in such matters as the imputation of Christ's righteousness, what the truth of the matter is—what both opposing parties *really* intend to say. On the surface, this method has the appearance of a mediating approach; in fact, his own opponents recognized it as a self-serving, if not devious, means of promoting his own position under the guise of having a "catholic spirit."

A contemporary anti-Methodist caricature of George Whitefield being inspired by a demon.

These two sermons signal the maturing of Wesley's theology. He recognized their significance and specifically requested that the Assistants disperse them among the people (*Minutes*, 58). He was becoming more self-assured in the details of his theological views and at the same time more willing to state his position unequivocally, with less concern for the reactions of clergy who might disagree with him. After the fruitless attempts at united action in 1764, he seems to have practically given up on forming any working relationship with the evangelical clergy for a time and was ready to be more explicit in differentiating the emphases of his (Methodist) theology on certain key points, though he still maintained that his views were in fact those of the Church.

Wesley had not entirely abandoned the idea of unity, but his realization that the Church clergy were "as a rope of sand" led him to concentrate on his relationships within the "Methodist" family of revivalists—those who could agree that a stress on holiness was a key to their unified efforts. In February 1766, Wesley had written to John Fletcher, "Unity and holiness are the two things I want among the Methodists" (*JWL*, 5:4). In August, using the same metaphor he had used in 1748, Charles expressed the hope that the two Wesleys could continue to work with Whitefield: "The threefold cord, we trust, will never more be broken" (*JWJ*, 5:182n).

John Wesley's public theological statements may have taken on a new tone of certitude, but his own spiritual pilgrimage was experiencing some low points. One letter to his brother in June 1766 suggests a winter solstice of his soul. One paragraph, with some phrases written in shorthand to conceal his personal agony from unwanted readers, reveals his turmoil (the Greek terms are transliterated in brackets):

> In one of my last, I was saying I do not feel the wrath of God abiding on me; nor can I believe it does. And yet (this is the mystery), I do not love God. I never did. Therefore I never believed, in the Christian sense of the word. Therefore I am only an honest heathen, a proselyte of the Temple, one of the [God-fearers]. And yet, to be so employed of God! and so hedged in that I can neither get forward nor backward! Surely there never was such an instance before, from the beginning of the world! If I ever have had *that faith*, it would not be so strange. But I never had any other [evidence] of the eternal or invisible world than I have now; and that is none at all, unless such as faintly shines from reason's glimmering ray. I have no direct witness (I do not say, that I am a child of God, but) of anything invisible or eternal.

This is an unusual baring of his soul to his brother. The public viewed him variously as a rampant enthusiast, an autocratic leader, a spiritual giant, a confident preacher of *sola fide*. But here we see him, in a moment of honest introspection, despairing of his own faithlessness, sensing a loneliness in his predicament, and relying upon the meager consolations of reason. On occasion, others had glimpsed this side of Wesley. In 1739, Charles Delamotte (speaking as an arch-Moravian) had told John, "You do not yet believe in, or build on, the rock Christ. Your peace is not a true peace. If death were to approach, you would find all your fears return" (*J&D*, 19:363). And William Briggs had written to him in 1750: "I think you have the knowledge of all you experience; but not the experience of all you know" (*Letters*, 26:415) Wesley always seems to have had the ability to preach beyond the limits of his own faith. This heart-wrenching letter to his younger brother in 1766, however, may be John's own experiential version of the mystics' "dark night of the soul," which was not so much a moment of spiritual desperation as it was a passage to higher levels of spiritual experience. The subsequent paragraph furnishes the evidence:

> And yet I dare not preach otherwise than I do, either concerning faith, or love, or justification, or perfection. And yet I find rather an increase than a decrease of zeal for the whole work of God and every

part of it. I am [borne along], I know not how, that I can't stand still.
I want all the world to come to [what I do not know] (*JWL*, 5:16).

In the light of these sentiments, it is not surprising that, in the months before and following this letter, his schedule and enthusiasm show no perceptible slackening. Since the first days of his field preaching, John Wesley's own sense of assurance had been buoyed up by the response to the work of the Holy Spirit by those to whom he preached the gospel. He considered this evidence of God's activity in other persons as an important means of his perceiving God's providence and of knowing God's will. And he was becoming more aware that God's presence in his life did not always depend upon his perception of it.

One continuing focus of activity and source of strength for Wesley was his annual conversation and interaction with many of his preachers at Conference. The Conference of 1765, held in Manchester in August, was notable for producing the first set of published **annual Minutes**. They were actually entitled, *Minutes of Some Late Conversations between the Rev. Mr. Wesleys and Others*, but were sometimes referred to as "penny Minutes," since copies of them sold for a penny. The format of these annual *Minutes*—question and answer—was the same as the minutes of the Conferences two decades earlier, which had provided the basis of the "Large" *Minutes* of 1753 and 1763 (entitled *Minutes of Several Conversations. . .*), which were compilations of selected doctrinal and disciplinary policies and rules from previous annual Conferences.

But the content of the annual *Minutes* was expanded to include more business matters of a timely sort. The first questions dealt with the preachers, who were listed first by categories (admitted, on trial, Assistants, travelling) and then by place stationed (thirty-nine circuits with ninety-two preachers). The annual listing was necessary, since their appointment was normally for only one year (two at the very most). Then came financial matters: balances of and rules for various funds (Kingswood Collection, Preachers' Fund, Yearly Subscription) and issues associated with the heavy debt incurred by the building program of the connection. Subsequent questions dealt with topics similar to the early Conferences: matters of building, discipline, worship, publishing, and temperance. Excerpts from the Conference in Ireland were also included, which note such things as which rules the preachers were not observing and how the leaders might handle those who take snuff and drink drams.

Some of the Answers in these *Minutes* furnish an interesting picture of early Methodism. As for the preaching-houses (never to be called "churches"), for instance: "1) Let all the windows be sashed,

Charles Wesley on horseback. He was constantly thinking in poetic terms and was known to come off his horse into a home asking for a pen to write down a verse.

opening downwards. 2) Let there be no tub-pulpits; and 3) No backs to the seats." The men and women should sit apart. Evening preaching should not begin after seven. Everyone should be home from the love-feasts by nine. And the preachers ought to be merciful to their horses, making sure that they are rubbed, fed, bedded, and never ridden hard (*Minutes*, 48–53).

No matter was too small to warrant attention—four rules were given to improve singing in the congregation. No matter was too controversial to consider—women were encouraged to speak in the band meetings, though not as public teachers in the congregation. No matter was too personal to mention—people who talk too much and read too little should be reproved publicly and privately to reverse the trend. No matter escaped Wesley's control—preachers were not to print anything without Wesley's permission; the penalty was exclusion from the connection.

Some of the preachers chafed at Wesley's tight leadership of the movement and control of the Conference. Wesley had an answer, expressed in typically historical fashion: at the 1765 Conference, he reiterated the history of the movement, going back to himself and his brother at Oxford. At the next Conference, he answered the question, "But what power is this, which you exercise over all the Methodists in Great Britain and Ireland?" with another political/historical sketch that starts with November 1738 and effectively leaves out Charles. He makes it very clear that he did not seek power: the people came to him for leadership—"It was merely in obedience to the providence of God and for the good of the people that I at first accepted this power, which I never sought, nay, a hundred times labored to throw off." It was also Wesley that initiated the Conference (to advise, not govern him), and the preachers agreed from the beginning to serve him "as sons in the Gospel." "They do me no favor in being directed by me," he pointed out, "At present I have nothing from it but trouble and care, and often a burden I scarce know how to bear." But the preachers should not feel like they are shackled, even though they have no vote in Conference, at least "not while I live." After all, he says, "Every preacher and every member may leave me when he pleases" (*Minutes*, 60–62).

Wesley also used that particular occasion to deliver a short discourse on the state of Methodism and made some suggestions for its future in the form of a farewell message, on the assumption that, at 63 years of age, he could not depend on seeing another Conference. It is a powerful plea to the preachers to tighten the reins and work harder at being faithful to the work. One subsequent entry in the *Minutes* illustrates how the depth of his concern has turned his mind on some issues. In answer to the question, "Why are we not more knowing?" he says, in effect, because we do not work hard enough. To cure this evil, he first prescribes that the preachers read the more useful books—steadily all morning, or at least five hours a day. The reaction of the preachers (using Wesley's own *homo unius libri* principle) and Wesley's responses reveals that Wesley is not hesitant to use sarcasm to make his point:

> "But I read *only* the Bible." Then you ought to teach others to read only the Bible, and, by parity of reason, to *hear only* the Bible. But if so, you need preach no more. Just so said George Bell. And what is the fruit? Why, now he neither reads the Bible nor anything else.
>
> This is rank enthusiasm. If you need no book but the Bible, you are got above St. Paul. He wanted others too. "Bring the books," says he, "but especially the parchments. . . ."
>
> "But different men have different tastes." Therefore some may read less than others; but none should read less than this.

"But I have no books." I will give each of you, as fast as you will read them, books to the value of five pounds.

And if there were any question as to whether Wesley was serious about the preachers' attitude on this matter, he responds to the comment, "But I have no taste for reading," by saying, "Contract a taste for it by use, or return to your trade" (*Minutes*, 68). Wesley had no time for those who stretched or twisted his principles for their own convenience, no matter whether it was Christian perfection or *sola scriptura*.

In the meantime, Wesley continued to provide his people with more publications. He had been producing an average of about six items a year for the previous decade; after 1765, he began to increase the output. Among the important works during that period were the summary of his most distinctive doctrine in *A Plain Account of Christian Perfection* (1766) and two more sermonic discourses in 1767, "The Witness of the Spirit, II" and "The Repentance of Believers," both of which added significant revisions to his earlier sermons on those topics.

The discourse on the **witness of the Spirit** is more than a restatement of his earlier sermon on the same topic. The intervening twenty years had witnessed a radical disregard among some Methodists for his attempt to avoid subjective "enthusiasm" in the doctrine of assurance by balancing such individual "feeling" with the objective ground of any such experience in the prior and direct testimony of the Holy Spirit (*Sermons*, 1:269–84). In this second treatment of the subject, he sets out to prove (from Scripture and experience) that there is, in fact, a direct testimony of the Spirit, distinct from one's own sense of the fruit of the Spirit, of one's being a child of God. He also brings to bear a theological principle that he had begun to use regularly when considering questions of the gifts of the Spirit (such as speaking in tongues or faith-healing): any purported gifts of the Spirit, including assurance, are to be judged by whether or not they result in the fruits of the Spirit—love, joy, peace, long-suffering, gentleness, goodness. Without these, he says, "the testimony cannot continue." Both witnesses are therefore necessary: the direct testimony of God's Spirit and the testimony of our own spirit, "the consciousness of our walking in all righteousness and true holiness" (*Sermons*, 285–98).

The discourse on **repentance** is a sequel to his sermon "On Sin in Believers" (1763). Having already pointed out that the power of sin, though broken, is not totally destroyed in the believer after justification, Wesley now more fully explains the sin that "remains but no longer reigns" after justification and the nature and consequences of repentance and belief in that light. He is challenging both the Reformed view of *simul iustus et peccator* (that the remains of sin can never be erased, but the believer's subsequent repented sins are covered by the imputed righteousness of Christ and thus inculpable), and the Moravian view (held by some Methodists as well, such as Maxfield and Bell) that justification results in total freedom from sin and guilt. Wesley presses home three points: 1) our hearts are not wholly sanctified or cleansed from sin at justification; 2) a conviction of our demerit after justification is necessary to a full acceptance of the atonement; and 3) a deep conviction of our utter helplessness teaches us "truly to live upon Christ by faith" (*Sermons*, 1:335–52). Wesley's continuing definition of sin as a willful, voluntary transgression of the known will of God, expressed as early as in his sermon on "Salvation by Faith" in 1738, is crucial to this argument as well as to his understanding of Christian perfection (*Sermons*, 1:124, 315; cf. 3:79).

The **revisionist** approach of Wesley's sermons in the 1760s belies his frequent claim that he had been totally consistent in his teachings over the years. These assertions are often repeated in works like *A Plain Account of Christian Perfection*, where he describes, and gives excerpts from, his writings during the period 1725–65 with such comments as, "This was the view of religion I then had. . . . This is the view I have of it now, without any material addition or diminution. . . . This is the very same doctrine which I believe and teach at this day, not adding one point." Anyone who had read the material closely could easily spot changes, as was the case with one clergyman who had a keen eye for theological distinctions—Thomas Rutherforth, Regius Professor of Divinity at Cambridge. In 1768, Wesley responded to the professor's published charge of his "maintaining contradictions." In a rare moment of candor, Wesley admitted that during the latter part of the period 1725–68, he had indeed "relinquished several of my former sentiments," perhaps even varied in some of them "without observing it," and would certainly not defend all the expressions he had used during that time. He even admits that he had many years previously given up the idea of assurance as essential to justifying faith. Wesley's inevitable retort to the Doctor's charge, however, is twofold: 1) Seeming contradictions are bound to appear when he was answering so many different critics at once, "one pushing this way, another that"; nevertheless, 2) "few if any real contradictions" will be found in his publications during the last thirty years (*Societies*, 9:375–76). Wesley then goes on in typical fashion to explain how, if one really understands his ideas, they would be seen as being consistent, scriptural, and in keeping with the teachings of the Church.

One of the interesting variations in Wesley's views can be seen in his fluctuating perspective over the years toward those who are **nominal Christians** (as distinguished from real Christians). Wesley frequently uses one of three phrases in reference to these "almost Christians": 1) those who "fear God and work righteousness," and 2) those who think religion consists of "doing good, avoiding sin, saying their prayers, and attending church" (strikingly similar to the outline of the *General Rules*), and 3) those who "have the form of godliness, but deny the power thereof." In the 1720s and early 1730s, Wesley speaks critically of the "half Christians," but refers to the real Christians (including himself) by using the first two phrases above, viewed as describing means of producing inward as well as outward holiness. By the late 1730s and early 1740s, however, he has begun to follow the Moravians in making a radical distinction between the "almost" and the "altogether" Christian (the point of his sermon on that topic in 1741), the former being no better than honest heathens. Charles was even more forceful in describing the second group as "self-deceivers" who are "an abomination in the sight of God," and anyone who had not received assurance is "not yet a Christian" (*Sermons*, 1:144, 149). By 1744, however, John was describing the Methodists as those "having the form and seeking the power of godliness" (*Societies*, 9:69). By 1749, he described his giving of class tickets to members as being as strong a recommendation as if he had written out on each, "I believe the bearer hereof to be one that fears God and works righteousness" (*Societies*, 9:265).

And in 1768, he tells Dr. Rutherforth that he thinks assurance is "the common privilege of Christians fearing God and working righteousness" (*Societies*, 9:376). The reconstitution of a place in Wesley's scheme for the formerly deprecated nominal Christians (even if as a second tier) is one of the revisions that had important implications for **evangelism** in the Wesleyan movement. While becoming more theologically sophisticated himself, he began to realize that the goal of the movement "to reform the nation . . . and to spread scriptural holiness over the land" did not depend on the people's acceptance or understanding of technical theological language or concepts. In December 1767, Wesley had deduced that a person could be saved who had no clear conception of (or even denied) imputed righteousness or justification by faith. He therefore concluded that it was high time for the Methodist preachers to give up bombast and "big words that have no determinate meaning" and "return to the plain word, 'He that feareth God, and worketh righteousness, *is* accepted with Him'" (Acts 10:35; *J&D*, 22:114–15). And the nurturing fellowship of the societies, more than the loud preaching in the fields, was the place where this word could be instilled in the believers.

In order to implant Methodist teaching in the minds and memories of the people, the Wesleys had for many years incorporated **hymn-singing** into their services and had published dozens of hymn books and pamphlets. At the beginning of this decade, they had produced an important book, *Select Hymns with Tunes Annext*, that included not only the words for 133 hymns but also (in various combinations) *Sacred Melody* (with many tunes), and *The Gamut, or Scale of Music*, along with *The Grounds of Vocal Music* and *Directions for Singing*.

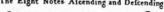

The Gamut was a music primer that gave examples for singers.

By mid-decade, they had published a second edition of this work, as well as Charles's *Short Hymns on Select Passages of the Holy Scriptures* and his *Hymns for Children*. These were then followed by *Hymns for the Use of Families* and *Hymns on the Trinity* in 1767, the last two together containing more than three hundred hymns.

Singing also gave believers an opportunity to testify to their shared spiritual experience: "What we have felt and seen / With confidence we tell" (*Collection*, 62). Wesley warned against "formality" in singing—the complex tunes that are not possible to sing with devotion, the "long quavering Hallelujah" that was sometimes annexed to tunes, the repetition of words that shocks all common sense and "has no more religion in it than a Lancashire hornpipe" (*Minutes*, 80). In the "Directions," Wesley outlined in some detail his expectations for Methodist singing:

> Sing them *exactly* as they are printed here, without altering or mending them at all. . . .
> Sing *all*. See that you join with the congregation as frequently as you can. . . .
> Sing *lustily* and with a good courage. Beware of singing as if you were half dead or half asleep, but lift up your voice with strength.

> Be no more afraid of your voice now . . . than when you sung the songs of Satan. . . .
>
> Sing *modestly*. Do not bawl so as to be heard above or distinct from the rest of the congregation. . . .
>
> Sing *in time:* . . . Do not run before nor stay behind it, but attend close to the leading voices and move therewith as exactly as you can. . . .
>
> Above all sing spiritually. Have an eye to God in every word you sing. Aim at pleasing him more than yourself or any other creature.
>
> (*Collection*, 765)

Wesley had a particular fondness for the "admirable" clear voices of children as early as his work with them at Oxford, and over the years he frequently noted his pleasure at hearing them sing.

John Wesley was becoming increasingly concerned about the Methodist work with the **children** and frequently exhorted the preachers to spend time with them. Whenever there were ten children in a society, he felt the preachers should establish a band and meet with them twice a week. The *Minutes* again reflect the preachers' hesitance on this matter: "But I have no gift for this." Wesley's response is firm: "Gift or no gift, you are to do it, else you are not called to be a Methodist preacher" (*Minutes*, 69). Wesley was certainly aware of the challenge that this task presented, and his own trials in this regard are reflected in his comment at St. Ives in August 1768: "I met the children, a work which will exercise all the talents of the most able preachers in England" (*J&D*, 22:156).

This concern for children was one of several matters incorporated into the series of questions asked of preachers before they were fully admitted into the connection. These questions were listed in the *Minutes* of 1766, as first asked of William Ellis (see box on p. 235).

The examination of preachers had for many years been Charles's task, but as his role in the leadership of the movement faded, John assumed more of these responsibilities. Charles had virtually stopped traveling throughout the connection by the 1760s, had become less regular in attending the annual Conference, and had begun to consider moving from Bristol to London (*CW*, 107). It was obvious that John was controlling the movement, but even he felt that as brothers they should form a united front. The tension between them continued to focus on matters that might or might not lead to separation, such as the licensing of preachers, the registering of the houses, and the holding of services during Church hours. Charles was particularly upset about a dozen Methodists who in 1764 had received ordination from "Bishop" Erasmus, a purported Orthodox hierarch who had also ordained John's Assistant, John Jones. Six of the ordinands were local preachers who had paid five guineas for the privilege of ordination in a tongue they did not understand. John had tossed them out of the society and refused to hear their appeal for reinstatement. Charles continued to be uneasy about many of these matters, however, knowing that on many of these issues his brother was barely being kept in check by political pressure from some of the clergy who were friendly to Methodism. Charles was keen to prevent separation from the Church at almost any cost; John was concerned but less anxious about the issue. Or, to use Charles's analysis of John: "His first object was the Methodists and then the Church; mine was first the Church, and then the Methodists" (*Church*, 208). In 1768, the Conference (with Charles in attendance) received twelve suggestions on reviving and enlarging the work, the last of which was to "keep to the Church": "They that leave the Church, leave the Methodists" (*Minutes*, 82).

There were other **differences** between the brothers, as they both recognized. John pointed out to Charles on one occasion, "In connexion I beat you; but in strong, pointed *sentences* you beat me. Go on, in your *own way*, what God has peculiarly called you to. Press the *instantaneous* blessing; then I shall have more time for my peculiar calling, enforcing the *gradual* work" (*JWL*, 5:16). But John also thought that Charles had "set perfection so high" as "effectually to renounce it." Charles himself could not point to any witnesses of such a perfection. And some of the expressions in Charles's hymns bothered John, especially those that echoed the amatory effusiveness of the Moravians or that gave comfort to the antinomians. At times, John became very perturbed at his brother, who seemed to waver between opposition and support. On one occasion, he complained to Charles that, although they seemed to be of a mind during their last conversation, "now you are all off the hooks again!—unless you only talk because you are in an humour of contradiction; and if so, I may as well blow against the wind as talk with you." Nevertheless, he again asked earnestly that Charles attend Conference the following month, and pointed out, "I will not be opposed at the Conference, for I will not dispute " (*JWL*, 5:18).

Doctrine, Discipline, and the Conference

The Conference had become, by the late 1760s, a more open body. Attendance, for some years by invitation only, was opened to any of the preachers by 1767. A few were *required* to come. All the Assistants, or heads of circuits, were expected to be there, and if possible at least one other preacher from each circuit (*Polity*, 244). The **circuit organization** was becoming more complex as the membership grew—nearly half of the thirty-four circuits in 1768 had more than eight hundred members. The numbers were reported to the Conference every year by the Assistant and recorded in the *Minutes*. Beginning in 1769, the membership chart included an asterisk beside any circuit that experienced a decline in membership (three that year).

A **General Steward** was appointed to handle finances on each circuit: to collect "quarterage" (assessment of quarterly collections) from the society stewards at the Quarterly Circuit Meeting and to pay expenses of the preachers (*Polity*, 240). In 1767, the connectional **Yearly Subscription** was over £804, of which £134 was spent for legal expenses, £148 for preachers' expenses, and £30 for "contingent expenses." The remaining £492 was divided among the seventy societies that petitioned for help with local expenses (*Minutes*, 72).

At this point, the preachers were contributing a total of about £50 annually to the **Preachers' Fund**, which included a guinea from each at entrance and a half-guinea every year thereafter. Once vested, at two guineas, a preacher was eligible, when "worn out" or **superannuated** (officially retired), to receive £10 a year; at his death, the widow and children would also be eligible for payment. No money from this Fund was returned to any preacher who left or was excluded from the connection, or lapsed payment for four years (*Minutes*, 50, 73). The **supernumerary** preachers (on temporary leave for personal reasons such as health) were not covered by this Fund.

Active traveling preachers received an annual allowance of £12 and expenses, and were expected to serve the connection full-time. In 1767, Wesley had closed the Conference with the comment, "Let us all be men of one business. We live only for this—to save our own souls and them that hear us." At the following Conference, Wesley gave the preachers who were following trades (some had been previously listed as "half-itinerants") one more year to leave their work, reminding them that "every traveling preacher solemnly professes to have nothing else to do, and receives his little allowance for this very end, that he may not need to do anything else." He especially singled out those who sold medicinal drops, saying that it might be all right for a wife to do so, but for any preacher to "hawk them about . . . does not suit the dignity of his calling" (*Minutes*, 75, 78–79). This problem, however, did not go away. At the 1770 Conference, Wesley reiterated the requirement for preachers to relinquish all trades or be excluded from the itinerancy, and put the preachers on notice that they would be questioned the following year as to whether they had entirely left off their trade or not. The offenders could become **local preachers** (no longer in full connection), to be sure, and many did. Between 1741 and 1765, only eighty-one of the preachers had remained in full connection until death; six were dismissed, about twenty became clergy, and nearly half either became or remained local preachers (*Polity*, 236).

None of the traveling or local preachers were **women**, however, even though some of the women were preaching, and at times beyond the meetings of their local society. A small group of women, led by Sarah Crosby, Sarah Ryan, and Mary Bosanquet, had in 1763 established a school and orphanage at Leytonstone, Essex, before moving their work to Cross Hall in Yorkshire five years later. Their home

---

1766 Examination of Preachers

Have you faith in Christ? Are you going on to perfection? Do you expect to be perfected in love in this life? Are you groaning after it? Are you resolved to devote yourself wholly to God and his work?

Do you know the Methodist doctrine? Have you read the Sermons? The Notes on the New Testament?

Do you know the Methodist plan? Have you read the Plain Account? The Appeals?

Do you know the Rules of the Society? Of the Bands? Do you keep them?

Do you take no snuff? Tobacco? Drams?

Do you constantly attend the church and sacrament?

Have you read the Minutes? Are you willing to conform to them?

Have you considered the Twelve Rules of a Helper; especially the first, tenth, and twelfth? Will you keep them for conscience' sake?

Are you determined to employ all your time in the work of God?

Will you preach every morning and evening? Endeavouring not to speak too loud or too long? Not lolling with your elbows? Have you read the "Rules of Action and Utterance"?

Will you meet the Society, the Bands, the Select Society, the Leaders (of Bands and Classes) in every place?

Will you diligently and earnestly instruct the children, and visit from house to house?

Will you recommend fasting, both by precept and example?

(*Minutes*, 1:54; cf. 1992 *Book of Discipline*, ¶425.)

provided a center of Methodist activity, including prayer services at which the women felt led to speak. Sarah Crosby, formerly a class-leader at the Foundery, had begun preaching when the class she organized grew to over two hundred persons, with no preacher in sight. She saw the need and began conducting a service, though unsure whether she should conduct herself in such a manner: "Yet I saw it impracticable to meet all these people by way of speaking to each individual. I therefore gave out an hymn, and prayed, and told them part of what the Lord had done for myself, persuading them to flee from all sin" (*People*, 34). The sermon was no doubt very similar to what many Methodist preachers were delivering. Sister Crosby's convictions in this regard were clear: "I do not think it wrong for women to speak in public provided they speak by the Spirit of God" (Chilcote, 128). But Wesley's hesitation on this matter can be seen in his advice to her in 1769 (which echoed similar advice to Grace Walton in 1761):

> (1) Pray in private or public as much as you can. (2) Even in public you may properly enough intermix *short exhortations* with prayer. But keep as far from what is called preaching as you can. Therefore never take a text; never speak in a continued discourse without some break, about four or five minutes. Tell the people, "We shall have another *prayer-meeting* at such a time and place." If Hannah Harrison had followed these few directions, she might have been as useful now as ever. (*JWL*, 5:130; cf. Chilcote, 297–98).

Wesley had also used this same distinction between preaching and exhorting with his first lay assistants when he was trying to keep them from preaching. And although Wesley had specifically told Sarah Crosby in 1761 that "the Methodists do not allow of women preachers," he had given her permission to read in public some portion of the *Notes* or the *Sermons* or to speak about her Christian experience (*JWL*, 4:133). The benefits of the latter he had also explained to Elizabeth Bennis in 1766: "One reason why those who are saved from sin should freely declare it to believers is because nothing is a stronger incitement to them to seek after the same blessing" (*JWL*, 5:6). Prayer, testimony, and exhortation were well within the limits of permissible women's activities. Wesley was well aware, however, that the religious establishment as well as most of the nonconformists felt that preaching by women transgressed both the social and religious conventions of the age (Chilcote, 8, 102). The fact that the Quakers defended the practice was little comfort to one who was trying to keep the Methodists within recognizable boundaries of the Church. Even though

Wesley supported women's education, gave women significant roles of leadership within Methodism, and even allowed them to the brink of preaching, he continued to stop short of officially recognizing their role. In that regard, he seems to have been driven by his concerns over the matter of separation, which were influenced in part by his recognition of the established prejudices of the Church as well as his sensitivity to the tension with his brother Charles over lay preaching in general.

Wesley's concern for and control of the preachers was managed by his annual itinerancy during the summer months and by his voluminous correspondence year-round. He wrote every preacher at least annually to prod, encourage, chastise, and exhort them to exercise their calling in more exacting ways. While visiting Ireland in 1769, he wrote a firm letter to Richard Steel with thirteen numbered suggestions on matters of preaching, visiting, health, deportment, and "several (comparatively) little things" to inculcate in his people. His concerns included health and cleanliness, in keeping with the rules circulated at the 1765 Conference. He prohibited tobacco and snuff (unless prescribed by a physician), the one as "uncleanly and unwhole-some self-indulgence," the other a "silly, nasty, dirty custom." He added "Touch no dram. It is liquid fire. It is a sure though slow poison." His suggestions on cleanliness were very specific, such as "Avoid all nastiness, dirt, slovenliness, both in your person, clothes, house, and all about you. . . . Clean yourselves of lice. . . . Cure your-self and your family of the itch." He saw a connection between outward and inward well-being: "Mend your clothes, or I shall never expect you to mend your lives. Let none ever see a ragged Methodist" (*JWL*, 5:132–34). Wesley summarized these suggestions in the 1770 "Large" *Minutes* by yet another memorable aphorism, "Tell them cleanliness is next to godliness" (*Minutes*, 538).

Concern for the conditions of his preachers and people, seen in Wesley's own personal contacts and comments, was becoming increas-ingly institutionalized in the Methodist movement. The annual distri-butions of the Preachers' Fund was only part of what was becoming a more extensive program of **connectional support** and philanthropy. The Kingswood School collection in the late 1760s began to approach £200 a year. A strong appeal by Wesley to donors in January 1767 had more than doubled the principal of the lending stock to £120. But the largest item of concern was the accumulating debt for building, which stood at nearly £12,000 in 1766. The Yearly Subscription helped meet this obligation, as did increasing restrictions on building new preaching-houses, culminating in a year-long construction moratorium in 1770.

Suggestions to fund remodelling or to reduce the debt at the local Society level were followed by Wesley's warning that such local financial initiatives should not diminish their contributions to the connectional Yearly Subscription: "Do not drop the substance by catching at a shadow."

Wesley's central position of leadership, combined with his increasing age and occasional bouts of illness, brought to the forefront the question of what would happen at his death. Many expected a splintering of the connection; others feared a power struggle. At the Conference in Leeds in August 1769, Wesley read a short paper (sent to Charles three months earlier for suggestions) that outlined his hopes for maintaining the unity of the connection. He recognized that he was presently the "centre of union to all our traveling as well as local preachers," but looked toward the situation after his death. Recognizing also that some would not realize their goals by staying in the connection, he expected that about a fourth of the preachers would become clergy ("procure preferment in the Church") and others would "turn Independents and get separate congregations." But for those who might remain, he suggested a plan of gathering in London to choose a committee of three, five, or seven (each to serve his turn as Moderator) to guide the connection. This committee would follow the methods Wesley had been using to "propose preachers to be tried, admitted, or excluded; fix the place of each preacher for the ensuing year, and the time of the next Conference."

This proposal is a modification of the Council concept that Wesley had suggested in 1760 and is much more specific than the Model Deed's stipulation (after 1763) that at Wesley's death the connectional control should pass to the "yearly Conference of the people called Methodists." At this point, Wesley felt it was important that the preachers at the Leeds Conference who were willing might sign some "**Articles of Agreement**." He had prepared a draft that included three resolutions:

> I. To devote ourselves entirely to God; denying ourselves, taking up our cross daily; steadily aiming at one thing, to save our own souls and them that hear us.
> II. To preach the old Methodist doctrines, and no other, contained in the Minutes of the Conferences.
> III. To observe and enforce the whole Methodist discipline, laid down in the said Minutes.

Nevertheless, the preachers desired that Wesley communicate an account of these actions at Conference to all the preachers "to be seriously considered." It is not clear what level of acceptance or what binding force, if any, this covenant had with the preachers.

The specification of the *Minutes* as the measure of doctrinal conformity might seem somewhat surprising, especially in the light of the Model Deed's similar stipulation concerning Wesley's *Sermons* and *Notes*. Certainly it was not simply the result of his observation that many people were "sermon-proof" (*J&D*, 22:189). In any case, the enforcement of the "old Methodist doctrine" was under Wesley's personal control at this point; Wesley could certainly make a decision on a preacher's doctrinal adequacy without reference to specific documents. And the *Minutes* did provide a measure for adequate preaching. Although the annual *Minutes* had taken on a very practical form (more discipline than doctrine), the "Large" *Minutes* still contained a good proportion of the doctrinal discussions from the various Conferences and therefore did reflect the basic shape of the "old Methodist doctrine."

In fact, Wesley produced a new edition of the "Large" *Minutes* in 1770. Of the 79 questions and answers, nearly three dozen were new (from the intervening Conferences) or amended from the previous edition of 1763. New items included the short history of Methodism, the provisions for worn-out preachers, and instructions on the care of horses (1765), on leaving off snuff and drams (1765), on visiting (1766), on working with children (1766), on extirpating smuggling and bribery (1767), on preachers leaving their trades (1768), on liquidating the old debt and the covenant of unity (1769), and on personal bankruptcy and the limitations on building (1770).

This new edition of the "Large" *Minutes* brought the doctrinal and disciplinary guidelines up to date, to the actions of the 1770 Conference, including the basic **agenda** of Conference itself, which was now spelled out in thirteen questions to be asked every year. Some items from the previous edition were omitted, such as the matter of meeting the bands every morning and the suggestions for ways to handle persecution, the bands and persecutions both becoming of less significance for the Methodists. The text of the Model Deed was also amended so as to omit William Grimshaw's name in the succession of leadership behind the Wesleys; he had died just before the previous edition had been published.

One item that the "Large" *Minutes* did not include from the 1770 penny *Minutes* was the final section on doctrine, the wording of which was a major source of **controversy** with Wesley's Calvinist detractors. The dispute had been heating up for at least two years, ever since the ejection of some Calvinist Methodists from St. Edmund's Hall in

Howell Harris's community, built in 1752 at Trevecca in Wales. Lady Huntingdon established a college nearby in 1769 for the training of preachers in her connection.

Oxford had resulted in a pamphlet war that galvanized Methodist opinion even more firmly into Arminian and Calvinist camps. Richard Hill (*Pietas Oxoniensis*) and Augustus Toplady (*Church of England Vindicated*) led the Calvinist writers into the fray. With the poor reception of Methodists at Oxford University, Wesley beefed up an "academical" course of training at Kingswood. At the same time in 1768, Lady Huntingdon established Trevecca College to help train Calvinist Methodist ministers, and soon chose two of Wesley's close associates to lead the school: John Fletcher as president and Joseph Benson (formerly at Kingswood) as headmaster. Benson and Fletcher soon became disenchanted with Trevecca. Wesley encouraged and shared their discontent, sarcastically warning Benson not even to mutter anything about Christian perfection in the Countess's presence— "heresy of heresies" (*JWL*, 5:166). Wesley himself was irritated by Calvinist Evangelicals such as Toplady, whose sermon in April 1770, "A Caveat against Unsound Doctrine," was aimed directly at him.

The 1770 Conference gave Wesley the opportunity to enter into the dispute. It came as the last point in the Answer to the closing Question: "What can be done to revive the work of God where it is decayed?": "Take heed to your doctrine." The explanation of this point took Wesley back twenty-six years, when he had asked the first Conference, "Have we not then unawares leaned too much towards Calvinism . . . [and] antinomianism?" The following year (1745), he had admitted that "the truth of the Gospel" lies "within a hair's breadth" of Calvinism and antinomianism (*Minutes*, 3, 9).

Now, in summary form, he enlarges that hair's breadth under the microscope, using ideas that he had stressed in the sermons of the 1760s. He mentions God's favor for those who "cease from evil and learn to do well"; he aligns the need for repentance with "works meet for repentance"; he speaks of God's acceptance of the person who "feareth God and worketh righteousness"; he claims that good works are a necessary "condition" of salvation. He finally asks the question, "What have we then been disputing about for these thirty years?" His answer: "I am afraid, about words."

Wesley was again primarily wrestling with the Calvinist aversion to anything that they thought bordered on works-righteousness. He was convinced that the Calvinist stress on God's predetermined activity in the one moment of justification (with its corollary of perseverance, "once saved, always saved") would normally result in spiritual conceit and moral laxity—in a word, antinomianism. In the *Minutes* in 1770, therefore, Wesley attempted to counter this attitude, particularly in the concluding comment, "We are every hour and every moment pleasing or displeasing to God, according to our works; according to the whole of our inward tempers and our outward behaviour" (*Minutes*, 96). This message coincides with Wesley's earlier comment to the Conference that reflects his life-long perspective: "No idleness can consist with growth in grace. Nay, without exactness in redeeming time, it is impossible to retain even the life you received in justification" (*Minutes*, 95).

The substance of what Wesley had said to the 1770 Conference echoes the essence of what he had been preaching consistently for nearly thirty years, and the details were those he had been pressing for a decade. But the shape, tone, and context of this particular Minute guaranteed an angry reaction from the Calvinists. However, an unexpected opportunity to placate the critics came to Wesley within weeks. Wesley was asked to preach the funeral sermon of his old Calvinist friend and antagonist, George Whitefield, who had died in America. Wesley mustered his diplomatic resources, retired to the country to write the sermon, and, on November 18, delivered the intended olive branch to an overflowing congregation at Whitefield's Tabernacle in upper Moorfields.

The sermon summarized Whitefield's life, character, and doctrine. Although Wesley ended with a strong call to emulate the "catholic spirit" that Whitefield embodied, it was in the doctrinal section that Wesley miscalculated. He portrayed Whitefield as a man who, from his beginnings as a Methodist at Oxford, had proclaimed essentially the same "grand doctrines" as Wesley himself, summarized here as "the new birth and justification by faith." In his elaboration of the point that humanity relies upon God's grace for salvation, however, Wesley reiterated the view that Christ's righteousness, seen in his passion, was the sole meritorious cause of justification (*Sermons*, 2:342). This point was at the heart of the controversy of the previous decade and was part of the very issue that had sparked the original controversy between the two in 1739.

That Wesley was asked to preach the funeral sermon was insult enough for some Calvinists, such as William Romaine, who were still bristling over the Wesleys' stridently self-conscious Arminianism during the previous decade. And many of Whitefield's friends resented the content of this particular eulogy, especially the omission of any mention of Whitefield's covenantal theology with its emphasis on absolute predestination.

But Wesley was convinced that his position on justification and sanctification was crucial to the goal of spreading scriptural holiness. His preaching and his organization had taken on quite a different shape from those of Whitefield over the years, in no small part because evangelism itself takes on a different form when holiness is the goal. The resulting tensions, both inside and outside the movement, had led Wesley to say at the 1768 Conference, "I ask, once for all, Shall we defend this perfection or give it up?" The preachers agreed to defend it. The possibility of perfection in love through grace was the distinctive and defining message in Wesley's revival, and the very organization of the movement itself, as a network of disciplined small groups, was designed to nurture that hope of perfection in the lives of the Methodists. The fact that many Calvinists and Evangelicals, within and without the Church, could not agree with this doctrine did not deter Wesley from his single-minded vision of reforming the land. He therefore set his mind to proceed in spite of them, or without them, to accomplish his goal.

Expansion, Controversy, and the Question of Control

John Wesley's self-evaluation on his sixty-eighth birthday is typical: "I am still a wonder to myself. My voice and strength are the same as at nine-and-twenty" (*J&D*, 22:282). The year before, he had also marveled, "[I] am now healthier than I was forty years ago." A quick check of his early diaries reveals that an annual review on his twenty-ninth birthday would have revealed several health problems during

The early Methodists in New York met in this small rigging-loft before they built a chapel in John Street.

the previous year, including "very lame" twice, "spit blood," and "my eye ill." Nevertheless, these later observations were not intended as an actual study of comparative strength or health. He was, among other things, trying to ascertain whether he should make the arduous trip back to America. He had been invited, and he understood that the field was ripe for harvest.

Whitefield had asked Wesley early in 1767 if there were any spare preachers to send to America to help him. Wesley's response was clear: we don't even have enough to supply the needs at home. But Wesley did point out that local preachers often are equal to the itinerants "both in grace and gifts," and hinted that they might be moved into "a larger field of action" (*JWL*, 5:45).

Whitefield's request was followed a year later (April 4, 1768) by a letter from **Thomas Taylor**, a Methodist in New York who described Whitefield's work in the New World: "his words were really as a hammer and as a fire" and enlivened the churches. But the people had not pressed on toward "holiness either of heart or life." Into that situation had come **Phillip Embury**, an Irish class-leader and local preacher who had emigrated to New York, and **Barbara Heck**, his cousin. They had followed the Wesleyan design of forming a little society (*W-A*, 42–43). They had also procured a rigging-loft in which to meet, but Taylor's letter asks Wesley for legal advice and financial assistance in order to build, in **John Street**, the "first preaching-house

Francis Asbury

on the original Methodist plan in all America (excepting Mr. Whitefield's Orphan-House in Georgia)." Taylor also asked Wesley to send an experienced preacher—"a man of wisdom, sound faith, and a good disciplinarian," adding that the Methodists in New York would be willing to sell their coats and shirts to pay for his passage (*W-A*, 79–80).

Wesley brought the matter to the 1768 Conference, along with a similar pressing appeal for help from some people in Maryland who had been awakened under the preaching of **Robert Strawbridge**, another Irish Methodist who had gone to America on his own around 1760. But nothing could be done. The shortage of preachers persisted, as Wesley noted in his *Journal*: "O what can we do for more labourers?" (*J&D*, 22:153). In the meantime, Wesley printed Taylor's letter for distribution to his Assistants. He even suggested to some of his itinerant preachers, such as Christopher Hopper and Joseph Cownley, that if they had a mind to "step over to New York," he would "not say you nay." They did not go. He also gave permission to others, Robert Williams and John King, who went on their own (*W-A*, 81).

At the next Conference, Wesley issued the challenge, "Who is willing to go?" After two days (and probably some arm-twisting by Wesley), Richard Boardman and Joseph Pilmore agreed (if not volunteered) to go—Pilmore to Philadelphia and Boardman to New York. The Conference collected about fifty pounds as a contribution toward the John Street debt (of £400) and another twenty or so for the preachers' passage (*Minutes*, 86). The *Minutes* then record (in answer to the very next Question) that the remaining debt for the connection was between five and six thousand pounds.

Before the year was out, Wesley was contemplating the possibility of going to America again himself (*JWL*, 5:167). At the beginning of

1770, he mentioned the possibility to several correspondents, saying that he had been strongly solicited by friends in Philadelphia and New York, and adding that his "age is no objection at all; for I bless God my health is not barely as good but abundantly better in several respects than when I was five-and-twenty" (*JWL*, 5:183). As the year came to a close, he was still talking about the possibility, but the likelihood becomes more remote during 1771.

Wesley had hoped in early 1770 that Whitefield would be able to take Wesley's place in America by encouraging the young preachers he was sending over. But Whitefield died within half a year, and the relatively in-

Captain Thomas Webb

experienced preachers were left without a leader. Pilmore, nevertheless, gathered together a society of nearly two hundred in less than a year and claimed that, with more preachers, "the American Methodists would soon equal, if not exceed, the Europeans" (Pilmore, 40). He sent to Wesley a strong plea for help, saying that there was work enough at that time for two preachers in each place. At the same time, Pilmore confided to a friend in England that the chief difficulty was lack of ordination, adding, "I believe we shall be obliged to procure it by some means or other" (*W-A*, 90).

There were other Methodist preachers in America, of course, including Williams and King, who had gone over on their own. And **Captain Thomas Webb**, who had retired early from the military with an injury that required an eye-patch, had sparked the early growth of the society in New York with his vibrant preaching (in full regimentals with his sword lying on the pulpit!). But Wesley tried to respond to Pilmore's call for help by recruiting regularly appointed itinerants. The inability to find one that was willing to go reinforced, for a time, Wesley's own inclination to cross the Atlantic. His own hesitance in this matter he attributed to his search for providential guidance. But at the 1771 Conference five volunteers came forward. He chose two:

Richard Wright and Francis Asbury, both only in their mid-twenties, with one and four years of service, respectively. The *Minutes* thus listed the four preachers sent to America (including the two sent in 1769) and a membership of five hundred.

But America was not all that was on Wesley's mind at this time. The Calvinists continued to pressure Wesley. In particular, their patron, Lady Huntingdon, had banned Wesley from her pulpits, complaining that the infamous 1770 Minute contradicted all his other writings. Wesley rightly disputed this point; but he strained his credibility when he tried to explain to her that the "ten lines" in question did not refer to "the condition of obtaining, but of continuing in, the favour of God" (*JWL*, 5:259). Wesley was also attacked by Walter Shirley's *Narrative* (1771) that recounted the main points of the controversy.

Shirley, an evangelical clergyman, was for a time an ally of the Wesleys. But early in 1770, Wesley warned Shirley not to contradict him when preaching in the Wesleyan preaching-houses. After the Conference in August of that year, Shirley entered the lists against Wesley. As the next Conference approached a year later, Wesley sent a circular letter that reprinted and defended the famous Minute, line by line. Walter Shirley likewise produced a circular letter, summoning many Calvinistic friends to a meeting in Bristol coincident with Wesley's Conference. The inevitable confrontation resulted in an explanatory document, signed by Wesley and fifty-three preachers, that seemed to be a Methodist retreat on the necessity of good works for justification. Shirley and his nine or ten friends accepted the olive branch as satisfactorily conciliatory. He then reciprocated by acknowledging publicly that he had been mistaken in his own interpretation of the *Minutes*.

In fact, the paper signed by Wesley and the preachers, which stated, "we abhor the doctrine of justification by works as a most perilous and abominable doctrine," was fully in keeping with Wesley's long-held views and made no new concessions whatsoever. Nevertheless, the carefully-worded final disclaimer seemed to satisfy the critics for the time being:

> And though no one is a real Christian believer (and consequently cannot be saved) who doth not good works when there is time and opportunity, yet our works have no part in meriting or purchasing our justification, from first to last, either in whole or in part (*JWJ*, 5:427).

Thomas Olivers, Wesley's Assistant in Derbyshire, also joined the fray by writing a defense of Wesley against Augustus Toplady (1771). But the mainstay of Wesley's defense was John Fletcher, who had resigned the presidency of Lady Huntingdon's college at Trevecca earlier in the year and whose *Vindication of the Rev. Mr. Wesley's Last Minutes*, published by Wesley right after the Conference of 1771, was the opening shot in a long series of volleys against the Calvinists. The main threat of the Calvinist view, as the Wesleyans saw it, was antinomianism, or neglect of the moral law. Fletcher's writing focused on this issue, starting with this series of five

Mary Bosanquet

letters to Walter Shirley, which became known as the first of his *Checks to Antinomianism* (*Documents*, 4:166).

In his defense of the Wesleyan position, Fletcher went farther than Wesley himself on several points: claiming a "second justification" by works as necessary for final salvation; defining four degrees of justification; referring to perfection as a "second blessing" (although Wesley also uses this term a few times during this period; *JWL*, 6:116). Fletcher's writings convinced the Calvinists that the Wesleyan scheme of salvation was dangerously tainted by a view of synergism that was both Roman Catholic and Pelagian. Olivers' attempt to defend Wesley actually helped substantiate the Calvinists' impression by equating Wesley's views on merit with the late medieval nominalist concept of *meritum de congruo* (Rack, 458). The opposition rose to the occasion with such anonymous publications as *The Jesuit Detected; or, The Church of Rome Discover'd in the Disguise of a Protestant* (1773).

This controversy was the backdrop for two other important developments. The first was a crucial shift in Wesley's attitude toward **women preachers**, spurred by arguments from Mary Bosanquet. Since moving to Yorkshire, she and Sarah Crosby had continued to hold prayer meetings and to speak at meetings in the area, as they worked together with John Oliver and other Methodist preachers. But occasionally, the meetings at which they spoke were held in preaching-houses, and their speaking took on the appearance of preaching. In the spring of 1771, one of the preachers objected to this by saying it was unscriptural for women to speak in the church. Soon, others joined in, using Pauline injunctions against women speaking and teaching.

Mary therefore wrote a letter to Wesley and outlined the various objections and her answers to each. The letter is a masterful combination of biblical exegesis and spiritual mandate. Her basic approach was not to challenge the prejudices against women's abilities or understanding, but rather to ask that they be given the same opportunity to follow their calling under similar rules and restraints. She felt that hers was an extraordinary call: "I do not believe every woman is called to speak publicly, no more than every man to be a Methodist preacher, yet some have an extraordinary call to it, and woe be to them if they obey it not" (*Documents*, 4:171). Wesley accepted the argument of the "**extraordinary call**," recognizing that not only Methodist lay preaching but also "the whole work of God termed Methodism" was an "extraordinary dispensation" of God's providence. Therefore Wesley was willing, like Paul, to make exceptions to the ordinary rules of discipline (*JWL*, 5:257). Wesley's acceptance of the preaching of certain women, however, was only a private accommodation and did not change the normal discipline of the connection as contained in the *Minutes*. His careful control of the issue seems intended to soften the prevailing prejudices on this matter in the mind of the public in order to maximize the benefit of the grace and gifts manifest in the ministry of these women (Chilcote, 171).

Another important development during this period of controversy was the actualization of a large publishing venture that Wesley had been considering for several years—a collected edition of his *Works*. The preface, dated March 1771, explains his intent to "methodize" his writings "under proper heads" so as to illustrate one another. He also wanted to correct them, not only the typographical errors (a problem which unfortunately the printer, William Pine, simply compounded) but also the rational and verbal mistakes. He also wished to correct "the sense," so as to present to the "serious and candid" public "my last and maturest thoughts, agreeable, I hope, to Scripture, reason, and Christian antiquity."

The first four volumes of the *Works* comprised a new edition of his sermons that incorporated nine of his sermons from the 1760s into the forty-three published in the previous four volumes. In keeping with his stated intentions to "methodize" the material, he juxtaposed these newer sermons to the earlier ones in such a way as to make clear that he had revised and clarified his position on many crucial points, notably those at issue with the Calvinists. As a final punctuation mark in this regard, the last sermon in the new collection was his funeral sermon "On the Death of George Whitefield."

These four volumes all appeared before the end of 1771. Another twenty-eight volumes appeared over the next three years, concluding with the latest Extract of his *Journal* (up to September 1770, save one Extract that was inadvertently omitted). One innovation ("a little out of the common way," as Wesley said) that makes these thirty-two volumes especially interesting is his marking with an asterisk those paragraphs that he "judged were most worthy of the reader's notice." Accounts of holy living and remarkable instances of God's providence are among the passages most frequently noted. It is remarkable, then, that Wesley chose not to mark the familiar account of his Aldersgate experience.

Some other preachers were not so hesitant to tout their own conversion experience, and sometimes in language resembling Wesley's own. John Walsh had sent an account of the revival in Everton in 1759, in which he noted how, in one instance, he had told the story of "how God had plucked such a brand as me out of the burning." Walsh then noted, "I have often found that nothing I can say makes so much impression on myself or others as thus repeating my own conversion" (*J&D*, 21:220).

The Methodist revival as a whole continued to depend upon the succession of local **revivals** such as that at Weardale in 1772. A growing feature of these outbreaks of spiritual fervor was the important role of local leaders who could keep the momentum of the revival going daily while the itinerant went on about the round. Wesley was impressed by what happened at Weardale, and in his *Journal* account, compared it favorably with what had happened at Everton over a decade earlier. He noted the similarities (its unexpected outbreak, swift progress, large number of conversions, violent emotions that attended it, and plain people who led it) but also the differences: this was a true revival of the work, not a beginning; the people were awakened and justified in much shorter time; a far greater number were converted; the number of visions and revelations "fatally counterfeited by the devil" were far fewer; and the leading instruments included three itinerant preachers who were "renewed in love" and several local leaders who were "deeply experienced in the work of God." Wesley not only included an account of the thirty children who were caught up in the revival (bringing to mind a similar outbreak at Kingswood when Joseph Benson was headmaster in 1768), but also pointed out that the children at Weardale typified the greater depth of revival there: they had "more constant fellowship with God than the oldest man or woman at Everton" (*J&D*, 22:335–37).

Not everyone was impressed by the Methodist prayer meetings that comprised the heart of many such revivals. James Lackington described the proceedings (after saying in effect you have to see it to believe it): "One wheedles and coaxes the Divine Being in his addresses; another is amorous and luscious; and a third so rude and commanding, he will tell the deity that he must be *a liar* if he does not grant all they ask." Then, he says, the believers, having thus "magnetized" one another's imagination into a state of spiritual intoxication, declare each others sins forgiven, or born again, or sanctified (*Memoirs*, 65).

Other critics of the Methodist people were motivated by more positive concern for the work. Elizabeth Marriott, wife of a London Methodist businessman, suggested to Wesley that not all the preachers were "alive unto God" and "heartily engaged in his work." She hoped that he might promote this end by meeting throughout the year with the preachers in small groups of three or four, as if in a band meeting. By giving strict reproof and clear advice to the preachers, Wesley could multiply his influence for good: one hour spent with the preachers would do more good than a week of writing or preaching. She pressed hard on Wesley's responsibility in this matter: "You are indeed the Father of the people; but the Preachers are in a peculiar sense your Sons in the Gospel. They therefore claim your first attention." And by stirring up one preacher, he might be instrumental in the conversion of hundreds (*Documents*, 4:174–75).

Wesley was, in fact, concerned about the numbers in the United Societies. The membership reports for 1772 and 1773 showed the smallest increases yet recorded in the *Minutes*—462 and 790 respectively (not including America). Many circuits showed decreases and were asterisked in the *Minutes*, five of them for two years in a row (Dublin losing 114, or nearly one-fourth of its members). He had described the problem in Dublin in 1771 in terms of "a general faintness" running through the society. For this, he held the leadership responsible, and met with them several times. On one occasion, he clearly enunciated their various responsibilities and authority in a scheme that also described the overall hierarchical scheme within which the society should work.

> In the Methodist discipline, the wheels regularly stand thus: the Assistant, the preachers, the stewards, the leaders, the people. But here the leaders, who are the lowest wheel but one, were got quite

out of their place. They were got at the top of all, above the stewards, the preachers, yea, and above the Assistant himself. To this chiefly I impute the gradual decay of the work of God in Dublin (*J&D*, 22:268–69).

The controversies seem to have taken their toll. But Wesley's enthusiasm for his Arminian message did not decrease. As he confided to his friend Charles Perronet late in 1774, "If we could once bring all our preachers, itinerant and local, uniformly and steadily to insist on those two points, 'Christ dying for us' and 'Christ reigning in us,' we should shake the trembling gates of hell" (*JWL*, 6:134). These two doctrines, justification and sanctification, still represented the dual thrust of the Methodist message, and Wesley was encouraged that most of the preachers were becoming clear on the matter, especially after reading Fletcher's *Checks* (four volumes of which had appeared by then).

Interest-free note from the Foundery lending-stock, intended to help Methodists improve their trade.

Through the working out of all of these issues, the Methodist mission proceeded apace. Wesley's success in soliciting more capital for the lending stock five years earlier allowed him in 1772 to raise the loans from one to five pounds each. This increase was not simply a response to inflation, but is one indication of the higher level of entrepreneurial involvement of those Methodists who were seeking temporary assistance in their small businesses. One beneficiary of the lending stock was James Lackington, who decided at age twenty-six in 1774 to start a business as a bookseller with three or four dozen of his own books, mostly works of divinity and valued at about five pounds. Being a Methodist (he "caught the infection" as an apprentice cobbler) and living near the Foundery, he arranged for one of the five-pound loans that, he says, were given by Mr. Wesley's people "to such of their society whose characters were good and who wanted [needed] temporary relief." Lackington became a success story, insofar as his business was concerned, increasing his stock five-fold in half a year (and before long, made a fortune), but within two years of getting the loan, he left the Methodists (*Memoirs*, 129–30, 151).

Lackington clearly felt that Wesley was "charitable to an extreme" and that he often gave money to unworthy objects. He noted that, to his knowledge, Wesley never denied relief to a poor person that asked him, and also knew for a fact that on some occasions Wesley gave ten or twenty pounds at once to needy tradesmen (*Memoirs*, 176). The largest portion of the poor to whom Wesley ministered were in the Methodist societies. Lackington himself noted with some astonishment that Wesley could not walk the few yards from his study to the pulpit without giving out coins to the "poor old people of his society" (*Memoirs*, 176). Many of the society who did join in the mission were poor, as Charles recognized in his poetry: "Gladly of that little give, / Poor thyself, the poor relieve" (*Poetical Works*, 9:177). And John pressed his more well-to-do followers also to have the same personal contact with the poor. Methodist charity was largely personal philanthropy. As he told Miss March, "Go and see the poor and sick in their own poor little hovels. Take up your cross, woman! Remember the faith! Jesus went before you, and will go with you" (*JWL*, 6:153). Half a year later, he was still pressing her to follow this aspect of the *imitatio Christi*: "Creep in among these in spite of dirt and an hundred disgusting circumstances, and thus put off the gentlewoman." The lesson was a hard one, and he understood that this was not the option most would prefer, even himself: "Do not confine your conversation to genteel and elegant people. I should like this as well as you do; but I cannot discover a precedent for it in the life of our Lord or any of his apostles" (*JWL*, 6:207). In a follow-up letter, Wesley explained to Miss March that he was not asking her to strike up friendships or acquaintances with "poor, inelegant, uneducated persons," but rather

> to visit the poor, the widow, the sick, the fatherless in their affliction; and this, although they should have nothing to recommend them but that they are bought with the blood of Christ. It is true this is not pleasing to flesh and blood. There are a thousand circumstances usually attending it which shock the delicacy of our nature, or rather of our education. But yet the blessing which follows this labour of love will more than balance the cross (*JWL*, 6:208–9).

The previous year, Wesley had instituted a plan of visitation for himself, starting at one end of the town and visiting each member of the society from house to house. He commented in his Journal, "I know of no branch of the pastoral office which is of greater importance than this." But he also recognized that it was so "grievous to flesh and blood" that he could prevail on few to undertake it, even the preachers (*J&D*, 22:396).

Wesley was not one to blame the poor themselves for their condition. In his "Thoughts on the Present Scarcity of Provisions" (1773), he blames the want of food and housing on a cycle of greed among the "haves" not the idleness of the "have-nots." The cause of the problem, he states more particularly, can be reduced to "distilling, taxes, and luxury," and the remedy entails the implementation of both personal and legal restraints in order to keep thousands of people from starving (*JWW*, 11:57–59).

The Methodists did their part to help alleviate this problem. Money raised in the societies was partly used for local charity—the stewards of the London society distributed seven or eight pounds a week to the poor. And the poor of the society were often exempted from various subscriptions, the Methodist internal revenue system. In 1771, Wesley instituted a connectional subscription as a "new method" to reduce the ongoing debt: have every Methodist give a penny a week for a year (or more if they are so minded). He also stipulated, however, "Let those who are not poor in each Society pay for those that are" (*Minutes*, 100). The result fell short of the projected £6500, but did represent a doubling of the previous year's contribution toward the debt to over three thousand pounds. The following year, he tried yet another method, using an annual collection in the autumn rather than the penny subscription, with the promise that every preaching-house that had a debt on it would receive back at least the amount that was collected there (*Minutes*, 105). That method did not work nearly so well, and the matter was quietly dropped for awhile.

During this same period, the attention of the preachers began to focus again on the question of the future organization of the connection. In 1772, Wesley's *Journal* has no birthday entry, with comments about his remarkable condition. Instead, there is a note that he was reading an ingenious *Treatise on the Hydrocele*. He had more than a passing interest in the subject, suffering at that time himself from this "awkward disorder," as he called it (edema of the scrotum). The problem stemmed from an accident the previous year, when his stumbling horse threw him against the pommel of his saddle. The resulting chronic infirmity served to heighten the realization that Wesley was older than his energetic schedule betrayed. Subsequently, several of his friends had tried to prevent him from riding on horseback and had raised money for a carriage (*JWL*, 5:310). Wesley and his preachers were well aware of the slender thread on which life hangs, and the issue of succession loomed larger.

Wesley felt that, regardless of the official plans laid out for organizing the lay preachers after his death, a clergyman or two should be at the head of the movement (*Church*, 208). His own choice at this point was the new champion of the Methodist cause, John Fletcher, whose own combination of knowledge and vital piety fit the model that Wesley had in mind. Wesley wrote to Fletcher in January 1773, exclaiming, "What an amazing work has God wrought in these kingdoms in less than forty years." But of course the real issue was, what would happen "when Mr. Wesley drops"? Who was sufficient to preside over the work? Wesley gave an extensive description of the perfect leader, and then asked if God had provided anyone so qualified: "Who is he? *Thou art the man!*" (cf. 2 Sam. 12:7; *JWL*, 6:10–11).

Wesley wanted Fletcher to start immediately working into the position, and Charles had reason to hope that this would happen. Charles even encouraged Mark Davis, a former itinerant who had left the connection to take holy orders, to come back in the summer of 1772, hoping that he might play some important role in the years to come. But Fletcher was not ready to leave his parish at Madeley. And the tensions between the lay preachers and the clergy were beginning to mount. The clergy, such as Davis, received a much higher allowance than the preachers, a matter of no small resentment. Also, there was some irritation over having some preachers in full connection who no longer travelled on their own circuit but served as part of a budding curia in London, such as Thomas Olivers, whose appointment as listed in the *Minutes* was, "travels with Mr. Wesley."

At the Conference of 1773, Wesley prevailed upon the preachers again (or at least forty-nine of those present) to sign the Articles of Agreement first drawn up in 1769 and thereby covenant to adhere to each other and to the old Methodist doctrine and discipline. The following year, seventy-two preachers signed, and eighty-one the year after that. Wesley's authoritarian style continued to grate on some. After the 1774 Conference, one of the preachers remarked that "Mr. Wesley seemed to do all the business himself" (*JWJ*, 6:35n). It was a well-known fact that Wesley was no friend to democracy. In his "Thoughts concerning the Origin of Power," Wesley demolished the prevalent myth that "the people" are the source of power. He further explained, in his "Thoughts upon Liberty" (1772), that the good order of King and Parliament were certainly more protective of true **liberty** than the roaring of the "patriot mob" following John Wilkes (fighting entrenched authority of the state) and the petitions emanating from Feathers' Tavern (for relief from subscription to the Articles). He was put off by libertarians and most reformers, and was suspicious of cries

John Fletcher,
Vicar of Madeley

for liberty. Anyone who "bawls for more religious liberty," said Wesley, "must be totally void of shame, and can have no excuse but want of understanding" (*JWW*, 11:34–53).

In the meantime, Wesley's health problems continued. He had succumbed to surgery to drain his hydrocele at the beginning of 1774, but months later his "complaint" was still bothersome, to the point of needing regular attention every nine or ten weeks (in place of the more "radical cure"; *J&D*, 22:395; *JWL*, 6:81). In June of 1775, during his usual biennial tour of Ireland, Wesley fell ill with a fever and was told by a physician to rest. Although he had just written to his brother Charles advising him to "preach as much as you can and no more than you can," John told his doctor that he must preach as long as he could speak (*JWL*, 6:152). He therefore pressed onward through his set itinerary for several days, using some of his "primitive remedies" to treat the ailments, but continually failing in health until he finally was put to bed for two or three days, "being more dead than alive" (by his own estimation). During that spell, Thomas Payne, a Methodist preacher, led a small group in prayer for their leader, asking God to prolong the life of his servant for fifteen years, as in the case of Hezekiah. But in spite of an English newspaper's report of his death at this time, Wesley did in fact respond to some medication given by his preacher companion, Joseph Bradford, and was on the road again in a week. The resulting loss of his hair and trembling of his hand were but temporary inconveniences (*JWJ*, 6:66–71).

In this context, **Joseph Benson**, sensitive to Wesley's condition as well as his outlook on separation from the Church but worried about the insufficiency of many of the preachers and concerned for the future of the connection, proposed a scheme for the regularization of Methodism along ecclesiastical lines. Benson's plan, developed in the summer of 1775, was to examine all the preachers, then set apart those who are qualified for the work of the ministry and set aside those who are deficient in gifts and grace. The borderline cases with potential could be sent to Kingswood School for further training.

John Fletcher, responding to Benson's draft of the "purge and ordain" plan, pointed out the positive implications ("it would cement our union, . . . make us stand more firm to our vocation, . . . give us an outward call to preach and administer the Sacraments") and the negative ("it would cut us off, in a great degree, from the national Churches of England and Scotland, which we are called to leaven"). He expressed some skepticism about "improvement" of the preachers by means of Kingswood, and suggested that the Wesleys might apply to the bishops for help, before "turning bishops" themselves, given their repeated declarations to stand by the Church. Nevertheless, time was running short, as he noted: "God has lately shook Mr. Wesley over the grave" (*JWJ*, 8:328–30).

Fletcher communicated the matter to Wesley, who agreed to hear the proposal at the Conference a fortnight later. In the meantime, Fletcher drew up his own proposal, incorporating some of Benson's ideas but going further toward suggesting the organization of a **"daughter church** of our holy mother." He appealed to Wesley's role as an "extraordinary messenger of God," playing on Wesley's view of the work of Methodism as the unfolding of God's providence. John was writing his *Concise History of England* at the time and had told his brother that he was thereby going to improve upon the work of Oliver Goldsmith and Nathaniel Hooke because, as he said, "My view in writing history (as in writing philosophy) is to bring God into it" (*JWL*, 6:67). Fletcher could do the same.

The plan that Fletcher sent to Wesley on the opening day of the Conference of 1775 proposed an alternative to the Feathers' Tavern approach, one that would reform "without perverting" the Church. Fletcher suggested that the "general society" of Methodists ("the Methodist church of England") should "recede" from the Church only in some "palpable defects about doctrine, discipline, and unevangelical hierarchy," but still approve of her ordination, partake of her Sacraments, and attend her services at every convenient opportunity. This reform would entail publishing a revised Thirty-nine Articles, "rectified according to the purity of the gospel," along with some "needful alterations in the liturgy [Book of Common Prayer] and the Homilies." The rectified Articles, the most spiritual part of the prayer book, and the *Minutes* would then represent (next to the Bible) the *vade mecum* or handbook of the Methodist preachers, for whom Kingswood School would become a center of education, renewal, and retirement.

This action would not be considered a schism, but rather a return to "the purity of the gospel, the strictness of primitive discipline, and the original design of the Church of England." The bishops would be asked to ordain preachers certified by "Messrs. Wesley and some more clergymen," and if this were not granted, the Wesleys would be obliged to take the "irregular (not unevangelical) step" of ordaining those preachers, who would serve as Assistants in the circuits (worthy Helpers would be ordained Deacons). Confirmation would be performed by Wesley, or by three or five Moderators who would be appointed to succeed Wesley at his death.

This whole scheme was designed to enable the "grand plan" for

Time Line 7
The Maturing of Methodism

1760	1765	1770	1775
George II		George III	
Seven Years' War			
	Stamp Act	Whitefield dies	American Revolution begins
Voltaire's *Candide*	"Large" *Minutes*	Watt's steam engine	JW's *Works*
Sermons, vol. 4	Annual *Minutes*		
Mozart born	Model Deed	Asbury to America	City Road Chapel
Select Hymns with Tunes		"Scripture Way of Salvation"	*Calm Address*
	Perfection controversy	Calvinist controversy	
Women preachers		Preachers	First	British preachers
	Plain Account of Christian Perfection	to America	American Conference	leave America
Original Sin	Preachers' Fund	"Articles of Agreement"	Benson/Fletcher plan
	Heptonstall octagon built		
"On the Use of Money"		Methodist Sunday School	

the preachers: "to preach the doctrine of grace against the Socinians, the doctrine of justice against the Calvinists, and the doctrine of holiness against all the world" (*JWJ*, 8:331–34). Fletcher's letter apparently did not reach Wesley at Leeds during the Conference. Benson did propose his plan at the Conference, and a committee of preachers did examine all and set aside some ("I fear not all who ought," complained Benson). A fortnight later, Wesley wrote to Fletcher, "We followed your advice and were more exact than ever in examining the preachers both as to grace and gifts" (*JWL*, 6:174). But neither the *Minutes* nor the correspondence makes any mention of Fletcher's proposal, which Wesley apparently left in his pocket for the time being. The session ended with eighty-one preachers signing the Articles of Agreement.

The organizational problem that had caught Wesley's attention in the meantime was the situation in America. In April 1773, Wesley had sent **Thomas Rankin** to the colonies as his General Assistant in order to correct difficulties caused by Boardman's and Pilmore's failure to continue as "genuine Methodists both in doctrine and discipline" (*JWL*, 6:57). Shortly after his arrival, Rankin held the first Conference of Methodist preachers in America. His agenda was to the point; the *Minutes* were short (two pages): three questions for the preachers, six rules, and the list of preachers and numbers in society. The opening questions tied the preachers to the authority of Mr. Wesley and specified their rules of doctrine and discipline to be those in the *Minutes*. The six particular rules listed were aimed at specific problems, persons, and places, including an injunction against administering the Sacraments (especially in Maryland and Virginia) and a prohibition on reprinting any of Wesley's books without his authority (which Robert Williams had done). It was an intimate gathering, reminiscent of a similar occasion nearly thirty years earlier. In America now, they were organizing in a Conference with ten preachers who served 1,160 members in five circuits.

The political unrest in the American colonies over the previous decade in the aftermath of military action against the French, continued to escalate, from the protests against the Stamp Act in 1765 to the Boston Tea Party in 1773. In March 1775, Wesley had advised the preachers in America to "be peace-makers, to be loving and tender to all, but to addict yourselves to no party" (*JWL*, 6:142). He told his brother Charles that his view of the situation had remained unchanged: "If a blow is struck, I give America for lost, and perhaps England too" (*JWL*, 6:152). But within days, word reached England that rioting had given way to warfare: the gunfire at Concord and

Lexington had been heard across the Atlantic, and the colonists' resolve at Bunker Hill would send a signal to Parliament.

In mid-June, just before his illness in Ireland, Wesley wrote a letter to the **Earl of Dartmouth** (Secretary of State for the Colonies) and then sent a copy to **Lord North** (prime minister and First Lord of the Treasury). His sentiments are clear.

> I do not intend to enter upon the question whether the Americans are in the right or in the wrong. Here all my prejudices are against the Americans; for I am an High Churchman, the son of an High Churchman, bred up from my childhood in the highest notions of passive obedience and non-resistance. And yet, in spite of all my long-rooted prejudices, I cannot avoid thinking, if I think at all, these, an oppressed people, asked for nothing more than their legal rights, and that in the most modest and inoffensive manner that the nature of the thing would allow (*JWL*, 6:161).

Wesley, cautiously echoing the opposition sentiments of Edmund Burke and William Pitt, then argued for conciliation and spoke against pressing the military cause in the American colonies as a losing proposition. He went on to point out that the real enemies were at home and were spreading sedition such that the bulk of the population (including multitudes who have nothing to do and nothing to eat) had been "effectually cured of all love and reverence for the King" and only awaited a leader to effect a revolution (*JWL*, 6:161–63).

The Methodists in America had been placed in an awkward position. Part of a British movement led by a staunchly loyal Tory, they had been asked to be peacemakers by their leader, which many colonists saw (along with pacifism) as equivalent to being a Loyalist, and treasonous to the American cause. Wesley's actual position, as expressed to North and Dartmouth, was not known in the colonies, and the communications across the ocean were slow. Wesley had begun to suggest to Rankin early in the spring of 1775 that Francis Asbury be sent back to England. At the Conference in August, he learned that Asbury would be staying in America for another year. Wesley wrote to Rankin that he was not sorry: "In that time it will be seen what God will do with North America, and you will easily judge whether our preachers are called to remain any longer therein" (*JWL*, 6:173).

Chapter 5—Suggested Additional Reading

Chilcote, Paul, *John Wesley and the Women Preachers of Early Methodism* (Metuchen, NJ: Scarecrow Press, 1991).

Church, Leslie, *The Early Methodist People* (London: Epworth Press, 1948).

HAM — Bucke, Emory Stevens, ed., *The History of American Methodism*, 3 vols. (Nashville: Abingdon Press, 1964).

Lyles, Albert M. *Methodism Mocked; The Satiric Reaction to Methodism in the Eighteenth Century* (London: Epworth Press, 1960).

Maser, Frederick E., *Robert Strawbridge, First American Circuit Rider* (Rutland, VT: Academy Books, 1983).

Memoirs — Lackington, James, *Memoirs of James Lackington, in Forty-seven Letters to a Friend* (London, 1794).

Poetical Works — John Wesley and Charles Wesley, *The Poetical Works of John and Charles Wesley*, ed. George Osborn, 13 vols. (London: Wesleyan Methodist Conference Office, 1868–71).

Pilmore, Joseph, *The Journal of Joseph Pilmore*, ed. Frederick E. Maser and Howard T. Maag (Philadelphia: Historical Society, 1969).

W-A — Baker, Frank, *From Wesley to Asbury; Studies in Early American Methodism* (Durham, NC: Duke University Press, 1976).

CHAPTER 6

Tensions and Transitions (1775–1791)

John Wesley prided himself in his lifelong consistency. As he grew older, his writings were sprinkled with comments like "just as I did thirty or forty years ago." As the century wore on, however, his longevity challenged his persistence. The rate of social, industrial, and political change began to accelerate. Revolutionary ideas at home and abroad quickened the pace at which important issues were reconsidered. Although Wesley did not easily admit to changes, he was always open to new truths and was at times constrained to rethink many of his own positions on crucial issues as situations changed and his own perceptions matured. Sometimes his revisions were slow and subtle over the years; at other times they were quick and forceful.

Theological and Political Polemics

The maturation of Wesley's theology reflected the unfolding procession of his spiritual pilgrimage. His long struggle with the questions of faith and assurance led to some modifications of his earlier Moravian-influenced positions. Although he struggled with these views for many years in the light of his personal experience, he was not inclined to discuss these matters explicitly in the successive extracts of his published *Journal*, which resembles a chronicle of events more than a reflective autobiography. Nevertheless, the *Journal* attracted many readers over the years, so that Wesley continued to reissue the early extracts.

By 1775, in the fifth edition of the earliest two extracts, he felt compelled to note that his earlier accounts from around the time of his Aldersgate experience were not quite accurate, from his later vantage point. Even at this stage, however, he did not feel obliged to revise the earlier text. Instead, he simply chose to add an errata sheet that included some very significant disclaimers to his earlier evaluations published in 1740: "I who went to America to convert others, was never myself converted to God" (1775—"I am not sure of this"); "[I lack] faith in Christ" (1775—"I had even then the faith of a *servant*, though not that of a *son*"); "I am 'a child of wrath.'" (1775—"I believe not"); "I was persuaded that . . . I was even then [1728–29] in a state of salvation" (1775—"And I believe I was"); "I had been all this time building on the sand" (1775—"Not so: I was right, as far as I went").

Although in 1738, Wesley had told Mrs. Hutton that previous to his Aldersgate experience he had not been a Christian, nearly forty

years later he was now willing to grant that those who had the "faith of a servant" (as well as many believers who had not yet received assurance) should be considered as Christians, accepted of God (Acts 10:35). These emendations represent the culmination of a series of shifts in perspective, and although somewhat unusual in their public form of admission, they are fully in keeping with Wesley's life-long habit of self-examination and reflection on his own spiritual condition.

This seal with Wesley's initials, used during the period 1774-85, is only one of over forty that he used during his lifetime.

On the other hand, Wesley changed his mind on the political situation in America almost overnight. At the end of September 1775, after reading Samuel Johnson's *Taxation no Tyranny*, he decided that the colonists' arguments, such as "no taxation without representation," held no moral or legal weight and that their cries for liberty were as irresponsible as those of Wilkes and others in England itself. He quickly published an extract and paraphrase of Johnson's work under the title, *A Calm Address to our American Colonies*. The "provoking" tract sold briskly— above 40,000 copies in three weeks (*JWL*, 6:182).

Although Dr. Johnson was apparently flattered by this unacknowledged borrowing, the critics charged Wesley with blatant plagiarism, as well as with reversing his position. The Calvinist, Augustus Toplady, relished the opportunity to blast his Arminian nemesis. A strong supporter of the Americans, Toplady published *An Old Fox Tarr'd and Feather'd* (1775), a fanciful and satiric account that tried to expose Wesley's motives and tactics as "a low and puny TADPOLE in Divinity, which proudly seeks to disembowel an high and mighty WHALE in Politics" (*EMW*, 117). This attack was followed by a similar literary assault from Caleb Evans in a letter to Wesley. But once again, John Fletcher stood by Wesley's side, this time on the American issue, and returned a blast in Evans' direction with *A Vindication of the Rev. Mr. Wesley's "Calm Address to Our American Colonies"* (1776). Fletcher agreed with Wesley that the real threat was at home in the "flame of malice and rage against the King and almost all that are in authority," spread by the seditious words of the libertarians. The response that Fletcher's attack elicited from Toplady is no surprise, either in tone or content: "The Switz mountain is, at length, delivered of its mice; which were begotten upon it, by the pressing necessity of Mr. John Wesley. And, to give the little squeakers their due, they resemble their progenitors to an hair" (*Documents*, 4:186).

Wesley did not lay down his own pen, however, and soon countered with another short treatise, *Some Observations on Liberty* (1776), in which he argues that the Americans have always enjoyed liberty; what they are asking for is independence, based on a concept of popular democracy that is not really democratic (excluding from power the women, youth, poor, etc.) and that will bring nothing but anarchy and confusion. Wesley falls back on the same principle again and again: "There is no power but of God" (*JWW*, 11:98–105).

Then in a sequel to his earlier essay, Wesley published *A Calm Address to the Inhabitants of England* (1777), in which he recounts the state of affairs in America, from the time his brother Charles heard the inhabitants of Boston crying for independence from the "English yoke," to the current military confrontation in which the Americans "roar like a wild bull in a net." His point is simple—such a position holds no prospect for real liberty: "Do you not observe, wherever these bawlers for liberty govern, there is the vilest slavery?" Moreover, he specifically encouraged those who are "vulgarly called Methodists" (who, he points out to friend and foe, do not blaspheme God or the King if they intend to stay in connection with him) to savor the unique civil and religious liberty that they enjoy as British subjects. He echoes points he made in a letter to Lord Dartmouth in which he warns against governmental complacency on matters of trade and employment. Wesley says that, in his travels across the length and breadth of the land, he has found thousands of unemployed people perishing and "creeping up and down like walking shadows," full of the spirit of murder and rebellion and heartily despising the king. Moreover, Wesley claims to be in a small minority (one or two of twenty) who felt at all constrained to defend the king (*JWL*, 6:176). In this context, Wesley was indeed active in helping to quell a spirit of revolt among the potentially rebellious segments of British society.

In the midst of these political polemics, Wesley was asked to preach a **charity sermon** at St. Matthew's Church, Bethnal Green, to benefit the widows and children of war victims. There he spread the blame a bit further: the British, he said, were suffering the miseries of war in

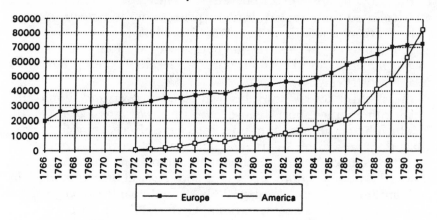

Membership of Methodist Societies

The Methodist movement in the British Isles showed a relatively slow but steady growth over the years; in America, the movement started later but grew faster.

the current conflagration as a result of the sins of all the people. His prescriptive message was clear: repent, fear God, and honour the king. Anticipating that "many would seek offense" at his words, he carefully wrote down the sermon in advance (No. 111, "National Sins and Miseries," *Sermons*, 3:564–76).

But negative reaction did not deter him from his campaign. Wesley soon reiterated this theme in a pamphlet with a typical eighteenth-century title: *A Seasonable Address to the more Serious Part of the Inhabitants of Great Britain, respecting the Unhappy Contest between Us and our American Brethren: with an Occasional Word interspersed to Those of a Different Complexion. By a Lover of Peace* (1776). The point was simple: no one could be exempt from blame, since the "universal impiety" of the people was "the first and principal cause of our misery and wretchedness in general and of the present distress in particular" (*JWW*, 11:127–28).

Wesley's explicit anti-American stance added more strain to the tenuous political position of his Methodist followers in America. Many of them were consequently suspected, by association, of having Loyalist sympathies. All of the Methodist preachers who had been appointed to the American colonies by Wesley, therefore, returned to England by 1777, except Francis Asbury, whose sympathies rested with the Americans. His convictions, however (in keeping with Wesley's explicit comments in his treatise on *Original Sin*), were pacifist, and he was therefore misunderstood by many of the more rabid "patriots" as being non-supportive of, if not traitorous to, the American revolutionary cause. Both Wesley's and Asbury's political views seemed to hurt the Methodist societies in the northern American circuits, which lost nearly half their members during the period 1775–77. But such views by their leaders did not prevent a swelling of revival spirit in 1776 among the Methodists in the south, where the membership grew by more than two thousand.

In England, the Methodist societies continued their steady but uneven growth of about sixteen hundred members a year. About a fourth of the circuits showed a yearly decrease (and were thus asterisked in the *Minutes*), but many of the others showed sizeable gains. In 1775, Leeds became the second circuit, along with London, to have over two thousand members, its size having doubled over the previous decade while London remained at 2500, the same as twenty years earlier. Within the societies, classes that had increased to more than thirty persons were required to divide (*Minutes*, 120).

Now a septuagenarian, Wesley was still a vital and active leader. In his 1776 birthday self-evaluation, he noted that he was able to preach even better than at twenty-three because of the exercise and fresh air from his constant traveling, the ability to sleep easily and regularly, and an evenness of temper. As he said, "I *feel* and *grieve*, but by the grace of God, I *fret* at nothing" (*JWJ*, 6:113–14). He still cultivated a lively interest in medicine and health. *Primitive Physick*, his book of home remedies, had by 1776 gone through at least 17 editions (each one expanded and several reprinted in America; see *EMW*, 1:134–44). It was then attacked by a young London physician, William Hawes, who was just coming into his own through his well-publicized efforts to develop successful methods of treating asphyxia. Hawes' often heavy-handed attack portrayed Wesley as a quack who was not only ineffectual but a definite menace to society. Hawes did have some right on his side, however. Through a continued misprint, Wesley had unwittingly prescribed as a vomit for poisoning "one or two drams of distilled verdigris" (enough to kill forty people) in error for "one or two grains"—a correction which he immediately made in the 1776 edition (see *EMW*, 2:136–37). Wesley's fondness for electrifying, also one of Hawes' own particular interests, escaped criticism. Hawes also ignored Wesley's suggestion of using mouth-to-mouth resuscitation for asphyxia or drowning, even though Hawes had two years earlier founded the Society for the Recovery of Persons Apparently Dead by Drowning (later the Royal Humane Society), which offered monetary rewards for workable methods of resuscitation.

Wesley himself, however, was more interested in reviving souls than in saving drowning bodies. One among several hindrances to the revival work that especially concerned him was the presence of un-qualified preachers. At the Conference of 1776, the examination of the preachers became more pointed, because of the acknowledged objection "that some are utterly unqualified for the work, and that others do it negligently, as if they imagined they had nothing to do but to preach once or twice a day." To meet this complaint, Wesley examined with special care those about whom there was some doubt. The results were recorded in the *Minutes*: "One was excluded for insufficiency, two for misbehaviour. And we were thoroughly satisfied that all the rest had both grace and gifts for the work wherein they are engaged. I hope, therefore, we shall hear of this objection no more."

The following year, the same question concerning the preachers resulted in another general objection, that "most of them are not called of God to preach," or at least may have "forfeited their calling." John knew that the preachers were crucial to the success of the revival. From Bristol, where the Conference was being held, he stated his position clearly in a letter to Alexander Mather, one of his Assistants: "Give me one hundred preachers who fear nothing but sin and desire nothing but God, and I care not a straw whether they be clergymen or laymen, such alone will shake the gates of hell and set up the kingdom of heaven upon earth" (*JWL*, 6:272; cf. 6:134).

Perhaps the American situation had prejudiced Wesley's view of overseas work, however, for when his new Assistant, Thomas Coke, recently from Ireland, suggested a Methodist mission to Africa, Wesley decided that "the call seems doubtful." Thomas Taylor, who noted this decision in his diary, also reported that although the Conference discussed the issue for an hour and a half, it "might have been done in five minutes." He went on to say, "We are vastly tedious, and have many long speeches to little purpose" (*JWJ*, 6:206n).

At this same 1777 Conference, Wesley for the first time memori-alized the preachers who had died in the work during the previous year. The *Minutes* lists those preachers, with brief comments (some less than tributes) sufficing as **obituaries**: "John Slocomb, at Clones: an old labourer, worn out in the service. John Harrison, near Lisburn: a promising youth, serious, modest, and much devoted to God. William Lumley, in Hexham: a blessed young man, a happy witness of the full liberty of the children of God. And William Minethorp, near Dunbar: an Israelite indeed, in whom was no guile" (*Minutes*, 127).

In addition to unqualified preachers, Wesley saw the continuing presence of Calvinism among the Methodists as a hindrance to the work. Speaking to this threat at the 1776 Conference, Wesley had noted that many people readily swallowed the Calvinist line because it was "so pleasing to flesh and blood," especially the doctrine of final perseverance. To stop its progress, Wesley suggested that the preachers read Fletcher's writings carefully, preach universal redemption explicitly, and visit the people diligently, but by no means imitate the Calvinists themselves by "screaming, allegorizing, calling themselves ordained," or a number of other temptations. His concluding suggestion was to pray that "God would stop the plague" of Calvinism, which he soon came to recognize as "the direct antidote to Methodism" (*Minutes*, 126–27, 667).

Often using the *The Spiritual Magazine* and *The Gospel Magazine* as vehicles of their venom, the Calvinists continued their concerted attacks upon Wesley. "The Serpent and the Fox," published anonymously in the latter in 1777, exemplifies the scurrility that appeared under the guise of light-hearted criticism. Using the format of a conversation between Old Nick the fiend and Old John the priest, the author portrays the two as plotting to obliterate the Calvinists, who represent a threat to both of them (*EMW*, 2:122–25). The published attacks took a number of other forms as well. One anonymous author, using the reaction to Wesley's *Calm Address* as the initial occasion, published a series of six pamphlets, each containing a lengthy satirical poem that mocked the enthusiastical mob of fanatics called Methodists, as well as their leader. The resulting caricature of Wesley and his followers is at times crudely obscene, as are the frontispieces that illustrate the text of each (*EMW*, 2:103–15). The Methodists may have opened themselves to criticism by the secretive (if not subversive) appearance of limiting their meetings to members with class tickets (*JWL*, 6:265). But even a gullible public would probably not have taken seriously the critic's portrayal, in *Fanatical Conversion*, of the Methodist love-feast as an orgy where "virgins are debauch'd in *sainted* dreams." The satirical picture of the Methodists typically builds upon a misconstrual of their terms and practices:

> To Reynard's Tabernacle lent at last,
> Infecting converts with its pois'nous blast;
> Whose strong effluviae young and old confound,
> And stretch the passive virgin on the ground;
> Chiefly on Watch-Nights, or Love's annual Feast,
> When victims fall before lewd Murcia's priest,
> Celestial impregnation to receive,
> And share those gifts which all who feel believe.
> (*EMW,* 2:108–9)

The author planned to produce more poems, but he seems to have saturated his market with the first half-dozen, and the Methodists were spared his further ridicule.

In November 1777, Wesley decided to meet the Calvinist challenge head-on by producing a monthly magazine himself. His introductory comments to the reader of the *Arminian Magazine* are aimed directly at his competitors, the two Calvinist magazines. He points out that writers in the two magazines not only have championed the doctrine that "Christ did not die for all, but for one in ten, for the elect only," but also have defended their "dear decrees with arguments worthy of Bedlam and with language worthy of Billingsgate" (the notorious mental hospital and the infamous fish market, respectively). Wesley's monthly magazine would have four parts: 1) writings that defended universal redemption (atonement); 2) biographies of holy persons; 3) letters and accounts of the experience of pious living persons; and 4) poetry that explained and confirmed the essential doctrines. The whole was designed to be a primer in holy living and holy dying, a handbook of the spiritual pilgrimage. The first issue began with the life of that great defender of universal atonement, Arminius, which set the tone of, as well as gave the title to, the whole series. Wesley was aware that its name would offend some, but he was confident that ninety-nine in a hundred persons in England rejected absolute predestination and would thus not take offense at his choice of title (*JWW*, 14:278–81).

The increased demands of the Wesleyan publishing program called for a full-time editor. Thomas Olivers had become the connectional "corrector of the press" by 1776 and was stationed at Wesley's side in London. He was not the only preacher who was part of a budding Methodist bureaucracy: Joseph Bradford was assigned to travel with Mr. Wesley and John Atlay to keep his accounts and soon to become "book steward." In the meantime, the Foundery, the London headquarters of the movement and the location of everything from preaching to printing (as well as the Sacrament since 1774), faced the prospect of being torn down. Planning for a new building had begun in March 1776, and later that year Wesley appealed to the whole connection to help the society in London. In April 1777, he laid the foundation for a new Methodist **chapel in City Road** across from Bunhill Fields, the Dissenter burial grounds.

He also used that occasion to preach a sermon outlining the history of Methodism (with some convenient revisions) as "the rise and progress" of an "extraordinary work of God." His main point was that Methodism was not a new religion but was simply the "old" religion

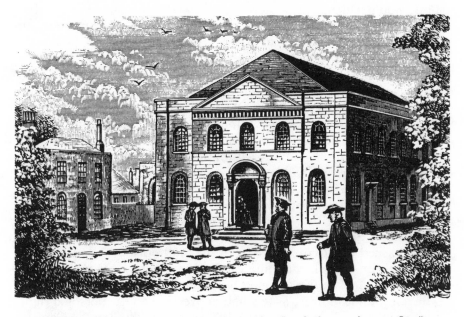

Wesley described the New Chapel in City Road as "perfectly neat, but not fine."
Opened in November 1778, it held as many worshipers as Whitefield's tabernacle
and replaced the smaller Foundery as Wesley's headquarters in London.

of the Bible, of the Primitive Church, and indeed of the Church of
England (*Sermons*, 3:577–92). He especially stressed that Methodists
never had any intention of separating from the Church. The very
architecture of the new chapel belied his argument, however. In spite
of suggestions in the 1776 *Minutes* that the preaching-houses should
be built either in the octagon style as at Yarm or as the square model
at Scarborough, Wesley built the chapel in City Road on the traditional
basilica plan that represented more traditional, if not to say sacramental, ecclesiastical architecture. The premises, with Wesley's new house
alongside, became a center of preaching, fellowship, and social service,
as well as of sacramental worship, and thus, with a high level of
self-sufficiency, functioned like a parish church (even with a burial
ground on the site). It was, however, unconsecrated and totally outside
the diocesan control of the Church (*Church*, 213-14). The trustees, who
did control the property, were an interesting mix of twenty-five men,
who included five weavers, a silk broker, three merchants, a gentleman, and a banker, and came from over a dozen different parishes
(*People*, 83).

The pulpit at City Road was, nevertheless, virtually restricted to
Methodist preachers who were ordained clergy. This constraint itself

presented problems, since there were so few who qualified under that limitation. Charles Wesley seems to have quickly monopolized the pulpit in City Road, much to the chagrin of some of the senior itinerants, such as John Pawson and Thomas Rankin, who disliked both Charles's "dry and lifeless" preaching and his distrust of itinerants. Other preachers, such as John Whitehead, began to push for the administration of the Sacrament at City Road during Church hours on Sunday morning, a move which John Wesley still managed to resist.

The tension between clergy and lay preachers within Methodism tested Wesley's resolve to stay within the Church. Edward Smyth, an Irish clergyman who had been dismissed from his curacy because of his Methodist practices, had publicly stated at the Irish Conference in 1778 his desire to separate from the "corrupt" Church. Wesley managed to reinforce the other preachers' resolve to stay within the Church on that occasion. When Smyth moved his family to Bath, Wesley asked him to preach there at the Methodist preaching-house, much to the chagrin of some of the lay itinerants there, such as Alexander McNab, the Assistant appointed to supervise that circuit. The question thus arose as to whether Wesley had the personal right to appoint preachers or whether that right was vested in the Conference, as McNab began to claim.

In November 1779, Wesley tried to resolve the problem in the Bristol/Bath area. Upon visiting the Bath society, he read a paper prepared nearly twenty years earlier (perhaps for the Norwich Society in 1760; see above, pp. 206f.), pointed out that "the rules of our preachers were fixed by me before any Conference existed," and noted in particular the twelfth rule: "Above all, you are to preach when and where I appoint." Wesley then relieved McNab of his preaching responsibilities "till he was of another mind" (*JWJ*, 6:262–63).

Charles saw the McNab affair as part of a larger conspiracy among the lay preachers, who were infected with "a spirit of pride and self-seeking." By overthrowing John Wesley, they would hasten a separation from the Church and thereby increase the possibility of ordination for themselves. John Pawson, challenging Charles's interpretation of events, claimed that the matter was a local squabble at Bath. Charles saw Pawson as one of the ring-leaders and warned brother John. John reinforced Charles's worries when he reinstated McNab within three months and essentially ignored the warning that it would hasten the day of ordinations and separation. Charles, however, not inclined to "stand by and see the ruin of our cause" (*Church*, 216), had produced a strongly worded poem against the lay preachers, part of which reads:

They now preeminence affect
　Eager to form the rising Sect,
Some better thing to gain:
　Like hireling priests, they serve for hire,
And thro' ambition blind, aspire
　Without the cross to reign.
(*Documents*, 4:190)

This increasing tension between the preachers, and consequently between the Wesley brothers, strengthened a growing tendency among the opposing parties to use historical reflections to undergird their positions. John Wesley now told the story of the rise of Methodism as the story of his own singular quest for holiness at Oxford, as described in his sermon at City Road in 1777. As he said on this occasion (using the third person to describe himself), "For several years [after 1725] he was constrained to travel alone, having no man either to guide or to help him. But in the year 1729, he found one who had the same desire" (*Sermons*, 3:581). Writing to Thomas Taylor in 1779, he expands upon this part of the story: "It pleased God by me to awaken, first my brother, and then a few others; who severally desired of me as a favour that I would direct them in all things." The rest of John's story unfolds in similar fashion, with various other "sons in the gospel" asking him to direct them, and the various structures of Methodism resulting from his efforts. The conclusion is obvious: "Whoever, therefore, violates the conditions, particularly that of being directed by me in the work, does *ipso facto* disjoin himself from me" (*JWL*, 6:375). In Wesley's mind, primacy in the history could easily be translated into primacy in the present.

Charles, however, used a contrary translation of those events. His account of the beginnings was becoming quite different from John's, especially in the context of these disputes. Charles wrote a letter to Dr. Thomas Chandler, an American clergyman, in which he tried with some subtlety to insinuate his own position of power in the 1770s by showing that he himself was the instigator of Methodism at Oxford. Charles carefully arranged the order of events in his story so as to portray John coming back onto the scene at Oxford after the movement was well underway (*Documents*, 4:204). Neither Charles nor his version of Methodist origins carried the day, perhaps in part because his story did not coincide with records of those early events. Moreover, his political clout was no match for that of his brother within Methodism.

In spite of all the tensions, John exhibited his concern for the preachers in a variety of ways, not least of which was to give advice to

The new cast iron bridge at Coalbrookdale was a fitting symbol of the developing industrial strength of the Midlands in the 1770s.

them concerning their **health**. At the Conference in 1778, John asked the question, "Why do so many of our preachers fall into nervous disorders?" The answer, "Because they do not sufficiently observe Dr. Cadogan's rules: To avoid indolence and intemperance." In order to promote good health through exercise and temperance, Wesley gave six bits of advice that no doubt reflected his own practice:

1. Touch no dram, tea, tobacco, or snuff.
2. Eat very light, if any, supper.
3. Breakfast on nettle or orange-peel tea.
4. Lie down before ten; rise before six.
5. Every day use as much exercise as you can bear; or
6. Murder yourself by inches.

In many of these matters, Wesley tried to keep up to date as much as possible, such as by reading the latest publications in medicine and science. In April 1779, after preaching in Shrewsbury, he walked to Coalbrookdale to look at the construction site for a new bridge over the Severn. The world's first cast-iron bridge, it consisted of a hundred-foot arch, fifty-two feet high and thirty-four feet wide, and weighed 378 tons. He was appropriately impressed: "I doubt whether the Colossus at Rhodes weighed much more" (*JWJ*, 6:226).

Many of his interests, of course, were quite directly related to his work with the Methodists. So his article, "Thoughts upon the Power of Music" (1779), was not simply theory, but had a practical application. That he favored a strong melody line to raise the passions in the human mind is clearly implied also in the negative: "What has counterpoint to do with the passions?" One should initiate nature in its melodic simplicity (*Collection,* 767).

This work was prefatory to the production of a new *Collection of Hymns* in 1780, the largest of the Wesleyan hymn publications. The 525 hymns were not ordered with the typical Anglican deference to the liturgical calendar, but rather were "carefully ranged under proper heads according to the experience of real Christians." The book was, in effect (to use Wesley's words), "a little body of experimental and practical divinity," exhibiting the *via salutis*. It also contained "no doggerel, no botches, ... nothing turgid or bombast on the one hand, nor low and creeping on the other." One would find no "*cant* expressions." Rather, here one would find "the purity, the strength, and the elegance of the English language." In fact, John had excluded a few of Charles's hymns (such as "Jesu, Lover of my Soul") from the collection on these very grounds. Wesley felt that he and Charles had produced an incomparable collection that breathed the true spirit of poetry, which, however, was properly kept in its place as "the hand-maid of piety" (*Collection,* 56, 74-75).

The *Collection of Hymns* had no musical notation, but Wesley produced *Sacred Harmony* almost simultaneously. This tune-book was basically a reissue of the tunes from *Sacred Melody* (1761), but with the music "in two or three parts for the voice, harpsichord, and organ" (*Collection,* 25). More often than not, of course, there would be no harpsichord or organ available; the hymns would be "lined out" by the leader, one line at a time. Wesley was known occasionally to have used an oboe player to assist the people with the tunes.

At this time, Wesley also became embroiled in another political controversy, now through his opposition to the Catholic Relief Act of 1778. His own treatise, *Popery Calmly Considered* (1779), reflected the traditional English Protestant bias. He reiterated this view in a strongly worded letter to the editor of *The Public Advertiser* in January 1780, in which he supported the work of the newly-formed Protestant Association, headed by **Lord George Gordon**. While not ready to persecute any person for their religious principles, Wesley was quick to insist that "no [non-Catholic] government ought to tolerate men of the Roman Catholic persuasion." The reason was simple: no Roman Catholic could give security for their allegiance or peaceable behavior, since they hold to the maxim, "no faith is to be kept with heretics" and since the pope has the power to dispense with any promise, oath, or vow (*JWL,* 6:370-73).

Many were "grievously offended" by his letter; others, including his old Calvinist protagonists in the *Gospel Magazine,* heartily approved it and circulated it as a broadside. Wesley was absent from London in June 1780 when Lord Gordon led twenty thousand supporters on a march to Parliament with a petition to repeal the Catholic Relief Act. When the House of Commons adjourned rather than consider the appeal, riots broke out. For four days London suffered pillaging and burning. Lord Gordon was thrown into the Tower prison, where Wesley visited him in December, talked with him about popery, and noted that such confinement would no doubt "prove a lasting blessing to him" (*JWJ*, 6:301).

Controversy of a different sort had been brewing among the Methodists in America. The outbreak of military conflict that had sent Wesley's preachers back to England also reduced the number of Church of England priests in the American colonies. Their departure left not only the Anglicans but also the Methodists without the administration of the Sacrament. In 1777, the question of Methodists administering the Sacrament arose, but was deferred. In 1779, after having laid the question over another year, the Methodist preachers who met in **Conference at Fluvanna**, Virginia, voted 19 to 10 to form a presbytery of four to ordain each other, and then the rest, in order to provide clergy to administer the Sacrament to the people. This action was, in part, the consequence of two Wesleyan principles: the necessity of constant Communion and the prerequisite of ordination for administration of the Sacrament. Wesley himself would have strongly opposed this action, however, since it was so blatant a breach of the ordered structures of the Church and represented a palpable step towards separation. Francis Asbury, in political seclusion in Delaware and unable to attend the southern Conference, also strongly opposed this action. He viewed the proceedings as "effecting a lame separation from the Episcopal Church that will last about one year" (*Asbury*, 1:304).

The following year, the northern preachers, under Asbury's guidance, voted "to sit in Conference on the original plan, as Methodists." Asbury proposed to attend the southern Conference with a request that they suspend their sacramental actions for a year, during which time Mr. Wesley would be consulted. To support his point, Asbury then read to the group Mr. Wesley's thoughts against separation, as well as Wesley's private letters of instruction to him as General Assistant (the northern preachers had named him General Superintendent). After some initial resistance, the Conference agreed to the terms and asked Asbury to ride through the circuits to help reinforce the union. By taking these actions, the American preachers recognized Wesley's authority over the connection and, at the same time, reinforced Asbury's leadership in America.

Asbury's letters to Wesley during the following six months stressed that the people were under great disadvantages through want of the Sacrament. Under those circumstances, he felt that "want of opportunity suspends the force of duty to receive the Lord's Supper" (*Asbury*, 3:25). In this situation, Asbury was willing to view proper ordination as a more important principle than constant Communion. He was at the same time, however, putting Wesley on notice to do something about the matter of ordination.

Wesley was, in fact, becoming more aggressive in his attempts to obtain ordination for his preachers through proper channels. Brian Bury Collins was denied ordination by the Bishop of Chester because, as the bishop explained to him, "you have never once expressed to me . . . the least degree of concern for your wandering mode of life and of preaching" (*Church*, 261). And another Methodist preacher, John Hoskins, who was intending to go to America, was denied ordination by Robert Lowth, Bishop of London, because of his lack of education. Wesley wrote an impassioned letter to Bishop Lowth, pointing out the great needs in America. He was especially piqued at the Bishop's priorities: "Your Lordship did see good to ordain and send into America other persons who knew something of Greek and Latin, but who knew no more of saving souls than of catching whales" (*JWL*, 7:31; cf. *JWJ*, 21:248).

At the same time that this correspondence was in progress, the 1780 Conference was meeting in Bristol. It was consumed with the task of reordering and revising the "Large" *Minutes*, a major endeavor that entailed extending the usual length of the meeting to more than a week. The new expanded document, the first revision in eight years, incorporated several additional questions from the deliberations of the previous four or five Conferences, and included several revisions and additions to previously included items. Among the new items were some specific suggestions on fasting (Q. 35), reasons against separation from the Church (Q. 47), and advice against talking in the preaching-houses before and after service (Q. 68). Among the addenda to previous items is a firm resolve never to drop the morning preaching, at 5 a.m. wherever it is practicable, as well as an admonition to preach only if twenty hearers are present; otherwise sing and pray (Q. 25). Wesley also added some specific suggestions on how preachers' wives should be not only "a pattern of cleanliness" but also "a pattern of industry" so as to prevent the preaching-houses from being spoiled by "sluts" (i.e., slovenly women; Q. 69). The married preachers (at least twenty-five percent at that point) had been admonished in 1779 not to hasten home after preaching to see their wives; they must first meet the society (*Minutes*, 141). This problem did not effect Wesley personally; at this point, he had been separated from his wife, Molly, for several years. Nevertheless, the problems of providing for over forty spouses soon led to a restriction against admitting any more married preachers, "unless in defect of single preachers" (*Minutes*, 151).

Wesley also decided to revoke his earlier "permission" for everyone to attend Conference. Charles Wesley did attend this Conference, which partially accounts for the strong reiteration of the principle that "none who leave the Church shall remain with us" (*JWL*, 7:29). There are also some other evident structural innovations, such as Christopher Hopper, his Assistant at Colne, being elected to preside over some of the sessions, and a cabinet of six persons, including Coke and Fletcher, being set up to assist Wesley (*Church*, 220). Shortly after the Conference, however, he made it very clear just who was still in control. To one of his preachers, Zachariah Yewdall, he wrote (still chafing from the McNab squabble), "It is I, not the Conference (according to the twelfth rule), that station the preachers; but I do it at the time of the Conference that I may have the advice of my brethren" (*JWL*, 7:40). It is clear that, as with most of the agenda, Wesley came to the Conference with appointment list in hand, though he was open to alterations on the spot (*Polity*, 251n). He was not, however, willing to allow unauthorized preaching in the connection, especially by women. In March 1780, he had sent instructions to John Peacock, the Assistant at Grimsby, to put a "final stop to the preaching of women" in his circuit. "If it were suffered," Wesley added, "it would grow, and we know not where it would end" (*JWL*, 7:8–9).

Despite continuing tensions and problems throughout the connection, the Methodist societies managed to spread and grow. The reported membership in 1781 of 44,461 was an increase of 631 over the previous year. There were 178 preachers, one for every 250 members, a fairly constant ratio since 1767. The number of circuits had nearly doubled to sixty-three, but still only about a dozen had over a thousand members. The asterisks in the *Minutes*, formerly marking the declining circuits, were now shifted to designate the thirty-three circuits that had grown, perhaps to put as positive a light as possible on a grim situation. More than twice as many circuits as in the worst previous year had lost members. Although six circuits had each grown by more than a hundred, another six had lost more than a hundred each.

Local growth, however, often brought the need for a new or larger meeting space. For years, the Methodists had taken over a number of different types of buildings that would accommodate a crowd—theatres, blacksmith shops, barns. An old slaughter-house in Belfast had been the site for Methodist meetings in 1764 during which a teen-ager had felt God's love in that "holy place." When his companions made fun of him and reminded him it was just a slaughter-house, he responded, "Maybe, but it was the house of God to me" (*People*, 42). About 1780, John Sutcliffe, who had joined a class in Ewood during the previous decade after hearing Wesley preach, needed to find a bigger place for the prayer meeting that he had later organized, which had outgrown his home in Pilling. He soon found a solid but unused barn at Luddenden that was seven by twelve yards, and although it was ten miles away, he moved there, bought the barn, dug rooms under it in which to live, and began to use the building for Methodist meetings (*People*, 36–37).

One of the growing circuits was Epworth, where a revival had broken out, especially among the children. The industrialization of the area had brought in four factories for spinning and weaving that employed large numbers of boys and girls. Some of these, "stumbling in at a prayer meeting," were "cut to the heart." Their efforts among their companions then changed the conditions in three of the factories, as described by Wesley: "No more lewdness or profaneness were found, for God had put a new song in their mouth, and blasphemies were turned to praise" (*JWJ*, 6:352–53). As Wesley soon discovered, here as elsewhere, the "fire kindled and ran from heart to heart," and thus started, "the flame spreads to those of riper years" (*JWJ*, 6:514–15). On occasion, however, he discovered what he called "wildfire" mixed with the genuine; each local revival had to be judged on its own character.

One of the circuits that showed a temporary decline was **Birstall**, where the preaching-house in the town was "awkwardly settled" on a deed that allowed the trustees to "place and displace" the preachers, a practice contrary to the Wesleyan scheme. When the society decided to construct a larger building in order to reclaim their earlier growth, Wesley tried to get the people to use the form of the Model Deed in the "Large" *Minutes*. This action would have bound the property to the Methodist connection and limited its pulpit to preachers appointed by John Wesley. But the Birstall people claimed they could not legally alter the nature of the deed. Consequently, at the 1782 Conference, Wesley insisted that all new preaching-houses be settled, "without meddling with lawyers," using the form of the Model Deed. He also stipulated that if the trustees at Birstall refused to settle it "on the Methodist plan," he would raise money throughout England "to purchase ground and to build another preaching-house as near the present as may be" (*Minutes*, 157).

Wesley felt that such firm action was required in order to protect the itinerant system. If trustees have the power to place and displace preachers, he pointed out, then "itinerant preaching is no more": the rotation of preachers is at an end, and while they stay, the bridle is in their mouth. To the critics who saw this action as a power play on the part of an aging patriarch, Wesley answered that these requirements were simply intended to protect the freedom of successive generations of itinerant preachers, to keep them from being turned out of their pulpits at the whims of trustees who might not like their preaching, a power that even noble patrons did not have in the Church (*Societies*, 507–9).

Wesley was not ready to support any and all types of preaching from Methodist pulpits, of course. The Model Deed stipulated that his *Sermons* and *Notes* would be the doctrinal standards for measuring proper Methodist preaching. And early in 1782, in the wake of the Gordon riots, he had written a short paper entitled, "How Far is it the Duty of a Christian Minister to Preach Politics?" Wesley felt that although their main task was to "preach Jesus Christ, and him crucified," the preachers should certainly defend the king and his advisors against unjust censure among the people, even though many people would then cry, "O, he is preaching politics!" (*JWW*, 11:155).

Not all Methodists agreed with Wesley on matters of politics. At Plymouth Dock in 1775, Wesley had spoken freely to some who were "deeply prejudiced against the King and all his ministers." His evaluation of their reaction to his argument was that "God applied it to their hearts," and "there is not one of them now who does not see things in another light" (*JWJ*, 6:78). In 1779, he had explained the decrease in some circuits as owing "partly to prejudice against the King and speaking evil of dignities," and prescribed a solution: "Suffer none that speak evil of those in authority, or that prophesy evil to the nation, to preach with us" (*Minutes*, 140).

Control of the preachers was a key to unity in the connection. The Conference had long been the means of promulgating and enforcing the various regulations. During this period, Wesley (in the Conference) reinforced proscriptions against the preachers publishing anything on their own, singing hymns of their own composition, powdering their hair or wearing artificial curls (*Minutes*, 151, 157–59). At the same time, if they could not preach twice a day, morning and evening, they were no longer considered as itinerant preachers (but might be listed as supernumeraries). The Assistants were also ex-

Preaching plan for the Grimsby circuit, 1782, by Thomas Wride, with days and locations (homes) listed.

pected to turn in quarterly "circuit plans" listing the several societies with columns for the members in each (indicating new members, backsliders, and band members), as well as the conversions, deaths, marriages, and "removes," with a total for each column (*JWL*, 6:374; *Minutes*, 140). These charts were different from the quarterly preaching plans modelled on Wesley's 1754 chart, which were just beginning to become more prevalent at this time and soon came to be known as "circuit plans."

Some of the regulations also applied directly to the Methodist people. Men and women were to sit apart in services; they were not to visit a hairdresser on Sunday; and they should not watch, much less perform, military exercises on the Lord's Day (*Minutes*, 157–59). In 1782, Wesley began to relax his previous rules concerning attendance at Church. While he praised Thomas Brisco for changing the hours of the Methodist service, Wesley went on to say that he would "encourage all persons to go to church as much as they possibly can" (*JWL*, 7:115). This was hardly the tone of Wesley's former injunctions on the matter of Church attendance. His own practice also began to reflect this new, more lenient attitude that seemed to encourage local option on the matter: he was now more likely to find himself attending Methodist services that extended into Church hours, especially in London or Bristol (*Church*, 291–92).

About this time, Wesley also published one of his longest descriptive **histories** of his movement, "A Short History of the People Called Methodists" (1781). It was actually an addendum to his edition of *A Concise Ecclesiastical History* and formed the last section of this four-volume abridgement of J. L. von Mosheim's work. He begins the account with a simplified description of the "three rises of Methodism": Oxford, Georgia, and London (*Societies*, 430). The remainder of the story, 132 numbered paragraphs, is largely taken from his *Journal*. Stories of countless Methodists reinforce the main point that they all aim at one point: to spread true religion through the three kingdoms. This "truly rational religion," grounded in Scripture, Wesley describes as "the love of God and our neighbour, filling the heart with humility, meekness, contentedness" (*Societies*, 502). Just like the *Journal* itself, which by this time had appeared in seventeen installments, or "extracts" (up through 1775), this "Short History" was a concise *apologia* that served as useful propaganda for the Wesleyan movement.

The people in the Methodist societies that Wesley described were by this time beginning to show the marks of increasing prosperity. While this development might have been reason for rejoicing, it also presented theological problems in the Wesleyan scheme of things. In fact, Wesley's analysis of declining membership in some societies had included "increase of worldly-mindedness and conformity to the world" as a chief reason (*Minutes*, 140). And anything that resembled the surplus accumulation of **wealth** by any Methodist, Wesley readily denounced.

For years, he had consistently urged Methodists to give away everything but their "necessaries and conveniences." He felt strongly enough about this issue that he initiated a new feature in his *Arminian Magazine* in January 1781—publishing original sermons by himself, each in two monthly installments. The first one to be included was a sermon on 1 Timothy 6:9, "They that will be rich fall into temptation and a snare" (*Sermons*, 3:228–46). He redefines "rich" to include all who have anything more than food to eat, clothes to wear, a roof over their heads. This sermon, later entitled "The Danger of Riches," furnished the opportunity to reiterate his three-fold principle asserted earlier in "The Use of Money" (1760): earn all you can, save all you can, (but especially) give all you can. He pleads with the Methodists, above all, to hear this word of the Lord. And as was often the case,

Thomas Coke,
"Apostle of Methodism"

the principle once enunciated soon found its way into the *Minutes* as an aphorism: "Everyone is covetous whose beneficence does not increase in the same proportion as his substance" (*Minutes*, 158).

Although Wesley was still able to keep most things fairly well within his oversight, the increasing pace of change in society, and the size and spread of Methodism, were such that personal management of the movement by one individual was becoming even more difficult.

Conference and Ministry

Thomas Coke, an ordained Anglican priest born in Wales, had come to London in 1777 to help Wesley at the time the new chapel in City Road was under construction. He quickly became Wesley's primary lieutenant in place of John Fletcher, whose health was failing. Unlike Fletcher, Coke was not associated with a parish, having been dismissed from his curacy in South Petherton, which he had in effect transformed into a Methodist circuit. Coke provided leadership in several important enterprises. He directed the Tract Society, which Wesley had begun in January 1782 as a means of printing and distributing free literature. Supporters of the project purchased the pamphlets, Wesleyan publications that cost a penny or less, which were then distributed to the poor. A penny was only the cost of a watch key for the wealthy, but for the poor it meant the value of a bag of sugar or a loaf of bread. Within two years, specially printed copies of thirty Wesleyan pamphlets were being distributed, all identified by the notation on the cover, "Not to be sold, but given away."

Coke was also the force behind early attempts to initiate foreign mission projects among the Methodists, having unsuccessfully proposed a mission to Africa in 1777. Six years later, he proposed the formation of the Society for the Establishment of Missions among the Heathen, a non-denominational group, and tried to encourage the Methodists to send missionaries to the East Indies. Wesley squelched the idea at this point by suggesting that there was "no call thither yet, no invitation, no providential opening of any kind" (*JWJ*, 6:476). Wesley was in favor of the general concept of **missions** to every part of the globe, as he exhibited in his sermon on "The General Spread of the Gospel" (1783; *Sermons*, 2:493), but at this particular time, he had other more pressing problems closer to home.

Not least of these was the need to assure some order and continuity in the connection beyond his lifetime. The Birstall case had foreshadowed the potential division and chaos that might follow his death. The trustees of the New Room at Bristol also balked at resettling their house on the Model Deed. Coke, whose Oxford degree was Doctor of Civil Law, had served as Wesley's deputy in both of those sensitive negotiations, as well as others. There were now nearly four hundred Methodist preaching-houses, with about two dozen applications a year for new houses (*Church*, 293). At the 1783 Conference, Wesley suggested that "the needless multiplying of preaching-houses" had been a great evil, and that Coke should travel throughout England for the purpose of getting them all "settled on the Conference plan" (*Minutes*, 165).

The Deed of Declaration

Coke had already come to realize that beyond Wesley there was no legal locus of authority in Methodism upon which to settle issues of property or polity. Coke, together with William Clulow, a young solicitor and Methodist, sought legal advice from John Madocks, a barrister of Lincoln's Inn, who informed them that the Conference as it presently existed could not legally assume Wesley's power or property. Therefore, there was no provision for a center of union among the people called Methodists after Wesley's death. Madocks suggested that Wesley prepare a declaration that would legally clarify these issues, with all the necessary details of organization spelled out in full, and enroll it in the Court of Chancery. The Conference of 1783 concurred with this opinion.

With Coke's help at the beginning of 1784, Wesley prepared the **Deed of Declaration**, a deed poll entitled "The Rev. John Wesley's Declaration and Appointment of the Conference of the People called Methodists." The key sentence in the eight-page document, in typical legalese, stated that

> John Wesley doth hereby declare that the Conference of the people called Methodists in London, Bristol, or Leeds, ever since there hath been any yearly Conference of the said people called Methodists in any of the said places, hath always heretofore consisted of the preachers and expounders of God's Holy Word, commonly called Methodist preachers, in connexion with and under the care of the said John Wesley, whom he hath thought expedient year after year to summons to meet him in one or other of the said places of London, Bristol, or Leeds, to advise with them for the promotion of the Gospel of Christ, to appoint the said persons so summoned, and the other preachers and expounders of God's Holy Word, also in connexion with and under the care of the said John Wesley, not summoned to the said yearly Conference, to the use and enjoyment of the said chapels and premises so given and conveyed . . . and for the expulsion of unworthy and admission of new persons under his care and into his connexion (*JWJ*, 8:335–36).

The practical function of the document was to list one hundred of the preachers (the "**Legal Hundred**") who, with "their successors for ever, to be chosen as hereafter mentioned, are and shall for ever be construed, taken, and be, The **Conference** of the People called Methodists" (*JWJ*, 8:338). The constitutional role of the Deed, which was enrolled in the High Court of Chancery on February 28, 1784, was to enumerate fifteen regulations for the conduct of the Conference. These specify an annual meeting, with forty present as a necessary quorum, a President and Secretary as officers, a three-year limit on appointments, and such other procedures as methods for admission and expulsion of preachers. The official record of actions was to be a Journal (from which the *Minutes* were then published). The final clause, however, stipulated that nothing therein should be construed "to extend, to extinguish, lessen, or abridge the life-estate of the said John Wesley and Charles Wesley" in any of the chapels where they "now have or may have any estate or interest, power, or authority whatsoever" (*JWJ*, 8:341). In other words, the document would not take full effect until after both of the Wesley brothers had died.

The Deed had some apparent implications for the future of the connection, however. The three-year limit on appointments was an extension of Wesley's traditional one or two, and the change satisfied many people. The legal Conference now became a delimited body of named preachers, rather than a group arbitrarily and annually invited by Wesley, although he still continued with the personal invitations for the time being. Coke had been opposed to restricting the Conference to the "Legal Hundred," and felt that all preachers in full connection should be members, as had been the case for over a dozen years before 1780. When Coke sent a copy of the Deed to the Assistant at Sarum, John Moon, he attached a disclaimer that stated clearly, "I had no hand in nominating or omitting any of my brethren." Since there were nearly two hundred lay itinerant preachers in the connection, almost half had been left off the list, including fourteen of the older Assistants. Although it is difficult to ascertain Wesley's criteria for choosing the hundred, it is apparent that seniority played little if any role. To those who thought some others might have been more suitable to be named, he replied, "True, if I had thought as well of them as they did of themselves" (*JWW*, 13:249). That he omitted several of the more contentious preachers did nothing, of course, to allay their discontent.

This Deed contains no mention of doctrinal standards, which were still specified within the Model Deed in the "Large" *Minutes*. And although Wesley continued to refer to the Methodist buildings as "preaching-houses," the Deed used the term "chapels," a subtle indicator of more conscious ecclesiastical self-sufficiency. There is no mention whatsoever of relationship to the Church of England. Wesley soon made clear, however, that no change of attitude had taken place. The following month, he sent a message to John Murlin, Assistant in Manchester, that if any of the lay preachers talked either in public or private against the Church or the clergy, or read the Church Prayers, or baptized children, they should promise to desist: "If they will not promise, let them preach no more. And if they break their promise, let them be expelled [from] the society." Another message to Zachariah Yewdall at Liverpool was more succinct: "You must mend or end that local preacher" (*JWL*, 7:213, 215).

John Hampson, one of the more cantankerous of the disgruntled preachers, published "An Appeal" to the Wesleys on behalf of "the excluded ninety-one." He tried to get those preachers to come to Conference in order to throw out the Deed and restore the old order. Most of the preachers, including the dying Fletcher, stood with Wesley and the new plan. A handful resigned, including Hampson and Pilmore. In order to allay some fears, Wesley promised to write a document that would assure equal footing to all the preachers (this letter he entrusted to Joseph Benson, to be read at the first Conference after his death). The note that concludes Wesley's account in his *Journal* can be read more than one way: "Our Conference concluded in much love, to the great disappointment of all" (*JWJ*, 7:7).

With this Deed, Wesley had taken a major step to help settle the future of the Methodist movement in Britain, even though the document did not resolve all the operational issues that were causing tensions from year to year. And although this particular step did nothing in itself to meet the growing pressure from the American Methodists (with membership nearly doubled to fifteen thousand in the five years since the Fluvanna Conference), it did allow Wesley to give more attention to the problems overseas.

A New Church in the New World

By the early 1780s, **Francis Asbury** was the only preacher appointed by Wesley who remained in America. At the conclusion of military hostilities, Wesley had written to Edward Dromgoole in Virginia, expressing his confidence in the young Asbury: "I am persuaded brother Asbury is raised up to preserve order among you, and to do just what I should do myself, if it pleased God to bring me to America." In September 1783, following the political conclusion of the Revolutionary War with the signing of the Peace of Paris, Wesley designated Asbury as his General Assistant for America. The letter conveying the appointment also included an appeal: "Let all of you be determined to abide by the Methodist doctrine and discipline published in the four volumes of *Sermons* and the *Notes Upon the New Testament*, together with the Large *Minutes* of the Conference" (*W-A*, 128). The Americans dutifully acknowledged their acquiescence to these requirements at their regular Conference in April 1784, adding some additional stipulations that the preachers must "keep the circuits they are appointed to, follow the directions of the London and American *Minutes*, and be subject to Francis Asbury as General Assistant, whilst he stands approved by Mr. Wesley and the Conference."

These attempts by Wesley to extend his personal influence across the Atlantic fell somewhat short of the expectations of American Methodists for relief on the matter of **ordination**. Asbury reported to Wesley that thousands of children remained unbaptized in America, and that some members of Methodist societies "had not partaken of the Lord's Supper for many years" (Coke and Moore, 468). Their Church of England compatriots were also frustrated by the inability of Samuel Seabury, one of their own leaders, to obtain episcopal

Spa Fields Chapel in Clerkenwell, London, formerly a theater, was purchased by Lady Huntingdon's connection in 1777.

orders in England during 1783. The American Methodists' sentiment was echoed by Seabury's complaint from England—"Nobody here will risk anything for the sake of the Church" (*Church*, 274).

Lady Huntingdon's connection had apparently reached the brink of dissent in March 1783 by ordaining some of its lay preachers. Their chapel in Spa Fields had already been registered as a dissenting chapel the previous year. Peter King's argument in his *Enquiry* was used as the rationale. Wesley had for some time been convinced, by the same arguments of King and Edward Stillingfleet, that he also had the right to ordain, but he had felt that it was not expedient to break with the traditional order of the Church. Wesley thought there might be extraordinary prophets, but not extraordinary priests. By 1783, however, the situation had changed; the need was critical. And no one who held the traditional power of ordaining would exercise it on behalf of the Methodists, who were in dire straits for lack of anyone to administer the sacraments. The American situation had now become a "case of necessity," not simply expediency (*JWL*, 7:262).

During the fall and winter of 1783/84, Wesley discussed the American problem with Coke, including a possible plan for Wesley to ordain episcopal leaders to supervise the Methodist work in America. At this point, Wesley seems to have been ready to move faster than

Coke, who wanted first to observe the American scene and report back to Wesley. Coke finally gave in to Wesley's plan, which included his own ordination before going to America. During the Conference at Leeds in August, 1784, Wesley asked for volunteers to accompany Coke to America, and from the volunteers chose two, Thomas Vasey and Richard Whatcoat. Wesley discussed the possibility of ordinations with only his senior advisors, or cabinet. According to one of them, John Pawson, the group advised against the idea but could tell that Wesley had made up his mind. Wesley consulted Fletcher, who was against it; a group of clergy in Leeds, who were against it; James Creighton, a new clergy assistant from Ireland, who was against it. Charles Wesley was not consulted at all.

In spite of all the opposition and in recognition of the potential criticism, Wesley pressed ahead with the plan. Although already an ordained presbyter of the Church of England, Coke agreed after the Conference that it was expedient to receive what amounted to epis-copal ordination, that is, "the power of ordaining others," by the imposition of Wesley's hands. Coke agreed that the action was in keeping with Scripture and the Primitive Church. On the more practical side, Coke had heard that Asbury did not want to share the superintendency of the work in America, and therefore an "authority formally received" from Wesley would allow Coke to overcome any unforeseen opposition (*Documents*, 4:198–99). The two also agreed that Wesley should ordain Whatcoat and Vasey.

In Bristol on September 1, therefore, Wesley, with the assistance of Coke and Creighton (who was less than enthusiastic), ordained the two preachers as deacons. On Thursday, they were ordained as presbyters, and Coke was set apart (Wesley's diary says "ordained") as a "Superintendent," using the Latinized translation of the Greek word *episcopos*. The argument could be made that Coke did not need such an ordination, since he was already, as was Wesley, a presbyter and could presumably use the same rationale as Wesley to ordain others as a scriptural bishop in cases of necessity. But it is clear that Coke was receiving more than simply ordination in this act by Wesley; it served as a formal designation of authority from Wesley that was necessary in order for Coke to exercise leadership in America.

Charles had been kept out of the picture throughout all these developments. Although he had been in Bristol at the beginning of September, he did not know about the ordinations. His reaction, upon hearing of the drastic action, was predictable in form and tone. He chided his brother and Coke in a published poem entitled "Epigram," which included a very quotable satire on John:

So easily are Bishops made
  By man's or woman's whim?
W[esley] his hands on C[oke] hath laid,
  But who laid hands on him?

Charles also decried Coke's ordination of Asbury:

A Roman emperor, 'tis said,
  His favourite horse a consul made;
But Coke brings other things to pass,
  He makes a bishop of an ass.
                    (*Rep. Verse*, 367–68)

Charles notwithstanding, the die was now cast. With these three clergymen, Wesley sent to America a plan for setting up a Methodist church separate from the Church of England. The new organization would have all the essential ecclesiological features of a "church" denomination: an ordained clergy to administer the sacraments, an official service book containing the liturgy, and doctrinal standards in the form of Articles of Religion. The "sketch" that Wesley sent looked very much like the Benson/Fletcher plan for a separate "Methodist Church of England" in the 1770s, which would have featured a clergy ordained by the Wesleys (if necessary), a prayer book with "needful alterations," and Articles of Religion "rectified according to the purity of the gospel" (*JWJ*, 8:332–33).

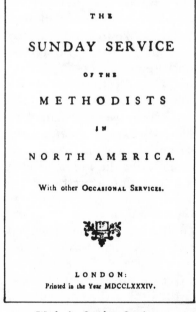

THE

SUNDAY SERVICE

OF THE

METHODISTS

IN

NORTH AMERICA.

With other Occasional Services.

LONDON:
Printed in the Year MDCCLXXXIV.

Wesley's *Sunday Service* was shipped to America with Coke as unbound sheets in order to save the export duty on books.

The new **prayer book**, *The Sunday Service for the Methodists in North America*, was Wesley's abridgement of the Book of Common Prayer. He had wished to improve the prayer book ever since his association with Thomas Deacon and the Manchester nonjurors during his Oxford days, when they were trying to pattern liturgy and worship after the Early Church. Wesley's diary indicates that he also experimented with the order of the service while in Georgia. And when quoting the Psalms, he had almost always used the language of the prayer book

Psalter, derived from the early Coverdale text, rather than the Authorized Version (King James). His reverence for the traditional BCP is evident in the way he preserved the tone and much of the text of the work in the *Sunday Service*.

Wesley's method for this revision followed his usual practice of abridgement by deletion, which Coke then refined with a few "little alterations." In the preface of this recension for American Methodists, Wesley explained that he had omitted many of the holy days (they served no "valuable end"), shortened the Sunday Service (formerly called Morning Prayer, "the length of which has been often complained of"), left out some Psalms and deleted parts of others (as "highly improper for the mouths of a Christian congregation"), and omitted some other sentences here and there (*Documents*, 4:201). In fact, he also left out the liturgical calendar, the catechism, the confirmation service, the Athanasian Creed, the visitation of the sick, and several other parts of the BCP. He chose to use the term "elder" rather than "priest" or "presbyter," and "superintendent" rather than "bishop," in the ordination services.

In the service of baptism, sprinkling was allowed as an alternative to immersion, the first known instance of such practice in a baptismal rite. A last minute change, entailing the substitution of new pages, restored the BCP rubric that instructed the baptizing minister to make a sign of the cross on the infant's forehead. An example of other subtle but important changes is the softening of regeneration language by changing "that he being born again" to "that he may be born again."

Up to this point, Methodism in America had been part of the British connection, which Wesley always insisted maintained no doctrine but what was in the Book of Common Prayer, the Homilies, and the Thirty-nine Articles. The Articles were standards of doctrine for the Church, those official teachings by which other statements of faith could be measured for orthodoxy. Methodist preachers, as part of a group within the Church of England, were measured by an even narrower delimitation within those boundaries: Methodists were to preach no doctrine but what was in Wesley's *Sermons* and *Notes*. This restriction also followed the Anglican pattern of limiting unordained, uneducated curates (without an M.A.) to reading sermons from the Book of Homilies.

Now that the Methodists in America were to have a separate denomination with an ordained clergy, Wesley decided to provide them with doctrinal standards in the more traditional ecclesiastical form. The *Sunday Service* thus included Wesley's revision of the Thirty-nine Articles of Religion, "rectified" and reduced to twenty-four in number. Of the fifteen that were omitted, six had been questioned at the Conference of 1744 as possibly disagreeing with Scripture (Of the Three Creeds, Of Works before Justification, Of Christ alone without Sin, Of Predestination and Election, Of the Authority of General Councils, Of Ministering in the Congregation). Wesley now revised or abridged several others and changed two of the titles. The whole was thereby reduced to half the original length.

Traditionally, the BCP was bound together with a psalm-book such as the Sternhold and Hopkins Psalter. It is not surprising, then, that Wesley also provided the Americans with a new version of *A Collection of Psalms and Hymns for the Lord's Day*. This book was selected from previous works, especially the popular 1743 collection. At just over a hundred pages, it was one-fifth the size of the 1780 *Collection of Hymns* that the Wesleys had just recently produced.

Wesley had thus provided the basic documents he felt the Methodists in America needed in order to form a church. When Coke, Vasey, and Whatcoat embarked from Bristol for America on September 18, they took these materials with them. They also had a letter from Wesley entitled, "To Dr. Coke, Mr. Asbury, and our Brethren in North America," dated September 10, 1784, a week after the ordinations and the day after he wrote the preface to the Sunday Service. In six numbered paragraphs, Wesley explained the rationale for the actions he had taken. The new political situation in America, brought about by "a very uncommon train of providences," had resulted in the American Methodists being "totally disentangled both from the State and from the English hierarchy." In those circumstances, Wesley had taken several actions, therein explained, as a scriptural and rational means of "feeding and guiding those poor sheep in the wilderness." He then pronounced their emancipation: "They are now at full liberty simply to follow the Scriptures and the Primitive Church." To that, he added a benediction, proclaiming that "they should stand fast in that liberty, wherewith God has so strangely made them free" (cf. Gal. 5:1; *JWL*, 7:238–39).

The "full liberty" of which Wesley spoke was, of course, a delimited freedom, not only bounded by the two authorities mentioned, but also by Wesley's own continuing influence. At the end of October, Wesley wrote to Asbury a very typical letter with several specific directions. He also warned of the possible dangers that lay ahead, of the preachers either "turning Independents and gathering congregations each for himself; or procuring ordination in a regular way and accepting parochial cures." The result of both options, he pointed out, would be the end of the Methodist itinerant plan, which Wesley trusted that

The "Christmas Conference" met at Lovely Lane Chapel in Baltimore, where Coke and Asbury were elected as superintendents (bishops) and Asbury was ordained as deacon, presbyter, and superintendent on three successive days.

Coke and Asbury would be able to avoid by forming a "regular connexion" (*HAM*, 1:211).

When Coke met with Asbury at **Barratt's Chapel**, Delaware, on November 14, 1784, they talked about the design that Wesley had prepared for the new church in America. What neither Coke nor Wesley had anticipated was Asbury's response. Based on the advice of a council of preachers he had gathered in anticipation of this meeting, and in the light of the southern preachers' determination to be self-sufficient in 1779, Asbury suggested that Wesley's plan should be approved by a Conference of all the Methodist preachers in America. He himself would submit to ordination if the preachers agreed, and he and Coke should serve as superintendents only if elected by an American Conference. Coke finally agreed that a Conference should be called to begin at Lovely Lane Chapel in Baltimore on Christmas Eve. In the meantime, Asbury introduced Coke to his new circuit by sending him on a nine-hundred-mile horseback tour of American Methodism (*HAM*, 1:208). Whatcoat and Vasey also went on a preaching tour in Maryland until time for the Conference.

The "**Christmas Conference**" met as planned on Christmas Eve and continued for nearly two weeks to consider Wesley's plan and to adapt the latest version of the "Large" *Minutes* (1780) to the American scene. Asbury's sentiments in the matter were "union but no subordination; connexion but no subjection" (*Asbury*, 3:63). He wrote to George Shadford, who had spent some time in America but was now back in England: "Mr. Wesley and I are like Caesar and Pompey: he will bear no equal, and I will bear no superior" (*Asbury*, 3:75). Yet, when the Conference revised the British *Minutes* to create the first American "Form of Discipline," they acknowledged in the "**binding Minute**" (Q. 2) that they were, during Wesley's lifetime, "his Sons in the Gospel, ready in matters belonging to church government, to obey his commands."

Wesley could not have anticipated that such an explicit stipulation would be necessary; the idea of the American Conference having this much control of their connection was not part of his plan. In fact, the American Methodists recognized Wesley's leadership in a number of obvious and intangible ways. During the Conference, Coke and Asbury had met with two representatives of the newly forming Protestant Episcopal Church, who recognized that the Methodists had the same liturgy, same Articles, and same discipline as they did and felt that some sort of merger or working relationship might be worked out. In the end, John Andrews, one of the Episcopalians, admitted that their negotiations failed, since the Methodists were bound that "Mr. Wesley be the first link of the chain upon which their church is suspended" (Vickers, 90–91). In the meantime, Samuel Seabury had been consecrated an Episcopalian bishop in Scotland in November, though it had little effect on the American Methodist developments since he did not return to America until the following summer.

The actions of the Christmas Conference established a new and separate denomination, the **Methodist Episcopal Church**. But although it had all the prerequisites of a church, it looked like a church, and acted like a church, its soul was still Wesleyan in that it still thought of itself as a society. It relied heavily upon the precedents of the British Wesleyans and acknowledged a polite respect for Wesley. Nevertheless, American Methodism already bore the indelible marks of American liberty on its foundation, some of which Wesley could never understand.

The Final Phase

In his October 1784 instructional letter to Asbury, Wesley had closed with a bit of news from home: "Those who hoped for a division among the Methodists here, are totally disappointed" (*HAM*, 1:212). This piece of optimistic hyperbole overlooked the continuing reactions to the Deed of Declaration and the ordinations. The charges against Wesley ranged from personal pomposity to *de facto* separation from the Church. Although the membership in the British Isles was now growing more rapidly, all the old tensions among the preachers were heightened, and the connection once again stood in jeopardy of unravelling.

At the beginning of 1784, John had expressed encouragement at the **revival** that was taking place among the Methodists in England: "Whom has God owned in Great Britain, Ireland, and America like them? . . . Truly these are the tokens of our mission, the proof that God hath sent us. Threescore thousand persons setting their faces heavenward, and many of them rejoicing in God their Saviour" (*JWL*, 7:206). He compared the work of the Holy Spirit among the Methodists with the revivals in New England under Jonathan Edwards and that described in Virginia by John Gillies. But many people, including Charles Wesley, saw Methodism as entering a dark period of storm and stress.

In April 1785, Charles wrote a telling letter to Thomas Chandler, a clergyman who was setting out for America, in which he gave a short account of himself and his brother John, who, he said, "always had the ascendant over me." Charles, enumerating the various developments in Methodism, with special attention to the question of separation from the Church of England, noted that "for fifty years we kept the sheep in the fold." Then came John's ordinations, which, Charles felt, were tantamount to separation from the Church. The result was also a tremendous personal strain: "Thus our partnership dissolved, but not our friendship" (*Documents*, 4:204–5).

From John's point of view, nothing essential had changed. Charles's tantrums notwithstanding, John was probably right in claiming that the ordinations for America had little impact on the question of British Methodist separation from the Church of England. To the 1785 Conference, he invited seventy preachers, several of whom were not members of the Legal Hundred. His letter of invitation to Thomas Wride made a larger point: "A Conference, while I live, is 'The preachers whom I *invite* to confer with me.' . . . No contentious persons shall for the future meet in any Conference. They may *dispute* elsewhere if they please" (*JWL*, 7:279).

The two most controversial issues arose again at the Conference. On the first, Wesley again announced that he had given up no power whatsoever by executing the Deed of Declaration. From those present, he solicited signatures of thirty-nine persons (twenty percent of whom were not named in the Deed) to a statement affirming the substance and design of that document. This list was later bolstered by thirty signatures from absentees, forty per cent of whom were not members of the Legal Hundred (*Minutes*, 181–82). On the second issue, **ordination**, he proceeded to ordain three preachers for the work in **Scotland**, John Pawson, Thomas Hanby, and Joseph Taylor. He rationalized his action by saying that Scotland was not under the Church of England (which would have thus entailed separation). Under this principle, he refused to ordain any for England, even "a desolate place" in Yorkshire. And to those who complained that all his careful rationalizations would be for naught if there were a separation after his death, he replied, "I dare not avoid doing what good I can while I live, for fear of evil that may follow when I am dead" (*Minutes*, 193).

John's protestations notwithstanding, his power was beginning to wane. Again he allowed Christopher Hopper to preside over sessions of the Conference. He was also less apt to stand in the way of a majority of the preachers there: "I will not run my head against all the Conference by reversing what they determined" (*JWL*, 7:286). And his diary for that week contains several references to his consultations with his "cabinet" (*JWJ*, 7:100). It is difficult to know whether John was slowly loosening or inevitably losing his grip. In any case, he certainly intended to avoid divisions and separation during his lifetime, if at all possible.

Charles Wesley did not attend the Conference, nor did he sign the statement concerning the Deed. Instead, he sent a note to John suggesting that John read over his own "Reasons against a Separation" (1758). John replied at some length, arguing that he still had done nothing to effect a separation from the Church. He also pointed out that no one he ordained was to use the powers conferred by that ordination while they were in England (either before or after being in Scotland, a somewhat awkward expectation on Wesley's part). Then he added a poignant personal appeal to Charles: "If you will go hand in hand with me, do. But do not hinder me if you will not help. Perhaps, if you had kept close to me, I might have done better. However, with or without help, I creep on" (*JWL*, 7:285).

The following month, when rumors spread that Wesley was intending to separate from the Church, he declared to the society in Bristol, "I had now no more thought of separating from the Church than I had forty years ago" (*JWJ*, 7:112). Within the month, Wesley finished a sermon, later entitled "Of the Church." Although he claims to agree with Article XIX of the Church, his assumptions in this sermon follow those in his letter to Charles, which show some affinity to more radical definitions of a fellowship of true believers (*Sermons*, 3:46).

But Wesley was not totally absorbed with matters of polity. In a sermon published in the *Arminian Magazine* that same month, on the text, "Work out your own salvation with fear and trembling" (Phil. 2:12), Wesley gave one of his most complete and mature delineations of the *via salutis*, the result of at least forty years of reflection. In this description of the divine-human interaction, Wesley makes it abundantly clear that synergism is not grounded in human effort but in divine grace, "preventing, accompanying, and following" (*Sermons*, 3:209). In another important sermon, on "Behold I make all things new" (Rev. 21:5; later called "The New Creation"), reiterates his belief in the restoration of all creation through God's boundless love. He even considers the nature of the changes that might take place to air, fire, water, and earth in this new creation. But his focus is turned on animate nature, and he gives a portrait of the peaceable kingdom. But, of course, the most glorious change will take place among humankind, who will "arise in an unmixed state of holiness and happiness far superior to what Adam enjoyed in paradise" (*Sermons*, 2:510). Wesley's eschatology, though infrequently expressed, was generally optimistic.

Although many of Wesley's sermons were now written primarily for his magazine, he continued to preach regularly. In some cases, the preached sermons were the same as the published, such as the one "On Charity" (*Sermons*, 4:515). He never had been an outstanding preacher, but many people now attended his preaching just to see the venerable patriarch, by now an almost legendary phenomenon. Horace Walpole, who had heard him several years earlier, was unimpressed: "He spoke his sermon, but so fast and with so little accent that I am sure he has often uttered it, for it was like a lesson" (*Documents*, 4:159–60). One observer in Lincolnshire in 1788 noted that Wesley preached with little effort, so that "but for an occasional lifting of his right hand, he might have been a speaking statue." But Mary Bosanquet, now married to John Fletcher, heard Wesley that same year and thought that "each sermon was indeed spirit and life" (*M&M*, 163–64).

In the spring of 1786, Wesley produced a sermon "On Schism," in which he again protested his innocence: "I have no desire nor design to separate from [the Church] till my soul separates from my body." He also called upon all true Christians to persevere in their attempts to be peacemakers, reiterating a familiar phrase from his Oxford days: "*Fac quod in te est; et Deus aderit bonae tuae voluntati*"—"Do what in thee lies, and God will be present and bring thy good desires to good effect" (*Sermons*, 3:69).

This perennial subject also came up at the 1786 Conference, at which Wesley insisted again that Methodists should not hold services during Church hours, so that Methodists could attend their parish church. He was willing to make some concessions, however, especially when the Church of England minister was wicked or preached "pernicious doctrine" such as Arianism, and when there were not sufficient churches within two or three miles (*Minutes*, 193). His opposition to some of the current preaching of his day, tinged with Deism, reinforced his prejudices on matters relating to supernatural phenomena, on which he was not willing to give way. As he told Thomas Tattershall: "While I live I will bear the most public testimony I can to the reality of **witchcraft**. The denial of this springs originally from the Deists, and simple Christians lick up their spittle" (cf. *JWL*, 7:300). This assertion simply reiterates a comment he had made ten years earlier: "I cannot give up to all the Deists in Great Britain the existence of witchcraft till I give up the credit of all history, sacred and profane. And at the present time, I have not only as strong, but stronger proofs of this, from eye and ear witnesses, than I have of murder; so that I cannot rationally doubt of one any more than the other" (*JWJ*, 6:109).

John's own experience of hearing Anglican clergy preach helped soften his position on the necessity of weekly attendance at the parish church, as he had noted earlier that year to Charles: "The last time I was at Scarborough, I earnestly exhorted our people to go to church, and I went myself. But the wretched minister preached such a sermon that I could not in conscience advise them to hear him any more" (*JWL*, 7:326). A month later, he clarified the point: "One may leave *a* church (which I would advise in some cases) without leaving *the* Church" (*JWL*, 7:327). In the *Minutes* for that Conference, he published his most recent thoughts, "Of Separation from the Church," and appended his rationale for his ordinations of preachers for Scotland, which followed a similar argument as that for America. To these, he added some wide-ranging advice for the preachers (see box).

The question of hearing an inadequate preacher, however, was quite a different question from that of receiving the Sacrament from such a person. In a sermon, "On Attending the Church Service" (1787), Wesley repeated his view from over thirty years earlier, that people should not hesitate to take the Sacrament, even if administered by a **wicked minister**. He pointed out, from a practical point of view, that many (if not most) of the ministers in his acquaintance for the last half century did not measure up to his basic criteria; they had "not been eminent either for knowledge or piety" (*Sermons*, 3:471). But his principle in this matter is clear: "The unworthiness of the minister doth not hinder the efficacy of God's ordinance. The reason is plain; because the efficacy is derived, not from him that administers, but from him that ordains it" (*Sermons*, 3:475). This statement not only was in keeping with Article XXVI of his own Church, but also had been fixed in Western Christendom as early as Augustine's response to the Donatists. Still smarting from the refusal of any bishop to ordain any preachers in his connection, Wesley also took this opportunity to point out that, although many would see them as a "set of poor, stupid, illiterate men that scarce know their right hand from their left"; yet they in fact had more knowledge of Scriptures, of themselves, and of God and the things of God, than nine in ten clergymen (*Sermons*, 3:471).

Advice to Preachers, August 1, 1786

1. Always to conclude the service in about an hour.
2. Never scream.
3. Never lean upon or beat the Bible.
4. Wherever you preach, meet the Society.
5. Do not, without the utmost necessity, go home at night.
6. Never take part against the Assistant.
7. Never preach a funeral sermon but for an eminently holy person; nor then, without consulting the Assistant. Preach none for hire. Beware of panegyric, particularly in London.
8. Have love-feasts in more places.
9. Introduce no new tunes. See that none sing too slow, and the women sing their parts. Exhort all to sing, and all to stand at singing, as well as to kneel at prayers.
10. Let none repeat the last line, unless the Preacher does.
11. Inform the Leaders, that every Assistant is to change both the Stewards and Leaders when he sees good. And that no Leader has power to put any person either into or out of the Society.

(*Minutes*, 193–94)

Wesley's attempts to extend his control over doctrine and discipline within the connection, as well as the quality of preaching in the local societies, can be seen in a minute from the 1787 Conference. Any person, in addition to the regular Methodist preachers, who desired to preach in any Methodist chapel or preaching house was required to have "a note from Mr. Wesley or from the Assistant of the circuit from whence he comes; which note must be renewed yearly" (*Minutes*, 203). Under this rubric, Sarah Mallett received such a note from Joseph Harper, Assistant for Norwich, permitting her to preach in that area "so long as she preaches the Methodist doctrines and attends to our discipline" (Chilcote, p. 195). Some of the itinerant preachers continued to oppose her contribution, perhaps following Wesley's own general inclinations (see above, p. 276). But in this case, Wesley tried to take the bite out of such widespread prejudice by encouraging her frequently. At the same time, he suggested that she go nowhere without the advice of his Assistant in the area. And he assisted her by means of specific advice on such matters as preaching, expanding upon his advice to the 1786 Conference: "Never scream. . . . It is disgustful to the hearers . . . and it is destroying yourself. It is offering God murder for sacrifice" (*JWL*, 8:190). She may not have been a regular preacher listed in the Minutes, but Wesley made it clear that she was still under his control in the connection.

Wesley continued to expand the work in other directions as well. His ordinations of preachers for the work in Scotland was part of a larger vision of **missions** that Thomas Coke was promoting at this time. Coke's earlier initiatives had failed for lack of support from Wesley. Now, in 1786, he avoided this problem by gaining Wesley's commendation before making his proposal (*Documents*, 4:209). He decided to follow Wesley's advice and, leaving aside the hazards of an Asian mission for the time being, pursue those fields of action that lay somewhat closer at hand. Coke's *Address . . . Proposing an Annual Subscription for the Support of the Missionaries* (1786) outlined the possibilities in the Highlands and adjacent islands of Scotland, the Channel Islands, Newfoundland, Nova Scotia, Quebec, and the West Indies. In all of these areas, the work had already begun and simply awaited encouragement and support. This subscription proposal was a connectional plan in that Coke specified the Assistants as the agents who were to collect and bring the money to the Conference annually. It was also a recruiting device in which he encouraged the preachers "to spend and be spent" in this cause. Coke hoped to spread these resources out "to the uttermost" so as to "leaven the whole lump of mankind" (*Documents*, 4:211–12).

Wesley's own mission focus was even closer at hand. At the end of 1785, he had encouraged John Gardner, one of the founders of the **Strangers' Friend Society**, in his work with the poor who had no parish or friends to help them. The plan was foundering because of opposition from Gardner's class-leader, but Wesley approved of the idea and subscribed threepence per week, with a guinea initial payment (*JWL*, 7:308). The following year, another group with the same name, and with the Methodists' support, was also established in Bristol (*More*, 194–95). While traveling in Holland during the summer of 1786, Wesley took a special interest in the manner whereby the deacons of Amsterdam relieve their two or three hundred poor every week. He noted in his Journal that "the whole was transacted with the utmost stillness and decency" (*JWJ*, 7:197).

The Methodists did not have to look for strangers to find the poor. Wesley's own continuing work among the poor Methodists is exemplified in his personal solicitation of funds in January 1787 to help about two hundred of the London society (nearly ten per cent) who were "in pressing want, yet had not weekly allowance." He went "a-begging" of the more well-to-do members over a period of five days but was disappointed to find only six or seven that would give as much as ten pounds apiece. The total of two hundred pounds he collected, although short of what was needed to implement the full design, did (as he said) allow "many sorrowful hearts to be made glad" (*JWJ*, 7:235–36; see also 6:451). In the matter of personal philanthropy, Charles did not follow John's pattern of publicly giving money to street beggars because he feared that someone would see him and think him ostentatious (*Documents*, 4:222).

The ongoing work of the Methodist connection was costing a significant amount of money overall. The *Minutes* for 1787 list the Kingswood Collection at about £740; contributions to the Preachers' Fund totalled over £458. The General Fund amounted to £1035, but still did not cover the yearly expenses. Wesley announced that English circuits would get only the number of preachers they could support financially. And in 1788, he appealed to the societies to support the preachers' wives, after noting that many of the circuits (claiming poverty) had not contributed the wives' allowance, and that he, Coke, and the Contingent Fund had been taking up the slack. The appeal ends with an observation that over the past fifty years, "the substance of the Methodists is increased in proportion to their numbers," and therefore there should be many who could cheerfully support "those who give up all their time, and strength, and labour to your service" (*Minutes*, 216). Wesley had recently repeated his view of stewardship in his sermon "On Riches" (1788), which confirmed the basic presupposition of his previous sermons on the topic, that everything beyond the necessities and conveniences of life should be considered riches (or "superfluities"). In this sermon, he went further and pointed out the many snares that await those who cleave to their riches, and ended with a word of advice: "Sit loose to all things here below as if you was a poor beggar" (*Sermons*, 3:528).

At age eighty-five, John Wesley was well aware how tenuous was the human grip on anything, including life itself. Charles Wesley expressed the brothers' feelings most succinctly as his own life ebbed away in the late winter of 1788. Unable to hold a pen, Charles dictated to his wife Sally some of his last lines:

> In age and feebleness extreme,
>   Who shall a helpless worm redeem?
> Jesus, my only hope Thou art,
>   Strength of my failing flesh and heart;
> O could I catch a smile from Thee,
> And drop into eternity!

Charles died on March 29, 1788. Samuel Bradburn's letter informing John, who was traveling in the Midlands, was misdirected, and John received it only the day before Charles's burial on April 5. John wrote to Sally, explaining his absence, but continued on his preaching tour. But two weeks later at a service in Bolton, while lining out his brother's hymn, "Come, O Thou Traveller Unknown" ("Wrestling Jacob"), John could not get past the words, "My company before is gone, / And I am left alone with Thee." He burst into tears and sat down in the pulpit, his face in his hands (*JWJ*, 7:376–77). The singing stopped, but John was finally able to continue. The power of this hymn is affirmed in Charles's obituary, given at Conference that year: "Dr. [Isaac] Watts did not scruple to say that 'that single poem, *Wrestling Jacob*, was worth all the verses he himself had written'" (*Minutes*, 205).

Advancing Years

John Wesley now began to prepare more in earnest for his own departure from the Methodist scene. At the conclusion of the 1788 Conference, at which he ordained six preachers for service abroad, he ordained Alexander Mather, presumably to provide continuity of ordained Methodist ministry in England after his death (*JWJ*, 7:422). Two months later, he appointed a committee to superintend the Book Room and manage his accounts. Four months later, he drew up a revised will.

The advancing years, however, did not diminish his energy for the work, which was becoming more demanding as time wore on. The connection had well over sixty thousand members in Great Britain, with over two hundred preachers. The American Methodists, now independent, were presenting problems he had not anticipated. Asbury and Coke had assumed the title "bishop" in preference to his term "superintendent," a change which moved Wesley to write to his "dear Franky" in 1788, "Men may call me a knave or a fool, a rascal, a scoundrel, and I am content; but they shall never by my consent call me a bishop! For my sake, for God's sake, for Christ's sake, put a full end to this!" (*JWL*, 8:91). Wesley compared himself to Coke and Asbury: "I creep; you strut along. I found a school; you a college!" The idea that they had incorporated their own names into Cokesbury College made Wesley shudder.

For their part, the Americans had put up with more than they could bear from Mr. Wesley. When Wesley instructed the Americans to have a Conference in Baltimore in 1787 to make Richard Whatcoat a General Superintendent, they reacted with less than polite disregard for his wishes. Not only did they ignore Wesley's instructions, but in doing so, they also rescinded the "binding minute" in order to be consistent and not be found in contempt of their previous pledge of loyalty to Mr. Wesley. Asbury expressed the attitude of the Americans: "For our old Daddy to appoint Conferences when and where he pleased, to appoint a joint superintendent with me, were strokes of power we did not understand" (*Asbury*, 3:63). When Wesley heard that the American Conference had rejected Whatcoat as superintendent, based on the assumption expressed by Asbury that no person in England could direct the Americans without being "omnipotent, omniscient, and omnipresent," he was stunned. Wesley also cringed when he heard of Asbury's comment, "Mr. Wesley and I are like Caesar and Pompey: he will bear no equal, and I will bear no superior." When Asbury allowed Wesley's name to be voted out of the American *Minutes*, the line was crossed, and Wesley reacted: "This completed the matter and showed that he had no connection with me" (*JWL*, 8:183).

Wesley himself was having enough trouble just directing the business of British Methodism. The demand for new preaching-houses had increased to a rate of more than twenty a year by the mid-1780s, which had resulted in a rash of special collections. In 1788, Wesley limited these collections to the circuits in which the houses were to be built. Within a year, however, he broke his own rule in this regard. The stipulation in the *Minutes* had been accompanied by a

reminder that all preaching-houses were to be settled on "the Conference plan," followed by a reprinting of the text of the Model Deed.
The information was directed primarily at the trustees of the **Dewsbury** society, who (like the Birstall trustees) refused to settle their new
preaching-house in the approved manner. Therefore, in 1789, Wesley
followed the precedent set earlier at Birstall and announced that they
would simply build another house at Dewsbury, to be properly settled,
assisted by a connectional collection. The *Minutes* list 115 preachers
who agreed that "the Methodist plan" should be followed for all
preaching-houses, followed by a list of 124 persons who had already
subscribed from 50 shillings to £50 each to the new house at Dewsbury.

But all was not simply business. Wesley was still producing sermons, both for the *Arminian Magazine* and for a new collection of
Sermons on Several Occasions (1787–88) in eight volumes that included
the previous four volumes and the sermons published in the magazine
over the previous decade. Among those produced in 1787 were a
revision of his Oxford sermon, "The Duty of Constant Communion"
(1732), and a new sermon, "The More Excellent Way." The first
contained his life-long emphasis on taking the Sacrament as often as
possible, although evidence indicates that, in many parts of England
at this time, finding a Communion service even once a month would
have been an unrealistic expectation.

The second sermon presents an obvious contrast to his earlier
sermon, "The Almost Christian" (1744), with its disparaging remarks
about nominal Christians. Now, some forty-four years later, while
Wesley is still emphasizing the life of the true Christian who walks the
upper path, he does not totally discard hope for "the lower order of
Christians." Part of the point now is to encourage "those who serve
God in a low degree" (*Sermons*, 3:266). In another sermon, "On the
Discoveries of Faith" (1788), he corrolates the two paths with the two
types of faith, that of a "servant" and that of a "son." It took only the
former to be accepted of God and be allowed into the Methodist
societies as one who "feared God and worked righteousness." But
those persons were expected to press on, so that they would obey God
out of love rather than fear (*Sermons*, 4:35).

This later explicit allowance for two orders of Christians, each with
its own hope of salvation, correlates with his post-Moravian allowance
of value in the searching faith of a "servant" as well as the assured faith
of a "son" or child of God. In 1788, in a sermon "On Faith," he could
acknowledge the mistake of his earlier approach: "Nearly fifty years
ago, when the preachers commonly called Methodists began to preach
that grand scriptural doctrine, salvation by faith, they were not suffi-

ciently apprised of the difference between a servant and a child of God. They did not clearly understand that even one 'who feared God and worketh righteousness, is accepted of him'" (*Sermons*, 3:497). At this later time, Wesley was especially proud that the Methodists were distinguished by their willingness to admit anyone as society members who had this searching faith of a servant (*Societies*, 536–37).

Time was beginning to take its toll on Wesley, however. On his return trip from Holland in 1786, the elderly Wesley had impressed a fellow traveler passenger with his good eyesight by reading a small-print edition. Sophie von la Roche's comment, published later that year in *Sophie in London*, was, "If the Methodists' principles keep their sight as clear as that to the age of 83, then I wish I had been educated in their sect." The timing of this comment is ironic, however. About the time it was published, Wesley himself noticed that he was having trouble reading—that he could not read his own large hymn book except by a large candle. Within another year, he could not read letters, if written with a small or bad hand (*JWJ*, 7:456). His birthday comment in 1789 is somewhat jarring, in the light of his previous optimism: "I now find I grow old." His sight was decayed; his strength was decayed; his memory was decayed. On New Year's day of 1790, he again admitted, "I am now an old man, decayed from head to foot," but added, "However, blessed be God, I do not slack my labour. I can preach and write still."

And Wesley continued to press many of his favorite themes, though sometimes with different nuancing. In a revision of the "Large" *Minutes* (1789), for instance, he prefaced the well-known sentence that gave the purpose of Methodism as "to spread scriptural holiness" with a new phrase, "not to form any new sect." In a sermon that same year on the prophetic and priestly offices, he characterized the Methodists in a manner similar to that of nearly fifty years earlier in *The Character of a Methodist*; this time he described them as "a body of people who, being of no sect or party, are friends to all parties, and endeavour to forward all in heart-religion, in the knowledge and love of God and man." In this sermon also, speaking to some Methodist preachers who were still ambitious for priestly powers, he pleaded with them, "O contain yourselves within your own bounds; be content with preaching the gospel." He pointed out that fifty years earlier, Methodist preachers were considered "extraordinary messengers of God" whom God had thrust out, "not to supersede, but to 'provoke to jealousy' the ordinary messengers." Then he added, "In God's name, stop there!" (*Sermons*, 4:82). He had also just recently, in his sermon "On a Single Eye" (1789), castigated as "vile, infamous wretches" the many worldly priests in the Church, saying (with Luther, if not Chrysostom) that "Hell is paved with the souls of Christian priests" (*Sermons*, 4:129).

Wesley's professed loyalty to the Church was still unshakable, as he wrote to Henry Moore: "I am a Church of England man; and, as I said fifty years ago so I say still, in the Church I will live and die" (*JWL*, 8:58). **Loyalty** was a basic trait that drove Wesley, as he had earlier told Walter Churchey: "Loyalty is with me an essential branch of religion, and which I am sorry any Methodist should forget. There is the closest connection, therefore, between my religious and my political conduct, the selfsame authority enjoining me to 'fear God' and to 'honour the King'" (*JWL*, 6:267). He was careful to point out that his Tory perspective was grounded in the idea that God, not the people, was the source of all power, including civil (*JWL*, 7:305). In 1756, he had volunteered to form two hundred of God's people into a Methodist militia to protect England against an invasion by the French (*JWL*, 3:165).

Wesley also rejected the principles of the **revolutionary fervor** that was beginning to tear apart France. To a preacher in America, he wrote that "the amazing revolutions" in Europe might be forerunners of a time when the knowledge and glory of the Lord might fill the earth, although "the poor infidels, it is true, who know nothing of God, have no such design or thought" (*JWL*, 8:199–200). Wesley had no time for the patriot's cry for "liberty," religious or political. With the Methodists who still wanted to choose their own leaders, Wesley had no patience:

> We have not, and never had, any such custom. We are no republi-
> cans, and never intend to be. It would be better for those that are so
> minded to go quietly away. I have been uniform both in doctrine
> and discipline for above these fifty years; and it is a little too late for
> me to turn into a new path now I am grey-headed (*JWL*, 8:196–97).

Although he certainly felt that his path had been adequate, Wesley did not always feel compelled to continue all of his practices. In July 1790, he decided to discontinue keeping his personal financial ac-

Wesley's last entry in his financial accounts at the back of his diary.

counts, in which he had listed receipts and expenditures from 1725 onwards. The last entry is followed by a note that makes a long-held point, if somewhat exaggerated in its chronology: "For upwards of eighty-six years, I have kept my accounts exactly. I will not attempt it any longer, being satisfied with the continual conviction that I save all I can and give all I can, that is, all I have" (*JWJ*, 8:80).

Moreover, Wesley was making increasing numbers of concessions. In 1788, Mr. Clulow, his solicitor, advised him to license all the preaching-houses and traveling preachers under the Conventicle Act, not as dissenters but as "preachers of the gospel." This decision, though thought to be politically necessary, was legally awkward, in the face of continuing protestation of loyalty to the Church, and therefore the licenses as dissenters were often not granted. Wesley protested one such confusing case to Dr. Tomline, Bishop of Lincoln, the following year: "The Methodists . . . desire a license to worship God after their own conscience. Your Lordship refuses it, and then punishes them for not having a license!" (*JWL*, 8:224). Wesley also began to give way increasingly on the matter of allowing services on Sunday morning during Church hours. His permission to do so in Dublin in 1789 caused a controversy throughout other parts of the connection that had pressed for the same. To some, he appeared to be preparing the way for a separation from the Church after his death. But in yet another treatise, "Farther Thoughts on Separation from the Church" (1789), he denied any such aim and professed his conviction: "I do not believe the Methodists in general design it when I am no more seen" (*Societies*, 540).

The Conference in 1790 was a severe test of that conviction. Wesley no longer had the commanding presence of his earlier years. John Pawson noted that Wesley was now "nearly worn out, and his faculties evidently were very much impaired, especially his memory" (*EMP*, 4:58). Even though Wesley did not preside over the sessions, Sutcliffe admits, "His presence sanctioned the whole." Sutcliffe described the "cabinet":

> A long table being placed across the chapel, which had no pews, Mr. Wesley sat in a chair at the head of the table, and about twenty venerable men on the benches, ten on each side, distinguished by bushy or cauliflower wigs, aged men that had borne the heat and burden of the day. Mr. Mather, as a sort of archdeacon . . . conducted the whole business of the Conference. Mr. Valton was the secretary, with his small quarto ledger (*Documents*, 4:233–34).

He also described the method of **stationing** of the preachers: "Mr. Wesley then put his hand into his pocket and pulled out the manuscript order of the stations, which it is believed no one had seen since he transcribed it in Newcastle on his way to the Conference." As the list was read, changes were made for the "mutual accommodation" of preachers and people. "All was paternal and fair," according to Sutcliffe's account.

The young preacher also described the examination of preachers "for admission into full connexion" at the end of Conference, which shows clearly that Coke played an important role: "The twelve young men . . . on one of the benches, spoke briefly of their experience, their call to preach; and confessed their faith. After this, Dr. Coke came on the fore bench with the Large *Minutes* on his left arm and delivered a copy to each, putting his right hand on each of our heads" (*Documents*, 4:233). Sutcliffe's own copy of the "Large" Minutes contains the standard inscription that had been used for about forty years: "As long as you continue to walk by these rules, we shall rejoice to acknowledge you as a fellow-labourer. John Wesley" (*Documents*, 4:231–32; cf. *Minutes*, 570).

Wesley may have been growing weak, but he still expected a full day's work from his preachers, who now numbered nearly three hundred in Great Britain alone (to guide 71,463 members). As he had

Wesley's wavering signature on the 1790 MS Journal of Conference.

told Jasper Winscom, a preacher on the Isle of Wight, earlier in the year, "I wish we had no circuit with fewer than three preachers in it or less than four hundred miles' riding in four weeks." Jasper noted that Wesley wanted the preachers on horseback again, which would contribute to their bodily and spiritual health. Wesley's own comment was placed in the negative: "If we do not take care, we shall all degenerate into milksops" (*JWL*, 8:206). Strong words for a man approaching his eighty-seventh birthday.

But age was not about to cause Wesley to mince words. He would also continue to proclaim the gospel. He thought that "On the Wedding Garment" (March 1790) might be his last written sermon: "My eyes are now waxed dim; my natural force is abated. However, while I can, I would fain do a little for God before I drop into the dust" (*JWJ*, 8:54). This sermon was his opportunity to say one more word about the relationship between the righteousness of Christ, which gives the believer a "claim" to heaven, and holiness, which gives the believer "fitness" for heaven. Holiness, then, is the true wedding garment, which Wesley describes in the same terms he used at Oxford sixty years before: having "the mind that was in Christ" and "walking as he walked." He dismisses the idea that holiness is supplanted by faith: "The imagination that faith *supersedes* holiness is the marrow of anti-nomianism." This sermon, then, is a rein-forcement of his emphasis on "faith which worketh by love," his mature alternative to the "faith alone" of the Moravians and Calvinists (*Sermons*, 4:147–48).

Seal used by Wesley in the 1780s, given to Elizabeth Ritchie.

In fact, Wesley wrote five more sermons, punctuating many of his favorite themes. "On Living Without God" repeats most strongly his assertion that holy living is more important than orthodox opinions (*Sermons*, 4:175). In "The Danger of Increasing Riches," he combines yet another denunciation of greed and surplus accumulation with a despairing realization that he has preached this message for over half a century and not convinced fifty misers of covetousness (*Sermons*, 4:181–82). And in "On Faith," which turns out to be his last, in mid-January 1791, he concludes with two verses from Charles's poem, "The Life of Faith" (1740):

> The things unknown to feeble sense,
>   Unseen by reason's glimmering ray,
> With strong, commanding evidence
>   Their heav'nly origin display.
>
> Faith lends its realizing light:
>   The clouds disperse, the shadows fly;
> Th' Invisible appears in sight,
>   And God is seen by mortal eye!
>   (*Sermons*, 4:200)

John's diary records another five weeks of fairly normal activity, preaching fairly regularly. In mid-February, he caught a cold, and on Sunday the 20th was unable to preach. He improved enough to preach the following Wednesday, the day of his last diary entry. That day, he also finished reading *Gustavus Vasa*, the life of a former Barbados slave, Olaudah Equiano. This book inspired Wesley to write, the following day, a word of encouragement to William Wilberforce, member of Parliament, in his fight against the slave trade: "Go on, in the name of God and in the power of his might, till even American slavery (the vilest that ever saw the sun) shall vanish away before it" (*JWL*, 8:265).

The next day, Wesley took a fever and began to decline rapidly. His housekeeper and companion, **Elizabeth Ritchie**, was at his side throughout the following week and recorded the events in some detail. The account reflects the *ars moriendi* tradition at its best, personifying the principles laid down in Jeremy Taylor's *Rules and Exercises for Holy Dying*. On March 1, the feeble Wesley gathered his strength and began singing Isaac Watts' hymn, "I'll praise my Maker while I've breath," which astonished those attending him. Further attempts to sing or speak were quite unsuccessful; "those lips which used to feed many were no longer able to convey their accustomed sounds." He was able to gather up his strength for one of his last utterances, "The best of all is, God is with us." On the following morning, March 2, 1791, he uttered his last, "Farewell" (*JWJ*, 8:138–44).

Wesley's quest for assurance, which gave impetus to his spiritual pilgrimage, was over. His search for peace had known both the despair of fear and the hope of faith. His warmed heart had experienced both the assurance of God's loving forgiveness and the continuing struggle with doubt. His restless heart that had found a trusting and confident faith but had on occasion wavered, had now found its rest with God. Wesley had long lived in the presence of his Maker, in fear of God's judgment and yet trusting in divine justice, in awe of God's majesty and yet confident in his gracious love, in expectation of continual surprises from God's Spirit and yet hoping through it all for guidance and comfort. So that at his death, Wesley knew of what he spoke when, from a heart that had long sought peace, he uttered his final testimony of faith, "The best of all is, God is with us."

Chapter 6—Suggested Additional Reading

Asbury — Asbury, Francis, *The Journal and Letters of Francis Asbury*, ed. Elmer T. Clark, J. Manning Potts, and Jacob S. Payton, 3 vols. (Nashville: Abingdon Press, 1958).

Coke, Thomas, and Henry Moore, *The Life of John Wesley* (London: Paramore, 1792 [facsimile edition, Nashville: Abingdon Press, 1992]).

George, A. Raymond. "Ordination," in vol. 2 of *A History of The Methodist Church in Great Britain*, ed. Rupert Davies, A. Raymond George, Gordon Rupp (London: Epworth Press, 1978).

More — Church, Leslie, *More about the Early Methodist People* (London: Epworth Press, 1949).

Rep. Verse — Wesley, Charles. *Representative Verse of Charles Wesley*, ed. Frank Baker (London: Epworth Press, 1962).

Vickers, John A., *Thomas Coke, Apostle of Methodism* (Nashville: Abingdon Press, 1969).

Epilogue

Wesley's death changed the boundaries of power and propriety with regard to actions by and comments about the people called Methodists. Everyone, including Wesley himself, had anticipated that the tensions within the movement during his life might escalate to the breaking point at his death. Wesley had stated as early as 1769 what he had recognized for some time, that he was the "centre of union," and that at his death many of the preachers would separate from the connection, either taking ordination in the Church or taking independent congregations. This prediction was followed, of course, by a succession of plans to avert such fracturing, and reinforced by continual pleas for unity. As late as a month before his death, he wrote to Ezekiel Cooper in Philadelphia, "Lose no opportunity of declaring to all men that the Methodists are one people in all the world; and that it is their full determination so to continue" (*JWL*, 8:260).

These words had a hollow ring to them in the new landscape of American Methodism. The Methodist Episcopal Church in the United States had long since exhibited, if not declared, their independence from Wesley and the British. Their changes from the British pattern in their initial Form of Discipline in 1785, their repeal of the binding minute shortly thereafter, their choice of nomenclature for the episcopal office, and a succession of other intentional actions declared that their new denomination was free from British control. Asbury's propensity to call Wesley, somewhat irreverently, "our Old Daddy" signals the future stance of American Methodists—touched by a familial love for Wesley's personal legacy, but no longer dependent upon their British patriarch's leadership. The American preachers may have been content to preach Wesleyan doctrines, but they were happy to be free from his political control. And Asbury was certainly ready to help the American Methodists fulfill Wesley's instructions to be "at full liberty simply to follow the Scriptures and the Primitive Church." Moreover, the process of practical disengagement that started in the late 1780s continued after Wesley's death, typified by the American Conference's approval in 1792 of a new order of worship, in effect setting aside the *Sunday Service* Wesley had sent over.

309

John Wesley's burial at 5 a.m. behind the New Chapel in City Road was attended by only a few close friends.

The situation was, in many ways, much more complicated in Great Britain. During an earlier period, as when Wesley was first writing his own epitaph in the 1753, of course no one could have predicted the almost universal outpouring of tribute and acclamation that would flow forth for the fallen leader nearly forty years later at his death. As his obituary in the *Gentleman's Magazine* put it, he was "one of the few characters who outlived enmity and prejudice, and received, in his latter years, every mark of respect from every denomination" (*EMW*, 2:154).

Internal jealousies and animosities were laid aside for the moment as the Methodist family paid their respects to their father in God, revered more in death than in life. A week after his death, Wesley's closest friends anticipated anything but calmness at the funeral, announced for March 9. Large numbers of people arrived in the area the day before, and prompted the leaders, late at night, to make arrangements for the burial to occur in private the next morning at 5 a.m. in the grounds behind the chapel on City Road. About twenty close friends knew the plan and were at graveside. Wesley's will followed a long-standing tradition and specified that six poor people should carry his body to the grave, each to be given a pound.

Wesley also had requested a simple funeral ceremony with "no pomp, except the tears of them that loved me and are following me to Abraham's bosom" (*JWJ*, 8:343). The public service in the Chapel at 10 a.m. was accompanied by an outdoor throng that, despite its combined numbers of curious and disconsolate, was quiet and peaceful, thanks in part to the care of a "vast number of constables" (*Death*, 15). Dr. John Whitehead, Wesley's personal physician and a local preacher in London, delivered the funeral sermon. He emphasized the steadying effect that Methodism had exerted on the population, a point rediscovered by biographers and historians during the following century and subsequently repeated as an aphorism. He also read excerpts from Elizabeth Ritchie's account of Wesley's last days. The sermon and account were printed within hours and were read from Methodist pulpits throughout the British Isles within days. The black drapings for the Chapel were remade into dresses and distributed to poor women (*Rack*, 533).

Methodism After Wesley

Another document, however, circulated among Methodists before the month was out, was of more significance to the future of the movement. A circular letter, drawn up at Halifax on March 30 by nine leading itinerant preachers, tried to set forth what they considered to be the proper course of action for the Conference to follow. Despite Wesley's careful planning, he had left many procedural ambiguities unsettled. The months following his death witnessed a variety of suggestions as to what the appropriate "Wesleyan" method might be in these circumstances. This "Halifax circular" proposed a procedure that was based upon that which Wesley had suggested in 1769. It supported the Deed of Declaration's concept of the Conference plan, but with significant adjustments in its implementation, such as the suggestion that districts be organized and that vacant places in the Legal Hundred be filled with preachers "according to their *seniority in the Work*." In effect, this document proposed a temporary set of by-laws aimed at preserving central control of the movement by the Conference, in part to perpetuate "the continuation of itinerancy among the Methodists" (*Documents*, 4:241–42). Other plans, such as one drawn up at Redruth, Cornwall, and signed by fifty-one "delegates" from the societies in the County of Cornwall, played upon the spreading popular democratic sentiment to amend the Methodist discipline in order to strengthen local control of the societies (*Documents*, 4:243–44).

At the Conference of 1791, meeting in Manchester in July, Samuel Bradburn read a letter that Wesley had written in 1785, the purpose of which was to assure the preachers that the Deed of Declaration was not intended to allow any of them to assume superiority over the others. The Conference responded with a firm resolve to endeavor to follow and imitate their "esteemed Father and Friend" in doctrine, discipline, and life (*Minutes*, 243). Thereupon, they proceeded to adopt most of the proposals in the Halifax circular. Of the nine persons who had signed the document, several of them subsequently became president of Conference, including the first signatory, William Thompson, who was elected that year as President of the Conference (to the surprise of Thomas Coke, Alexander Mather, Henry Moore, and some other obvious choices). The Conference also decided to divide the three kingdoms into twenty-seven districts and "to follow strictly the plan which Mr. Wesley left us at his death." This decision did not solve the problems, however, because Wesley had not made any provisions, in the Deed of Declaration or elsewhere, for many such important matters as the calling and operation of Conferences in Scotland and Ireland, much less the handling of pressure for separation from the Church, which enjoyed growing support.

The "Methodist plan as Mr. Wesley left it" included a large number of contradictory practices in different places. The resulting ambiguity as to general principles had been the result of a long period of local adaptations to particular needs. Over a period of more than sixty years, Wesley had developed methods and procedures that, while intended to "reform" the Church of England, in fact gave the Methodists a self-conscious identity distinct from the Church. While Charles always emphasized the negative impact of these developments upon the Methodists' relationship with the Church, John tried to focus on the positive results in the lives of the Methodists who were affected. The many variations of practice that resulted within this tension and that were evident in the connection at Wesley's death did not bother everyone. Some preachers, such as William Thompson, wanted to leave things just as they were—where they preach during Church hours and where they don't, continue in like manner; where they baptize and bury the dead, continue to do so, and otherwise don't; where they read from the BCP and where they pray "without book," continue in like manner (*Documents*, 4:247).

In this conservative atmosphere, many of the developments that had begun under Wesley were actually reversed. The Conference of 1792 (after drawing lots) strictly limited the administration of the Sacrament among Methodists (except in London and a few other designated places) and for all practical purposes did away with ordination for the time being. The following year, they decided to prohibit the use of the title "Reverend" by preachers and to drop the distinction between ordained and unordained preachers. The informal role of women as preachers, never very prevalent, began to disappear completely for the time being.

At the same time, several people had already begun to recirculate ideas that the Wesleys had suppressed for over forty years—proposals that would have radically changed the nature of Methodism into a more openly dissenting group with its own clergy and sacraments. Most of these proposals were opposed by the traditional "**Church Methodists**," who had long followed Charles Wesley's concerns for maintaining close relationships with the Church of England. Many of the latter, however, found themselves opposing another Wesleyan principle, the central control of Conference, while many (though not all) of those leaning toward dissent were supporters of the Conference.

The confusion of parties became evident in a particular controversy over the opening of Portland Chapel in Bristol in 1792. Samuel Bradburn, though unordained, wore a preaching gown when he delivered the opening sermon on August 26, 1792. The trustees of two other Bristol preaching-houses, Guinea Street and the New Room, criticized Bradburn for acting the priest and jeopardizing Methodism's connection with the Church, and cited Wesley to support their position. Bradburn defended his actions and the stance of "**Conference Methodists**" in *The Question, Are The Methodists Dissenters?*

Time Line 8

Tensions and Transitions

1780	1785	1790	1795
		George III	
Fluvanna Conference	Treaty of Paris	CW dies JW dies	Wordsworth and
			Bristol controversy Coleridge
Arminian Magazine started	"Christmas Conference"	French Revolution	*Lyrical Ballads*
	Tract Society		
Collection of Hymns	Deed of Declaration	*Sermons* in 8 vols.	Halifax Circular Plan of Pacification
	Ordinations for America	Biography Controversy	
Coke joins Methodists	Case of Birstall House		
		Portland Chapel Dispute	Kilham's *Progress of Liberty*
	Sunday Service Strangers' Friend Society		
Smith's *Wealth of Nations*	Revival in Epworth		
	Ordinations for Scotland	Coke to West Indies	Methodist New Connexion

which argued that Wesley himself was ambiguous on the matter of separation. Bradburn also signed a circular that defended the actions at Portland Chapel and criticized the trustees of the other two chapels, some of whom were wealthy men, had friends who were Church members, and took their stand based on their social perspective. The circular was co-signed by thirty-one other preachers, trustees, and male leaders at Portland, with the note, "We did not think it necessary to trouble the Women Leaders" (*Death*, 64).

Another controversy, which pitted preacher against preacher, revolved around an attempt to produce an official biography of Wesley. In order to counteract the influence of a three-volume biography that appeared in June 1791 by a disgruntled former preacher, John Hampson, the Book Committee appointed Dr. Whitehead to write one for the connection. Whitehead was one of a committee of three, with Coke and Moore, who had been charged by Wesley, in his will, with the disposition of his manuscripts.

After Whitehead was given the manuscripts, he began making demands for royalties and fees that were not in keeping with the connectional tradition of giving all profits from the publishing enterprise to the Preachers' Fund. When Whitehead refused to give up the manuscripts or allow a review of his writing, his services were discontinued by the Book Committee, and he was expelled from the London pulpits by Thomas Coke. Coke and Moore proceeded to write a competing biography, largely from Wesley's *Journal* and their own recollections. The latter work was written within six months, published in April 1792, and sold out its first printing of 10,000 copies before the Conference met that July (and nearly a year before Whitehead's first volume appeared).

The biography controversy was not simply over manuscripts, fees, and author's rights, however. Whitehead was a local preacher who disliked "the black-robed boys" (his term for itinerants, such as Coke and Moore) who exercised their power through the Conference. He saw the Deed of Declaration as the cause of Methodism's "corruption and final dissolution," and attacked the 1784 ordinations as being Coke's "stalking-horse to gain influence and dominion" (*Death*, 26–28). If alliances could be figured easily, this anti-Conference, anti-clerical stance would seem to have made him a friend of the "Church Methodists," but he was not. Whitehead's preface also described the "cruel" treatment he had received from some of the preachers in the matter of the biography. Many of the laity and local preachers sided with Whitehead and even formed a committee to further his cause. Most of the London preachers opposed him. Henry Moore later wrote

"A Plain Account of the Conduct of Dr. Whitehead Respecting Mr. Wesley's Manuscripts," a rebuttal of Whitehead's description of events, but chose not to publish it (*Death*, 83–125).

Henry Moore also became embroiled in another controversy in 1794, when he administered Communion in Portland Chapel, Bristol, according to permissions given by the Conference. His actions were opposed by the trustees of the other two Methodist chapels in Bristol, even though Moore had been ordained by Wesley in 1787. Those trustees suggested that such actions contradicted the "Old Plan" of Methodism and implied separation from the Church. They tried to bar Moore from their pulpits and actually did expel him from the pulpit of the New Room in August of that year. On that occasion, Moore simply removed to Portland Chapel to continue and took most of the congregation with him.

The struggle between Conference control and local control thus blurred the lines between the Church and the Dissent parties. There were Church Methodists who hoped that strong Conference control would suppress dissenting tendencies, but there were others (such as at Bristol) who felt that local control could best keep good relations with the Church. Some **Dissent Methodists** relied on the Conference to move in their direction, but others felt that power at the local level was essential to their democratic intentions. A new rhetoric appeared on the Methodist landscape, one that spoke of "the natural order of society," the desire for "just and natural rights" and "those privileges which are our inalienable rights."

The strongest statements of dissent/democracy/local power came from Alexander Kilham, who had been the champion of liberty within the Methodist movement for several years. He felt that Methodism should completely separate from the Church of England, have its own ordinations, and provide the Sacrament regularly to its people. He also felt that the Conference was run by rich preachers who conspired to perpetuate their own power. In his work, *An Earnest Address to the Preachers assembled in Conference* (1795), he pleaded for a return to the status quo at Wesley's death, which the Conference of 1791 had affirmed but which he felt had been abrogated by successive Conferences.

Kilham's views were not accepted by the majority of the Conference in 1795, which tried to resolve the long-standing tensions by passing a compromise document, "Articles of Agreement for General Pacification." This **Plan of Pacification**, as it came to be known, brought an uneasy peace to Methodism. Among other provisions, it allowed the Sacrament to be administered in chapels where a majority

John Wesley's portrait
in the *European Magazine*, April 1791.

of the trustees, along with a majority of the stewards (representing the sentiment of the people), approved such a step. The Conference was also required to approve these arrangements in each instance. It also reaffirmed the provisions of the Deed of Declaration, including the power of Conference alone to appoint preachers. In substance, the Plan was a victory for Conference control of Methodism (*Documents*, 4:264–67). In effect, the Plan represented an acknowledgment of British Methodism's final ecclesiastical separation from the Church of England.

If this solution satisfied anyone, it certainly did not satisfy Alexander Kilham, who responded with a treatise, *The Progress of Liberty Among the People Called Methodists*, wherein he proposed "Outlines of a Constitution" for the Wesleyan movement, built upon his understanding of democratic principles. Upon his expulsion from the Conference in 1796, these proposals became the basis for the formation of the Methodist New Connexion, a new denomination into which two other Methodist preachers and five thousand members followed him.

Those who had called loudest for dissenting, separatist actions in order to preserve their view of a vital Wesleyan tradition had now found it necessary to organize separately from the Conference that Wesley himself had established. This offshoot represented only the beginning of a process that continued through the following century, with various groups becoming independent in order to preserve one or another fundamental principle that they thought was essentially Methodist or Wesleyan.

The Wesleyan Heritage

These convulsions within Methodism in the months and years following Wesley's death illustrate some of the political difficulties that his followers experienced in an attempt to carry on what they understood to be the Wesleyan tradition. Nearly everyone understood that somehow, authenticity of the movement for the future depended on some continuity with the past. And just as Wesley had been perceived as the "centre of union" among the people called Methodists during his lifetime, the recollection of his life and thought has furnished the precedents for the Wesleyan tradition or heritage that has been at the heart of Methodism since his death. Although Methodism is more than the lengthened shadow of Wesley, the movement continues to bear the indelible marks of his heart and mind. In order to understand the Methodist heritage, it is necessary to catch the spirit of Wesley, the man and his message.

Despite the official Methodist antipathy for Hampson's biography of Wesley in 1791, it provided a first-hand description of their leader that has been quoted by successive generations of writers:

> His face, for an old man, was one of the finest we have seen. A clear, smooth forehead, an aquiline nose, an eye the brightest and most piercing that can be conceived; and a freshness of complexion scarcely ever to be found at his years, and impressive of the most perfect health—conspired to render him a venerable and interesting figure. Few have seen him without being struck with his appearance; and many who had been greatly prejudiced against him have been known to change their opinion the moment they have been introduced into his presence. . . . In dress, he was a pattern of neatness and simplicity. A narrow, plaited stock; a coat with a small upright collar; no buckles at his knees; no silk or velvet in any part of his

apparel, and a head as white as snow, gave an idea of something primitive and apostolic; while an air of neatness and cleanliness was diffused over his whole person (*EMW*, 2:84).

Though small in stature, Wesley had a presence that was commanding and a reputation for energy that was near legendary. The statistics of his industriousness became a matter of widespread fascination. He had published hundreds of books, preached tens of thousands of sermons, traveled hundreds of thousands of miles. His obituary in the *Gentleman's Magazine* is a telling tribute, even if discounted for polite hyperbole: "His personal influence was greater than, perhaps, that of any other private gentleman in any country. . . . As the founder of the most numerous sect in the kingdom, as a man, and as a writer, he must be considered as one of the most extraordinary characters this or any age ever produced" (*EMW*, 2:154–56). Even "excluded preachers" who might have been hostile to him because they were not included in the Legal Hundred, such as John Pawson, acknowledged at his death that "now the whole world did him honour, and all sorts and all degrees of men spoke well of him" (*WHS*, 49:16).

Wesley was important for who he was as a person, as well as for what he thought and what he did. But he also bore that mark of genius that prevents observers from ever getting a complete grasp of just who he was or what he thought. His associations cut across normal party lines and his ideas bridged many polemical positions. There are, however, several significant characteristics of his life and thought that provide useful clues to a fuller understanding of the heritage that bears his name.

From his Oxford days, Wesley was conscious of living in the presence of God, with all of the potential comfort and discomfort that such a realization might bring. He was also keenly aware that God's presence might be consciously sensed by an individual; he came to feel that the "spiritual senses" could be just as reliable and vivid as any empirical sense perception. To the typical Anglican trilogy of authorities (Scripture, tradition, reason) he added direct human experience of divine reality as an important criterion for understanding religious truth. He also came to realize, however, that the reality of God's presence did not depend upon human perception.

It is no surprise, then, that Wesley's understanding of the Christian life took shape quite self-consciously within his own spiritual pilgrimage and focused on the way of salvation—the drama of the divine-human relationship. Wesley himself preferred the phrase, "the *Scripture* way of salvation," since his perception of truth was based on a view of reality that was grounded in a biblical perspective. His words and actions breathe the teachings, the imagery, the very vocabulary of Scripture. But his purpose was not to replicate the first century in eighteenth-century England, but rather to live in his own day a life that was faithful to the love that God had shown for humankind in Jesus Christ.

But he also observed God's actions in the lives of other persons as important means of understanding God's will and providence. In some ways, his understanding of the gospel was confirmed as much or more in the lives of others as it was in his own. In an age when most of the population was suspicious of religious fanaticism, Wesley was not hesitant to accept radical manifestations of the work of the Holy Spirit, but he also was cautious enough to measure such experiences by biblical norms to test their authenticity. Although he allowed for extraordinary gifts of the Spirit, Wesley was prone to emphasize the ordinary gifts—love, peace, joy. Although his aim was to reform and renew the Church, the limits of his reverence for ecclesial authority and order were determined as much by his understanding of the Early Church as by the rules of the Church of England. Insofar as the latter perpetuated the mission and tradition of the former, he was a staunch advocate for loyalty to the established order. If current forms and regulations interfered with his call to minister to those who had spiritual and physical needs, however, he was willing to consider certain options to deviate, innovate, or otherwise press the limits of normal propriety.

Many of the tensions within the Methodist connection were caused by Wesley's particular priorities in these matters. For instance, he felt strongly that Christians should receive the Sacrament frequently ("constantly"), but not at the cost of either lay administration or improper ordination. Many of his decisions in specific instances were driven by the matter of "necessity," and the resulting variations of practice often gave the appearance of inconsistency as to principle or priority. The difficulty was in part due to Wesley's attempt, over a long lifetime, to deal with organizational and missional questions from a theological perspective, which itself was open to development and change. The close interweaving of these three areas provided the matrix for the movement of the people called Methodists.

God's love is at the heart of the Wesleyan tradition. It is the ground of its theology, it is the impetus for its mission, and it is the reason for its organization. To speak of God's love is to speak of grace; to speak of grace is to speak in relational terms of God's loving relationship to humankind. Wesley's own brand of synergism within that divine-human relationship was grounded in a "sure trust and confidence" in God's forgiving and redeeming activity through Jesus Christ as well as God's sustaining and empowering activity through the Holy Spirit.

For Wesley, justification and sanctification were both necessary parts of the daily drama of salvation. And the exercise of "faith working through love" meant not simply love of God but also love of neighbor, works of piety and also works of mercy. And just as Wesley would point out to the Calvinists that faith itself is made possible by grace, so also he would stress that these works are made possible by grace. Wesleyan theology is a thoroughgoing theology of grace.

Wesley's distinction between justification and sanctification meant that pardon did not necessarily mean perfection. There was more to the Christian experience than faith and forgiveness. The new birth that resulted from God's forgiveness was only the threshold of holiness, which then entailed a process of continued openness to God's grace and the exercise of love within a fellowship of believers that would provide a nurturing environment for growth in grace and in service to the world.

Wesleyan theology, while grounded in Scripture, emerged from Wesley's experience; it attempts to explain life in the presence of God. Wesleyan organization arose from the need to nurture daily the seeds of faith that give new life. Wesleyan mission developed to spread the love of God to every neighbor, that is, to everyone who had a need (although especially to those in the family of faith who had the greatest needs). And Wesley viewed this whole development, including his leadership role, as a part of God's providential activity in the world.

The people called Methodists, of course, did not always agree with Wesley, from his days at Oxford to his dying day. Many of them heard only what they wanted to hear, or heard his message as they wanted to hear it. Some, perhaps, did not fully understand his message or completely share his vision. The horizon of his concern included many seemingly disparate emphases that had typically not been held together: knowledge and vital piety, sacramentalism and evangelism, faith and good works, justification and sanctification, *sola fide* and *sola gratia*, piety and mercy, personal holiness and social holiness. Some who did not share the same comprehensive perspective considered Wesley to be a confusing if not elusive figure. It is not difficult at all to portray him as a "reasonable enthusiast" or a "radical conservative," as Henry Rack and Frank Baker have done.

The unifying focus for Wesley was a concern for spreading scriptural holiness. This emphasis on "practical divinity" was a central feature of the "holy living" tradition that for centuries had bridged many of the traditional divisions within Christianity. Wesley, therefore, could feel a strong kinship with many of the French Catholic mystics, the German Lutherans, the English Calvinists, the American revivalists, and the Scottish evangelicals, all of whom shared a heritage of holiness that could be traced back through Ignatius of Loyola and Thomas à Kempis to the leaders of the Early Church. One common thread in that lineage is a holistic concern for the well-being of God's creatures—mind, body, and soul. The Methodist program of medical clinics and interest-free loans, orphanages and schools, housing for the widows and meals for the poor, were of a piece with Wesley's understanding of "love of neighbor."

The irony of Wesley's attempt to reform the Church by spreading scriptural holiness is that most of his well-intentioned steps toward that goal led to an increasing self-conscious identity among the Methodists themselves, which resulted in intensified pressure for separation from the Church. Charles tended to fret about this tendency and worried about the negative consequences of separation. Despite that risk, John continued to hope for the intended results and cherished any positive signs of renewal. The strength of this double-sided concern persisted into successive generations of Methodists who had difficulty fully conceiving of themselves as a separate church.

The amalgam that was Methodism was never a fully unified movement in the eighteenth century, as hard as Wesley tried to hold the diverse elements together. Preachers and people alike often went their own way, regardless of Wesley's convictions and control. Tensions often resulted from people hearing only part of what Wesley was saying or not being able to grasp the manner by which he held disparate emphases together. And although Wesley was generally a good listener, he sometimes did not hear the people or fully appreciate their frailties. Methodism never achieved a large membership during Wesley's lifetime, partly because of the strict discipline that was required in order to have a quarterly class ticket renewed. But that the movement survived at all, much less, beyond his death, is a testimony to the persistence of his efforts to lead people into an experience of what he felt was a true vision of Christian living.

The Wesleyan heritage takes its vital energy from the dynamic imagery of the spiritual pilgrimage. It is the story of a people struggling together to understand God and themselves as they move from birth to death, from new birth to eternal life, from fear to joy, from doubt to confidence. Wesley himself was on this same pilgrimage, and as he moved along life's path, he often gained a new perspective that would help clarify the whole picture of where he had been and where he was going. He was willing to test doctrines, challenge traditions, reinterpret Scripture, and be open to the Holy Spirit. His theology is therefore an interesting combination of polemic and *apologia* that is more occasional than systematic.

But one should not therefore discount Wesley's thought as not having any consistency or as not being based on some pattern of thinking. The task of discerning his theology, however, is not so much one of deriving the principles of his thought and action as it is one of discerning the impulse for and direction of his spiritual pilgrimage as a maturing person in company with a band of fellow-travellers who were trying to embody the *imitatio Christi* in order to transform the world, which was at the same time a transforming experience for them. Wesley was not so much interested in speculative theology; his concern was "practical divinity," as he called it—the practice of Christian discipleship, "having the mind of Christ and walking as he walked." Adherence to a set of rules or adoption of a set of beliefs was not as important as conforming to a divine pattern of virtue and walking in the footsteps of Christ.

Although Wesley was a strong leader, his concern was not primarily to develop a band of faithful "Wesleyans," but of faithful Christians. The fact that he could equate "genuine Christianity" with Methodism should not be understood in the sectarian sense that Methodists held the secret of true religion. Rather, the mark of the people called Methodists was that they loved God and neighbor, which was simply the mark of a true Christian who had the faith of a "child of God."

The Wesleyan ethic of love was as much a virtue ethic as it was an obligation ethic. The Methodists' actions were produced by their responsiveness to what God had done for them in Christ and with them through the Holy Spirit: who they were prompted what they did. The various lists of rules were simply a means of measuring the sincerity of their faith and the depth of discipleship as followers of Christ. The many acts of charity and mercy were in imitation of the love of Christ, "who went about doing good."

The term "Methodist" had a previous history that indicated an Arminian way of thinking as well as a methodical way of living. Wesley's accent on "faith working through love" necessitated a synthesis of belief and action. He is often seen as a pragmatic leader who could perceive and respond to needs. He viewed himself as a person who was conscious of providential direction. Perhaps there is no contradiction between the two views.

Wesley's own self-understanding of his calling, seldom constrained by humility, was visibly stamped upon his long and energetic life, and was reflected in the inscription carved onto his tombstone behind City Road Chapel:

> This great light arose,
> by the singular providence of God,
> to enlighten these nations,
> and to revive, enforce, and defend,
> the pure apostolical doctrine and practice of
> the Primitive Church,
> which he continued to defend, both by his
> labours and his writings,
> for more than half a century;
> and who, to his inexpressible joy,
> not only beheld their influence extending,
> and their efficacy witnessed
> in the hearts and lives of many thousands,
> as well in the Western world as in these kingdoms,
> but also, far above all human power or expectation,
> lived to see provision made, by the singular grace of God,
> for their continuance and establishment,
> to the joy of future generations.
> Reader, if thou art constrain'd to bless the instrument,
> give God the glory.

Epilogue—Suggested Additional Reading

Death — Heitzenrater, Richard P. *"Faithful Unto Death": Last Years and Legacy of John Wesley* (Dallas: Bridwell Library, 1991).

Field, Clive. "Bibliography," Part 2 of vol. 4, *A History of The Methodist Church in Great Britain*, ed. Rupert Davies, A. Raymond George, Gordon Rupp (London: Epworth Press, 1988).

Hempton, David. *Methodism and Politics in British Society, 1750–1850* (London: Hutchinson, 1984).

Jarboe, Betty M. *John and Charles Wesley: A Bibliography* (Metuchen, NJ: Scarecrow Press, 1987).

Walsh, John. "Methodism at the End of the Eighteenth Century," in vol. 1 of *A History of The Methodist Church in Great Britain*, ed. Rupert Davies and Gordon Rupp (London: Epworth Press, 1965).

Selected Bibliography

Abbey, Charles John, and John H. Overton. *The English Church in the Eighteenth Century*. London: Longmans, Green, 1878.

Allen, W. O. B., and Edmund McClure. *Two Hundred Years: The History of the Society for Promoting Christian Knowledge, 1698–1898*. London: SPCK, 1898.

Allison, Christopher F. *The Rise of Moralism; the Proclamation of the Gospel from Hooker to Baxter*. New York: Seabury Press, 1966.

Appeals — Wesley, John. *The Appeals to Men of Reason and Religion, and Certain Related Open Letters*, ed. Gerald R. Cragg (vol. 11 in *The Bicentennial Edition of the Works of John Wesley*). Nashville: Abingdon Press, 1989.

Asbury — Asbury, Francis. *The Journal and Letters of Francis Asbury*, ed. Elmer T. Clark, J. Manning Potts, and Jacob S. Payton. 3 vols. Nashville: Abingdon Press, 1958.

Baker, Frank. *Charles Wesley as Revealed by his Letters*. London: Epworth Press, 1948. (*CW*)

Baker, Frank. *From Wesley to Asbury; Studies in Early American Methodism*. Durham, NC: Duke University Press, 1976. (*W-A*)

Baker, Frank. *John Wesley and the Church of England*. Nashville: Abingdon Press, 1970. (*Church*)

Baker, Frank. "The People Called Methodists: Polity," in vol. 1 of *A History of the Methodist Church in Great Britain*, ed. Rupert Davies and Gordon Rupp. London: Epworth Press, 1965. Pp. 213–55. (*Polity*)

Baker, Frank, ed. *Representative Verse of Charles Wesley*. London: Epworth Press, 1962. (*Rep. Verse*)

Baker, Frank. *William Grimshaw*. London: Epworth Press, 1963. (*Grimshaw*)

Bangs, Carl. *Arminius*. Nashville: Abingdon Press, 1971.

BCP — Book of Common Prayer.

Beynon, Tom. *Howell Harris, Reformer and Soldier*. Caenarvon: Calvinistic Methodist Bookroom, 1958.

Böhler, Peter. "Diary," trans. by W. N. Schwarze and S. H. Gapp, in "Peter Böhler and the Wesleys," *World Parish* 2 (November 1949).

Bucke, Emory Stevens, ed. *The History of American Methodism*, 3 vols. Nashville: Abingdon Press, 1964. (*HAM*)

324

Butterfield, Herbert. "England in the Eighteenth Century," in vol. 1 of *A History of The Methodist Church in Great Britain*, ed. Rupert Davies and Gordon Rupp. 4 vols. London: Epworth Press, 1965. Pp. 3–33.

Cambridge — see Walsh, John.

Campbell, Ted A. *John Wesley and Christian Antiquity*. Nashville: Kingswood Books, 1991.

Chilcote, Paul Wesley. *John Wesley and the Women Preachers of Early Methodism*. Metuchen, NJ: Scarecrow Press, 1991.

City Road — see Stevenson, George J.

Church — see Baker, Frank.

Church, Leslie. *The Early Methodist People*. London: Epworth Press, 1948. (*People*)

Church, Leslie. *More about the Early Methodist People*. London: Epworth Press, 1949. (*More*)

Clarke, W. K. Lowther. *Eighteenth-Century Piety*. London: SPCK, 1962.

Coke, Thomas, and Henry Moore. *The Life of John Wesley*. London: Paramore, 1792; facs. Nashville: Abingdon Press, 1992.

Collection — Wesley, John, and Charles Wesley. *A Collection of Hymns for the Use of the People Called Methodists*, ed. Franz Hildebrandt and Oliver A. Beckerlegge (vol. 7 in *The Bicentennial Edition of the Works of John Wesley*). Nashville: Abingdon, 1989.

Cragg, Gerald R. *The Church and the Age of Reason*. Baltimore: Penguin Books, 1966.

Crookshank, C. H. *History of Methodism in Ireland*, 3 vols. Belfast: Allen, 1885.

CW — see Baker, Frank.

CWJ — Wesley, Charles. *The Journal of the Rev. Charles Wesley*, ed. Thomas Jackson. 2 vols. London: Mason, 1849.

Davies, Rupert, A. Raymond George, Gordon Rupp. *A History of The Methodist Church in Great Britain*. 4 vols. London: Epworth Press, 1965–88.

Death — see Heitzenrater, Richard P.

Dickens, Arthur G. *The English Reformation*. New York: Schocken, 1964.

Documents — see Vickers, John A.

Egmont — John Percival, Earl of Egmont. *Diary*. 3 vols. London: HMC, 1923.

EMP — see Jackson, Thomas, ed.

EMW — see Heitzenrater, Richard P.

Field, Clive. "Bibliography," Part 2 of vol. 4, *A History of The Methodist Church in Great Britain*, ed. Rupert Davies, A. Raymond George, Gordon Rupp. London: Epworth Press, 1988. Pp. 653–830.

George, A. Raymond. "Ordination," in vol. 2 of *A History of The Methodist Church in Great Britain*, ed. Rupert Davies, A. Raymond George, Gordon Rupp. London: Epworth Press, 1978. Pp. 143–60.

Grimshaw — see Baker, Frank.

Gunter, W. Stephen. *The Limits of "Love Divine": John Wesley's Response to Antinomianism and Enthusiasm.* Nashville: Kingswood Books, 1989.

HAM — see Bucke, Emory Stevens, ed.

Heitzenrater, Richard P. *The Elusive Mr. Wesley.* 2 vols. Nashville: Abingdon Press, 1984. (*EMW*)

Heitzenrater, Richard P. *"Faithful Unto Death": Last Years and Legacy of John Wesley.* Dallas: Bridwell Library, 1991. (*Death*)

Heitzenrater, Richard P. *Mirror and Memory; Reflections on Early Methodist History.* Nashville: Kingswood Books, 1989. (*M&M*)

Hutton, James. "James Hutton's Account of 'The Beginning of the Lord's Work in England to 1741,'" *WHS* 15 (1926).

Ingham — Ingham, Benjamin. *Diary of an Oxford Methodist: Benjamin Ingham, 1733–1734,* ed. Richard P. Heitzenrater. Durham, NC: Duke University Press, 1985.

J&D — Wesley, John. *Journal and Diaries,* ed. W. Reginald Ward and Richard P. Heitzenrater. 7 vols. (vols. 18–24 in *The Bicentennial Edition of the Works of John Wesley*). Nashville: Abingdon, 1988–.

Jackson, Thomas, ed. *Lives of Early Methodist Preachers.* 6 vols. London: Wesleyan Conference Office, 1849. (*EMP*)

Jarboe, Betty M., ed. *John and Charles Wesley: A Bibliography.* Metuchen, NJ: Scarecrow Press, 1987.

Jarboe, Betty M., ed. *Wesley Quotations: Excerpts from the Writings of John Wesley and Other Family Members.* Metuchen, NJ: Scarecrow Press, 1990.

JWJ — Wesley, John. *The Journal of the Rev. John Wesley,* ed. Nehemiah Curnock. 8 vols. London: Epworth Press, 1938.

JWL — Wesley, John. *The Letters of the Rev. John Wesley,* ed. John Telford. 8 vols. London: Epworth Press, 1931.

JWW — Wesley, John. *The Works of John Wesley,* ed. Thomas Jackson. 14 vols. London: Conference Office, 1872.

Kimbrough, S T, ed. *Charles Wesley, Poet and Theologian.* Nashville: Kingswood Books, 1992.

Lackington, James. *Memoirs of James Lackington, in Forty-seven Letters to a Friend.* London: 1794.

Legg, J. Wickham. *English Church Life from the Restoration to the Tractarian Movement.* London: Longmans, Green, 1914.

Letters — Wesley, John. *Letters,* ed. Frank Baker. 7 vols. (vols. 25–31 in *The Bicentennial Edition of the Works of John Wesley*). Oxford: Clarendon Press, 1980–.

Lyles, Albert M. *Methodism Mocked: The Satiric Reaction to Methodism in the Eighteenth Century.* London: Epworth Press, 1960.

M&M — see Heitzenrater, Richard P.

Maddox, Randy L. *Aldersgate Reconsidered*. Nashville: Kingswood Books, 1990.

McAdoo, Henry R. *The Spirit of Anglicanism*. New York: Scribner's, 1965.

Maser, Frederick E. *Robert Strawbridge, First American Circuit Rider*. Rutland, VT: Academy Books, 1983.

Memoirs — see Lackington, James.

Memorials — see Stevenson, George J.

Minutes — *Minutes of the Methodist Conferences* (vol. 1, 1744–1798). London: Mason, 1862.

Moore, Henry. *The Life of the Rev. John Wesley*. 2 vols. London: John Kershaw, 1824.

More, Paul E., and F. L. Cross. *Anglicanism*. London: SPCK, 1962.

More — see Church, Leslie.

OM — see Tyerman, Luke.

People — see Church, Leslie.

Perkins, E. Benson. *Methodist Preaching Houses and the Law; The Story of the Model Deed*. London: Epworth Press, 1952.

Pilmore, Joseph. *The Journal of Joseph Pilmore*, ed. Frederick E. Maser and Howard T. Maag. Philadelphia: Historical Society, 1969.

Plumb, J. H. *England in the Eighteenth Century, 1714–1815*. Baltimore: Penguin, 1964.

Poetical Works — John Wesley and Charles Wesley, *The Poetical Works of John and Charles Wesley*, ed. George Osborn, 13 vols. London: Wesleyan Methodist Conference Office, 1868–71.

Polity — see Baker, Frank.

Portus, Garnet Vere. *Caritas Anglicana*. London: Mowbray, 1912.

Rack, Henry D. *Reasonable Enthusiast; John Wesley and the Rise of Methodism*. 2nd edition. Nashville: Abingdon Press, 1992.

Rep. Verse — see Baker, Frank.

Rowe, Kenneth E., ed. *The Place of Wesley in the Christian Tradition*. Metuchen, NJ: Scarecrow Press, 1976.

Rupp, Ernest Gordon. *Religion in England, 1688–1791*. Oxford: Clarendon Press, 1986.

Schmidt, Martin. *John Wesley; A Theological Biography*. 2 vols. London: Epworth Press, 1963–73.

Sermons — Wesley, John. *Sermons*, ed. Albert C. Outler. 4 vols. (vols. 1–4 in *The Bicentennial Edition of the Works of John Wesley*). Nashville: Abingdon, 1984–87.

Societies — Wesley, John. *The Methodist Societies; History, Nature, and Design*, ed. Rupert E. Davies (vol. 9 in *The Bicentennial Edition of the Works of John Wesley*). Nashville: Abingdon, 1989.

Stevenson, George J. *City Road Chapel, London, and its Associations, Historical, Biographical, and Memorial*. London: Stevenson, 1872. (*City Road*)

Stevenson, George J. *Memorials of the Wesley Family*. London: Partridge, 1876.

Sutherland, Lucy S., and L. G. Mitchell. *The Eighteenth Century*. Volume 5 of *The History of the University of Oxford*, ed. T. H. Aston. Oxford: Clarendon Press, 1986.

Tyerman, Luke. *The Oxford Methodists*. New York: Harper, 1873.

Vickers, John A., "Documents and Source Material," in vol. 4 of *A History of the Methodist Church in Great Britain*, ed. Rupert Davies, A. Raymond George, and Gordon Rupp, 4 vols. London: Epworth Press, 1988. Pp. 3–649. (*Documents*)

Vickers, John A. *Thomas Coke, Apostle of Methodism*. Nashville: Abingdon Press, 1969.

W-A — see Baker, Frank.

Walsh, John. "The Cambridge Methodists," in *Christian Spirituality*, ed. Peter Brooks. London: SCM Press, 1975. (*Cambridge*)

Walsh, John. "Origins of the Evangelical Revival," in *Essays in Modern English Church History*, ed. G. V. Bennet and John Walsh. New York: Oxford University Press, 1966.

Walsh, John. "Methodism at the End of the Eighteenth Century," in vol. 1 of *A History of The Methodist Church in Great Britain*, ed. Rupert Davies and Gordon Rupp. 4 vols. London: Epworth Press, 1965. Pp. 277–315.

Ward, W. Reginald. *The Protestant Evangelical Awakening*. Cambridge: Cambridge University Press, 1992.

Watson, David L. *The Early Methodist Class Meeting*. Nashville: Discipleship Resources, 1985.

Whitefield, George. *George Whitefield's Journals*. London: Banner of Truth Trust, 1960.

WHS — *Proceedings of the Wesley Historical Society* (Burnley and Chester, 1989–).

Willey, Basil. *The Eighteenth Century Background*. Boston: Beacon Press, 1964.

Index

Italic type indicates pages that contain illustrations; **bold type** indicates pages with definitions or significant references.